THE 'SOUL' OF THE PRIMITIVE
Lucien Lévy-Bruhl

Foreword by
Professor E. E. Evans-Pritchard

"It is not uncommon for students, friends, and admirers to present a scholar with a *Festschrift* to please him when he is old, but it is rare, when he is no longer there to be pleased, that the centenary of his birth is commemorated by a similar volume, as was done for Lévy-Bruhl" (from the Foreword). So great was his influence and so important his work that several of his books first issued in the 1920's are now being reprinted to meet the needs of students, for (again in the words of Professor Evans-Pritchard) "his vigorous, penetrating, and imaginative ideas live on."

Lévy-Bruhl held that the collective representations of primitive peoples are prelogical and mystical. Persons and things in primitive thought form part of one another to the point of identity. A man participates in his social group, in his name, in his totem animal, in his shadow. In this volume, Lévy-Bruhl develops his theory of participation in relation to primitive conceptions of the human personality.

THE 'SOUL' OF THE PRIMITIVE

How Natives Think

(LES FONCTIONS MENTALES DANS LES SOCIÉTÉS
INFÉRIEURES)

Authorized translation by LILIAN A. CLARE

"Every student to whom it has hitherto been inaccessible in the original tongue will welcome the chance of making the acquaintance of what is on all sides acknowledged to be an anthropological classic."— *Times*.

"A fascinating volume. . . . The facts which he has collected are of the greatest value."—*New Statesman*.

"Students of primitive psychology owe a debt of gratitude to Mrs. Clare for her excellent translation of this stimulating book."—*Theology*.

THE 'SOUL' OF THE PRIMITIVE

By

LUCIEN ·LÉVY-BRUHL

AUTHORIZED TRANSLATION BY
LILIAN A. CLARE

WITH A FOREWORD BY
PROFESSOR E. E. EVANS-PRITCHARD
F.B.A.

FREDERICK A. PRAEGER
Publishers
NEW YORK . WASHINGTON

BOOKS THAT MATTER

Published in the United States of America in 1966
by Frederick A. Praeger, Inc., Publishers

111 Fourth Avenue, New York 3, N.Y.

© *George Allen and Unwin Ltd. 1966*

Library of Congress Catalog Card Number: 66–12985

PRINTED IN GREAT BRITAIN

FOREWORD

BY E. E. EVANS-PRITCHARD, F.B.A.

LUCIEN LÉVY-BRUHL (1857–1939) was a scholar whose influence has been great. His books were widely read—by philosophers, psychologists, anthropologists and historians. He was himself a philosopher by training; his books on Jacobi and Comte are still considered to be important. And it was as a philosopher that he entered the field of what we in England call social anthropology, the central questions in which he was interested being those of formal logic.

In 1910 appeared *Les fonctions mentale dans les sociétés inférieures* (translated: *How natives think*, 1926) and in 1922 *La mentalité primitive* (translated: *Primitive Mentalité*, 1923). These are his best known books and they were much criticized, some of the criticism arising from a misunderstanding of what he was saying. Other volumes followed which were an amplification of his earlier views, and also a refinement of them, as he made use of information about ideas of primitive peoples not available to him when he wrote his earlier books. One of these is that of which the present volume is a translation (*L'âme primitive*, 1927: translated as *The "Soul" of the Primitive*, 1928). It was followed by *Le surnaturel et le nature dans la mentalité primitive*, 1931 (translated as *Primitives and the Supernatural*, 1936), *La mythologie primitive* (1935), and *L'expérience mystique et des symbols chez les primitifs* (1938). A summary of his views about primtive thought is to be found in his Herbert Spencer Lecture delivered in Oxford: *La mentalité primitive* (1931). His last reflections on primitive mentality were published from his notebooks in 1949 after his death: *Les carnets de Lucien Lévy-Bruhl* (1949). Whether he would have published these final reflections as they stand might be questioned, but as they are set forth they would seem to some degree to reverse his earlier position.

This position is, to put it in his own language, that the collective representations of primitive peoples are prelogical and mystical. By "representations" he means the ideas people accept in any given society. By "prelogical" he means that their thought does not conform to the rules of logic accepted by us, and by "mystical" he means belief in supra-sensible forces of one sort or another as manifested in what he calls the "law of participation." By this he means that persons and things in primitive thought form part of one another to the point even of identity. A man participates in his social group, in his name, in his totem animal, in his shadow, to give a few examples, in such a way that his mentality may be said to be formed by these many "mystical" links.

In this volume he develops his theory of participation in relation to primitive conceptions of the human personality. He set himself a very difficult task, as he fully realized, because here the problem of translation from primitive languages into our own is most acute. We are dealing with conceptions such as those which we translate as "soul" and "spirit." That is as near as we can get to their meaning in our own language, but what the words in their own languages mean to those who speak them may not correspond exactly, or even at all, with what the words by which we translate them mean to us. In the process of translation, or mistranslation, we may easily put into the thought of primitive people ideas quite foreign to them, and that is what Lévy-Bruhl holds has only too often happened.

It is now held by most, perhaps all, anthropologists that Lévy-Bruhl overstated his case in making too strong a contrast between primitive mentality and civilized mentality. If this is so, the fault does not lie entirely with him, for, having had himself no experience of primitive peoples, he had to rely on reports which were sometimes based on misunderstandings between writers about primitive peoples and those about whom they wrote, especially with regard to the topics discussed in this book, conceptions about which neither could communicate without great difficulty with the other.

Nevertheless, the evidence cited by Lévy-Bruhl is impressive and much of it is given by authorities who beyond question must be respected as knowledgeable and trustworthy. So, even if Lévy-Bruhl's conclusions about primitive mentality can no longer be accepted quite in the terms in which he set them forth, it is a plain fact that much of the thought of primitive peoples is difficult, sometimes almost impossible, for us to understand, in that we cannot follow their lines of reasoning because the underlying assumptions on which they are based, while taken for granted by them, are totally alien to us. So the problem still remains—in his words "the primitive's thought proceeds along a path in which we find it very difficult to follow it," as this fascinating book well illustrates.

It is not uncommon for students, friends and admirers to present a scholar with a *Festschrift* to please him when he is old, but it is rarely that, when he is no longer there to be pleased, the centenary of his birth is commemorated by a similar volume, as was done for Lévy-Bruhl in a special number of the *Revue Philosophique* in 1957, to which I had the honour of contributing. His vigorous, penetrating, and imaginative ideas live on: "For Death—he taketh all away, but them he cannot take."

AUTHOR'S PREFACE TO THE
ORIGINAL EDITION

THE object of this book is a study of the ways in which those whom we have agreed to call "primitives" conceive of their own individuality. Guided by results obtained in previous researches, I propose to inquire into the notions they possess of their life-principle, their soul, and their personality. An examination of the facts available has led me to recognize that, properly speaking, they have not any notions of them. I find myself face to face with "pre-notions."

To do away with all ambiguity, therefore, I must define at the outset what is meant by the title *The Soul of the Primitive*. We are dealing here with the ideas which, among the peoples termed primitive, correspond more or less closely with those which the word "soul" implies to our minds.

CONTENTS

I. The need for recourse to an indirect method.—The same essence, that of *mana*, inherent in all persons and objects.—The *imunu* of New Guinea.

II. The Dschaggas s rites of apiculture.—Invocation of all the beings interested therein.

III. Mystic powers of rocks and stones.—Stones that live and grow and reproduce their kind.

IV. Plants and trees that are reservoirs of mystic powers.—The fea. and respect they inspire.—The attempts made to assimilate their qualities.

V. Human beings and animals only slightly different.—Animals living in human fashion and taking on human forms: tigers, elephants, crocodiles, etc. (Malaya).—Similar ideas in South Africa and among the Eskimo.

VI. Mythical beings, half-human and half-animal, of Australia and the Andaman Islands.—Totemic ancestors.—Inspiration and significance of primitive art.

PART I

CHAPTER I

I. The principle or genius of the vegetable and animal species.—The individual's relations with it in New France, Malaya, South and East Africa.

II. The real unit the *group* and not the individual.—The importance of hierarchic order in primitive societies.—The chief's mystic functions.

III. The pronominal suffix in the Melanesian languages.—Substantives denoting relationship or parts of the body also used with the personal pronoun in a similar way.

IV. Group-relationship and the classificatory system in Melanesia, New Guinea, and among the Yakuts, etc.

PART II

CHAPTER VII

CHAPTER VIII

CHAPTER IX

CONTENTS

INTRODUCTION

THE PRIMITIVE'S IDEA OF THE HOMOGENEITY IN ESSENCE OF ALL BEINGS

I

It is scarcely likely that primitives have ever given a form, however indefinite, to the more or less implicit idea they may have of their own personality. At any rate it would be quite useless to question them about it, for ambiguity and misunderstanding would be the only result. Their replies would bring out but one thing clearly—that the meaning of the question had altogether escaped them. We must therefore proceed in another fashion. The study of certain of their institutions and customs, the analysis of certain of their collective representations[1]—these will allow of our defining, with as much exactitude as the subject permits, the way in which primitives conceive of the human individual, either in himself or in his relations to his group.

If we follow this indirect method—the only one which permits us to attain our end—we shall have to go very far back. We must start from the collective representations in which all beings, whether living or not, and all objects that surround the primitive are ranged, for to him his own personality is but one of such beings or objects. He has undoubtedly "a lively inner sense" of his personal existence. He refers the sensations, pleasures, pains he experiences, to himself, just as he does the acts of which he knows himself to be the doer. But from this it does not follow that he apprehends himself as a "subject," nor especially that he is conscious that he apprehends himself as anything different from "objects" not himself. To attribute to him these differentiations and distinctions of which he knows nothing, would be to fall into what William James called "the psychologist's fallacy." At the same time it would be a failure

---

[1] Reviewers of the author's earlier studies often suggest that to the ordinary reader the term "collective representations" is unnecessarily cumbersome, and may not be understood. Such readers can easily substitute the words "tribal concept" or "group-idea" for the term in general use by scientists.—TRANSLATOR.

to recognize the collective nature of these representations. In the vague idea which the primitive has of himself, elements arising out of individual self-reflection count, as we know, for very little.

The apparent similarities between the primitive and the child, so often noted, may be deceitful. We must not make use of them save cautiously and with certain reservations; yet, upon the question now confronting us, they are singularly striking. Is it not a significant fact that, as observers are unanimous in asserting, the idea of himself as a subject does not appear in a child until fairly late? His little personality asserts itself early, however, and demands its own satisfactions energetically. The tiny individual's feelings regarding himself are evinced by lively reactions, imperious demands, signs of jealousy, and so forth. Nevertheless, the child apprehends himself only as a being or an object like those surrounding him. He still speaks of himself in the third person. He has quite naturally adopted, with the language of the persons he hears and understands, the ideas which they have concerning him. Some years have to pass before he says: "*I* want this or that." Though already an observer, he is very far from making any psychological analysis.

We may say the same of the primitive. We shall have numerous proofs that he, too, appears to himself as he appears to others and they to him, without distinguishing himself from the beings and objects of the world around. To determine as best we can the idea he forms of his own individuality, we will therefore begin by studying how he represents other beings, living or otherwise, to himself, and in particular the members of his social group.

Without entering here upon the old dispute, now almost settled, between the theories of animism and preanimism, it will suffice to recall the fundamental idea inherent, as it were, in primitive mentality, the existence and importance of which are no longer called in question. To the mind of the primitive there is existent and permeating, on earth, in the air and in the water, in all the divers forms assumed by persons and objects, one and the same essential reality, both one and multiple, both material and spiritual. It is continually passing from one to another, and by means of it may be explained (as far as such minds trouble about explanation), the existence and activities of all forms of being, their permanence and their metamorphoses, their life and death. This mystic reality which permeates everywhere and which is felt rather than represented, properly speaking, cannot be put into a conceptual form like the "substance" of our metaphysicians. Codrington first made it known under the name of *mana*, which Speiser in the New Hebrides translates by *Lebenskraft*. Neuhauss and the German missionaries of New Guinea call it *Seelenstoff*; it is the *zielstof* of Kruijt and many other Dutch scientists, the *Potenz* of Dr. Pechuël-Loesche in Loango, and so on. There is no term in our languages which exactly corresponds with the expressions used by primitives to designate this essence, so difficult to define. It will be best to rely upon descriptions which complete and corroborate each other.

Codrington's description is well-known. The following are derived from British New Guinea. Holmes, explaining what the natives of the Purari Delta understand by *imunu*, emphasizes the point that this principle is present everywhere at once like an impersonal force, and yet it is individual in certain persons. "It was associated with everything, nothing arrived apart from it . . . nothing animate or inanimate could exist apart from it. It was the soul of things. . . . It had personality, but it was only such as resembled the specific characteristics of its habitat. . . . It could be kind or malign, it could cause pain and suffer pain, it could possess and be dispossessed. It was intangible, but like air, wind, it could manifest its presence. It permeated everything that made up life to the people of the Purari Delta, yet it was not *rokoa*, life, energy, but *imunu*, which I have ventured to translate as soul, living principle, that which enables everything to exist as we know it, and distinct from other things which, too, exist by it."[1]

Another writer who has observed the same natives has very clearly brought out, if I may venture to put it thus, the essential obscurity surrounding the idea. "*Imunu*," says he, "is one of those wide and indistinct categories whose emotional implications are clearer than the intellectual. Masques and bull-roarers are *imunu*. So also many other things, hunting charms, old relics, grotesque carvings, freaks of nature, etc., are commonly

[1] J. H. Holmes, *In Primitive New Guinea*, p. 150.

B

said to be *imunu*. So, too, are an exceptionally large tree, the vast rivers. . . . *Imunu* is neither material nor spiritual. Nor can it be said that the real *imunu* is something immaterial, and the concrete object an earthly tenement for it. . . .

"The only fair and satisfactory way of dealing with the *imunu* concept would be to enumerate all the applications of the word. . . . In short, it seems better to regard the term in its wider application as adjectival rather than substantive; it stands for a quality, or complex of qualities, rather than a thing. If asked 'What is an *imunu*?' a native informant is, of course, completely nonplussed, but pointing to this or that— and a perplexingly varied assortment of things they may be— he will say 'This is *imunu*.' "[1]

These two descriptions are as instructive on account of their differences as they are through their similarities. Holmes seems to lay stress on that aspect of the *imunu* in which it appears as the substance of all forms of being, and accordingly he prefers to make the word a substantive. Williams, who emphasizes its emotional side, sees in *imunu* a quality rather than a substance, and he would consider it an adjective. Both these observers recognize that this class of representation has no exact equivalent in our conceptual thought. The idea of *imunu*, at once abstract and concrete, and permeated by emotional elements, must perforce remain indistinct to our minds, although it completely satisfies the mentality of the primitive.

So, too, Sir Everard im Thurn, speaking of the natives of British Guiana, remarks: "To the Indian all objects, animate and inanimate, seem exactly of the same nature except that they differ in the accident of bodily form. . . . It is very

---

[1] F. E. Williams, "The Paimara ceremony in the Purari Delta" (*Journal of the Royal Anthropological Institute* (henceforth *J.A.I.*), liii (1923), pp. 362–3. Cf. F. E. Williams, *The Natives of the Purari Delta*, pp. 243–5. Territory of Papua. Anthropology, Report No. 5, 1924.—Similar ideas seem to subsist as the basis of what are termed "fetish beliefs" in West Africa. If the natives are asked what they regard as fetish, an intelligent convert, after a moment's reflection, answers: "What heathens call *Vôdun* is everything that surpasses man's power and intelligence, everything that is astonishing, out of the ordinary, terrible, prodigious, such as the great whirlpools, the rainbow, the vast and ever-moving ocean, the big rivers like the Mono, lakes like the Ahémé, thunder and lightning, the tiger known to the Fons, the boa-constrictor of the inhabitants of Grand Popo, the snake-fetish of the Pédahs, the smallpox in Sakpata, crocodiles, etc., . . . all these are fetishes. Our ancestors believed that they were all endowed with superhuman virtues, and that they were the dwelling-place of mysterious powers and spirits." G. Kiti, "Le Fétichisme au Dahomey," *La Reconnaissance africaine*, ii, No. 25, pp. 2, 3 (1926).

difficult for us to realize the Indian conceptions of this identity, in everything but bodily form, of men and other animals; and it is still more difficult to realize that the Indian conception is wider even than this in that it knows of no difference, except again in bodily form, between animate and inanimate objects."[1]

Thus primitive mentality considers and at the same time feels all beings and objects to be homogeneous, that is, he regards them all as participating either in the same essential nature, or in the same ensemble of qualities. To his mind it matters nothing to arrange them in a series of classes, genera, and species clearly distinct from each other and corresponding with a scale of concepts, logically defined in their extension and intension. His primary object is to discover in the objects which attract and retain his attention the presence and degree of intensity and (strange as it may appear to us) the kindly or malevolent disposition of that quality or principle or *mana* or *imunu*, or whatever name we may like to call it. It is necessary for him to be forearmed against the dangers by which he imagines and feels himself threatened at all times, and this fear of his regulates his attitude to beings and objects.

Thus it is not to the pursuit of knowledge that this dominating representation directs the primitive's mind. Undoubtedly the "native," especially the medicine-man or wizard, usually the most intelligent in the group and the most conversant with all its traditions, is hardly ever as ignorant as we may be tempted to imagine. Even among peoples whom we regard as very low down in the human family, he knows how to distinguish the genera and species of plants which interest him. He knows the characteristics and habitat of animals, insects, birds and fishes, etc. To give but one example, among the Papuans of Mailu Island in British New Guinea, "without any trouble the natives give me the names of one hundred and seventeen trees, including thirty-seven different edible fruit-bearing trees. They tell me in a very short space of time the names of one hundred and ninety-one fish, and sixty-nine edible crustaceans picked up on the reef or dug up from the sand beaches."[2] And other things are in keeping with this.

[1] Im Thurn, *Among the Indians of British Guiana*, pp. 350–5.
[2] W. J. V. Saville, *In Unknown New Guinea*, p. 191.

Yet the primitive, with all this somewhat exact knowledge that he possesses and utilizes, scarcely troubles about extending and investigating it. He is content with transmitting it as he has himself received it. While not failing to realize its practical value, he does not appraise it as we should do. The objective characteristics which permit of our differentiating beings very like each other, are of slight importance to him unless they bear a mystic significance. He makes use of the knowledge, often a very exact one, that he possesses, but only exceptionally is he interested in it, for it plays an altogether subordinate part in his actual doings. It is especially upon the power or powers, the mysterious, invisible, and everywhere present forces, that the success or failure of his hunting, fishing, agriculture, and in fact, of all the enterprises in which he may engage, depends. These it is that he must endeavour to subjugate, appease, and incline to his cause.

When primitives' understanding and emotions have from time immemorial taken this turn, it matters little to them that beings appear more or less approximate to or distinct from each other in their outward form and their objective qualities. Like ourselves, the primitive perceives the general differences between a stone and a tree, or a tree and a fish or a bird, but he does not heed them, because he does not feel them as we do. The form of objects interests him only so far as it permits him to divine how much *mana* or *imunu* they may possess. Accordingly he sees no difficulty in metamorphoses which are quite incredible to us: to him, all forms of matter may change their dimensions and their shape in the twinkling of an eye. All of them are receptacles, either potential or actual, of these mystic powers, and sometimes it happens that a being which is apparently insignificant may contain a formidable amount of *mana*. Thus beneath their seemingly strong diversity they present an essential homogeneity; the primitive has no need to examine or know them better to be certain of that fact. But, on the other hand, in his desire to attain the ends he proposes to himself, he cannot do enough to propitiate the mystic powers of which all these forms, animate or inanimate, differing so widely in our eyes, are the receptacles and vehicles.

II

Perhaps the best means of making such an attitude comprehensible, as well as the collective representations from which it proceeds, will be by giving an instance. I will borrow one from a noteworthy pamphlet written by the missionary Gutmann, entitled *Apiculture among the Dschagga*.[1] The writer is the author of a series of excellent works on the Bantus of Kilimandjaro.

Gutmann first of all recalls their proverb, "In all the relations of life bees are human beings," which well expresses the natives' admiration and respect for these wonderful insects. Nevertheless they have not penetrated the mystery of the life and activities of bees, and have but a very imperfect conception of their social organization and their work. They make up for the deficiency of their knowledge, and add to the powers they believe that bees can procure for them by many mystic practices, "inexhaustible in their abundance." I cannot enumerate them all, even in abridged form, but will quote the main ones only, the "headings."

The first adjuration is addressed to the axe destined to fell the tree, the trunk of which will be fashioned into beehives. The iron to form the axe is carried to the blacksmith with an offering of beer, the native being accompanied by his wives and children. As soon as he arrives he pronounces words of favourable omen, and they all imitate him. "Iron, provide us with oxen and sheep! (to be purchased with the sums the honey yields). Axe, provide us with a hive which will bring prosperity to our children!"

When he is to carry to the blacksmith the iron thus blessed, the man rises before dawn so that he may not meet anybody who could exercise a malign influence on the metal. The blacksmith at once sets to work, and while the bellows are in full blast there are fresh adjurations, in which the native recalls the names of all the beekeepers he knows, in order to attract their bees to his own hive. "Come, bees, come to the hive that I am going to make with my axe!" This axe must not be used for ordinary wood-cutting, and no hand must touch it except

[1] Br. Gutmann, "Die Imkerei bei den Dschagga," *Archiv für Anthropologie.* Neue Folge, xix, Brunswick, 1922.

that of the beekeeper, above all, never the hand of woman. Meticulous care is employed in fashioning the knife for dividing the honeycomb. This must be shaped like a pruning-knife, and have a handle formed of a piece of wood about sixteen to eighteen inches long. Whilst he is at work upon it, the smith expresses his desires as he strikes the iron: "May this knife serve its master faithfully! . . . May he enter the hive quietly, without disturbing the bees. . . . May his bees not forsake him! . . . May the hive not be shattered, nor the bees swarm elsewhere! When the beekeeper goes along the road with this knife, grant that he may not encounter anything unfavourable," and so on.[1]

When the usual gang of four natives goes to the forest to fell the tree, the trunk of which is to make the hive, the adjurations addressed to it before it is felled and sawn in pieces will vary according to its species. For preference they select the *msedi*, the king of the forest, whose wood is the most durable. The head of the gang applies his axe to the trunk saying, as he swings it four times: "*Msedi*, thou who art so great . . . it is poverty that brings me to thee. I need children. I need goats and oxen. . . . Thou, *Msedi*, if thou hast the chance, cause the bees to come hither!" (He then enumerates the places whence they are to be attracted.)

Another tree, the *mringa*, only to be found in the belt cultivated by the Dschagga, calls for special adjurations when it is to be felled. It is supposed to be the sister of the native who owns it, and he cannot take part in the felling operations. All that is done to make use of the tree is represented to it as if in preparation for its marriage. The day before it is to be cut down the owner betakes himself to the tree with offerings of milk, beer, honey and so forth. "My child, about to leave me, I am giving thee to a man who will wed thee, my daughter! . . . Do not think that I am forcing thee to this marriage, but now thou art fully grown. . . . My child, about to leave me, may all go well with thee!" . . . Next day he absents himself that he may not be obliged to be there when the tree is felled, when he who has acquired it shall arrive. In his place there is a master of ceremonies whose task it is to confide the tree, his

[1] Br. Gutmann, "Die Imkerei bei den Dschagga," *Archiv für Anthropologie.* Neue Folge, xix, Brunswick, 1922, p. 9.

sister, to those who come for it, just as a fiancée is confided to her husband's friends. When the rites have been accomplished they begin to strike the tree with the axe, and at this moment the head of the gang says: "O child of a man thou art about to leave, we are not hewing thee down, we are giving thee in marriage! Neither is it by force, but with kindness and gentleness." . . . He finishes up with the adjuration to the bees, as in the case of the *msedi*. At length the tree lies on the ground, and while the gang is busy around the fallen giantess, its owner arrives as if by chance. He is amazed at what he sees; he laments, as for a crime that he has come too late to prevent, exclaiming, "You have stolen my sister from me!" These words, and many similar expressions, are designed to persuade the tree of his sorrow. The others do all that they can to calm him. They are ardent in asseverations that all will be for the ultimate good of both his sister and himself, and finally peace is restored.

Whilst the trunk is being hollowed out to make the hives, new adjurations, to the rhythm of the blows, are addressed to the axe itself, to the bees in the hive and the bees of other beekeepers. They are accompanied by maledictions hurled against all who may, through their sorceries and witchcraft, seek to injure these bees and their home.

When the hive is finished it is furnished with a crook to hang it up by. This is made of the wood of certain trees, and there are the same ceremonies and adjurations to go through when these trees are felled. Those who cut them down excuse themselves by recalling the example set by their ancestors, who did the same through poverty and because they needed children and cattle.

It is now a matter of putting the hives in position. In the forest they are hung fairly low, sometimes within reach of the hand. They run no risk, for nobody passes by. But in the plains they are suspended from high branches, sometimes as much as twenty yards above the ground, at the extreme end of stout boughs. For the purpose of hanging the hives up there and for taking them down it has been necessary to arrange a special system, and to fabricate heavy ropes and cords by means of tree-bark and lianas. An "inexhaustible" series of adjurations is again required here, to assure the final success of the beekeeper—adjurations addressed to the baobab whence the bark will be taken, and to the rope that is being twisted, to name the chief ones only. When all is finished, an offering of food is made to it, and thus it is introduced to the common life of the village and brought into clan relationship. Whilst formulating good wishes for its success, the natives rub it with all sorts of edible fruits except those which bees do not frequent. The same thing is done for the cord which will serve to throw the plaited cable over the branch where the beekeeper will hang his hive, for the stone attached to this guy-rope, and so on. At the end of the day, all the cordage is hung in the "men's house." A curse is pronounced upon anyone who may touch it without having the right to do so, and may thus exercise a baneful influence over it. The beekeeper spends the night in its vicinity, and at this time the "senior rite-master" instructs him as to which foods, and especially which plants, he must avoid eating all the time he is looking after the bees. Plants which have a malign influence and those which the bees dislike are, above all, forbidden.

The tree in which the beekeeper hangs his hives is of special importance to him. By adjurations and sacrifices he places himself under its protection, and thus a bond is established between the arboreal family and his own.[1] The *mrie*, the king of the trees, is regarded as being particularly lucky, and its favour is sought by invocations. Appeal is made to the example of its brothers, who dispensed benefits to men, and to the poverty which emboldens the gang to approach it. It is entreated not to let the man who scales it fall, not to throw the hive to the ground, to protect the beekeeper against his enemies. They beg that he may not meet a leopard or a rhinoceros, etc., upon his route. Upon this occasion they confine themselves to marking the tree.

For climbing the tree and placing the hives a propitious day is always chosen. Before they begin, all species of bananas, except one, are eaten, and saliva, mingled with their juices and with honey, is thrown upon the tree trunk, while prayer is offered. Thereafter, with many rites and invocations, the placing of the hives is accomplished.

[1] Br. Gutmann, "Die Imkerei bei den Dschagga," *Archiv für Anthropologie.* Neue Folge, xix, Brunswick, 1922, p. 19.

I pass over a vast multitude of prayers and ceremonies and come straight to the gathering of the honey. The Dschagga beekeeper is not primarily concerned, as one of ours would be, in avoiding stings. He knows that he can keep free of them by working at night and with the help of the smoke of special torches. What he dreads is the warlike tribes or wild beasts that may be hovering near, and the cables and branches that may break. He therefore procures a good "traveller's charm," formed of the most varied ingredients calcined and reduced to soot. Should he perceive either men or beasts he will blow this soot in their direction, and thus render himself invisible. This magic talisman is likewise an oracle. Before setting out, the beekeeper puts some on the palm of his hand and blows it in the direction he is going to take. If the wind blows the soot back towards him, it is a sign that he will encounter misfortune on the way or upon arrival, and he remains at home. Another day he will consult the oracle again. When he is once near the tree, there will be fresh prayers and adjurations before he climbs it.

When all the hives have been brought down and everything has ended well, the oldest man in the gang seizes the axe with both hands, the others clasping his right arm. He rubs the axe against the trees four times, saying: "Rest in peace, *mrie*, king of the trees! We have given thee back thy queen-bee, guard her well as thou hast done until now! Be kind to us next time, as thou hast been now," and so forth.

Finally it goes without saying that during the operations, the details of which we have omitted, prayers and entreaties have been many times addressed to the bees themselves and to their queen.

All this, says Gutmann, is closely bound up with ancestor-worship—not only through an association of ideas which we can readily grasp and explain, but through a steady and profound sentiment which is difficult of definition. The Dschagga who in the course of his operations adjures the iron, axe, tree, cable, guy-rope, hive, bee, etc., to be favourable to him, is convinced that he will succeed because his ancestors went through the same procedure, and they obtained honey from the bees thus. He has, too, a feeling which, though vaguer, is no less certain, that the ancestors of the trees and of the bees have accomplished that which he is entreating their present descendants to accomplish, and that these are as much one with their ancestry as he with his own.

To us, who can hardly enter into it, this is a very strange emotional state, yet it is natural to the "primitive," because of the community of essence that he imagines, or rather, that he feels, in all the forms of being with which he is in relation. Someone may ask: "Do you really think that the Dschagga addresses his entreaties to the iron, axe, tree to be felled, liana, rope, cord, hive, or honeycomb cutter, as if these objects have the power to grant or to refuse him their favour and concurrence, and can secure, or prevent his success?"—To this we may answer: The Dschagga would certainly not think so any more than we do, if he had the same idea of these very different objects as we have—if, for instance, he knew how far the composition of a bar of iron differs from that of a tree or a creeper, and the nature of these vegetable products from that of insects like bees, or again, the nature of bees from that of man. But he does not know this, nor does he trouble about it. He has no idea of "the natural kingdoms," or of the essential properties of the forms of being included in them. To him all being is defined (as far as he thinks of defining it) by what it possesses of mystic force, either as a constant factor, or at a given moment. From this point of view, a piece of iron may have a beneficent or a malevolent influence upon the fate of the man using it, just as the tree he climbs may have. The man therefore will adjure both the iron and the tree; he will make offerings to them both, and will have recourse to all the means within his power to render their influence what he desires it to be. As to classifications, he knows only the mystic ones or, as Gutmann frequently says, the totemic ones.

Do not let us imagine therefore that the Dschagga first conceives of the iron, axe, tree, etc., as we do, and that afterwards he attributes to them a consciousness and the power of granting or of refusing what he is asking of them. When he speaks to them, when he flatters or deceives them, supplicates or adjures them, brings them offerings, and so on, it is not because he is making personalities out of inanimate objects; it is because he feels in them the presence of a force which is neither exactly personal nor impersonal, and which he does not differentiate from them.

III

This being so, we shall not be surprised to find that to the primitive the mineral kingdom, especially in the form of stones and boulders, is something quite different from what it is to us. According to the natives of the Dutch East Indies, Kruijt tells us, animals and plants die, but not stones. These are to the soil what bones are to the body. They accordingly partake of its nature, and are entitled to the same respect. Hence the trouble and uneasiness of the natives when they see Europeans attacking stones and boulders with hammers or in any other fashion—feelings which prospectors and miners have to reckon with. In Dutch New Guinea, for instance, some rocks had been dynamited in view of the construction of a road, and the Papuans thought there would be an outbreak of murrain among the pigs as a consequence.[1]

When he nears an ordinary boulder or stone of any sort the primitive will pass on without paying any attention to it, but should anything in it, either a curious shape or strange position or abnormal size, for instance, arrest his glance or strike his imagination, he at once invests it with the characteristics which, among the Papuans of the Purari Delta, make him call it *imunu*, among North American Indians *wakan*, and everywhere else by some name of that kind. Endowed with mystic powers, these boulders or stones may exert a favourable or an unfavourable influence upon the native and his family. Therefore, guided by circumstances, he will try to attract and dominate this influence, or else to avert it. Should he succeed in capturing it for himself, he increases his own *mana* or *imunu* to that extent.

Such, for instance, are the "sacred stones" which, in New Caledonia and many other places, are believed indispensable to the success of cultivation. In shape they more or less recall the taro or the sweet-potato tuber, of which an abundant crop is desired. At sowing time these are planted in the fields with elaborate ceremony, and when the harvest is reaped they are taken up and put away carefully until the following season. Their mystic powers are communicated

[1] A. C. Kruijt, *Het Animisme in den Indischen Archipel*, pp. 205–6.

to the soil and the plants growing in it, and these become fruitful.

Elsdon Best has noted a similar custom in New Zealand. He regards these stones as "talismanic objects" or *mauri* (a word whose significance we shall study later on). "These objects," he says, "are rudely hewn images of no great size, say from twelve to eighteen inches in height; a few are larger. . . . Such a stone image would be kept at the *tapu* place of the village at ordinary times, and when the crops were planted it would be taken to the field and placed at the *upoko* or head thereof. When the crop was lifted the stone was removed again to the *tapu* place.

"These stone figures were believed to have a most beneficent effect on the growing crops, and this because of the powers and influence of the gods which they represented. A portion of the produce of the first tuber planted was utilized as an offering to the talismanic stone." [1] Among the Maoris a real religion and even a theological system had been developed, and this is why Elsdon Best speaks of gods. In New Caledonia and among peoples of the same standard of civilization, the *mana* is regarded as immanent in the stone itself and revealed by its shape.

W. E. Armstrong, in his noteworthy writings upon the natives of Rossel Island, to the most easterly point of New Guinea, broaches some opinions concerning the representations, so difficult to define, that form the basis of beliefs of this kind. He lays stress upon one special conception peculiar to these natives, who speak of it as *yaba*. "In general, the *yaba* consists of a bit of ground or reef or even of sea, a visible stone or tree or some other object, and a guardian, usually a snake; a real snake may be interpreted by the native as the guardian, if there happen to be one of the right kind about. The stone or other object is, of course, a good deal more than it appears to the eye—it would seem to have a sort of dual existence in most cases, like that of the gods, for it has an existence in Temewe,[2] where it is human in form—in fact, there seems to be a vague idea that that which really is the stone may be at the

---

[1] Elsdon Best, *The Maori*, ii, pp. 386-7.
[2] A subterranean or submarine abode, which Armstrong compares with the mythical Alcheringa of Spencer and Gillen's Aruntas.

same time a stone on Rossel and a man, or perhaps it would be better to say, spirit or god, in Temewe." [1] Extraordinary as this conception may appear, we must not reject it as incredible or incomprehensible, for it reveals unsuspected complexes in the mentality of the primitive. For reasons easy to understand, the native keeps these as secret as he can, fearing to have them profaned by the indiscreet white man. We shall meet with many similar ideas.

In Kiwai Island, belonging to New Guinea, sacred stones play an important part in one of the initiation ceremonies known as *mimia abere*. "On entering the club, the initiates are led with all solemnity to the chief post of the house . . . to see the *mimia abere*, or sacred stones or wooden figures, as the case may be. The stones are carefully uncovered, and the initiates for the first time behold one of the most sacred treasures of the tribe—two old stones brought in from the sea, with rough sketches of human faces painted upon them. . . . The usual warning is given that should they divulge what they have now seen, or give any information whatever about it, they will be killed. The stones are again respectfully covered over with *mimia* plants. . . . After the feast, one of the elders addresses the stones as follows: 'We have made this feast for you. We have decorated all the houses for you. We want you to see to it that we do not get sick. We want you to look out for our good. You are now going to stop under the house.' " (They are in fact placed there.) "The speaker continues: 'You sleep under the house now. . . . We have danced for you, and the next time we make *mimia* we will bring you into the house again.' " [2] These sacred stones are evidently "reincarnations" of ancestors, possibly the original parents of the tribe.

In one of the eastern islands of the Torres Straits there are stones which have been men, and have the power of moving. "There were two stones called Kol, one at Zaub, the other at Er. Once a year these stones were supposed to roll across the island by themselves (so I was informed) and exchange places."[3] In the New Hebrides, "Sommerville writes," says Speiser,

[1] W. E. Armstrong, "Rossel Island Religion," *Anthropos*, xviii–xix, 1923–4, p. 5. Cf. W. E. Armstrong, "Territory of Papua," *Anthropology*, Report No. 2.
[2] E. B. Riley, *Among Papuan Head-Hunters*, pp. 231–3.
[3] *The Cambridge Expedition to Torres Straits*, vi, p. 11 (folk-tale).

"that in Malekula great blocks of stone are regarded as the corporeal form of ancestors, and this is the case almost everywhere where monoliths are erected over the tombs. . . . It is the same with the cliffs on the gloomy Tuki-Tuki promontory at Fate. This is looked upon as the entrance to Hades, and some large stones represent the souls of the ancestors. The natives were in special awe of a very high boulder of a conical form which rises out of the sea on the north-west coast of Fate. It was the 'incarnation' of a legendary chief called Namote, and when the boat passed by it, the natives lowered their heads in prayer and fear." [1]—In Timor stones are very frequently found to be objects of worship. Most of them, however, possess no power of their own. Those which are used in funeral rites merely represent the dead person, whilst others again are altars. . . . But the natives of Timor believe, too, in stones which have a certain power of rendering persons ill, or of making the crops fail. . . . It is the witch-doctor who diagnoses these stones, and when he discovers one in the vicinity of a house there is nothing to be done but to leave the house and settle somewhere else. . . . So, too, the stones which are war talismans have special virtues attributed to them." [2]

Similar notions are often to be met with in other districts. Two instances will suffice. "Among Nagas generally," says Hutton, "we find plenty of animatism (sic), particularly as regards stones. The Sema village of Lazemi boasts a pair of stones, male and female, that breed and produce offspring yearly, while similar beliefs may be found among all Naga tribes." [3]—There are "charm stones kept in granaries to ensure the prosperity of the owner, and as a guard against the depredations of mice." Stones known as agchucho (black stones with a white streak in the centre) "breed and beget young, in witness whereof there are numerous small stones always to be seen lying around the place where the agchucho are. These in time will grow up and become agchucho and breed in their turn. In most Sema villages, agchucho are prized only as giving

---

[1] Felix Speiser, Ethnologische Materialen aus den Neuen-Hebriden und den Banks-Inseln, p. 345.
[2] A. C. Kruijt, "De Timoreezen, Bijdragen tot de taal-, land- en volkenkunde van Nederlandsch-Indië, 1923, pp. 455–6.
[3] J. H. Hutton, The Angami Nagas, pp. 179–80. Cf. Ibid., pp. 408–9.

success in war." [1] "Like the *agchucho*, the charm-stones (*anagha*, *ashega*) breed and increase. *Anagha* are kept in the paddy and conduce to plentiful crops, ensure their lasting well, and among other duties fight the mice that come to eat and despoil. In proof of this every true *anagha* has on its surface the marks where mice have bitten it. . . . The irregular stones are compared to the hind leg of a pig, the head of a deer, etc., and contribute to plenteousness of flesh, whether wild or tame. These are called *ashega* and kept in the house to ensure success in hunting and the prosperity and fruitfulness of live stock." [2]—And lastly, another trait which slightly recalls what Armstrong has reported: "A black stone, about eighteen inches long, picked up in the fields . . . somewhere about the year 1906, had (in 1912) acquired a regular cult. It has an interpreter who communicates with it in dreams, in which it appears as a human being, the stone itself being said to walk about in human form by night. The stone has been put in a niche in a cliff where only one or two can approach it at a time. It is said to foretell success or failure in trading ventures. . . . This stone grows, and is incredibly reported to have increased its length by several inches since its first appearance. . . . Sacrifices are offered to it." [3]

To conclude our study of conceptions relating to stones, of the Bantus of the Ruanda, we are told that "the difficulty of making the negroes understand that the vegetable is superior to the mineral kingdom arises from the fact that they are persuaded that stones grow by 'intussusception,' and are endowed with veritable, though slow, powers of development." [4] This almost universal conviction makes the beliefs just related appear less strange than they seemed at first sight.

IV

Like the rocks and the stones, trees, too, may possess sacred characteristics. A belief in the close relationship of man with plants and trees is frequently to be found. I shall give a few significant examples merely. "The old-time Maori," says

[1] J. H. Hutton, *The Sema Nagas*, pp. 174–5.
[2] *Ibid.*, pp. 253–4. [3] *Ibid.*, p. 255.
[4] Fr. Alex. Arnoux, "Le culte de la société des Imandwa au Ruanda," *Anthropos*, vii, 1912, p. 287, note.

Elsdon Best, "looked upon trees in general with different eyes from ours. When the Maori entered a forest he felt that he was among his own kindred, for had not trees and man a common origin, both being the offspring of Tane? Hence he was among his own folk, as it were, and that forest possessed a *tapu* life-principle even as man does. Thus, when the Maori wished to fell a tree wherefrom to fashion a canoe or house timbers, for two reasons he was obliged to perform a placatory rite ere he could slay one of the offspring of Tane. He saw in the majestic trees living creatures of an older branch of the great family; he felt the strange old-world influences that spring from a belief in animatism, he heard the voices of unseen things in the rustling branches, in whispering winds, in the sound of rushing waters." [1]

To fell a tree, therefore, is a serious matter. We have just seen what ceremonies, supplications, adjurations and offerings the process demands from the Dschaggas. It is usually under-taken with the greatest precautions only, especially when, in addition to the general kinship between plant life and man, so to speak, there is a more direct and personal link with the tree in question. In Kiwai Island, "when clearing the ground for a new garden, the natives are afraid to cut down any big tree in case it may be the dwelling-place of an *étengena* (a kind of spirit). A large tree growing near a garden which one's parents have made, will never be touched. 'You cut him down,' said one of my informants, 'that is body belong you you cut him. That tree he dry; you dead too.' Sometimes a man who wants to cut down a tree, first asks the *étengena* to leave it, and go and live somewhere else. . . . It bears ill-will particularly to strangers, and that is one reason why people do not like to go alone to each other's gardens. A father will from time to time bring his son with him to his garden, and take him near the tree of the *étengena*, so that the spirit may learn to know the boy and become kindly disposed to him, it will understand 'that ground belong that boy, when father he finish, that boy he look out ground.'" [2] This observation has been rendered in the

---

[1] Elsdon Best, *The Maori*, ii, p. 452.
[2] G. Landtman in Beaver, *Unexplored New Guinea*, 2nd ed., pp. 309-10. Dr. Cremer has collected similar ideas and practices among the Bobo of French West Africa. "If a man wishes to clear fresh ground, he takes a fowl and sacrifices it to his ancestors, and then goes to consult the Revealer of secrets, asking him to tell

"pidgin-English," which is too restricted in vocabulary to bring out the delicate shades of meaning, for here the tree is somewhat too clearly differentiated from the spirit that dwells within it. If we are to enter fully into the native's idea, it is the tree itself (in its mystic nature) no less than the spirit immanent therein, whose malign influence he dreads for his son.

"Apparently dead and even seasoned timber may yet retain the soul which animated it during its lifetime. Thus, the instructions for the performance of the rites to be used at the launching of a boat involve an invocation to the timbers of the boat, which would therefore seem to be conceived as capable, to some extent, of receiving impressions and communications made in accordance with the appropriate forms and ceremonies." [1] This is (as usual with Skeat) translating into expressly animistic language conceptions which probably are not so definite and clear-cut in the natives' minds. The circumstance which Skeat is relating may be placed, quite naturally, side by side with the similar ones that Gutmann has described. It must no doubt be understood in somewhat the same way, taking into account of course the differences existing between the conceptions of the Malays and those of the Dschaggas.

In another work Gutmann had insisted at length upon the "feeling of unity of life with plants and animals" which a man in these societies experiences and his desire to be in communion with them. The primitive, says he, feels himself dependent upon plants and animals to an extent that we find it very difficult to imagine. "As an effect of this dependence he pictures to himself in a totally different fashion from ours the calm assurance and the certainty of their means of existence enjoyed by animals and plants as compared with himself. And in this way he

---

him where the field's special powers reside. The Revealer says that the first place is the top of the slope, and that he must be careful when he gets there; another is the tamarind tree that towers above the other trees, and he must sacrifice to it, and yet another is the hohu tree; the offering he makes to it will renew the field. . . . If he has burnt a sacred tree and wants to put the fire out he must bring thither some unfermented beer, buy a cotton bandage, and catch a goat. Then he ties the bandage and kills the goat. This is done to 'impress' the funeral rites of the tree, and to preserve his own health, for if he does not do it, some misfortune will ensue. . . . He apologizes to the sacred trees for burning them while clearing, 'he did it in ignorance.' "—J. Cremer, *Les Bobo*, pp. 88-90.

[1] W. Skeat, *Malay Magic*, pp. 194-5.

saw, clearly traced before him, the path he must follow to acquire their calm assurance and their certainty. It would not be by violent methods, but by veneration, by an effort to adapt himself to their modes of life." [1]

Gutmann justifies this original theory by a vast number of circumstances that he himself has noted. "Even to-day the Dschagga, when it is a question of marriage or of birth, attaches the greatest importance to his connection with certain trees, the chief of which is the banyan. This appears in a twofold aspect as the protector of young lives—on the one hand, on account of the power of rejuvenation afforded by its aerial roots, and on the other, because of its soothing and milky sap, which flows in such abundance that it heals all injuries to the bark. It is in material made from this bark that the mother and her suckling are wrapped, and from a tree of this species, re-garded as sacred in ground belonging to the Msiwu familial group, is acquired, with solemn rites, and prayers addressed to it, the material to be used for the newly circumcised, these, according to the ceremonial used, being regarded as new-born." [2]

There is one tree with which the Dschaggas, doubtless because of its importance to them, have preserved the same relations from time immemorial, and this is the banana. It demands assiduous care, and it is responsible for the ultimate settlement of the tribe in one place. The Dschagga venerates it to-day as his guardian and protector and as the link which binds one generation to another. In Gutmann's article we can see the importance of the rôle attributed to it in the initiation and marriage ceremonies. Infants and old men are under the special protection of the banana. The Dschagga believe, too, that cattle serve as an intermediary between plant-life and man. The banana plantation has special need of cattle manure, and it is on condition of being well-manured that it renews its products." [3]

In short, the human group regards itself as in close relation, if not of descent, at any rate of community of essence, with the beneficent plant world which has enabled it to lead a life

---

[1] Br. Gutmann, "Die Ehrerbietung der Dschagga Neger gegen ihre Nutz-pflanzen und Haustiere," *Archiv für die gesammte Psychologie* (1924), p. 124.
[2] *Ibid.*, p. 127.   [3] *Ibid.*, p. 136.

less rigorous than that of nomadic tribes. Its gratitude is embodied in a series of conceptions which their emotional and mystic character render difficult of description. "The primitive," says Gutmann, ". . . revered a tree as a higher associate to whom he owed his food, clothing and shelter, which provided him with weapons and tools . . . which gave flexibility to his bow, solidity to his club . . . which, once dead, gave him through its body (timber) the most effective defence against wild beasts and spectres—the red flower of fire. . . . He sought especially after a most intimate connection with trees which seemed to him to possess the supreme virtue of renewing and healing themselves, such as the banyan fig and the banana." [1]

His first ambition therefore is to gain the goodwill of the plants whose precious benefits have become indispensable to him and, while venerating them, to raise himself to their level. What his rites and ceremonies, adjurations and prayers are intended to bring him is that intimate communion with them which shall make him a participant in their mystic powers and the privileges which he esteems so highly.

These are far-sighted ideas of Gutmann's, and they help to throw light upon one aspect of primitive mentality, for the representations described as current among the Dschaggas are not exceptional. Similar ones, having animals for their object, are found in many peoples who live by cattle-rearing, such as Kafirs, Hereros, and many other Bantu tribes. We know how incredibly fervent are the sentiments with which cattle inspire them, how they care for, love and venerate them. Nothing is more precious in their eyes, and they are little short of being worshipped and adored.

But even when we are considering tribes much lower in the social scale than these Bantus, there is an analogy which cannot be denied, even though it be naturally a more remote one. When Von den Steinen, for instance, is accounting for the ideas and sentiments of the Brazilian Indians relative to the animals by means of which they live and to which they owe not only their food but their weapons, ornaments and implements, he uses words which strikingly recall Gutmann's own descriptions.

[1] Br. Gutmann, "Die Ehrerbietung der Dschagga Neger gegen ihre Nutz-pflanzen und Haustiere," *Archiv für die gesammte Psychologie* (1924), p. 124.

Yet one more fact will serve to stress the homogeneity of the vital essence in men and trees. "Not only," say Smith and Dale, "may a man live at the expense of others, but he may also by means of *musamo* draw life from trees. Once when Sezongo II was very ill, the doctor had men climb a Butaba tree, cut a thick branch and carry it, taking care not to allow it to touch the ground, to the chief's hut and plant it there. At the foot of the branch the doctor went through some incantations. The Butaba is a tree full of vitality, a stick from it readily takes root and grows: some of its vitality, by means of the doctor's magic, passed into Sezongo and he recovered. The tree then planted is still pointed out." [1]

V

Primitives' collective representations with regard to animals seem to us less singular than those we have just studied, no doubt because our folk-lore is very similar to theirs in this domain. From our own childhood our fairy-tales have accustomed us to viewing animals behaving like men, and vice versa. Looking into the matter more closely, however, our attitude differs more from that of the primitive than would at first sight appear. We amuse ourselves, as if in a game, by attributing to certain animals our passions and our methods of acting; we make of some of them—such as the fox, bear, lion, etc.—the living symbol of a characteristic and of a vice. But at the same time, the feeling of the gulf which separates the nature of the animal from that of man, is always more or less clearly present. To the primitive who also amuses himself with such tales this gulf does not exist. In his eyes the transit from animal to man and from man to animal is accomplished in the most natural way, without astonishing or shocking anybody. It is agreed, too, as self-evident, that the faculties of animals are no whit behind those of human beings. "The child-like mind," says Callaway, "has no theory to support; it makes no arbitrary distinctions between intelligence as manifested by man and intelligence as manifested by brutes: where it sees actions implying intelligence, there it believes intelligence exists." [2] To the Caribs of British Guiana, "animals, and

---

[1] Smith and Dale, *The Ila-Speaking Peoples of Northern Rhodesia*, i, p. 258.
[2] C. H. Callaway, *Zulu Nursery Tales*, p. 135.

plants, and lifeless beings live and act like man. In the morning
the animals go to 'their work,' like the Indians do. The tiger
and the snake and all other animals go out hunting, having
'to look after their family' like the Indian has. . . . The
swimming fish does nothing else but paddle onward. The
birds (and maybe all animals) are proprietors and have possessions. Every bird possesses 'its' plant. Kuano, the king of
the vultures, behaves like a real king too. Apakaui, the smallest
of the vultures, has to light the cigar for him, just as in the
Carib family the women and children have to light the cigar
for their husbands and fathers." [1]

Von den Steinen relates similar facts, and gives the reason
for them. "The Indian did not know that he was separated
from the animal world by a gulf. He merely perceived that all
created beings conducted themselves as he did in essentials:
they had their family life, they understood each other by means
of a language of their own, they had habitations, fought each
other, lived upon what they caught or upon fruits; in short, he
felt himself to be *primus inter pares*, but not above them." [2]—
Among Bantus, much more advanced, Junod sees in this way
of assimilating animals and men, at any rate in certain cases,
a deeper meaning, both symbolical and realistic. "The human
beings are represented by animals which resemble them in a
certain point: the reed-buck, wandering during the night,
signifies the wizards who do the same; the hyena, which eats
the remains of the feasts of the lion, is the parasite following the
chief, etc. There are thus signifying and signified objects: the
fate of the signifying will be the fate of the signified. This
conclusion, to which an enlightened mind would certainly
object, is forced upon the mind of the primitive, plunged in the
twilight of his animistic captions, by a kind of self-evidence.
He has a much deeper intuition of the unity of the animal and
human world than we have. Spoon once told me mysteriously:
'The astragalus of the goat truly represents the people of the
village, because these animals live in it, they know us, they
know what is in us.' This is probably the deep, hidden reason
why the diviners believe in their art." [3]

[1] W. Ahlbrinck, "Carib Life and Nature," *Reports of the Twenty-First Congress of Americanists* (1924), p. 221.
[2] K. von den Steinen, *Unter den Naturvölkern Zentral-Brasiliens*, p. 201.
[3] H. A. Junod, *The Life of a South African Tribe*, ii, p. 521.

If these representations, which cannot be distinct, have to be translated into our conceptual language, we should say, for instance, that "animals are represented as being like men." We should give these words the complete and distinctly definite sense they convey to us, whilst to the mentality of the primitive, which perceives instinctively the homogeneity of essence in all beings, and attaches little importance to their outward form, they convey a very different meaning. Thus we fail to recognize and, if we are not careful, we falsify the primitive's thought by the mere fact of expressing it. This is a point we must always bear in mind if we are to avoid distorting facts, even those which seem the simplest and most intelligible.

I shall relate here a small number only, and these obtained chiefly in Malaya, where the evidence is particularly abundant and detailed, though somewhat too much tinged with systematic animism. "To the Malays," says Skeat, "the tigers are human beings who assume, for purposes of their own, the tiger's shape, and who have, moreover, in various parts of the Peninsula (Mount Ophir, for instance) settlements of their own; the houses of which have their framework of human bones, covered over with human skin, and are thatched with women's hair. They even have a chief who, unlike his followers, never adopts what may be called the tiger disguise, but always appears in his own shape as a man. They are besides credited with having established a regular form of government, and are believed to be under an injunction or 'curse,' which prevents them from taking the life of any of their human neighbours, unless it has been 'given them.' . . . The tiger beliefs are not in any way exceptional; there is an elephant city, just as there is a city of the tigers . . . and it is the same for the rhinoceros, crocodile, wild deer, wild hog, etc." [1]—Elsewhere Skeat says, too: "All wild animals, more especially the larger and more dangerous species, are credited in Malay folk-lore with human or (occasionally) superhuman powers. . . . Hunting dogs are spoken to continually as if they were human beings." [2]

Among the Sakai of the Malay Peninsula, "for all I know," says Evans, "all tigers may be thought to be human beings

---

[1] W. Skeat, "Vestiges of Malay Totemism," *Transactions of the Third International Congress for the History of Religions*, i, pp. 98-9.

[2] W. Skeat, *Malay Magic*, pp. 149, 181.

who have assumed an animal shape." [1] "The Mantra of Johore, even in the face of their Christian teaching, believe that a tiger in their paths is invariably a human being who, having sold himself to the Evil Spirit, assumes by sorcery the shape of the beast to execute his vengeance or malignity. They assert that invariably before a tiger is met, a man has been or might have been seen to disappear in the direction from which the animal springs." [2]

Here already we have the belief which is so widespread, the belief in the sorcerer who takes the form of an animal (the werewolf). But it is often a case of animals who have not magical powers. "Far away in the jungle (as I have several times been told in Selangor) the tiger-folk (no less than the elephants) have a town of their own, where they live in houses, and act in every respect like human beings. There they live quietly enough until one of their periodical attacks of fierceness comes on, and causes them to break bounds and range the forest for their chosen prey."[3]— "At Labu, in Selangor, I heard on more than one occasion a story in which the elephant-folk were described as possessing, on the borders of Siam, a city of their own, where they live in houses like human beings, and wear their natural human shape." (Here follows the story of an elephant wounded in the foot, who is the daughter of a king, and who marries a human being and has children, but finally becomes an elephant again.). . . "Ghost elephants are not uncommon. They are popularly believed to be harmless, but invulnerable, and are generally supposed to exhibit some outward and visible sign of their sanctity, such as a stunted tusk or a shrunken foot. They are the tutelary genii of certain localities, and when they are killed the good fortune of the neighbourhood is supposed to depart too." [4]

In the same way crocodiles are supposed to act like human beings. "Whenever it effects a capture, the crocodile carries its victim at once below the surface, and either tries to smother him in the soft thick mud of the mangrove swamp, or pushes him under a snag or projecting root, with the object of l(+ting

[1] Evans, *Studies in Religion, Folk-lore and Custom of British North Borneo and the Malay Peninsula*, p. 240, note 2.
[2] W. Skeat and Blagden, *The Pagan Races of the Malay Peninsula*, ii, p. 325.
[3] W. Skeat, *Malay Magic*, p. 157.   [4] *Ibid.*, pp. 151–3.

him drown, while it retires to watch him from a short distance. After what it considers a sufficient interval to effect its purpose, the crocodile seizes the body of the drowned man and rises to the surface, when it 'calls upon the Sun, Moon and Stars to bear witness' that it was not guilty of the homicide:

> It was not I who killed you,
> It was water which killed you.

"After thrice repeating this strange performance, the crocodile again dives and proceeds to prepare the corpse for its prospective banquet."[1] This disowning of the homicide is an exact imitation of the action of the hunter when he is explaining to his victim that it is not he who has slain it, that it must not bear him ill-will nor hide itself from him in future.

Moreover—and this belief is frequently met with in Africa—the crocodile attacks only those victims that have been "delivered" over to him.[2] How does he recognize them? By having recourse to a process of divination which enables him to "see," as in a mirror, the human being destined to become his prey. "Whenever this process reveals to him the figure of his prospective victim without the head, he knows he can safely attack the person thus designated."[3] The same is said to be true of the tiger.

From among the Toradjas Kruijt has collected accounts equally instructive. There is one, for instance, of an immense crocodile, very well-disposed towards mankind and always ready to allow those who asked his permission to cross the river. There was a special formula to be used, and then he would appear on the surface of the water. If he opened his mouth, the traveller might quite safely cross the river on his back, but otherwise it was best to refrain, for that was a sign that the man had done some ill-deed for which he was to be punished by death. It is only those who have something on their conscience who are slain by crocodiles; nevertheless, if they do kill someone, the death should be avenged.

"It is related that there was once a regular war between crocodiles and men. A youth had killed a young crocodile and cut it in pieces, etc. Thereupon the crocodiles in a fury assemble

---

[1] W. Skeat, *Malay Magic*, p. 290.   [2] *Vide Primitive Mentality*, chap. i, sect. 2.
[3] W. Skeat and Blagden, *The Pagan Races of the Malay Peninsula*, ii, p. 154.

and besiege the capital city. Finally peace is made; a chief offers them a goat, which is accepted. . . . Certain Toradjas imagine crocodiles that are like men, who, when they come ashore, shed their crocodile 'garment' and take human shape. One of these had hung up his skin in the reeds. Someone sets fire to these reeds, and the skin is burnt up. The crocodile remains ashore, marries, and has descendants possessing the power to make crocodiles leave the water."[1]

According to what Hose and Macdougall have been told, crocodiles, like other animal species, talk to each other, and formerly they used to talk with men. "The Orang kaya Tummongong tells us that in the olden times the crocodiles used to speak to his people, warning them of danger, but that now they never speak, and he supposes that their silence is due to the fact that his people have intermarried with other tribes."[2] —"Like all other races of Sarawak, the Kenyahs regard the crocodiles . . . as more or less friendly creatures. They fear the crocodile, and do not like to mention it by name, especially if one be in sight, and refer to it as 'the old grandfather.' They regard those of their neighbourhood as more especially friendly, in spite of the fact that members of their household are occasionally taken by crocodiles. . . . When this happens, it is believed, either that the person taken has in some way offended or injured one or all of the crocodiles, or that he has been taken by a stranger crocodile, that has come from a distant part of the river, and therefore did not share in the friendly understanding usually subsisting between the people and the local crocodiles."[3]—A young Kayan chief tells the same writers that a crocodile may become a man just like themselves. "Sometimes a man dreams that a crocodile calls him to become his blood-brother, and after they have gone through the regular ceremony and changed names (in the dream) the man is quite safe from crocodiles. Usong's uncle has in this way become blood-brother to a crocodile, and is now called Baiya (the generic name for the crocodile), while some crocodile unknown is called Jok. Usong considers himself the nephew of the crocodile Jok. Usong's father has also become blood-brother to a crocodile, and Usong calls himself a son of this particular unknown crocodile. Sometimes he asks these two, his uncle and his father crocodiles, to give him a pig when he is out hunting, and once they did give him one. After relating this, Usong added: 'But who knows if this be true?' "[1] It was a noteworthy remark, and possibly the young chief only uttered it out of regard for the scepticism which he divined in the white man who was his interlocutor, without, however, sharing his view of the matter. "Although Kenyahs will not kill a hawk, they would not prevent us from shooting one if it stole their chickens, for they say that a hawk that will do that is a low-class fellow, a cad, in fact—for there are social grades among the hawks just as there are among themselves."[2]

The preceding facts, which could easily be multiplied, sufficiently prove that to primitive mentality it is neither unprecedented nor absurd that an animal should appear in human shape, just as it is neither surprising nor terrifying to see a man assuming the outward appearance of an animal. In all countries the medicine-men are experts at this sort of thing. Here is an instance. "One group (of Kalamatans), the Long Patas, claim the crocodile as a relative. The story goes that a certain man named Silau became a crocodile. First he became covered with itch, and he scratched himself till he bled and became rough all over. Then his feet began to look like a crocodile-tail, and as the change crept up from his feet to his body he called out to his relatives that he was becoming a crocodile and made them swear that they would never kill any crocodile. Many of the people in olden days knew that Silau became a crocodile because they saw him at times and spoke with him, and his teeth and tongue were always like those of a man. . . . Silau arranged with the other crocodiles that he would give a sign to his human relatives by which the crocodiles might always be able to recognize them when travelling on the rivers. . . . If a man of the Long Patas is taken by a crocodile they attribute this to the fact that they have intermarried to some extent with the Kayans."[3]

We shall find it necessary to call to mind this facility in

[1] Hose and Macdougall, "The Relations between Men and Animals in Sarawak," *J.A.I.* (1901), p. 190.   [2] *Ibid.*, pp. 178–9.   [3] *Ibid.*, pp. 193–4.

transformation when we study the case of dead persons who appear in animal form. But even now, when speaking of the living only, we find this on many an occasion presenting primitives with a problem which causes them grave anxiety. Every time that the movements, appearance, cries or gestures of an animal seem somewhat out of the ordinary they ask themselves in terror whether they may not be dealing with a human being —and they reply in the affirmative. A tiger or leopard which is bolder than the rest is assuredly a man, that is, a wizard. "Crocodiles," says Hardeland, "are beings like men, servants of the Djata, or water-divinities. They take the form of crocodiles only when they come to visit our world. For this reason a Dayak will never disturb—much less kill—a crocodile, except in the case when blood has to be avenged, one of his relatives having been killed by a crocodile."[1]

Beliefs of this kind, so frequent in the Malay Archipelago, are to be found elsewhere, in Africa as well as in South America, and among the Eskimos.

Among the Ba-ila, for instance, "some animals and birds are termed *bantu*, i.e. persons: and *baloghi*, i.e. warlocks. In them there is a quasi-personal quality. They are said to have *shingvule* (shadow souls), just as men have; but, unlike men, they are not reincarnated after death."[2] Here is something equally significant. "A Mukongo said to me one day: 'There are four different kinds of men: white, black, *ba-nganda* (crocodiles) and Portuguese.'"[3] In a note Father Van Wing explains that "crocodiles are ranged among men here because, according to a common belief, sorcerers are metamorphosed into these monsters that they may devour human beings." This is why, in naming them, the native can choose between "man" and "crocodile," because they can assume either form at pleasure. In calling them *ba-nganda* (crocodiles), he none the less does not fail to include them also in the number of human beings, of which they, like the Portuguese, form one class. Nothing could more clearly show that to his mind the form in which the crocodile-man or man-crocodile appears is a matter of in-

[1] A. Hardeland, *Versuch einer Grammatik der Dayakschen Sprache*, Anhang, p. 370.
[2] Smith and Dale, *The Ila-Speaking Peoples of Northern Rhodesia*, ii, p. 87.
[3] Fr. Van Wing, *Études Bakongo*, p. 113.

difference. He is man or animal at pleasure. Perhaps it would be more correct to say that he is both man and animal.[1]

"These people," says the traveller Magyar, when speaking of the Benguela negroes—and the same is true of nearly all the Bantu tribes and many other primitives—"believe that he who has been initiated into the secret arts of the wizard can assume at will the form and characteristics of any beast whatever."[2] He himself relates some characteristic instances. Here is one that shows how deeply rooted and active is this belief. "Two neighbours, Schakipera and Kimbiri, go to the wood to gather honey. Possibly Schakipera was the more adroit, or it may have been mere luck, but at any rate he found four big trees full of honey whilst Kimbiri could only find one. When he reached home again, Kimbiri was bewailing the fact that he had had such bad luck, while his neighbour had been so fortunate. Meanwhile Schakipera had returned to the wood at once with his relatives in order to bring away the honey he had found. In the evening he was attacked and torn in pieces by a lion. His companions hastily climbed trees and thus saved themselves.

"His affrighted relatives at once go to the *kimbanda* (sooth-sayer) to discover who was really responsible for his death. The *kimbanda* consults the oracle several times and finally declares that Kimbiri, jealous of his neighbour's rich harvest of honey, assumed the form of a lion in order to avenge himself. . . . The soothsayer's judgment was reported to the ruler of Kiakka, and he, in the face of the accused's strenuous denial, ordered the matter to be settled by the ordeal of poison." Matters then followed their usual course in affairs of this kind. The ordeal was unfavourable to the accused, he confesses, and succumbs to tortures.[3] This is an ordinary story, but the significant point about it is that the accusation appears quite natural

---

[1] Among the Jibaros of Ecuador, "there are instances of trophies having been made of the head of the jaguar. Many years ago an Indian woman was killed by a jaguar in the neighbourhood of Rio Zamora. The Jibaros regard a jaguar, which in this way attacks and kills people, as the incarnation of the soul of an evil sorcerer which has entered that wild beast with a view to harming or killing his enemies. The Indians consequently resolved to take revenge, arranged a hunting of the animal, and succeeded in killing it. They thereafter made a trophy of his head, and a victory feast was celebrated in the ordinary way." R. Karsten, *Blood-Revenge, War and Victory-Feasts among the Jibaro Indians of Eastern Ecuador*, Bureau of American Ethnology (henceforward designated as E.B.), Bulletin lxxix, pp. 33-4.
[2] L. Magyar, *Reisen in Süd-Afrika* (1849-57), p. 328.   [3] *Ibid.*, pp. 121-4.

to the soothsayer who formulates it, the prince who orders the trial by ordeal, the crowd of bystanders, to Kimbiri himself who has been transformed into a lion, in fact, to everybody except the European who happens to be present. It amounts to an accusation of wizardry, for who does not know that a wizard can assume the form of an animal when he pleases?

Major von Wissmann relates a similar story, adding: "The belief that human beings can assume the shape of wild beasts is universal in Africa. Whenever anybody is torn by a beast of prey, they find out by some manipulation who has been the sorcerer who had changed himself into a wild beast. On a former occasion, in a conversation with Tibbu Tibb, who is on the whole rather enlightened, I was astonished to find him clinging to this superstition."[1]

In Northern Nigeria, "when a child gets to the age of three or four without being able to walk, and keeps thin in spite of a large appetite, the case is considered a very serious one. The parents bring the child to the priest and consult him. He examines the child, and may inform the parents that it is not human, but 'the offspring of something in the bush or in the water.' If the offspring of something in the bush is indicated, the parents give the child to a friend to carry to the bush: he does so, leaves the child and hides to see what happens. The child left to himself will first cry and then, after looking round and seeing that no one is about, will change into a monkey and vanish among the trees; the watcher returns and reports. If the offspring of something in the water is indicated, the same procedure takes place; the child is left near the water, and finding itself alone, becomes a water-snake and disappears into the water."[2] Thus a disclosure, which appears passing strange to us, decides the parents upon abandoning a child to whom they have had time to grow attached. The statement seems quite natural to them. The outward appearance of the child, apparently normal, does not prevent it from being at the same time an animal, or even an animal rather than a human being. Since it possesses this dual nature it is or will become a sorcerer; it will bring misfortune to its relatives and to their social group. They must therefore rid themselves of it.

[1] Von Wissmann, *My Second Journey through Equatorial Africa*, p. 261.
[2] C. A. Woodhouse, "The Inhabitants of the Waja District of Bauchi Province," *Journal of the African Society* (1924), p. 113.

The idea that a child of normal appearance may nevertheless not be "human" is a familiar one to primitives. Among many peoples, when a woman gives birth to twins, one of them is sacrificed, and frequently for the reason that it is the offspring, not of the woman's husband, but of a spirit, or at any rate that it is not the child of a living human being. Moreover, Spencer and Gillen report the existence of the following belief: "On the very rare occasions on which the child is born at a very premature stage as the result of an accident, nothing will persuade the natives that it is an undeveloped human being; they are perfectly convinced that it is the young of some other animal, such as a kangaroo, which has by some mistake got inside the woman."[1] Junod incidentally alludes to a similar belief. "During pregnancy . . . conjugal relations . . . are recommended. I one day overheard the grieved outpourings of a young married man who was complaining bitterly that he had been bewitched by his maternal aunt" (he believed that she had rendered him impotent). " 'It is because my wife is pregnant, and my enemies wanted to jeopardize her pregnancy, and put in the place of a child that could not grow a snake or rabbit or quail or gazelle or something of that kind.' "[2]

These facts throw light upon the innumerable stories and legends in which a woman gives birth to a snake or crocodile, a bird, or an animal of some kind or other. To the primitive's mind the fact in itself has nothing that is incredible. Being unusual it calls for, and receives, a mystic interpretation, but it is not contrary to nature, and no one has any idea of throwing doubt upon it.

Thus for reasons which, in his own eyes, are sufficiently forcible, the primitive will always be ready to think that an animal is in reality a man who has changed his shape. "I have often tried to chide the Garenganze people," says Arnot, "for their want of bravery in not hunting down the many wild animals that prey around their towns, carrying off the sick people, and often attacking and seizing solitary strangers. They excused themselves by explaining that these wild animals are really 'men of other tribes,' turned, by the magic power

[1] Spencer and Gillen, *The Native Tribes of Central Australia*, p. 52.
[2] H. A. Junod, "Conceptions physiologiques des Bantous sud-africains," *Revue d'Ethnographie et de Sociologie* (1910), Nos. 5-7, p. 157.

they possess, into the form of lions, panthers, or tigers, who prowl about to take vengeance on those against whom they are embittered. In defending this absurd theory, one man said it was not possible for a Luba and Lamba man to go out into the country together without one stealing a march upon his neighbour, getting out of sight, and returning again in the form of a lion or leopard, and devouring his travelling companion. Such things, they say, are of daily occurrence among them; and this foolish superstition leads them not only to tolerate the wild animals around, but almost to hold them sacred."[1] It is the same with the Ba-rotze. "During our absence in the capital, the leopard had seized upon some of them. . . . Finally, during supper one night, he was caught in the trap which Andréas had already set many times in vain, and he escaped safe and sound, carrying away the bait. Our Zambesi boys at once exclaimed: 'This leopard is not an animal: it is a person.' "[2]

These men-beasts or beast-men have formidable powers, surpassing those of ordinary men or animals. They inspire very mixed feelings; fear and respect are the dominating ones, mingled with a strong desire to avoid contact with them if possible, and not to attract their attention, above all, not to excite their wrath. According to the Copper Eskimos, "birds and animals have extraordinary faculties and powers. Some of the shamans know their speech and can converse with them. Many animals have changed to human beings before the very eyes of the hunters, and changed as quickly back again. They can be offended by scornful words, and the hunter who mocks the caribou, for example, or the seal, will suddenly find himself stricken down by sickness or afflicted by constant ill-luck."[3]

Rasmussen relates the following circumstance in the very words used by the Eskimo who recounted the story. "A woman, while out for a long walk, once came to a house she had never seen before, and went inside. There was no one at home, but towards evening the people of the house came back, and they turned out to be bears in human shape. So she hurriedly hid

F. Arnot, *Garenganze*, pp. 236-7.
[2] A. and E. Jalla, *Pionniers parmi les Marotze*, p. 39.
[3] D. Jenness, *The Life of the Copper Eskimo*, p. 180 (The Canadian Arctic Expedition, vol. xii).

herself by creeping behind the skin hangings. The bears came home, and she saw that one of them was carrying a hunting-thong and a harpoon, just as men do. When the bears had eaten, they went to bed, and the bear that had carried the same hunting implements as a man lay down just in front of the woman.

" 'It is strange how the skin hangings on the wall bulge out!' said the bear once. And the woman, who was afraid she would be discovered, strangled her child, which was beginning to cry.

"The bear with the hunting implements was the soul of a bear that had just been killed by a man, and the implements it was carrying were the very ones the hunter had hung up over its skin.

"The woman could hear them talking about people, and they said: 'Yes, we cannot stand against them, for they bar the way for us with their dogs and they kill us with their arrows.'

"Next day, when the bears had gone out hunting, the woman fled home, and told the others what she had heard and seen.

"This happened long ago, in the days of our first forefathers, and that is how we know about the souls of the bears."[1]

Later on we shall have to inquire into the real meaning of the word "soul." For the time being we grasp here how it is that a non-conceptual representation, difficult for us to reproduce, comprises the essential characteristics of man and animal at the same time. These people who return home at night, talk, eat, and go to bed as men do, are known at once by the woman hiding behind the skin hangings to be animals. Possibly they had the form of bears until they had reached the very threshold. One of them is dead, but save for his carrying the hunting implements, he does not appear any different from the others. Finally, the woman is so much in dread of these bear-men or men-bears that she does not hesitate to strangle her child that its cries may not betray her presence.

The Chukchee, who have been so carefully studied by Bogoras, have similar ideas. "All kinds of wild animals are supposed to have a country and to keep households of their own. . . . The hunters of the Chukchee Peninsula are un-willing to dig out young foxes, because foxes 'have a household of their own' and might take vengeance by means of their household charms. . . . Black bears live in underground houses, and polar bears have a country of their own on the ice in the open sea. They live by hunting seal and walrus, and engage in quite extended expeditions for this purpose. They also build snow houses, which are lighted by oil-lamps, and have other human-like pursuits. Eagles have a separate country. . . . The smaller birds also have a country of their own, from which they go out in small toy-like skin boats to hunt worms and mussels. . . . Sea mammals have a large country of their own far away in the open sea.

"Animals, when personating human beings, can change their shape and size quite as easily as spirits do. The ermine, for instance, appears as a stately warrior clad in white armour. . . . The owl also becomes a warrior. Mice are people living in underground houses. (They have) reindeer and have sledges of grass. By a sudden transformation they become real hunters with regular sledges, and hunt polar bears. . . .

"A shaman who visits the land of mice finds that their ways of life are quite human. He is requested to help a woman who is suffering from a severe cold and a sharp pain in her throat." (On her neck the mouse has a thin noose of grass, having been taken in a snare, from which he frees her.) . . . "In most cases animals, while personating human beings, retain some of their former qualities, which identify them as beings of a special class acting in a human way, but different from mankind. . . . The fox-woman keeps her strong smell, etc."[1]

VI

To the primitive's mind, men and animals, taken in the widest sense of the words, are, as W. E. Roth felicitously puts it, "intimately interchangeable." From this it is an easy transition to the ideas of a special kind which are frequently encountered in primitive myths and legends. Those of the Arunta have been made well-known by Spencer and Gillen. The description given by them of the mythical ancestors of this tribe is in striking harmony with the ideas we have just been studying. "In the Alcheringa" (in the mythical and legendary

[1] W. Bogoras, *The Chukchee*, pp. 283-4.

D

period) "lived ancestors who, in the native mind, are so intimately associated with the animals or plants the name of which they bear, that an Alcheringa man of, say, the kangaroo totem may sometimes be spoken of either as a man-kangaroo or as a kangaroo-man. The identity of the human individual is often sunk in that of the animal or plant from which he is supposed to have originated.

"Going back to the far-away time, we find ourselves in the midst of semi-human creatures endowed with powers not possessed by their living descendants and inhabiting the same country which is now inhabited by the tribe."[1] . . . And a little farther on: "To the Australian native there is no difficulty in the assumption that an animal or a plant could be transformed directly into a human being, or that the spirit part which he supposes it to possess, just as he does in his own case, could remain, on the death of the animal, associated with such an object as a Churinga, and at some future time arise in the form of a human being."[2] And lastly, "the fundamental feature of the totemic system of the Arunta," according to these same writers, may be expressed thus: "Each individual is the direct reincarnation of an Alcheringa ancestor, or of the spirit part of some Alcheringa animal."[3] . . . "He was a member of a group of individuals, all of whom, just like himself, were the direct descendants or transformations of the animals, the name of which they bore. It is as a reincarnation of the never-dying spirit part of one of these semi-animal ancestors that every member of the tribe is born, and therefore, when born, he, or she, bears of necessity the name of the animal or plant of which the Alcheringa ancestor was a transformation or descendant."[4]

We shall come upon this notion of reincarnation again in further study. For the moment let us retain only that of the mythical beings in whom this Australian tradition sees the origin of its totemic groups. Theirs is no isolated case. With many peoples the ancestor who gave the tribe its existence is also a hybrid being, semi-human, semi-animal or vegetable. A similar feature is to be found in the legends of the Andaman Islands, and A. R. Brown has noted its significance. "Many of the actors in the legends bear the names of animals, but at the

[1] Spencer and Gillen, *The Native Tribes of Central Australia*, pp. 119–20.
[2] *Ibid.*, p. 127.   [3] *Ibid.*, p. 202.   [4] *Ibid.*, p. 228.

same time are spoken of as though they were human beings. Many of the legends explain how some species of animal arose from some one of the ancestors who became an animal and the progenitor of the species." (Here the author gives an instance.) "It is necessary to define as exactly as possible what meaning these stories have to the natives. It is not simply that the legendary person is a man with the name and some of the characteristics of an animal; nor is it simply that the legendary person is the ancestor of the species of which he bears the name. We can only adequately express the thought of the Andamanese by saying that he regards the whole species as if it were a human being. When, in the legends, he speaks of 'Sea-eagle,' he is thereby personifying the species . . . he is regarding the characteristics of the species as if they were characteristics or actions or results of actions of a person. Admittedly this is a vague description, but the vagueness is in the mental pheno-menon described; the Andamanese do not, in this matter, think clearly and analyse their own thoughts. However, we can help ourselves to understand their thoughts by recalling the tales that amused us as children, in which the fox or the rabbit of the tale was an embodiment of the whole species."[1]

We can help ourselves too, it seems, by the circumstances just related and explained, for they have demonstrated primi-tive mentality passing—on the very slightest inducement occa-sionally—from the idea of the human being to that of the animal, or inversely. It is accustomed to the assumption that the same being may be sometimes human, sometimes animal, or both together at the same time, and these are really no mere vague ideas. They certainly appear so from our point of view, used as we are to thinking by means of clear-cut concepts, and because we are trying to impose our logical forms upon the objects of primitive thought, but to the latter, ignorant of our logical exigencies, such ideas are on the contrary clear and lucid, if not definite. They determine action, often irresistibly, a fact of which we have had abundant proof. Consequently the semi-human, semi-animal mythical beings of the Australian aborigines are in all respects comparable with those of which we have already spoken, which proceed from a human form to that of a crocodile, lion, or screech-owl, and the reverse, or

[1] A. R. Brown, *The Andaman Islanders*, pp. 387–8.

those which are at the same time men and lions, men and crocodiles, and so on. These mythical beings, therefore, do not constitute a separate class, the product of a mental activity which is especially poetical or religious. Primitive mentality moves in the midst of such ideas as in its natural element. Whether it is a case of a dread wizard with the power of taking on the form of a tiger, or of the mythical ancestor possessed of both the human and animal nature, the mental process is exactly the same. The participation is imagined and felt in the same way in both cases.

When we fully comprehend the usual modality of the primitive mind in action these mythical beings no longer appear exceptional. We at once perceive how it has been able, indeed how it has been obliged, to create them. The assumption, at will, of divers forms, and the possession, all together or in turns, of the characteristics inherent in these forms, is one of the natural and unvarying privileges of persons who are endowed with an intensity of mystic force. In every social group the man who has been admitted, by a long and secret initiation, into the world of occult forces, and made to participate therein— the medicine-man, the wizard, the shaman, the "*piaé*," etc.— has at the same time acquired the power to assume, when he pleases, some other than the human form. Now the mythical ancestor is naturally represented as bearing within him the highest degree of mystic force. He is *par excellence* a reservoir and source of *mana*. He therefore possesses, *ipso facto*, the ability to appear, now in one form, and now in another, and to participate constantly in both forms at once.

When the animal or plant form is the predominating feature in such a representation, the ancestor is frequently said to be totemic. We know how many discussions and problems have gathered round totemism. It is not our purpose to treat here the problems which we consider are very often badly propounded, because they imply definitions and distinctions to which the primitive is a stranger. Dr. Rivers is entirely right when he says: "If, at the present time, you talk to a Melanesian about the totemic ancestor from whom he traces his descent, he will speak of this ancestor at one moment as if he were a human being and at another moment as if he were an animal. When you endeavour to ascertain when or how the change took place, you find that, so far as you can tell, there was no change, but the subject of the narrative has been thought throughout as both a human being and an animal. Your endeavours to give the narrative definiteness from your own point of view seem to your informant only evidence of failure to understand the whole matter; if you persist in these attempts, he loses heart, and may either refuse to say more, with the excuse that he has forgotten the story or does not know it properly, or he continues his narrative carelessly and gets out of difficulties by giving answers on lines suggested by the form of the inquiries."[1] The wise course, as Rivers shows us, is to seek definiteness from the Melanesian point of view only.

Among the Orokaiva of British New Guinea, "the *heratu*" (a plant-emblem) "of the clan is constantly referred to as 'our ancestor.' . . . When a man is dead and lies awaiting burial, the women may be heard crying to him as the offspring of his *heratu*: 'Child of Asava! Child of Hombiga!' " (Asava and Hombiga are plants.)

"Now I have many times asked the native what he means by calling the plant-emblem his ancestor. Sometimes he cannot give an answer, but very commonly he can, and then it is always the same: 'Our real ancestor,' he says, 'was a human being, not a tree; *it was a man with a tree-name.*' "[2] Nothing can be more definite than this explanation if we know how to understand it, and do not read into it distinctions which the native does not make. To this Papuan, as to the Australian aborigine and Rivers's Melanesian, the dual nature of the mythic ancestor is self-evident.

From what we have just formulated we shall retain but the consequence which follows. The totemic ancestor, whether it be lion, leopard, crocodile, witchetty-grub, eucalyptus, or anything else, is not merely the animal or plant ascertained to exist in the milieu in which the social group is living. It is, as A. R. Brown has realized, the mystic essence, both of the individual and of the species of this animal or plant, and at the same time it is a being with a human essence. If it is ordinarily represented

[1] W. H. R. Rivers, *History of the Melanesian Society*, ii, p. 359.
[2] F. E. Williams, "Plant-Emblems among the Orokaiva," *J.A.I.*, xlv (1925), p. 414.

with the attributes of such and such an animal species, if it appears as a kangaroo or a lion, that does not prevent it from being at the same time a man, nor indeed mean that its human form may not exist beneath the other, actually rather than potentially, and quite ready to manifest itself. Sometimes the two forms indeed coexist, as we see in the double masks of the Eskimo of the Mackenzie River and of Labrador, where the eye can perceive in such characteristic fashion the dual nature of the beings they represent.

The totemic ancestor properly so called must therefore be a particular instance of the mythical ancestor found almost everywhere, in whom the animal or the plant is indissolubly mingled with the man. This participation extends to the human group descended from him, and if this group renders the mythical ancestor the worship due to him, it receives benefits from him. His close relationship with the animal or plant species the form of which was possessed by the ancestor should assure it of his protection.

Do we not find, too, in these representations inherent in primitive mentality, the origin of one of the most persistent themes of their art? We see bodies of animals having human heads, human bodies surmounted by the heads of crocodiles, lions, whales, monkeys, birds, and human limbs side by side with the limbs of animals, etc. Accustomed as we ourselves may be to representations of sp'.inx, chimera, centaur, gryphon, mermaid, and other fantastic beings, the art of the primitive, in spite of the noteworthy objects it has produced, often appears monstrous to our minds. But this is a mistake which would at once disappear if we were able to place ourselves at the point of view taken by the primitive artist and those for whom his work has been done. In their eyes these hybrid beings are by no means fictitious monsters, but on the contrary they are ordinary and familiar objects. These drawings and sculptures express in the most explicit fashion the participation of one being in two natures, or rather, in two forms, both of which belong to it at the same time. This duality naturally remains merely potential when the being appears in one of its two forms, though it is nevertheless actual, since the form that is unseen is present there, even if not perceived. The work of art discloses it to the eyes. By uniting a man's body with the head or limbs or tail of a crocodile, a lion's body with a human head, it simply materializes the coexistence of the two forms.

These curious and at times wonderful results of primitive art are not, therefore, any more than myths, the product of an imagination directed towards fantastic creations. Among these peoples as among ourselves the artist is he who excels in expressing what all feel and perceive imperfectly. The anthropozoomorphic statues which to us appear to be the product of unbridled fantasy are for the most part faithful representations of traditional ideas. I might say, and without uttering a paradox, that such art is above all realistic. It endeavours to reproduce faithfully models which are in the minds of all.

Moreover, these mythical beings, half human and half animal, but at the same time superhuman and superanimal, which are both source and stay to the social group, are, as we know, the most copious well-springs of mystic force which the primitive mind can conceive. They are beings *par excellence*, the beings whence others derive their reality. Now the representation of them is in a certain sense their very selves. It participates in their mystic power, and causes it to radiate on all around. When they are carved on the pillars and the fronts of human dwellings in New Guinea, for instance, on the prow of their canoes, their tools and weapons, their seats (for there is no object at all, says Jenness, speaking of the natives of Entrecasteaux, which has not its ornamentation), we may be pretty certain of two things; firstly, the artistic embellishments, while destined to please the eye, first and foremost help objects to participate in the *mana* possessed by their models; secondly, the artist's fantasy has not been able to exercise itself save within fairly narrow limits. For, except in conventional designs, if he did not faithfully reproduce the type of mixed being which all have in mind, he would probably be exposed to considerable trouble, and assuredly he would not satisfy his fellows.

Thus the works of art are the plastic expression of the most sacred collective representations, just as certain myths are their poetic expression, and certain institutions their social one. If primitives frequently endeavour to reproduce beings who are half human and half animal, they are but interpreting the mystic coexistence of the human and the animal forms in the beings who are the revered objects of their thought.

PART I

CHAPTER I

THE SOLIDARITY OF THE INDIVIDUAL WITH HIS GROUP

I

AFTER having studied the instances given in the Introduction we are, I consider, authorized in presuming that the primitive does not conceive the connection between a living being and its species quite as we do. When a leopard, or a mouse, for instance, is actually present to his sight or is imagined by him, the representation of it is not differentiated in his mind from another, a more general image which, though not a concept, comprises all similar beings. This grasps them in their ensemble, dominates them and frequently, if his mind dwells upon them, seems to engender them. The representation of it is characterized both by the objective qualities which the primitive perceives in beings of this kind, and by the emotions they arouse in him. It is somewhat analogous to the way in which, during the Great War, many people would talk of "the Boche," and as many colonists in Algeria talk of "the Arab," or many Americans of "the black man." It denotes a kind of essence or type, too general to be an image, and too emotional to be a concept. Nevertheless it seems to be clearly defined, above all by the sentiments which the sight of an individual of the species evokes, and the reactions it sets up.

Similarly, the idea which primitives have of plants and animals is both positive and also mystic. They are able to select the edible fruits and nearly always, when their condition is a sufficiently settled one, they know how to cultivate certain plants and how to treat those which, like the manioc, are originally noxious; they can hunt or lay traps for the larger animals, birds, fishes, etc. But on the other hand, as Gutmann has clearly shown, they have a great respect for the outstanding faculties of plants and animals, which so marvellously suffice unto themselves, and which therefore possess an ability, or rather, a power that man would gladly share with them. Hence their attitude with regard to them, not in any way like ours, that of a superior being, an irresponsible master. Hence, too, the complex sentiments of astonishment and admiration and sometimes even of veneration, and the need, as it were, of assimilating themselves to them, which lend the primitives' images of these beings a semi-religious character.

Such an aspect of them necessarily escapes our consciousness. It contains affective elements which we do not experience, and, on the other hand, we are not able to think unless definite concepts of plants and animals occupy our thoughts. As a matter of fact, the primitive's mind does not picture either the individual or the species exactly, but both at the same time, one within the other. As I have already recalled above, and as many observers have noted—A. R. Brown in the Andaman Islands, Junod and others among the Bantus—we can get some idea of what is in their minds through the personages of our old fairy stories of childhood. The bear, the hare, fox, tortoise, etc., are at the same time individuals—Bruin, Reineke Fuchs, and so on—and the personification of their species. Thus, whatever may happen to an animal in the story, if he is killed, for instance, it does not prevent him from reappearing alive, often in the same story. As far as the individual is concerned, he undergoes all possible catastrophes, and even death, but in so far as he is a type, he is imperishable, indestructible, comprising in himself the infinite multiplicity of the individuals of his species. Smith and Dale have noted this trait in the folk-lore of the Ba-ila. "To us there is a lack of coherence in many of the details, and explicit contradictions pull us up and spoil our pleasure; as when Fulwe, after being cooked and eaten, gives Sulwe his doom. But such things do not worry the Ba-ila or detract from their enjoyment. For one thing, Fulwe, though dead, lives in his race; it is a mere accident that one individual dies; it is the ideal Fulwe, not the Fulwe who merely breathes, but the Fulwe in the narrator's mind, and *he* is immortal."[1] To use the terms of Plato, the Ba-ila represent to themselves the "idea" of him.

It is not in stories alone, but also in everyday life that the primitive mind tends to confuse the individual and the species. As Miss Benedict remarks of the Bagobo: "The killing of a

[1] Smith and Dale, *The Ila-Speaking Peoples of Northern Rhodesia*, ii, p. 344.

snake, though perhaps not carrying a direct prohibition, is regarded as unwise, in view of the attitude which the snake community might assume toward the offender. . . . They told me that if the snake had been put to death all its relatives and friends might have come to bite us."[1] (In this case a snake, encountered upon the road, had been carefully removed but not killed.) This solidarity among snakes implies that they are imagined, or rather, *felt*, to be all participating in the same essence.

Instead of snakes, it may be animals, of such a kind that man can hardly choose whether he is to spare or to kill them; he may be obliged to pursue them and take their lives that he may feed upon them. He will then take the greatest precautions not to offend his game, and, so that he may be forgiven the necessary slaughter, he will repudiate it. (We have already seen that the crocodile imitates man in this respect.) In a former volume we have examined into the meaning of the rites relating to hunting and fishing.[2] The invocations and charms before the departure and during the expedition, the excuses and supplications after the death of the animal, are not addressed solely to the one about to be pursued, or the one killed, but, through it, to all its species, and the species in its very essence or, as Smith and Dale express it, in the "idea" of it. The real individual is not such and such a stag or such and such a whale, but *the* Stag, *the* Whale.

This leads at once to two results. In the first place, a very close connection unites animals of the same species. Their individuality is but relative, and they are actually only multiple and transient expressions of a single and imperishable homogeneous essence. Offend one, and you incense them all. Should you be so unwise as to speak ill of one of them and irritate it, it is not that one alone of which you must beware, for all will avenge the insult. Or again, all will escape you. It is not one certain stag which will not let you perceive or approach him; the unlucky hunter will see none of them. So, too, if a forbidden word has been uttered, all the trees of a certain species become invisible to the eye. When at last the game has been captured he is entreated thus: "Do not tell your companions or your

[1] L. W. Benedict, *Bagobo Ceremonial, Magic and Myth*, pp. 238-9.
[2] *How Natives Think*, pp. 227-44.

fellow-creatures that we have injured you, for it is not we who have taken your life. On the contrary, we are offering you food, fresh water, weapons, everything that can please you. Tell the rest how well we have treated you," etc.

The hunter's concern in this particular is particularly well-depicted in the *Relations de la Nouvelle-France*. "The savages," says the missionary Le Jeune, "do not throw to the dogs the bones of beavers or female porcupines—at any rate, only certain specified bones; in short, they take very good care that the dogs do not eat the bones of the birds or any animals caught in the nets, for otherwise they would have immense difficulty in catching others of the species. Again, there are countless regulations to be observed in this respect, for it does not matter if the vertebræ and the rump are given to the dogs, but the rest must be thrown into the fire. In any case, for the beaver which is ensnared it is best to throw its bones into a river. It is remarkable that they collect these bones and preserve them so carefully, that you would think their hunt would be useless if they had contravened their superstitions.

"Whenever I laughed at them and told them that the beavers did not know what happened to their bones they used to say: 'You don't know how to trap beavers, and yet you want to tell us about them.' Before the beaver is actually dead, they told me, his spirit would come and look round the hut of the man who had taken him and he would notice very carefully what had been done with his bones. If they had been given to the dogs, the other beavers would have been warned, and that would make it very difficult to snare them, but they are quite content to have their bones thrown into the fire or into the river, and the net which has ensnared them is especially pleased about it. I told them that the Iroquois, according to the report given by the one who was with us, threw the bones of the beavers to the dogs, and yet they caught a good many, and that our French hunters took incomparably more than they did, nevertheless our dogs ate the bones. 'There is no sense in what you say,' was their reply; 'don't you see that both you and the Iroquois cultivate the soil and reap the harvest, and we do not; therefore it is not the same thing at all.' When I heard this irrelevant reply, I began to laugh."[1]

[1] *Relations de la Nouvelle-France* (1634), pp. 87-9.

No doubt the Indians wished the missionary to understand
that the Iroquois and the French alike did not depend, as they
did, on living by the good will of the animals they were hunting,
and thus had not the same urgent need to conciliate the species
to which their victims belonged. In the lines which follow the
passage just quoted, Father Le Jeune is deploring the fact that
he knows so little of the Indians' language. We may well ask
ourselves, therefore, if the expression he uses really renders
their thought when he is speaking of the "spirit" of the beaver
coming into the hut to see what has become of its bones. What
is certain is that the other beavers, according to the Indians,
have been told about it. The treatment meted out to one
animal is immediately known and resented by its companions.
The Indian is fully persuaded of this, and his actions bear
it out.

As to the sum-total of plants or animals of a certain species
living at present, the primitive does not even attempt to imagine
it. To him it represents an indefinite multiplicity, which he
regards collectively as he would his own hair, or the stars in
the sky. He does not think of this as an abstract idea, yet he
needs to represent it in some form or other to himself, since he
feels it to be more real than the individuals composing it. His
representation is reported to us in varied forms, although these
are all somewhat related to each other. It is probable that their
diversity depends, at any rate partially, on the greater or lesser
degree of exactness in the observations made, according to
whether the observers understand much or little of the language
and the mentality of the natives studied, and whether these are
more or less disposed to reveal what they really think, as well
as the degree of capability they possess in doing so when their
consent is obtained. For it often happens that the white man
is asking them to define for him something that they have
never yet formulated to themselves. We can therefore guess at
the value of the reply he is likely to get.

It is once again Father Le Jeune, one of the best of the Jesuit
observers of New France, from whom we borrow a fairly precise description of the idea we are now following up. "They
say that all animals of every kind have an elder brother who is
as it were the source and origin of all individuals, and that this
elder brother is wondrously great and powerful. The beavers'

elder brother, one of them told me, is about as big as our hut, whilst the young ones (by which I understand the ordinary beavers) are not quite as big as our sheep. It appears that the elders of all animals are the juniors of the Messou (the Manitou?). He is therefore well-connected, the worthy restorer of the universe is the elder brother of all the animals. If during sleep this eldest animal or principle of animal life is seen, the hunting will be successful; if the dreamer sees the senior of the beavers, he will trap beavers; if it be the senior moose-deer, he will catch them, and revel in the possession of the juniors by favour of the senior he has seen in his dreams. I asked them where these elder brothers were. 'We are not quite certain,' they said, 'but we believe that the senior birds are in the sky and the other seniors in the sea.' "

This principle, this "elder brother," then, is a kind of personified genius of the species, in whom individuals of the species, the younger brothers, participate, and which makes them what they are. Here it seems as if we can understand the primitive's thought without difficulty. The idea of the genius of a species is familiar to us, and even natural. It has some affinity with the "archetypes" of the philosophers. Let us be cautious, however, lest we be deceived by words. When *we* speak of the genius of a species, we have first represented to ourselves collectively the animals or plants which compose it, we have framed a general abstract idea of it. Later we interpret this concept of ours by a concrete, perceptible form, and thus the genius of the species is a more or less expressive and living symbol, according to the imaginations engaged upon it. In all cases, however, for us this personification of the species comes *after* the concept and presupposes it. The very language we speak would itself be enough to impose this order on us.

The processes through which the primitive mind works are quite different, however. To it the genius of a species is not a more or less concrete symbol which follows after the concept, for primitive mentality has no abstract general ideas, or at any rate, if it possesses any, they are vague and indefinite. The representation of the genius takes their place. Since it is veritably the source, as Father Le Jeune puts it, and the substance of the individuals which participate in it, it is this which constitutes the element of generality, and this which is at the very centre of the particular representation of each individual of the species.

It now becomes very difficult to locate ourselves at the point of view of primitive mentality. To tell the truth, we can hardly flatter ourselves that we ever really arrive there. We cannot expunge from our minds concepts which they have possessed from infancy, or suddenly do away with the use and the memory of words that we have always employed. How can we feel, as primitives do, that when an animal has been wounded or killed, not only are all the others of his species immediately warned, but that in reality it is not a particular individual but the very species personified in its essence and in its genius that has been struck down? If it were merely the case of a certain lion or a certain stag the hunter would not trouble any more about it. He would leave the wild beast there, he would eat the game, and there would be an end of the matter. But it is not solely a certain particular animal that he has killed; he has attacked the mystic essence of all lions or all stags, and this, as Father Le Jeune says, is "wondrously great and power-ful," and hence indestructible. A mortal man's blows cannot endanger it. The Eskimo who slays an immense number of caribou does not imagine that these animals will ever disappear. If they become scarce and he finally sees none at all, he will account for the fact by some mystic reason. The caribou con-tinue to exist and are no less numerous, even if they have been slain in thousands, but now they are refusing themselves, that is to say, the genius of their species has withdrawn his favour from the men whom he formerly permitted to track and slay them.

It is thus essential to retain his good graces at any price. If through some fault, such as the violation of a taboo, neglect of a rite or ceremony or incantation, a man has been unfor-tunate enough to lose them, it is absolutely necessary to regain them. The safety and well-being of the group depends upon its relations with these "genii," with the mystic principles of certain vegetable or animal species. If these relations are strained, he is in danger, and if they break, life is no longer possible for him. The hunter may then spend days and nights in the forest and the fisherman in his canoe; neither will catch anything. His wives, children, and he himself will die—unless

E

the tribe is no longer nomadic, at any rate at certain seasons, or unless his wives know how to cultivate plantations and fields. It is thus easy to account for the unusual honours rendered by the hunter and his family to the animal slain—that is, in reality, to the genius of its species. Since the rites have both a persuasive and a constraining influence, the primitive is sure that, if everything has been carried out as it should be, the relations between himself and this genius will remain satisfactory. Future hunting and fishing expeditions will once more turn out well.

In other regions, it is not of the genius of a species of plants or animals that a man talks, but of its ancestor, its chief, master, or king. He personifies the "mother of the rice" which bears it and makes it grow, and allows it to be gathered. Upon the subject of the "paddy spirit" Leslie Milne says: "His home is wherever the paddy is growing. He travels with the paddy as its bodyguard, and he is able to be in more than one place at the same time."[1] Kruijt relates that he was shown a "king of trees." On the east coast of Sumatra, the Bataks have planted large india-rubber trees. "At a place called Pematang Bandur, I found an enormous specimen of this kind of tree. They told me that this was the king of the heveas, and that it was forbidden to tap it except in times of the greatest need, for if this giant were ill-treated, the other trees would yield less latex."[2] This tree is to its congeners what the "mother of rice" is to the paddy.

Representations of the same kind are frequently encountered in the case of animal species. "Among the Atjeh natives, and in Macassar, Boegin, and with the Dayaks," says Kruijt too, "there is in each herd of buffaloes or cows one called 'the captain.' Most frequently it is an animal of a special form or colour. It keeps the troop together, that is, it holds fast the principle (zielstof) of the others, so that they remain with one another and keep healthy. If this captain-buffalo were to be slain, the others would certainly die or run away, and in any case the herd would be broken up."[3]

It is the same with wild animals. In Southern Nigeria, for instance, "among every thousand or so of bush-pig, one is to

---

[1] Leslie Milne, *The Home of an Eastern Clan*, p. 2
[2] A. C. Kruijt, *Het Animisme in den Indischen Archipel*, p. 155.   [3] *Ibid.*, p. 133.

be found, of great size and very splendid, with a skin marked like that of a leopard. . . . Such animals are the kings of the bush-pig. They are never allowed to walk at all, but are carried everywhere by those of the common sort. . . . Never do they seek for their own chop. This is brought by the lesser pigs, at dawn and evening time. . . . Each year the King Boar is carried away to a new place amid very thick bush, so that the hunters should never find him."[1] This king-boar, like the buffalo-captain, the giant hevea-tree, the "mother of the rice," the elder brother of the beavers, like all the "genii" of this kind, is a personification, if we may put it thus, of the mystic essence of which all the individuals of the species partake. He is the true "unit" of them all.

With the Dschagga the word used to designate the bees of a hive is in the singular, and perhaps we have here a linguistic trace of an idea akin to the foregoing. What interests the Dschagga especially is not any particular specimen of these insects, or their number: it is the Bee, the wonderful race that can produce wax and honey. It is certainly seen in a mass, but it is essentially a principle, genius, mystic power of which it is natural to speak in the singular.

II

Does a man's representation of himself in his relations with his group differ considerably from that he pictures of the plant or animal with respect to its species? It is hardly possible that such should be the case if it be true that the difference between men, animals, plants, and even inanimate objects, is not one of nature but merely of degree, and that the faculties possessed by animals are in no whit inferior to those of men. Moreover, as we have already seen,[2] the idea that an individual has of himself, in primitive communities as in our own, must be differentiated from the subjective feeling he possesses of his states of consciousness, emotions, thoughts, actions and re-actions, etc., in so far as he refers them to himself. From this latter point of view his personality is for him an individual clearly distinct from all the rest, opposed to them, and appre-

[1] P. A. Talbot, *Life in Southern Nigeria*, pp. 92–3.
[2] *Vide* Introduction, pp. 1–2.

hended by him in a way that is unique and very different from that in which he perceives individuals and objects around him. But this direct apprehension, vivid and constant as it may be, forms only a small part of the idea he has of his own personality. The predominating elements of it are collective in origin, and the individual hardly grasps himself save as a member of his social group. There are very many facts which prove this, and I shall cite but a small number only, choosing those which most clearly demonstrate it.

"A man," says Elsdon Best, "thought and acted in terms of family group, clan or tribe, according to the nature or gravity of the subject, and not of the individual himself. The welfare of the tribe was ever uppermost in his mind; he might quarrel with a clansman, but let that clansman be assailed in any way by an extra-tribal individual, or combination of such, and he at once put aside animosity and took his stand by his side."[1] Again: "A native so thoroughly identifies himself with his tribe that he is ever employing the first personal pronoun. In mentioning a fight that occurred possibly ten generations ago he will say: 'I defeated the enemy there,' mentioning the name of the tribe. In like manner he will carelessly indicate 10,000 acres of land with a wave of his hand, and remark: 'This is my land.' He would never suspect that any person would take it that he was the sole owner of such land, nor would any one but a European make such an error. When Europeans arrived on these shores many troubles arose owing to the inability of the Maori to understand individual possession of land, and land selling."[2]

It is the same in French West Africa. "The individual," says Monteil, "whatever he or his position may be, is of no importance save as a member of the community; the community exists and progresses, he only exists and progresses by it and, to a great extent, for it."[3] In the Belgian Congo, "at the same age, every free Azanda seems to know just as much as his fellows; they give the same replies and manifest the same psychology. Thus it is an excessively stable and conservative psychology. The value of the social group seems to them to be inviolably fixed. . . . Therefore any revolutionary, any man

---

[1] Elsdon Best, *The Maori*, i, p. 342.   [2] *Ibid.*, pp. 397–8.
[3] Ch. Monteil, *Les Bambara du Ségou et du Kaarta*, p. 220.

who on account of personal experiences was differentiated from the collective thought, was at once pitilessly destroyed. Sasa had one of his own sons executed for having changed a legal decision which was the customary one. The Azanda who has been in contact with us, or who has acquired a different mental outlook, no longer has a place in the social group. . . . As a rule, what strikes one most in the answers given by the semi-civilized with regard to their customs is the very slight importance attaching to individual opinion compared with the collective thought of the group. They do this or that, not because 'I' want it, but because 'we' desire it. Here, more than among Western peoples, whose individualization often masks a profound participation in the life of the community, we realize how intensely social the life of the Azanda is. All its rites, all its education tends to make the individual one with the community, to develop in him qualities exactly like those of the other individuals of his group."[1]

De Calonne-Beaufaict lays special stress upon the obligatory conformity which tends to make all the individuals of the same group alike. His testimony is supported by other witnesses, who show the subordination of the individual to his group among the Bantus. For instance, a missionary tells us: "In studying Bantu institutions, it is necessary at the outset to eliminate our idea of the individual. . . . A man's rights and duties are born with him, being conditioned by his precedence in the family and the precedence of the family in the tribe. Nothing is further from Bantu thought than the doctrine that all men are endowed by nature with fundamental equality and an inalienable right to liberty (whatever the definition of the term). . . . They cannot admit for a moment that any man but a chief is born free, and they cannot conceive how any two men can be born equal. Everything in their political system is built on status, and status is a matter of birth.—Well, all this means that the individual does not exist in Bantu society. The unit is the family."[2]

Smith and Dale say the same thing: "The clan is a natural mutual-aid society, the members being bound to render their fellows all the help they can in life. Members of one clan are,

[1] A. de Calonne-Beaufaict, *Azande*, pp. 20–4.
[2] Rev. W. C. Willoughby, *Race Problems in the New Africa*, pp. 82–3.

if we may use the Biblical language, members also one of another. A member belongs to the clan; he is not his own; if he is wronged they will right him; if he does wrong the responsibility is shared by them. If he is killed the clan takes up the feud, for he belongs to them. If a daughter of the clan is to be married they have to give their consent first. Ba-ila who have never met before will at once be friends if it turns out that they are of the same *mukoa*. If one has the misfortune to become a slave, his clansmen will contribute his redemption price," etc.[1]

Such a social organization at once involves a great difference between the idea of the individual animal and the human individual. Each animal is directly and immediately a participant in the mystic principle which is the essence of its species, and all have the same claim to it. Save for those which have something unusual about them, in which the primitive's mind suspects witchcraft, they all are, so to speak, similar and equivalent expressions of this "principle" or "genius." The human individual himself also exists by virtue of his participation in the essential principle of his group, but a community of human beings does not correspond at all points with an animal or vegetable species. First of all, it is not of an indefinite number in the same way as they are. Above all, it is articulated into sections and subsections. The individual occupies in turn several positions in his group. He attains them more or less quickly according to his birth and to his social importance during the course of his life. In short, in every human society there are ranks and a hierarchy, even if one of seniority only. The individual, whoever he may be, is dependent upon the group (except in the case of a chief where his absolute power has been accepted), but not in a way that is uniform.

The more deeply observers penetrate the minds of "primitive" or semi-civilized peoples, the more important does the rôle of this hierarchy appear to be. Spencer and Gillen have demonstrated it in the Central Australian tribes, Dr. Thurnwald in the Banaro of New Guinea, and Holmes in other Papuans of British New Guinea. The last-named relates the story of a man who kills his younger brother for having taken a place which belonged to the elder without asking permission.—Among

[1] Smith and Dale, *The Ila-Speaking Peoples of Northern Rhodesia*, i, p. 296.

the Bantus, the individual is both strictly subordinated to the social group and rigidly established in his own rank. The group, as we know, is composed of the living and of their dead, and the first place belongs to the latter. These must therefore be served first. It is to them that the first-fruits are offered, and none would fail in this obligation. "Bantus," as Junod observes, "do not think they dare enjoy the products of the soil if they have not first given a portion of them to their gods. Are these gods not those who make cereals grow? Have they not the power even of controlling the wizards who bewitch the fields? These rites are also evidently dictated by the *sense of hierarchy.*"[1] —Among the Hereros, no one dare drink of the morning's milk just drawn from the cows until the ritual libations have been performed. The ancestors must drink first.

The "village," that is, the familial group, among the Thonga people studied by Junod, "is a little organized community having its own laws, amongst which the most important seems the law of hierarchy. The elder brother is the uncontested master, and no one can supersede him. He is the owner of the village. . . . No one must 'steal it' from him. Should any one do so, the whole community would suffer and no children would be born; the life of the organism would be deeply affected; this is the reason why the headman must go first with his principal wife to have relations with her in the new village, and thus to *take possession* of it or *tie* it. For this same reason, when the headman dies, the village *must* move. As long as the inheritance has not yet been distributed, it is still *his home*; but as soon as the ceremony has taken place, the villagers must go away, and close the door with a thorny branch."[2] As Junod says elsewhere: "There is a mystic tie between this man and the social organism which is under him."[3] Should he die, the village dies also. This intimate dependence on him is expressed by the Thonga, not in abstract terms, but in striking images. "The chief is the Earth. He is the cock . . . he is the bull; without him the cows cannot bring forth. He is the husband; the country without him is like a woman without husband. He is the man of the village. . . . A clan without chief has lost its reason. It is dead. . . . The chief is our great warrior; he is

---

[1] H. A. Junod, *The Life of a South African Tribe*, i, p. 376.
[2] *Ibid.*, pp. 296-7.   [3] *Ibid.*, p. 289.

our forest where we hide ourselves, and from whom we ask for laws. . . . The chief is a magical being. He possesses special medicines with which he rubs himself or which he swallows, so that his body is taboo," etc.[1] Does not such a social organism recall—*mutatis mutandis*—a hive of bees? Is not the chief in certain respects to be compared with the captain-buffalo that "keeps the herd together," and by its own power so assures its well-being and cohesion, that when it is slain the herd perishes or is broken up?

Moreover, and here again is another aspect of the intimate and almost organic solidarity uniting members of the same social group, the individual which does not belong to it counts for nothing. We know how much attention the group shows to its dead, and how it hastens to render them all the honours that are their due. But "when a *stranger* dies in a Thonga village, when no one knows him, 'he does not matter'" (says Junod's informant). "The grown-up men will bury him. They dig a hole and drag the corpse into it with a rope. They do not touch it. There is no contagion, therefore no ceremony of purification. Among the Malukele and the Hlengwe such a corpse is burnt."[2]

III

Melanesian and Micronesian languages nearly all present a remarkable peculiarity, which Codrington sums up as follows: "It is most important to understand that all nouns in Melanesian languages are divided in native use into two classes: those that take the personal pronoun suffixed, and those that do not. . . . In Melanesian languages, excepting Savo, the distinction is based upon the notion of closeness or remoteness of connexion between the object possessed and the possessor, but the carrying out of this principle in detail is by no means easy to follow. . . . In some cases no doubt the same word may be used with or without the suffix; but never when the word is used in precisely the same meaning."[3]

The nouns which take this suffix, "according to a strict native use," are "nouns which generally signify members of the body,

[1] H. A. Junod, *The Life of a South African Tribe*, i, pp. 356-7.
[2] *Ibid.*, i, p. 166.　　[3] R. H. Codrington, *Melanesian Languages*, pp. 142-3.

parts of a thing, equipments of a man, or family relationship."[1] In the Tami language of German New Guinea, for instance, "an important class of nouns is composed of those which take a possessive suffix: they are nouns denoting degrees of relationship and parts of the body."[2] In Neu Pommern, on the north coast of the Gazelle Peninsula, Father Bley remarks: "The possessive pronouns are also used to denote relationship, the connection (*Zugehörigkeit*) of the part with the whole, particularly of the parts of the body to the body itself, and they are placed after the noun, partly as suffixes."[3] At the same time, Father Bley points out some exceptions to this rule.—In the Roro, a Melanesian language of British New Guinea, "the possessive suffixes may be used with or without the personal pronoun preceding the thing possessed. The suffixes are used only with special nouns such as parts of the body and relations."— In the Mekeo language of a neighbouring tribe "the possessive suffix is used in the case of parts of the body, relations, and a few other words."[4] We might cite other examples, but these will doubtless suffice to decide, as Codrington does, that this is an invariable rule in Melanesian languages.

Very often what seems to be an irregularity or an exception proceeds on the contrary from a very strict and precise application of the rule. This is so with the following irregularities, noted by Peekel:[5]

anugu tunan, my man (husband), instead of *tananagu*;
anugu hahin, my wife, instead of *hahinagu*;
a manuagu, my wound, instead of *anagu manua*;
a subanagu, the remains of my meal, instead of *anagu subana* (*gu* being the personal pronoun suffix of the first person).

From the natives' point of view, these are perfectly regular forms, and indeed the only correct ones. In fact, since exogamy is strictly observed in these tribes, husband and wife belong

[1] R. H. Codrington, *Melanesian Languages*, p. 128.
[2] Bamler, "Bemerkungen zur Grammatik der Tamisprache," *Zeitschrift für afrikanische und ozeanische Sprachen* (1900), v, p. 198.
[3] B. Bley, "Grundzüge der Grammatik der Neu-Pommerschen Sprache an der Nord-Küste der Gazelle Halbinsel," *Zeitschrift für afrikanische und ozeanische Sprachen* (1897), iii, pp. 101–2.
[4] Strong, "The Roro and Mekeo Languages of British New Guinea," *Zeitschrift für Kolonialsprachen*, iv, 4, p. 304.
[5] Peekel, *Versuch einer Grammatik der Neu-Mecklemburgischen Sprache*, pp. 68–9.

to different clans. Accordingly the husband is not and cannot be related to his wife, nor she to him, and it is quite natural that the possessive pronoun should not be suffixed after the nouns "husband" and "wife." These nouns are not among the class of substantives taking the pronominal suffix. Conversely, the wound which involves a part of my body, and the skin of the banana that I have eaten are, to the primitive's way of thinking, things which "belong" to me in the strictest sense of the word. They are literally parts of myself; therefore the nouns "wound" and "remains of the meal" must be followed by the suffix.—By virtue of the same principle we can understand why the native says *anugu hahin* (my wife) without the suffix, when speaking of the woman he has married, for she is not of his family. But he will say: *hahin i gu* (my sister) with the suffix, for his sister is of the same clan as himself; she "belongs" to him, in the sense that she makes, with him, part of the same whole, like two limbs belonging to the same body.

In Micronesian languages we find, too, a class of nouns taking the personal pronoun as a suffix. According to Thalheimer, who has made a special study of the subject, these are nouns denoting: (1) the parts of the body and the divers functions of man's mental activity; (2) relationship; (3) relation of a position in space and time; (4) the dependent parts of an independent whole; (5) personal adornments, weapons and instruments, the house, the garden; (6) possessive nouns, i.e. nouns provided with possessive suffixes, which serve in certain cases as possessive pronouns in a special sense (*Pronomina ediva et potativa*).[1]

This instructive list helps us to comprehend how the Melanesians picture the relations of kinship to themselves. Thalheimer himself remarks on this: "The solidarity of relatives among themselves is denoted in the same way as that of the various parts of an individual," and he accounts for this fact by the construction of the Melanesian *gens*, saying: "The individual is to the family what the limb—head, arm, leg—is to the living body."

Thus the fact to be found in their languages throws light upon ideas of which we can hardly suppose that Melanesians

[1] A. Thalheimer, *Beitrag zur Kenntniss der Pronomina personalia und possessiva der Sprachen Melanesiens*, pp. 52–7.

have a clear consciousness. They do not think in abstract terms, nor reflect upon concepts. They have never had any notion of the organic finality manifested by the structure and functions of a living body, nor of the special way in which the parts are subordinated to the whole, and the whole in its turn depends upon its parts. Neither have they ever analysed the solidarity uniting the individuals of the same family with one another. Nevertheless their languages testify that they do compare these. To them the familial group is a being which, by its unity, is like a living body. We too say: the "members" of a family, but to us it is a mere metaphor, though not an inapt one. To them, although they do not think about it, it is the literal expression of a fact. In their imaginings the individual does not depend less closely upon his familial group than the hand or foot depends upon the body of which it is a part.

As Codrington has noted, the division of substantives into two classes, one of which takes the possessive pronominal suffix, and the other not, is a feature peculiar to the languages of Melanesia and Micronesia. But in this very district, by way of exception, and in a good many others all over the world, one unvarying fact has been remarked. Certain substantives—usually the names of the parts of the body and the different relationships—are never used without a personal pronoun, whether it be prefixed or affixed or separated from the noun. Thus, in the Baining language, "there are words which are never used except conjoined with a personal pronoun. They are those which denote the parts of the body or the degrees of relationship. They are never to be met with standing alone . . . the possessive pronoun is placed before the noun. . . ."[1] In the other Melanesian and Polynesian languages known up to the present, he says, one is struck by finding a special possessive pronoun for a certain group of words denoting parts of the body and relationships. This kind of pronoun is used as a suffix for the nouns to which it refers. There is nothing like this in the Baining tongue. It knows no distinction between the possessive pronouns. It does not append a personal pronoun to any kind of substantive; the possessive pronoun is always

[1] Roscher, "Grundregeln der Baining Sprache," *Mitteilungen des Seminars für orientalische Sprachen*, vii, p. 38.

placed *before* its substantive. Moreover, the Baining recognizes also certain substantives (precisely those denoting parts of the body and relationships), which he never uses without a possessive pronoun. Thus we see that Baining thought coincides on this point with that of the surrounding peoples, but the way in which it is expressed is different.[1]

This remark holds good for hundreds, perhaps thousands, of languages: Oceanic, American, African, Asiatic, European, in which one cannot, according to Powell's way of putting it, say simply "hand" or "head," but must always indicate at the same time whose hand or head it is; languages in which one cannot say "father," "mother," "son," "brother," etc., without mentioning whose father, mother, son, or brother is in question. The fact is universal, as it were, and it has been noted scores of times. Everywhere the rule applies equally to the nouns denoting degrees of relationship and parts of the body, and usually to these two categories only. This, it appears, allows us to conclude, especially after analysing the more peculiar facts ascertained in Melanesian and Micronesian languages, and without being too bold in concluding, that in all parts of the world these two categories of nouns—names of relationships and names of parts of the body, make but one in reality. All proceeds as if, to those who speak these languages, the two relations are exactly alike. Not that they have ever taken this into account themselves. They apply this grammatical rule of theirs, of a grammar which is frequently so complex and so meticulous, with the same unreflecting rigidity and the same spontaneity as others. Yet the fact that the rule exists is only the more significant.

IV

How are we to understand the term "family relationship" in societies either "primitive" or "semi-civilized"? It is not very long since ethnologists first thought of putting this question to themselves, yet as long as it had not been considered, dire confusion was inevitable in the matter. Up to a fairly recent period it has been accepted, as if it were a self-evident fact,

[1] Roscher, "Grundregeln der Baining Sprache," *Mitteilungen des Seminars für orientalische Sprachen*, vii, p. 33.

that all existing human families were of essentially the same type as our own. Both history and observation seemed to agree with this instinctive conviction. What we knew of the Roman, Greek, Slav, Semitic, Chinese, and other families seemed to confirm the idea that the fundamental structure of the family is everywhere the same.

Now to-day we know that in a great many of the social communities which are more or less "primitive," what we call the family, in the traditional and current sense of the word, does not exist. In its place ethnologists have found an institution that we can designate by the same name, but only on condition that we remember that it is radically different. A careful study of the vocabularies of these societies will suffice to establish this fact. Among the Banaro, as Dr. Thurnwald rightly remarks, "the absence of the family (in our sense of the word) is accompanied by the absence of the expressions which correspond with this idea."[1]

The family which is noted in these societies is of the type called "classificatory." We find it of the same kind in all its essential features in all latitudes, and in districts most remote from each other. It has been described in North America, where Morgan discovered it; in South America (among the Araucans, for instance); in Australia, Melanesia, Papua, Equatorial and South Africa; among the Ashanti (where Captain Rattray recently confirmed its existence); among the Yakuts in Siberia, and so forth. In short, the classificatory "family" or system seems to have been no less widespread than our own type of family, which we held to be universal.

Its primary characteristic, as Howitt so aptly puts it, is that "the social unit is not the individual, but the group; and the former merely takes the relationships of his group, which are of group to group."[2] The individual does not form a part of a certain group because he has this or that tie of relationship; on the contrary, he has this or that tie because he forms part of a certain group. This family constitution is so different from our own and so foreign to ideas and sentiments which have been natural to us from childhood's days, that we can understand how it happened that it should have been unrecognized for

[1] Dr. R. Thurnwald, *Die Gemeinde der Banaro*, pp. 133–4.
[2] A. W. Howitt, *The Native Tribes of South-East Australia*, p. 157.

so long, even by the observers who saw it daily. It demands a persevering effort to grasp the idea thoroughly. Nevertheless, if we do not accustom ourselves to the idea of "group relationship," the way in which many primitives picture to themselves their relations with other members of their familial group (known to the Germans as *Sippe*) will be unintelligible to us.

"It is absolutely essential," say Spencer and Gillen, "in dealing with these people to lay aside all ideas of relationship as counted amongst ourselves. . . . The primitive has no idea of relationships as we understand them. He does not discriminate between his actual father and mother and the men and women who belong to the group, each member of which might have lawfully been either his father or his mother."[1] Codrington says too: "It is the knowledge of this that forms probably the first social conception in the mind of the young Melanesian. It stands foremost in the native view of mankind, and is the foundation on which the fabric of society is built up. To the Melanesian man it may almost be said that all women, of his own generation at least, are either sisters or wives—to the Melanesian women, that all men are brothers or husbands."[2] In other words, all with whom marriage is forbidden her are her brothers; all the rest are her potential husbands.

Elsewhere Codrington has given a detailed description of this family constitution. Its fundamental feature is the following: "All of one generation, within the family connexion, are called fathers and mothers of all who form the generation below them; a man's brothers are called fathers of his children, a woman's sisters are called mothers of her children. . . . This wide use of the terms father and mother does not at all signify any looseness in the actual view of proper paternity and maternity . . . the one who speaks has no confusion in his mind, and will correct a misconception with the explanation: 'my own child' *tur natuk ; tur tasina*, his brother, not his cousin."[3]—A. R. Brown notes the same thing. "Although a given person applies the name *mama* (father) to a large number of individuals, if he is asked 'Who is your *mama*?' he immediately replies by giving the name of his actual father, unless his father died during his

[1] Spencer and Gillen, *The Northern Tribes of Central Australia*, p. 95.
[2] R. H. Codrington, "On Social Regulations in Melanesia, *J.A.I.*, xviii, 4, pp. 306–7.   [3] R. H. Codrington, *The Melanesians*, pp. 36–7.

THE INDIVIDUAL AND HIS GROUP

infancy, in which case he gives the name of his foster-father.
. . . Each term, therefore, has what we may call a primary or
specific meaning. The primary meaning of *mama* is father and
that of *maeli* is father's father. . . . Just as we use the word
'cousin,' so the Kariera native uses his word *mama*, speaking
of a large number of different related persons by the one name,
but distinguishing in thought, though not in words, those of
his 'fathers,' who are more nearly related to him from those
who are more distantly related. . . . This distinction between
nearer and more distant relatives of the same kind (that is,
denoted by the same term) is of the greatest importance in the
social life of the Kariera tribe. It seems probable that it is
equally important in other tribes of Australia, though I do not
know that it has been specifically pointed out by previous
writers."[1]

With this reservation, and taking into account the special
affection that children nearly always feel permanently for their
real mother, and frequently, too, for their father, it remains a
fact that it is by no means from mere politeness, or in a purely
conventional manner, that the primitive calls the brothers of
his father "fathers," the sisters of his mother "mothers," and
the children of his father's brothers and of his mother's sisters
"brothers and sisters," and "wives" (at any rate potential ones),
the women that he can lawfully marry, and so on. It is in this
manner that family relations impose themselves on him, and
his language testifies to the fact. In all the tribes of Queensland
studied by Dr. Roth, for instance, "son, daughter, brother's
son, brother's daughter, have no distinctive terms: every
language has but one word to denote them all. Similarly, the
sister's son and the sister's daughter are described by the same
word." In these tribes, too, Roth shows that the father's
father is denoted by the same word as the son's son, the mother's
mother by the same word as the son's daughter. These extraordinary circumstances are explained when we study the
classes and sub-classes between which alone marriage is permitted. We cannot enter into details about these classes, but
the nomenclature set forth by Roth suffices to show how
greatly the group-relationship of the Australian aborigines
differs from our own ideas of kindred.

[1] A. R. Brown, "Three Tribes of Western Australia, *J.A.I.*, xliii (1912), p. 150.

Codrington lays considerable stress upon this difference. In a passage where it is so marked as to be difficult to follow, he notes that in certain Melanesian languages the words "mother," "husband," "wife" are plural in form. "In the Mota language the form is very clear; *ra* is the plural prefix; the division, side, or kin, is the *veve*; and mother is *ra veve*; *soai* is a member, as of a body, or a component part of a house or of a tree, and *ra soai* is either husband or wife. To interpret *ra* as a prefix of dignity is forbidden by the full consciousness of the natives themselves that it expresses plurality. The kin is the *veve*, a child's mother is 'they of the kin,' his kindred. A man's kindred are not called his *veve* because they are his mother's people; she is called his *veve*, in the plural, his kindred, as if she were the representative of the kin; as if he were not the child of the particular woman who bore him, but of the whole kindred for whom she brought him into the world. By a parallel use to this a plural form is given to the Mota word for child, *reremera*, with a doubled plural sign; a single boy is called not child, but children, as if his individuality were not distinguished from the common offspring of his *veve*. The same plural prefix is found in other Banks' Island words meaning mother: *rave* in Santa Maria, *retve* in Vanua Lava, *reme* in Torres Islands. The mother is called *ratahi* in Whitsuntide, and *ratahigi* in Lepers' Island, i.e. the sisters, the sisterhood, because she represents the sister members of the social group who are the mothers generally of the children. Similarly the one word used for husband or wife has the plural form. In Mota a man does not call his wife a member of him, a component part of him, but his members, his component parts; and so a wife speaks of her husband. It is not that the man and his wife make up a composite body between them, but that the men on the one side and the women on the other make up a composite married body. The Mota people know that the word they use means this; it was owned to myself with a blush that it was so, with a Melanesian blush! and a protestation that the word did not represent a fact."[1] This is quite true. But it is no less so that it was the missionary who had taught them to blush about it. The existence of plural words to express "husband," "wife," etc., would not be accounted for if they had never corresponded with a reality,

[1] R. H. Codrington, *op. cit.*, pp. 28–9.

to which we have other testimony moreover. That there should be no word of singular form in these languages to express mother, child, husband, or wife, etc., is a feature (quite compatible, as we have seen, with the natural feelings of maternal or filial love) that of itself throws strong light upon the constitution of the Melanesian family.

After this the facts related by Thurnwald in his study of the Banaro of New Guinea will seem less singular. "Children," says he, "except the one who is called the child of the 'spirit' (*Geistkind*) give each other names according to their respective ages, and their sex, and the sex of the speaker is also taken into account. . . . As *aia* and *néin* mean merely 'older' and 'younger,' special expressions to express fraternal relationship properly so called are altogether lacking. The entire generation of children regards itself as a unit for the two halves of the clan, and the only distinction between them is their relative age. The feeling of belonging to some kind of paternal or maternal family is not contained in it."[1] As a matter of fact, among the Banaro, lineage does not call for the conception of the fixed relation which two complementary terms, like father and son, would arouse in us. The charge of caring for the generation which is growing up is the concern of the familial group (*Sippe*) and of the clan. *The absence of a family in our sense of the word* is on all fours with the absence of the words corresponding with these ideas (of father and son).[2]

A study of the words denoting family relationships would lead to similar results.[3] Paternity is conceived in a very different fashion from ours, and one which, in certain cases, has nothing to do with the act of procreation. Just as in the Australian and Melanesian tribes of which we have already spoken, among the Banaro there are no clearly definite words to denote married pairs, that is, words which do not at the same time serve to denote other persons. The word for woman (wife) properly signifies "mother." The word *mu-mona* (husband) is also used for other quasi-marital relations. In all that relates to the etymology of this word, we should hardly be in error in assimilating it to *nram* or *nam*: the other, the stranger, i.e. the man who comes from the other clan. (The Banaro practise exogamy.)

---

[1] R. Thurnwald, *Die Gemeinde der Banaro*, pp. 111, 115.
[2] *Ibid.*, p. 133.   [3] *Ibid.*, pp. 136, 145, 148.

Among them, as in all regions where the classificatory system is in existence, "we do not find any sharp boundary between relatives in the direct line and the collateral branches. No doubt this confusion of the two lines arises out of the circumstance that all social ties are conceived, not according to the relation of one individual to another, but according to *totals*, relations of groups and sub-groups of individuals. Thus it is not a consequence of the principle of exogamy in itself, but indeed of the idea they hold of society. Yet this must not be interpreted to mean that the individual is wholly left out of account. Closely connected individuals who stand in a definite relation to one another are comprised in the same term."[1]—"The principle according to which these groups and sub-groups are formed is moreover not unique. There is no characteristic which of itself determines it in a definite way. The predominating factor is the social relations between one person and another, for in the construction of the Banaro system these have had preponderating influence. Persons are afterwards grouped according to consanguinity and to age."[2] The young people who are growing up are ranked primarily and principally according to their age, and only afterwards according to their sex. "For adults, it is the sexual relations which are of the most importance. It is their position from the sexual point of view that determines the relation between two persons; it is decided according to whether sexual relations are allowed or prohibited between them, or with a certain third person. It is on these grounds that each individual is classed in a group relationship bearing a certain name."[3]

Before we leave the study of the Banaro I shall quote one more reflection of Dr. Thurnwald's which strikingly bears out what I have been trying to show here: "This method of grouping is closely bound up with the whole way of thinking of primitive peoples, and the latter is manifested in their general method of reckoning. In forming their groups the Banaro do not make use of general number-concepts as we do when we wish to distinguish the members of a family according to the universally applicable scheme of finding the distance between the degrees of relationship calculated from the precise

[1] R. Thurnwald, *Die Gemeinde der Banaro*, p. 149.
[2] *Ibid.*, p. 154.   [3] *Ibid.*, p. 158.

number of births separating one person from another of the same blood. The number-concepts of the primitive are mere aids to memory, or else they are the images of a mass, as for instance a basket full of things, a bearer's load, a pack of wolves, a band of men, and these images are formed according to the impression made upon the imagination by external objects. . . . In their method of classing and grouping, the classificatory systems of relationship reflect the characteristic of primitive mentality, which at once seizes upon the concrete and is quite aloof from any theoretical abstraction." And finally, this concise summing-up: "Relationship is not a matter of calculation, but of grouping."[1]

Thurnwald knows and discusses the works of Codrington, of Rivers and others who have recently studied the classificatory system. It may perhaps be interesting to recall, after this description of his, one which was given more than twenty-five years ago by a Russian savant, Sieroshevski.[2] It shows that the earlier Yakuts possessed a familial constitution strikingly similar to that just related, without the author's having had, apparently, the slightest suspicion of the resemblance, or even of the existence of the classificatory system in general. "The ancient words for family relationships had different senses from what the same words have now. For instance, the Yakuts have no word for the general sense of brother or sister. . . . They have special names for older brothers, younger brothers, older sisters, younger sisters. These words, with some attributives which are generally omitted in vituperative speech, are used to address uncles, nephews, aunts, grandchildren of different grades, and even stepfathers and stepmothers, although the two latter are commonly called father and mother. It follows from this that the family falls into two groups—those who were born earlier and those who were born later. These groups form the background of the terminology for family relationship. . . . The author thinks that in the beginning the Yakuts had no words at all for brother or sister, and that the words used now for younger brother, younger sister, etc., were terms, not so much for family relationships, as for *sib* relationships, and

[1] R. Thurnwald, *Die Gemeinde der Banaro*, pp. 123–4.
[2] W. G. Sumner, *The Yakuts*. Abridged from the Russian of Sieroshevski. *J.A.I.* (1901), p. 89.

meant simply older or younger *sib* comrades." Here we recognize the "group relationship" characteristic of the classificatory system.

"The Yakuts employ the term child or my child" (probably "child" is always accompanied by a possessive pronoun) "not only to their own proper children, but also to the children of brothers or of sisters, or even to brothers and sisters themselves, if they are very much younger. They have not, therefore, in their genealogical terminology, any words for son and daughter which testify directly to a blood relationship between specific persons. The word which we translate 'son' strictly means boy, youth, young person. It was formerly used as a collective for the body of warriors, or the young men of the tribe or *sib*. . . .

"This lack of words to distinguish between son and boy, daughter and girl, is not due to the poverty of the language; on the contrary, their genealogical terms astonish us by their abundance and variety." The same remark has often been made about Melanesia, Australia, and it applies almost everywhere where the existence of the classificatory system has been ascertained.[1] Not only do they distinguish those of earlier and later birth, but they have a special denomination for younger brothers which is only used by women. They have a special name for the wife of a husband's older brother, and another for the wife of the husband's younger brother, and other similar peculiarities, which seem incomprehensible not only to us, but also to the Yakuts of to-day.

"Accordingly . . . we infer beyond a doubt that, at the time when the present system of genealogical relationships took its origin amongst the Yakuts, *the precise genetic connection of any given boy with his parents had no especial denomination.* All the old

[1] With the Ba-Ila, for instance. "The secret of understanding the system is first of all to rid one's mind of the terms one is used to, and to grasp firmly the principle that the words *tata* and *bama* do not mean what father and mother mean to us, but rather indicate certain positions in a table of genealogy; and the same with regard to *mwanangu, mukwesu*, etc.

"The terms applied vary as—

(1) whether I am the person speaking, or spoken to, or spoken of;
(2) whether I am directly addressing my relation, or referring to him or her;
(3) whether I am speaking of myself as one person or including others with me;
(4) whether the speaker is older or younger than the person spoken to; or of
(5) whether the person speaking, or the person spoken to, is male or female.

"The vocabulary is equally extensive on other points."

Smith and Dale, *The Ila-Speaking Peoples of Northern Rhodesia*, i, pp. 316–17.

people in the *sib* called all the young people in the *sib*, up to a certain point of growth, by the same denominatives."

So, too: "There is no word for father which admits of a natural and simple explanation, like the word for mother (procreatress)—the word for father should be translated 'old man.' This vagueness in regard to the male blood tie, side by side with the definiteness of the female connection with the offspring, is very significant. . . .

"Unions between them, inside of the *sib*, were exceedingly free and non-permanent. The children could know only their mothers, and they could know them only up to a certain point of their age; after that they forgot this relationship. It was supplanted by a feeling of belonging to a certain group. Within that group there were only 'men' and 'women,' older or younger than the person in question. There are out-of-the-way places amongst them now where the current word of the language for 'wife' is unknown; they meet it with laughter. A word for 'husband' exists nowhere amongst the Yakuts. The current word means properly 'man.' "

To sum up on this point, in places where the classificatory system exists, relationship is "of the group" only. It is not individuals, but groups that are inter-related; individuals are related only because they belong to related groups. Thus the relationship is social rather than familial, in our sense of the word. In Western Australia, "When a stranger comes to a camp that he has never visited before, he does not enter the camp, but remains at some distance. A few of the older men, after a while, approach him, and the first thing they proceed to do is to find out who the stranger is. The commonest question that is put to him is: 'Who is your *maeli?*' (father's father). The discussion proceeds on genealogical lines until all parties are satisfied of the exact relation of the stranger to each of the natives present in the camp. When this point is reached, the stranger can be admitted to the camp, and the different men and women are pointed out to him, and their relation to him defined. . . . I took with me on my journey a native of the Talainji tribe, and at each native camp we came to the same process had to be gone through. In one case, after a long discussion, they were still unable to discover any traceable relationship between my servant and the men of the camp. That night my 'boy' refused to sleep in the native camp, as was his usual custom, and on talking to him I found that he was frightened. These men were not his relatives, and they were therefore his enemies."[1] The relationship in question here is evidently a social relationship and not, like our own, based mainly upon ties of blood.

The classificatory system also constitutes indeed, as Junod has pointed out, a hierarchy. No doubt natural sentiments are not stifled beneath this social structure, for all observers agree in telling us that "primitives" adore their children, that they indulge them and love to play with them. Filial, fraternal and conjugal affection exist among them as with us, though perhaps somewhat differently and with fine distinctions that it is often difficult to define precisely. But it is above all the implicit "idea" of the individual in his relations with his social group that differs from ours. To convince ourselves of this, we have only to remember the difficulty we experience in entering into the sentiments and ideas Codrington described for us, which appear so natural to the Melanesians.

[1] A. R. Brown, "Three Tribes of Western Australia," *J.A.I.*, xliii (1913), p. 151.

CHAPTER II

THE SOLIDARITY AMONG MEMBERS OF THE SOCIAL GROUP

I

THAT the social group, clan, or *sib* is the real unit of which the individual is a mere element is proved in many cases not only by the familial structure; the daily life of the primitive is another testimony to it.

Of the Indians of Guiana, for instance, Dr. W. E. Roth relates an observation made by Father Gumilla, and since confirmed: "The idea that not only the patient but also his relatives and others should abstain from certain diets was very widespread. The *piache's* first prescription is to impose a general fast on the patient and all his kinsfolk."[1] "With the Caribs, Arawaks, and Warraus, the whole family—father, mother, brothers and sisters—is dieted on exactly the same line as the invalid. If a man (a Carib Islander) gets wounded or ill, he will ask his brother, sister or some relation to abstain from eating such and such a thing. This would make the pain worse even if they were fifty miles off."—"Among the Jibros and Canelos Indians, when one member of the family is sick, the rest have to diet in the same way as the patient himself, for if they ate unsuitable food, it would be the same as if the patient ate that food, and his condition would grow worse."[2] We know that these same Indians practise *couvade*. After the birth of a child the parents, especially the father, must submit to a great many taboos, for fear of compromising the life of the newborn infant.

In certain peoples this intimate solidarity of father and child continues until the age of initiation. "Even the men have to submit to certain restrictions as regards the eating of poultry.

[1] Fr. J. Gumilla, *El Orinoco ilustrado*, i, p. 210, quoted by W. E. Roth, *An Inquiry into the Animism and Folk-lore of the Guiana Indians*, E.B. Bulletin, xxx, p. 352.
[2] R. Karsten, *Blood-Revenge, War and Victory-Feasts among the Jibaro Indians of Eastern Ecuador*, E.B. Bulletin, lxxix (1923), p. 12.

If the bird be a female, it may be divided among several persons, but if it be a male, it must all be eaten by the same man, or sickness will ensue. The man in question may give some of it to his son, if the latter be not yet circumcised. This is a particularly interesting fact, since it shows that before circumcision a male child is not regarded as possessing an individuality distinct from that of his father, although he is considered to belong to his father's village."[1]

This solidarity, which is, as it were, physiological, presents itself in other forms. Junod tells us that "when a younger brother cuts his teeth, they are considered as pushing away or putting forth the teeth of the elder, as the younger brother comes into the world, as a rule, three years after the elder."[2]— Among the Basutos, "when it is noticed that a young girl (whose duty it is to keep awake all night) falls asleep, they inquire very carefully whether among her relatives there may not be someone who is sleeping. If they find one of them has stolen away to have a sleep, they wake him so that he may return to join in the songs; it is really the fault of that person that the young girl has fallen asleep."[3] Finally, in North America, on the north-west coast, among the Indians of Cape Flattery, where a man had been wounded in the arm by a bullet which passed through the arm, injuring but not breaking the bone, "I advised the friends," says Swan, "to take him immediately to the hospital . . . where he could have surgical advice, but they concluded to try their own remedies first. . . . They next went to where the young man's father was buried, and dug up the bone of the upper part of the left arm, which they washed, and then sawed or split in two, lengthwise, and formed splints of it. These were scraped, and the scrapings of the bone applied as a dressing. The bone splints were applied and the arm bandaged firmly. The Indians assured me that the bone from the father's arm would renew or replace the wounded one in the boy's arm; that they always tried it in the case of a broken bone, and it always effected a cure. Thus, if a leg, an arm or a rib is broken, they take a similar one from the body of the nearest relative

---

[1] Torday and Joyce, "Notes ethnographiques sur les populations habitant les bassins du Kasai et du Kwango oriental," *Annales du Musée du Congo belge*, Série iii, 2, pp. 305–6.   [2] H. A. Junod, *The Life of a South African Tribe*, i, p. 50.
[3] E. Jacottet, "Mœurs, coutumes et superstitions des Basoutos," *Bulletin de la Société de Géographie de Neuchâtel*, ix (1897), p. 130.

who has been dead over a year, and apply it either as a dressing by scraping, or in the form of splints. I have, however, seen none but the instance above quoted, when the splints were applied."[1]—A fact closely resembling this was observed in South Africa. "A Berg Damara, angry with his son, threw his cudgel at him when he was running away, and seriously wounded him. I treated the wound with an antiseptic, but when I examined it in renewing the bandage I found it septic and inflamed. I insisted on knowing what had caused this, and at last the boy confessed that his father had scraped with a knife the handle of his cudgel, to which the perspiration and greasy matter from his hand had adhered" (that is, his *Seelenstoff* or vital principle), "and that he had put these little shavings of wood in the wound. I looked at the cudgel, and realized that the boy had told the truth. This dirty mess was intended to heal the wound that the father's cudgel had made."[2] The perspiration and the greasy matter from the body of a man are the man himself, and here they were playing the same rôle as the bone from the arm in the case of the Cape Flattery Indian. In the ideas which urge the Damara to action, and also the Indian, there is little differentiation between the individuality of father and son.

II

The community in essence thus felt by the members of a group, and particularly by persons most nearly related—father and son, brother, etc.—induces these to consider their quasi-identity as a self-evident thing. There is not much wanting for them to be substituted for one another: they are almost "interchangeable." The results of this "multiple individuality" are often strange, and sometimes tragic. Stories popular in Gaboon throw light on this. "There were a husband and wife who had been married a number of years. She had a child, a little boy. The husband had a brother, and this brother had taken a strong fancy to the woman, and wanted to possess her. Secretly he was asking her to live with him. But the woman always refused, saying, 'No, I don't want it.' Then this brother's love

[1] J. G. Swan, *The Indians of Cape Flattery*, p. 78.
[2] Missionary Kuhlmann, *Berichte der rheinischen Missionsgesellschaft* (1914), pp. 60–1.

began to change to anger. He cherished vexation in his heart toward the woman, and asked her, 'Why do you always refuse me? You are the wife, not of a stranger, but of my brother. He and I are one, and you ought to accept me.' But she persisted: 'No, I don't want it.' Finally he tried to enter her hut, and she killed him."[1]

In another story (of the Ogoué region) a brother, angry with his brother's wife, who was resisting his advances, killed her one night in the forest whilst she was on the way to visit her parents. He was seen and denounced by the woman's son. "Then all the townspeople gathered around him, being horrified at the news of the woman's death. The husband called them all to a council, and the palaver was held at his house. There the grandfather and the lad told the whole story.

"The brother-in-law began to enter a denial, but the husband said: 'No! you are guilty! And because we are brothers, and we are one, the guilt is also mine, and I will confess for you.'

"But the wife's family said to the husband: 'We have no quarrel with you. We want only the person who killed our sister, and a fine of money for our loss.'"[2]

These two stories show clearly that among these natives a very strong sense of their own personality is at the same time coexistent with an idea which makes, as it were, the two brothers into one individual. In the first one, passion, in order to obtain satisfaction, makes an appeal to this belief. The husband's brother cannot understand why the wife should repel his advances, seeing that he is his brother's *alter ego*, and he thinks that she has no right to do it. In the second, this idea of the quasi-identity of the two brothers is so pronounced that the husband of the murdered woman, far from expressing a desire for vengeance upon his brother, feels that he shares his guilt.

In fact, in many social aggregates, particularly in the parts of Africa inhabited by black races, there exists a kind of potential right, accruing to the younger brother, over his elder brother's wives. They are among those whom he has the right to marry: they are his "potential wives." The brother may say,

[1] W. H. Nassau, *Fetichism in West Africa*, pp. 287–9.   [2] *Ibid.*, p. 293.

and often does, to his brother's wife: "*ukento amo :* my wife."
In the same way, the wife calls her husband's brother: *yakala
di nzila*, the husband from outside, as opposed to her husband,
whom she calls *yakala di nzo*: the husband inside. These appella-
tions are no mere empty forms. They correspond with the
familiar relations which are lawfully established between the
nzadi, and not allowed between other unmarried persons.
Such familiarity is the cause of many adulteries, and the
blacks express this abuse of it by the proverb: "The louse in the
nzemba bites both mother and child, and the *nzadi*, either man
or woman, comes between husband and wife."[1] So, too, in the
district between the great lakes: "The twofold expression
current throughout our western area: *bayi-babange* (my husbands), and *mukasi wayitu* (our wife), used by the wife and her
brothers-in-law, are not so much a deferential plural as an
expression of customs in the highest degree immoral.

"In Bunyoro, conscience protests, by means of the adage:
'The wife is the guardian of her husband's taboos in his absence'
(and therefore ought to remain faithful to him), but only too
often concupiscence gains the upper hand, aided by the consideration that the family, having helped the future bridegroom
to settle himself matrimonially, has thereby acquired a quasi-
right, against which, in practice, the man interested will be
careful not to appeal."[2]

The brother often exercises this right with the husband's
permission, during his absence, or, even without the latter's
having left the village, with his more or less explicit consent.
Where this permission is wanting, the relations of the wife with
her husband's brothers are not regarded as adultery. As a
matter of fact, in "primitive" societies, what *we* call adultery is
merely a theft, and, like many thefts, may have serious mystic
consequences for the one who is the victim of it. But when a
brother takes something belonging to his brother, even if it be
the wife who is lawfully his, it is not theft, properly speaking.
The two brothers make but one person: one does not steal
from oneself. And Father Gorju rightly remarks that the wife

[1] Fr. Van Wing, *Études Bakongo*, p. 133. The *nzemba* is the cloth covering the
child which the mother carries on her back.
[2] Fr. J. Gorju, *Entre le Victoria, l'Albert et l'Edouard*, p. 289. Cf. H. Rehse,
Kiziba, Land und Leute, p. 93.—"The husband sometimes leaves his wife to his
unmarried brother."

has not been acquired at the husband's cost alone, for his whole family has contributed towards the payment of the *dot*.

Death does not rupture this intimate solidarity existing between brothers. This fact accounts for many of the customs relating to widows—the right, for instance, which in certain cases becomes the obligation, of the brother to espouse the widow. Without entering into detail upon these questions, which are not part of our subject, let us simply quote the explanation given by Lindblom with respect to the customs of the Akamba. "He who takes over his brother's widow looks upon her children in every way as his own. If they are girls, he receives all the purchase-money when they are married. However, the children always call him *mwendwasa* (uncle). What is more interesting is that, if he himself gets any children by the woman, they also say uncle and not *nau* (father). The property of a dead man who was childless does not go to the brother, but to the son the latter may have by the mother. Thus it can be said that in a way the deceased is looked upon as the child's father. The question then is whether the son is really looked upon as actually begotten by the dead man— the idea does not seem to be altogether unreasonable in the case of people that worship ancestral spirits—or whether the essential factor is the right of ownership, which may be supposed to continue even after death."[1] Lindblom himself prefers the second explanation. It is true, as we shall presently see, that among Bantus the dead frequently preserve their rights of ownership. But it seems to be truer still that the Akamba are scarcely likely to put to themselves the question to which Lindblom seeks an answer. By virtue of the quasi-identity of brothers, the living brother, who has married his dead brother's widow, is both himself and his brother. The two make but one, and the children belong equally to both. Out of respect for the dead, they will all call the second husband "uncle," whether he be really their uncle or their father.

"Among the Jibaros when a man dies his brother must marry the widow. The departed husband, who is still jealous of the wife he left behind, does not cede her to any other man than his brother, who with himself forms one personality and represents him in the most real sense of the word. When a younger

[1] G. Lindblom, *The Akamba*, p. 83.

Jibaro is murdered by his enemies, the duty of revenging his death is also first of all incumbent on his brothers."[1]

What will happen, then, in the case of fratricide? The answer to this is given in a legend related by Dr. Malinowski: "Toweyre'i, in spite of having killed his brother, is still the man who has to arrange the mortuary proceedings, act as master of ceremonies, and pay for the functions performed in them by others. He personally may neither touch the corpse nor perform any act of mourning or burial; nevertheless, he, as the nearest of kin of the dead man, is the bereaved one, is the one from whom a limb has been severed, so to speak. A man whose brother has died cannot mourn any more than he could mourn for himself."[2] Fratricide, therefore, is a kind of partial suicide. It may appear inexplicable, mad; nevertheless it does not incite avenging wrath. In a fine Basuto story reported by Casalis, we hear of the younger brother, killed by the elder, reappearing in the form of a bird to unmask the murderer, but without any idea of avenging himself.[3] In British Equatorial Africa, "if a man kill his younger brother, or any one under his charge, there is no case against the murderer. For one thing there is no prosecutor, and, moreover, relatives may be treated as slaves."[4] Hutereau says explicitly: "Fratricide and parricide are not punished; they are always regarded as accidental, and if the murderer inherits, he has as much right as anybody else to the inheritance of his victim. Very often, indeed, the wives may choose him as their husband."[5]

If it be the case, not of a brother or father, but of a more distant relative, compensation for the murder will be demanded. To the great surprise of most observers, however, it is less than it would be for one who is a stranger to the familial group. For instance, among the Waniaturu, Eberhard von Sick notes: "For the murder of a near relative the penalty, far from being increased as one might suppose, is, strange to relate, diminished

[1] R. Karsten, *Blood-Revenge, War and Victory-Feasts among the Jibaro Indians of Eastern Ecuador*, E.B. Bulletin, lxxix (1923), p. 12.
[2] B. Malinowski, *Argonauts in the Western Pacific*, p. 320.
[3] E. Casalis, *Les Bassoutos*, pp. 358–9.
[4] D. Macdonald, *Africana*, i, pp. 168–9.
[5] A. Hutereau, "Notes sur la vie familiale et juridique de quelques populations du Congo belge," *Annales du Musée du Congo belge, Ethnographie et Anthropologie*, Série iii, Documents ethnographiques concernant les populations du Congo belge, i, 1, p. 100.

by half, and reduced to seven head of cattle. No one has been able to give me an explanation of this strange custom."[1]

The key to this enigma will be found in what has just been said. For the murder of a brother there is no possible compensation, because the murderer himself would have to demand it. If it is a case of a near relative, the murderer has done a wrong to others at the same time as to himself, and owes them compensation, but a lesser one.—In Kavirondo (still in Basutoland), "generally the murder of a relative is punished less heavily than that of a stranger; the fine varying in proportion to the degree of ownership the murderer has in the victim. The reason being, of course, that the death of a relative is regarded more in the light of a private loss than from the point of view of the community."[2]—It is the same with the Kikuyu. "If a man murders his cousin on his mother's side of the family, the father of the murderer collects fifty sheep or goats, and pays them to the head of the family of the deceased . . . the elaborate ritual described above is not observed because of the blood relationship which exists. (The compensation is much reduced.)" Hobley adds: "If a man kills his brother or sister by the same mother, there is no compensation—the case very rarely arises; the father would, however, kill a sheep and make his children eat it together."[3]

In South America the same ideas have led to the same results. "No tribal notice is taken of a murder committed intra-family, such as the murder of a son or a wife, as no revenge is necessary; the loss only affects the murderers, and it is simply arranged by the family itself. The loss of one member does not suggest itself as a reasonable cause for compelling the loss of another. The one exception to this would be if the murdered man were a noted warrior whose death would constitute a serious tribal loss. Action might then be taken by the whole tribe. . . ."[4] Among the Jibaros "it sometimes occurs that a man kills his brother, if the latter, for instance, has seduced his wife or bewitched one of his children. But in this case blood revenge generally fails, inasmuch as the natural avengers—i.e. the

[1] Eberhard von Sick, "Die Waniaturu," Bässler-Archiv, v (1915), Heft 1-2, 31.
[2] K. H. Dundas, "The Wawanga and Other Tribes of the Elgon District, British East Africa," J.A.I., xliii (1913), pp. 52-3.
[3] C. W. Hobley, Bantu Beliefs and Magic, p. 234.
[4] Ch. Whiffen, The North-Western Amazons, pp. 172-3.

father and the remaining brothers, abstain from carrying it out. 'It is enough that one member of our family has died,' they say, 'why should we deprive ourselves of one more?' The slayer is consequently pardoned."[1]

To conclude, in the extreme north-east of Asia Bogoras has noted, not without surprise, the same custom. "In the beginning of my acquaintance with the Chukchee tribe, I was astonished to find that all murders are divided into two categories—those committed within the family group and those outside of it. Only those of the second category are liable to blood-revenge. Those in the first category were exempt from it, or, indeed, from any punishment at all."[2]

Although it is not stated as a general rule, it is probable that after murders of members of the family it is necessary to have recourse to rites of purification to appease the justly incensed ancestors, who are ready to punish the homicide in his own person or those of his relatives. Upon this point Dr. Cremer says: "With many of the river-tribes of the Volta, theft, outrage, murder of relatives, which do not give occasion for civil action, must be expiated by offerings and sacrifices, and these are the more considerable the closer the tie of blood between the guilty person and his victim."[3]—"*Chikuto*," write Smith and Dale, "is the special kind of curse that falls upon a person who sins against close relations. . . . Of any one who kills his father, mother, maternal uncle, brother, sister, the people say: 'That cursed one! He will not live long on the earth; no. He will die of *chikuto*, he will die a violent death in the veld. A lion will take him, or he will be drowned,' " etc.[4]

III

Since in these societies the true unit is the social group (clan, family or *sib*), of which individuals are merely the component elements, it is quite natural that these should not be sole arbiters of the most important actions of their lives. It is the group, or its chief, who will decide for the individuals. Marriage, for instance, often appears to be the conclusion and outlying result

---

[1] E. Karsten, *Blood-Revenge, War and Victory-Feasts among the Jibaro Indians*, E.B. Bulletin, lxxix, p. 13.　　[2] W. Bogoras, *The Chukchee*, p p. 663-4.
[3] J. Cremer, *Les Bobo*, pp. 69-70.　　[4] Smith and Dale, *op. cit.*, p. 416.

of the ceremonies of initiation of the young men. It may happen that all do not marry at once. Sometimes the number of women whom they may legitimately marry is too small—for example, where the older men or the chiefs keep the young women for themselves, and possess veritable harems. But in principle and, if we may use the term, in right, the young man, when initiated, marries if he can find a wife.

Would it not be more correct to say that he *is* married? Does he choose his wife for himself? Is there a previous understanding between the two persons concerned? Assuredly personal inclinations play some part therein, varying with circumstances, but undeniably existing. The young girl, who as a rule is not consulted, often finds means of suggesting to her mother, and even to her father, what her inclinations are, and of getting rid of a suitor who does not please her. Most frequently she attains her end. Individual preferences often exercise an influence—we have seen proofs of this—but with this reserve, which we must never overlook, it is the familial group that decides the matter.

Nearly everywhere the choice is primarily limited by the exogamy of the clan and also by the inhibition of sexual relations between blood relatives. In primitive societies incest is the crime *par excellence*, and the one most severely punished. It is not defined among them exactly as it is with us. In the primitive's eyes, a man's relations with a very distant cousin, or even with a person who is not related to him (as we understand relationship), but who belongs to the same totem, may be incestuous. On the other hand, in certain communities, the marriage of grandfather and granddaughter is lawful. Accordingly it is not solely kinship (in our sense) upon which incest depends. To the primitive, wherever the classificatory system exists, the women of his social group are divided into two classes: those with whom sexual relations are permitted, and the others. If he infringes the interdict upon the latter class, he is committing incest. All the rest are "potentially" his wives, just as he and his comrades are the "potential" husbands of each of them. It is from these that his wife (or wives, if he has several) will be chosen. Let us put on one side the question, which is at the present time possibly incapable of solution, as to whether a group-marriage has ever existed (that is, whether the men of a certain group have ever been the husbands, collectively, of a certain group of women). Nowhere do we find, as Westermarck has shown, anything exactly like this. In all primitive societies about which we have reliable testimony, a more or less complete appropriation of one woman by one man, recognized by the group, constitutes marriage. This man and this woman, belonging to sub-groups or classes between which sexual relations are permitted, go to live together, and the woman will belong to that man alone, save in cases allowed for by tribal institutions. But how is the selection made?

Let us take as an example the Queensland tribes described by Dr. Roth. Each man after having passed through the successive stages of initiation may have at least two wives. The one will be "official," assigned to him as a member of the community, in the general camp-council; the other, "non-official," whom he chooses for himself, and who requites his love, if we may use the expression. . . . The marriage is not the occasion for any "corroboree" or public festivity. Here are the different ways in which the choice is made. 1. "Supposing that the camp-council consider a man fit and suitable to have . . . a wife, he has to take whomsoever is assigned to him thus: the brothers or mother's brothers of the young woman talk among themselves concerning that particular individual . . . and convene all the other males available of a certain rank to a sort of camp-council. . . . The person *sub judice* can be present to listen only, but more usually he will leave camp to go on some fishing or hunting expedition. If all is found to be proper and satisfactory . . . the woman's brothers and mother's brothers after sundown direct the bride to her future husband's hut, whither it is obligatory on her to go and remain. This ceremony is binding on both sides and except by mutual agreement, the couple can only be parted by death.

2. "A man can exchange his true blood-sister, i.e. by the same mother, for the blood-sister of another individual. This arrangement only holds good, however, provided that the respective inhibitions are observed, and that the unanimous vote of the camp-council has sanctioned it."

Roth then examines into (3) the form of marriage by capture, either of a young girl or of a married woman, and notes the cases in which these unions, in certain conditions, may be accepted or tolerated by the tribe.[1]

In Central Australia Spencer and Gillen, and in German New Guinea Thurnwald, have described in detail the conditions of what we, in default of another word, must term marriage, or (according to Roth's expression) "the permanent sexual union." We are obliged to refer the reader to their works, and it will be found that there again, when it is a question of the "official" wife, it is the group that decides the matter. Certain rites prove, too, that the appropriation of the woman by the man is not absolute. The "potential" right of other men upon the woman who is their "potential" wife is actually exercised, either at the very time of the marriage, before the husband, or, later, on the occasion of certain festivals and ceremonies.

In the Indian Archipelago, where the wife is usually acquired by the payment of purchase-money, a young man is rarely rich enough to provide it personally. His family advances him the necessary sum, on condition that he himself contributes when another young man desires to marry in his turn. The family, having paid for the acquisition of his wife, has certain rights over her. In any case, the woman does not belong to her husband's family until the agreed purchase-money has been paid in full. Up to that time she continues to belong to her own family. The purchase-money is not given to the father and mother of the young wife; they receive but a small portion of it, but all members of the family group have a share in it, according to very definite and complicated regulations. Thus marriage is primarily a transaction between two families, a combining of interests which have been discussed by seniors possessed of authority, upon whom the younger members depend. The seniors do not appear to take preferences much into account.

The Bantus will afford us one more example. Among the Thonga of South Africa, "for the black man legal marriage is and remains the one object in life. It is through his wife and children that he becomes somebody in the society. This fact does not as yet appear during the first year of wedlock, for

[1] W. E. Roth, *Ethnological Studies among the North-West Central Queensland Aborigines*, No. 323, p. 181.

the newly married woman must cook at the fireplace of her mother-in-law. . . . He is not yet a lord. But if he is rich, he will not be long in buying a second and third wife. For each new wife he will build a hut. . . . This will end in forming a kraal."[1]

Now "the Bantu idea of matrimony is that the son of a commoner has no voice in choosing his first or 'great wife,' who is to be the mother of his heir; and that no daughter should be allowed to choose her husband. The main consideration in selecting a spouse is not the suitability of the individuals to one another . . . but the desirability of an alliance between two families. . . . But young men and maidens, even in Bantu families, are often able to work the oracle so that its pronouncement shall not be alarming. . . . Once a man has married his 'great wife,' however, he is free to look about for himself, and in a year or two, if the bride-price is available, the family council is ready to negotiate a marriage of his choice. (As a rule, a man's wives have no objection to the arrival of a 'new wife.')"[2]—With the Bechuana, "rarely is marriage a matter of mutual choice on the part of bride and groom. It is invariably a matter of arrangement between the elders of both; and it is no unusual thing for children to be betrothed before they are born, an agreement being made between two families that the son of one shall marry the daughter of the other, while as yet there is neither son nor daughter. So from their earliest years children are accustomed to look upon each other as already betrothed. This does not keep either from promiscuous intercourse, but the agreement will usually be carried out, even if the woman should have a child by some other man, or the man be the father of a child born through some other woman."[3]

Without laying more stress on circumstances which are frequently described, we may come to the same conclusion as Junod does. "Marriage in primitive or semi-civilized tribes is not an individual affair as it has become with us. It is an affair of the community. It is a kind of contract between two groups, the husband's family and the wife's family. What is the respective position of the two groups or families? One of the

[1] H. A. Junod, *op. cit.*, i, p. 125.
[2] W. C. Willoughby, *Race Problems in the New Africa*, pp. 113-15.
[3] J. Tom Brown, *Among the Bantu Nomads*, p. 59.

groups loses a member, the other gains one. To save itself from undue diminution, the first group claims compensation, and the second grants it under the form of *lobola*. This remittance of money, oxen or hoes will allow the first group to acquire a new member in place of the one they have lost, and so the balance will be kept. This conception of the *lobola* as being a compensation, a means of restoring the equilibrium between the two groups, is certainly the right one."[1] And in another passage, Junod further insists: "The only way of understanding the *lobola*, as well as other similar payments in kind which we meet with amongst a great number of un-civilized or semi-civilized nations, is to consider it as *a compensation given by one group to another group*, in order to restore the equilibrium between the various collective units composing the clan. The first group acquires a new member; the second one feels itself diminished, and claims something which permits it to reconstruct itself, in its turn, by the acquisition of another woman. This collectivist conception alone explains all the facts."[2] So, too, the *bogadi* (among the Bechuanas, the counter-part of the *lobola*) "is an equivalent handed over to a family for the loss that family has sustained by the passing of a woman child of theirs into another family. Behind it lies the question of loss and the means of repairing that loss. The cattle given to a family enables it to pass on *bogadi* to some other family for a wife for one of the sons."[3]

In the course of time, no doubt, secondary ideas have been engrafted upon the earlier one, yet this remains the real root of the matter. The way in which these affairs are conducted in many other social aggregates, less civilized than the Bantus, leaves little doubt on the subject. A woman's entry into another group by marriage always involves compensation for the group losing her, and it most frequently demands another woman in return. That which has now become *lobola* with the Bantus was originally an exchange of women. One clan obtains a wife for one of its members on condition that the latter on his side gives one of his sisters (in the "classificatory" sense of the word) as a wife for one of the second clan, and thus neither clan will gain or lose. Roth noted this form of marriage among Queens-

[1] H. A. Junod, *op. cit.*, i, pp. 121–2.　　　　[2] *Ibid.*, pp. 262–3.
[3] J. Tom Brown, *op. cit.*, pp. 60–1.

land tribes. Howitt writes : "I have shown how universal, among Australian tribes, is the exchange of a sister for a wife, and that every wife is, as it were, the 'dot' that allows of the acquisition of another."[1]—Thurnwald considers reciprocity to be the essential principle regulating marriage among the Banaro. In the island of Kiwai (British New Guinea), " it is almost a fixed law that brothers and sisters are exchanged in marriage, a law holding good to the present day. The bridegroom's sister, if he has one, must be given to the bride's brother, or, failing a brother, to her nearest male relative. This rule was very strict, and no attention was paid at all to the feelings of the lady in the matter. . . . When there are no brothers or sisters available, the bridegroom has to pay for his wife."[2]—"Hely has noted that a wife is bound to adopt her husband's totem, and this is the reason why a man must always give one of his relatives in exchange for her, in order that the comparative strength of the respective clans may be maintained."[3]—In the same district, Riley tells us : "All the unmarried girls receive very strict instructions *re* their marriage proposals. They are commanded not to propose to any youth who is unfortunate enough not to possess a sister whom he can give in exchange for her. If a young woman marries into another family, the latter must provide a maiden in her place. . . . In this way the strength of the clans is kept up, and consanguinity avoided. A girl may not marry a man of her own clan."[4]

In short, this custom, "universal" in Australia, and widespread in New Guinea, is found again in other districts, especially among the Bantu tribes, who generally give it the form of the *lobola*. Of the Bambwa Roscoe says : "Wives were as a rule obtained by exchange, and if a youth had sisters it was an easy matter to obtain wives. He would arrange with his parents to give one of his sisters to some man of another clan, who would arrange with *his* parents to give one of his sisters in exchange. . . . When a man had no sister to exchange, he got the permission of some man or woman to marry their daughter, and promised in return a number of goats. . . ."[5]

[1] A. W. Howitt, *The Native Tribes of South-East Australia*, p. 293. Cf. pp.360–2.
[2] W. N. Beaver, *Unexplored New Guinea*, pp. 64–5 (Mawatta and Turituri tribes).
[3] *Ibid.*, p. 181.   [4] E. B. Riley, *Among Papuan Head-Hunters*, p. 48.
[5] J. Roscoe, *The Bagesu*, p. 153.

Thus in these societies, except in cases where a group procured wives by violent measures, or raids upon their neighbours, what we call marriage usually involved originally an
exchange of woman for woman between exogamic clans.
Usually several couples were thus united at the same time—
four at any rate among the Banaro, Thurnwald tells us. It is
indeed the simplest way to maintain an equilibrium between
the clans, and possibly, too, to assure the woman's fair treatment in the group she is to live amongst—since an equal number
of women run the same risk on each side. In case of necessity,
reprisals would present no difficulties. But what is to be done,
if there are only enough lawfully marriageable women upon
one side? Compensation must then take another form, one
which will allow those who do not receive wives in exchange
for their sisters to procure them elsewhere with what they have
obtained. This is no doubt the origin and one of the essential
reasons of the *lobola*.

Thurnwald has many times insisted on the important part
played in primitive aggregates by the ideas of "reciprocity"
and "compensation" (*Vergeltung*). They are closely connected
with the ever-present need to react against any attack, to
avenge any injury, and repair any loss. A story related by
Landtman throws strong light on this point. A man pursued
by a snake took refuge at a friend's house. In the night the snake
arrived and carried off the friend, taking him for the man
against whom it was incensed. "In the morning the people
saw the tracks of the snake and found that a man was missing.
They said to the new-comer: 'What's the matter you no speak
first time?' 'Snake he come behind, that's why I run away,
come here.' 'You no more go home, you take place belong that
man snake he been take him. Pickaninny there, woman there
belong that man, you take him.' Therefore the man could never
go back again to his proper home."[1]—In Neu Pommern, "when
a child dies, his father is obliged to make the uncle on the
mother's side a present consisting of cowries, bracelets, etc. . . .
It is payment for the loss of a member of his group."[2] As a
matter of fact, the child belongs to his mother's clan. This

---

[1] G. Landtman, *The Folk-tales of the Kiwai Papuans*, p. 463.
[2] R. Parkinson, *Dreissig Jahre in der Südsee*, p. 187.

clan is thus deprived of a unit, and the father who brought up
the child and is responsible for it owes the clan an indemnity, to
compensate it for this loss, just as the Papuans kept the man
pursued by a snake because he had been the cause of the loss
of a member of their group. So, too, the clan does not cede
one of its women in marriage unless it receives another in
return, or is otherwise compensated. In all these instances,
which seem widely different to us, the individual is of importance only in so far as he is a member of a group. It is the
destiny, the needs, the safety of the living unit which constitutes the group, that determine the lot of any given individual
member.

IV

If this unit has suffered an irreparable loss, either from the
aggression or the witchcraft of another group, what form will
the demand for compensation take? What reparation can re-
establish the equilibrium that has been upset? To obtain a wife,
another was given in exchange. To satisfy vengeance, it must
be corpse for corpse. The group from which one of its members
has been snatched will know no rest until the guilty group has
also been deprived of one of its own. And in the same way as
when an exchange of sisters was impossible, they consented to
grant a wife for compensation received, the injured group will
in certain cases renounce the taking of a human life. They will
be content to receive the price of blood.

In Southern Nigeria, two tribes at war cannot be persuaded
to conclude peace as long as the number of the slain is not the
same on both sides. From reasons of *amour-propre*, with which
no doubt are mingled mystic representations respecting the
dead, they will not resign themselves to any upsetting of the
balance between them. "When Government tried to bring
about the cessation of hostilities, the men of Afaha Esak
answered stubbornly: 'No, not until an equal number have
been slain on their side.' If one of the parties failed to inflict
the same loss upon the enemy, peace could only be bought by
paying heavy compensation."[1] It is the conquerors who pay
this kind of war indemnity. It is all the greater, according to

[1] P. A. Talbot, *Life in Southern Nigeria*, p. 241.

the greater difference in number between their dead and those of the conquered.

The vendetta therefore seems to be, primarily, a mystic settling of accounts. "When a man has been killed by a man of another tribe, this last must expect to see killed, at the first opportunity, not the assassin, but some man or other of his tribe. . . . Body for body is the rule. As a matter of fact, it is usually known in the district that such and such a tribe owes the other a corpse, and that the people of the former dare not go to certain places because they would have to pass in front of an enemy village." Here is one story among hundreds. "Two villages had killed each other's men; one had two corpses, the other but one. The story came to the ears of the Governor, who meted out justice by deporting the chief of the second village. Since this man disappeared, he became the second corpse; the people had accepted the idea, and went away satisfied. Now this year, that chief was pardoned and returned to his village. Ever since, there have been complaints from the other village, which declared, logically enough, 'One of your corpses has arisen from the dead; raise one of ours, and we shall be satisfied.' "[1] With these same Pahouins, "the father of one of our boys came to me one day saying he wished to take his boy back again for some time. 'I am growing old, you see,' said he, 'and before I die, I must tell him all about our quarrels, so that he may know which tribes owe us corpses.' "[2]

These accounts, the settling of which sometimes extends over a score of years, are never personal matters. By the death of one of its members a group has been injured, and satisfaction can only be procured by inflicting a similar injury on the group which is responsible. But it is not necessary that the very author of the injury should be struck down. It is all a *collective* matter: the injury, the harm suffered, the duty of vengeance, and the subject upon whom it is to be exercised.

In face of this obligation of a collective and superior order, individual feelings at once disappear. In Australia, "friendship is seldom allowed to interfere with the sacred duty of revenge. A man would consider it his bounden duty to kill his most intimate friend for the purpose of avenging a brother's

---

[1] *Missions évangéliques*, lxxiv, 2 (1899), pp. 429-30 (Lantz).
[2] *Ibid.*, lxx (1895), p. 255 (Allégret).

death, and would do so without the slightest hesitation. But if an intimate friend should be killed, he would leave revenge to the relatives of the deceased."[1] The same characteristic has been noted among the Bantus. "A man came on a visit to a place where he happened to quarrel with another man. Some friends of the latter came up and were about to settle accounts with the stranger, but he was undismayed, and shouted, 'Come on, then, enemies of . . . (and here he mentioned the name of his clan); here you shall see one who is not afraid!' There was by chance among his assailants one of the same clan as the stranger, and when he heard that they were clan-kinsmen, he immediately went over to the stranger's side, and helped him against his own friends!"[2]

These facts sufficiently demonstrate that the feeling of solidarity in the group is supreme over all others. Hence it is easy to see that the responsibility would be collective, and vengeance would be exercised indifferently upon one or another, provided he belonged to the group. "The Jibaro certainly first of all wants to take revenge on the person who committed the crime; but if he cannot be caught, it may instead be directed against one of his relatives—his brother, his father, even his mother or sister. To understand this we have to consider that the conception of individual personality and consequently of individual responsibility does not exist among the primitive Indians in the same sense as among civilized peoples. . . . The members of the same family are regarded as, so to speak, organically coherent with each other, so that one part stands for all, and all for one. What happens to one member of that social unit happens to all, and for the deed of one member the rest are held equally responsible."[3]

This principle does not apply in cases of homicide alone. Thus, "in cases of theft (or indeed of any other crimes to which the principle of collective responsibility is applicable) it is not necessary to identify the thief, nor is it necessary that he should be produced, or even known. It is sufficient, if a case has been clearly established against a kraal."[4] The latter considers it

---

[1] Dawson, *Australian Aborigines*, p. 71.   [2] G. Lindbolm, *The Akamba*, p. 114.
[3] R. Karsten, *op. cit.*, pp. 11–12.
[4] Col. Maclean, *A Compendium of Kafir Law and Customs* (Mr. Werner's notes), p. 67.

quite natural, besides, that it should be held wholly responsible for the shortcomings of one of its members. It is this semi-organic solidarity which renders the violation of certain taboos so terrible. Incest, for example, "involves overwhelming disorders, droughts, famines, sterility among the women throughout the clan."[1] Doubtless the ancestors, incensed by the crime, manifest their anger, and do not distinguish between the guilty and those whom *we* consider innocent, precisely because to them, that is, to native ideas, innocent and guilty are not separated. They are mingled in the group-unit.

In conformity with a well-recognized psychological law, the very fact of being thus, or of believing themselves to be, punished without discrimination, strengthens the feeling of their collective responsibility in the minds of all. "The natives," writes a missionary to the New Hebrides, one of the first to enter into relations with them, in the island of Aniwa, "had an extraordinary dread of violating the taboo, and believed that it meant death to the offender or someone of his family."[2] A public calamity, such as an epidemic and succession of deaths occurring shortly after one another, would be cause for believing that someone had committed a crime of this kind. Then there would be recourse to divination, perhaps not so much for the purpose of discovering the culprit or culprits, as for finding out exactly which of the taboos had been infringed, and proceeding to the needful expiatory rites.[3]

V

From the same principle it follows that primitives cannot understand that land may be an individual and inalienable property. That which may be granted to individuals, and pass from one to another, is the use of the soil and the appropriation of its fruits, as well as that of trees, but nothing more. Hence arise indeterminable conflicts between white men and natives. The white men inveigh against the bad faith of natives who have sold their lands and received and spent the

---

[1] Fr. Van Wing, *Études Bakongo*, p. 175.
[2] J. G. Paton, missionary to the New Hebrides, *An Autobiography*, Part II, p. 213.
[3] Cf. Fr. Fauconnet, *La Responsabilité*, for the subject of this paragraph.

price of them, and yet refuse to give them up to the purchasers. The natives, on their side, are indignant at an act of spoliation that their ancestors would not have allowed them to tolerate, and at the supposition that they had ever had any idea of submitting to it. The land, as a matter of fact, belongs—and this in the fullest sense of the word—to the social group in its entirety, that is, to the living and dead collectively. "The owner-ship of the soil," says Fr. Van Wing, "is collective, but the conception of this is very complex. It is the clan or family which owns the undivided soil, but the clan or family is not merely the living; it is also, and primarily, the dead, that is, the *Bakulu*. The *Bakulu* are not *all* the dead of the clan; they are only its worthy ancestors, those who are leading a happy and successful life in their villages under the earth. It is the *Bakulu* who have acquired the clan's domain with its forests and rivers, its pools and its springs; they have been buried in their property. They continue to rule there; they often return to their springs and rivers and pools. The wild beasts of the bush and the forest are their goats, the birds are their poultry. It is they, too, who 'give' the edible grubs of the trees, the fish of the rivers, the palm-wine, the field-crops. The members of the clan living above ground can cultivate, reap, hunt, fish: they make use of the ancestral domain, but it is the dead who remain its owners.—The clan and the soil it occupies constitute an indi-visible thing, and the whole is under the rule of the *Bakulu*. It follows accordingly that the total alienation of the land or of a part of it is contrary to Bakongo mentality."[1]

In the same way, with the Ashantis, the ancestors "are the real landowners, who, though long departed, still continue to take a lively interest in the land from which they had their origin or which they once owned. The Ashanti land laws of to-day appear but the logical outcome of a belief which, in the not very remote past, considered the living landowners as but holding as it were tenancies at will from the dead, and as being the trustees of the latter. I believe it may be this religious aspect which largely accounts for the reluctance in the West African mind to the total alienation by sale of land to a foreigner, or even to one of their own race."[2]

[1] Fr. Van Wing, *Études Bakongo*, pp. 127–8.
[2] Capt. R. S. Rattray, *Ashanti*, p. 216.

Thus the black races do not conceive that the land can be really sold. But no more do the white understand how it is that so simple a transaction should be unintelligible to natives, and hence there are misunderstandings, disputes, violent measures on both sides, reprisals, evictions, and finally the extermination of the former masters of the soil. When conflict breaks out, the white men as a rule are in ignorance of the mystic obligations which the natives cannot refuse to obey, and they really believe themselves cheated. This failure to recognize what primitive mentality is, is soon followed by bad faith and the abuse of power. This chapter of the history of the relations between white and black races portrays a spectacle as monotonous as it is revolting.

In the most "primitive" societies, in black Australia, for instance, there is, as a rule, "very little idea" of individual ownership, as Spencer says. What one member of the group has acquired belongs to them all. "If you give a man a stick of tobacco, there are certain individuals, such as men who might lawfully be his fathers-in-law, to whom he is obliged to give some, and even if they are not on the spot, he will immediately share it with others. Give a man a shirt in return for work that he has done for you, and the chances are that you will find a friend of his, who has done nothing except ask for it, wearing it next day. On many of the cattle stations the work is done by a few natives, but everyone at hand shares in the proceeds, whether these be clothes, food, or tobacco; and it never occurs to them that the lazy loafer is living at the expense of his more industrious brother."[1]—Taplin had already written: "In the clan there can be no personal property—all implements, weapons, etc., belong to the members collectively; every individual regards them as possessions of his clan, and to be employed for its welfare and defence as occasion may require. If he has a weapon, or net, or canoe which is in some sense his own, he knows that his property in it is subject to the superior rights of his clan."[2]

When a native has entered upon a more or less voluntary

---

[1] B. Spencer, *The Native Tribes of the Northern Territory of Australia*, p. 36.
[2] G. Taplin, *The Folk-lore, Manners, Customs and Languages of the South Australian Aborigines*, pp. 11–12.

contract to work for white men, if he does not die before the end of it, he returns to his own home with a certain amount of property. But, say Jenness and Ballantyne, "a work boy's 'trade' is not his personal property; it belongs to all the family in common, and as many as can will gather round to see it opened out. Besides the loin-cloth and the belt and knife that the lad is wearing—these he is usually allowed to keep, at least for a time—he will probably bring a mirror and a pair of scissors and second knife perhaps, and red-shell ear-pendants manufactured by the whites. One thing is never lacking, the stick-tobacco varying from ten to thirty pounds in weight, according to the time that he has served at work. His elder brother presides over the distribution of all this wealth, and the rest of the kinsfolk aid him with copious suggestions; as for the boy, he must content himself with looking on, and take with proper gratitude the tiny fraction of all his gains that may be allotted to him."[1]

Thurnwald observed the same thing in the Solomon Islands, and explains the reason for it. "Men who have taken service with a European divide their total gains between the members of their family on returning home. This is because the latter, during their absence, have been deprived of their strength and their assistance. What a man has earned during his absence from home has been earned as a member of his group (*Sippe*), from which his working power and collaboration have been withdrawn."[2] In fact, the individual belongs to his group, and not to himself. When he enters into an engagement it is, as it were, the whole group which goes in his person to work for the white man. It is the group that earns the wages, and consequently the group that will divide it up, when the worker returns to his tribe. The latter has no more idea of claiming a personal ownership in his gains than he would have of protesting his innocence when collective responsibility causes him to be punished for the fault of some other member of the group.

[1] D. Jenness and A. Ballantyne, *The Northern d'Entrecasteaux*, pp. 95–6.
[2] R. Thurnwald, *Forschungen auf den Solomon Inseln und dem Bismarck Archipel*, iii, p. 36.

CHAPTER III

THE COMPONENT PARTS OF THE INDI-
VIDUALITY, AND ITS LIMITS (I)

I

WE are now approaching the most difficult part of our task. An analysis of their institutions and customs permitted of our determining with some degree of precision how primitives picture to themselves the relations of the individual with the persons and objects surrounding him, and in particular his relations with his social group. But what, in their eyes, constitutes the individual himself, of what spiritual and material elements he is compounded, how he lives and how he dies— these are problems which are much more difficult to solve. The reasons for this are clear. In the first place, we cannot attribute to the primitive on this subject, any more than on others, any speculative curiosity, or need of knowledge for the sake of knowledge. Where such a need does exist, it is extremely slight. The primitive is sufficiently satisfied with the mystic explanations ever present in his mind, to suit all cases.

Thus we find ourselves faced by collective representations which are far from distinct, in which the emotional elements predominate, concealing gross contradictions which are neither perceived nor felt by primitives. Hence arise two causes of error, both equally difficult to avoid: either we have to be satisfied with confused and contradictory notions (which are not so for primitive mentality), and by this apparent fidelity give a false idea of its representations—or else we must endow it with a clarity and inner coherence of which it feels no need, and thus betray it in another way. To try to avoid both dangers, there is but one course open to us, and that is, to place ourselves as best we can at the point of view of this primitive mentality, so that we may reconstitute individuality as it pictures it and, as far as is possible, throw light upon what

therein appears confused and contradictory through the
ensemble of its collective representations, and the general
principles governing them.

In the second place, upon such a subject we can scarcely
hope for altogether satisfactory testimony. Even attributing
to the observers sufficient competence and a sincere desire
to describe facts as they really are, and not as they would like
them to be, we are obliged to exercise the very greatest precaution in trusting what they say. They nearly all accept as
true, without having reflected upon the matter, and as if no
other hypothesis were possible, that primitives have beliefs
similar to their own, that in their eyes the human individual
is composed of soul and body, that is, of two elements very
different from each other, although joined together in this life.
Thus there would seem to be a kind of innate metaphysics in
the human mind: upon these problems the light of nature
would enlighten every man coming into the world. The missionaries above all, even those who are most concerned about
exactitude and most possessed of the critical faculty, expect to
find in the natives among whom they live the familiar distinction between body and soul. It is rare—and the reason for
this we shall discover later—for them to have to confess themselves mistaken. When they do not verify distinct conceptions
of body and soul, they believe at any rate that they discover
traces of them, and even recognizable vestiges. How often
testimony, which they alone are in a position to furnish,
remains entirely useless, because those who offer it have
imagined beforehand that the minds of primitives deal with
concepts really unknown to them! And even when it is actually
possible to make use of the testimony, how difficult it is to
extract the real content of the primitives' thought in its own
setting and with its fine shades of meaning!

As a matter of fact, *do* primitives picture to themselves
individualities as such, in any definite fashion? The persons
belonging to their group or neighbouring groups appear to
them as more or less strong, formidable, and enduring, according to the proportion of mystic force or *mana* possessed by
them. Those who have most of this quality—the chiefs, medicine-men, old men who have long resisted the advance of time
—are distinctly delineated individualities. A young child, a

youth not yet initiated, a woman who has not yet borne children, possess but little *mana*, and their individuality does not impose itself—far from it—with the same strength and vigour as those just defined. In short, the general concept of the human individual, as it exists in our minds, remains obscure to the primitive.

Thus by another road we return to one of the principal conclusions to which the preceding chapters have led. If primitive mentality pictures the individual as such, it does so in a way that is wholly relative. The individual is apprehended only by virtue of his being an element of the group of which he is a part, which alone is the true unit. According to the relative importance of the place he occupies in the group, this element will stand out more or less in the picture.

Two preliminary observations will possibly help to dissipate the obscurity inherent in the subject.

1. Although individuals—whether human or otherwise—are represented from a certain point of view as vehicles of mystic power, bearers of *mana*, whenever the primitive wishes to account for their physical or mental faculties he will always do so by attributing these to special beings dwelling within them and charged with the performance of them. According to the Ba-ila, for instance, if we are able to hear, it is because there are in our ears little beings called *bapuka*, who are in charge of the faculty of hearing. When a terrible noise, like the discharge of a gun close by, deafens us, it is because these *bapuka* have been stunned by the shock of the detonation, and if an old man loses his hearing, it is because his *bapuka* are dead.[1] The processes of reproduction are to be explained in the same way. To primitive mentality all the functions of the body are really accounted for by "*actions de présence.*" These have, moreover, not the faintest resemblance to catalysis. The primitive has no notion of a more or less complex concatenation of phenomena which condition themselves. He believes in the real and concrete presence of one or more complete little beings within the individual, and this idea exempts him from paying any attention to actual processes.

In the same way the adult Koryak very easily accounts for

[1] Smith and Dale, *The Ila-Speaking Peoples of Northern Rhodesia*, i, pp. 224–6.

the phonograph. "The grown-up people explained it very simply, thus: 'A living being, capable of imitating humans, is sitting in the box.' They used to call it 'the old man.' "[1] Among the Lenguas of Chaco it was the same with regard to the compass. "I explained to them that the little blue hand always pointed to the north wherever I happened to be." The Indians remained incredulous, and one old man made various experiments, finding, to his intense surprise, that the needle invariably pointed to the north. "A lively discussion ensued. . . . After a great deal of talking, the old man declared it to be his firm opinion that, before I had left my own land, I had caught a little blue devil and had secured it in this case, and that it was constantly pointing out my road homewards with its finger."[2]

Similarly, to the extent that primitives differentiate animate beings from inanimate objects, they will explain life by the presence of an organ or of a being, and death by the destruction or definite departure of this organ or being. It is not the cessation of the functions, respiratory, circulatory, and so forth, which entails as a consequence the end of life. On the contrary, if the functions cease, their cessation is due to the departure of the being whose presence was maintaining life, or to its destruction through some cause or other. This is an idea that we must never lose sight of when observers are speaking of the "soul," as primitives know it.

2. The antithesis of matter and spirit, so familiar to us as to appear almost natural, does not exist in primitive mentality—or, at any rate, it interprets it differently from ourselves. The primitive has no conception of matter, or of a body, whence *some* mystic force, which we should term spiritual, does not emanate. To him, too, there is no spiritual reality which is not a complete being, that is, a concrete thing, with a bodily form, even if this be invisible, intangible, without consistency or density. Here are some proofs of this, selected from many. "The African does not believe in anything being soul-less, he regards even matter itself as a form of soul, low, because not lively, a thing other spirit-forms use as they please. . . . This conception is, as far as I know, constant in both Negro and

[1] Jochelson, *The Koryak*, p. 427.
[2] W. B. Grubb, *An Unknown People in an Unknown Land*, pp. 100–1.

H

Bantu."[1] In Canada "the Ten'a do not conceive the spirits as really spiritual, or immaterial, substances. For them the spirits have a sort of subtle body, a kind of aerial fluid, so to speak, capable of endless transformations, moving from place to place almost instantaneously, rendering itself visible or invisible at will, penetrating into other bodies, and passing through them as though they were no obstacles, in short, possessed of the qualities proper to real spirits. But the conception of a real spiritual substance is beyond the Ten'a intelligence."[2]

It is to Elsdon Best that we are indebted for the most concise and comprehensible summing-up on this point. "Confusion is caused in our minds by the native terms denoting both material representations of immaterial qualities and immaterial representations of material objects."[3] Representations, we may add, that are extremely difficult, if not impossible, for minds fashioned like our own to reconstitute. Hence what likelihood is there that representations of the body, the soul, and of their interdependence should be, I do not say similar, but even comparable, in primitives and in ourselves?

II

Every one of us believes that he knows exactly what constitutes his personal individuality, and where he would consider that it ended. My feelings, thought, recollections, are myself. My head, arms, legs, internal organs, etc., are still I myself. All the rest that I perceive is not I. Thus my individuality is grasped by my consciousness and circumscribed by my bodily exterior, and I believe that my neighbour's is precisely so, too.

With primitives also, each person relates his states of consciousness, his limbs and his organs to himself. Certain languages, as we have already seen, even express this fact by adding personal pronouns as suffixes to substantives which denote these individual elements. But this suffixing extends further. It is applied also to the names of objects intimately connected with the individual, and forming, as it were, one

---

[1] Mary Kingsley, *West African Studies*, p. 199.
[2] Fr. Julius Jetté, "On the Superstitions of the Ten'a Indians," *Anthropos*, vi (1911), p. 97.   [3] Elsdon Best, *The Maori*, i, p. 299.

body with him. In fact, as has often been noted, in the representations of the primitives, each man's individuality does not stop short at his personal exterior. The limits which surround it are indecisive, ill-defined, and even variable according to the amount of mystic force or *mana* which an individual may possess.

First of all the primitive's idea of individuality comprises, in addition to his own body, all that grows upon it, all that comes from it, its secretions and its excretions: hair of the head and body, nails, tears, urine, excreta, seminal fluid, perspiration, etc. We need only recall the well-known articles in *Globus* in which K. Th. Preuss[1] demonstrated that magical practices exercised on these bodily products reacted upon the personality itself, of which they are integral parts. This is the reason that in many social aggregates so much care is taken to avoid hair or nail-parings or excreta falling into the hands of a third party who might possibly be malevolently inclined. To have the disposal of these would be to have the man's life in one's hands. The hair and secretions, etc., of the individual are his very self, just as his feet or his hands, his heart or his head, are. They "belong" to him in the fullest sense of the word. Henceforth I shall speak of them as his "appurtenances."

To these parts of the individuality we must add the impressions a body leaves upon a seat or on the ground, and especially the traces of his footsteps. Thus, in a popular legend of Kiwai Island, we are told: "He was out of reach when the people got to know of his visit, and the only thing they could do was to shoot off their arrows into his foot-traces, thus trying to hurt him."[2] In another part of New Guinea, where a rain-maker had been successful, "on his return the hero was met at the village with loud beating of drums, the mothers taking their babies and setting them down in his footprints, thinking perhaps that their little bodies might gather up some of the knowledge of this marvellous man."[3]

We find the same ideas with respect to these appurtenances in Equatorial Africa and in South America. Among the

---

[1] "Der Ursprung der Religion und Kunst," *Globus*, lxxxvi, No. 19, *et seq.*; lxxxvi, No. 20, *et seq.*
[2] G. Landtman, *The Folk-tales of the Kiwai Papuans*, p. 418.
[3] *Annual Report*, Papua (South-Eastern Division), 1910, p. 78.

Pangwe, "a man had set a snare close to a path. When he came back next morning he saw the fresh tracks of a man in the grass, but he found nothing in the snare. He accordingly thought that someone had stolen the animal that had been ensnared. He then took this track (i.e. the grass with a little of the soil on which the man had walked) and placed it in a leper's privy, so that the supposed robber might be contaminated with leprosy. Then the others said to him: 'What are you thinking about? For all you know, it might have been your brother or one of your friends.' "[1]—In the Warrau tribes of Guiana, there is a popular story in which "the mother, looking around, carefully examined the fresh tracks, and said: 'This is the man who has killed my child.' Her next move was to dig up a bit of the soil marked by one of the fresh footprints, wrap it up in a leaf tied with bush rope, and hang it on a branch while she went for firewood. . . . When the woman returned . . . she made a big fire, and threw the bundle into the flames, saying as she did so: 'Curse the person whose footprint I now burn! May the owner fall into this fire also!' She thought that if she burnt the 'footmark,' so would the person's shadow be drawn to the fire." (Now while she had been away looking for wood, someone had substituted her footprint for the one she had dug up, and she felt herself drawn to the fire.) "Twice was she thus dragged toward it against her will, and yet she succeeded in resisting. But on the third occasion she could not draw back; she fell in and was burnt to ashes."[2]

The imprint of other parts of the body must be watched over with not less care than the footprints. "When they have been sitting down, the New Hebrideans take great care before going away to rub out with their feet the impression left by their posteriors in the dust, and they do this from fear of witchcraft."[3] In this last case, as with the footprints, the appurtenance is a reproduction of part of the individual, and therefore the individual himself. Later we shall see what profound significance this identity bears for primitives.[4]

[1] Tessmann, "Sprichwörter der Pangwe, West Afrika," *Anthropos*, viii (1913), p. 405.
[2] W. E. Roth, *An Inquiry into the Animism and Folk-lore of the Guiana Indians*. E.B. Bulletin, xxx, p. 128. Cf. W. J. V. Saville, *In Unknown New Guinea*, p. 268.
[3] J. Bt. Suas, "Notes ethnographiques sur les indigènes des Nouvelles Hébrides," *Anthropos*, ix (1914), p. 763.   [4] Cf. Chap. iv, pp. 153–7.

To the number of a man's appurtenances belong, too, as we know, the remains of his food. That a consubstantiality between the individual and what he eats should be established, we can understand without difficulty: he becomes, he is, what he feeds upon and assimilates. This participation, in the primitive mind, extends to the remains of his food; it is as true of what is not consumed as of what is. This is a well-known fact, and I shall give a few examples only. In Melanesia, at Saa, in Malanta, "before the circle was complete the Saa people learnt their danger, gathered their women and children, and escaped unseen and unheard in the darkness. . . . But when they were clear of the enemy and safe outside their line, they remembered that a bunch of areca nuts from which Paucelo Paima (their chief) had already taken some to chew with his betel leaves, was left behind. The two brothers of Paucelo Paima agreed that one of them, if he died for it, must go for the nuts to save the elder brother."[1]—In Neu-Mecklenburg, "if a native is on a journey, or if he takes a meal in a strange compound, he will be seen to put away carefully in the basket he carries on his arm his banana-skins, the betel-nut he has finished chewing, as well as the remains of his meal, and carry it all off to burn it at home."[2] And the missionary adds: "To the Neu-Mecklenburger's mind, the remains of his food and the man are, so to speak, the same person, and this is why he says: '*di te ru iau*' (they have picked me up) and not: '*di te ru ra subanagu*' (they have picked up the remains of my food)." It is a striking expression, and no metaphor: the remains, like other appurtenances, are literally comprised in the native's individuality.

We can say as much, strange as it may appear, of the clothes worn by an individual, and impregnated with his perspiration. Thus, in the Island of Kiwai, "one day the girls on their way home from fishing came to Baidam's abode, and picked up the leaves which he had used when dancing. They stuck them inside their grass-petticoats and went home to sleep, and from Baidam's 'smell' they all became pregnant."[3]—A similar belief has been found in Madagascar. "The father's lamba must not be worn by his daughter; so, too, the sister must not

[1] R. H. Codrington, *The Melanesians*, p. 49.
[2] P. G. Peekel, *Religion und Zauberei auf dem mittlern Neu-Mecklenburg*, p. 102.
[3] G. Landtman, *op. cit.*, p. 268.

wear her brother's lamba,"[1] and with the Baghirmi people:
"The Kozzam are related to a greater tribe called the Hémat.
About their origin there is a story told that they are descended
from an Arab, Ali Ouèmit, who set out for Mecca accompanied
by his daughter, who had reached the age of puberty but was
still a virgin. The girl's loincloth having worn out, her father
gave her his trousers, that she might conceal her nakedness.
Sometime afterwards the maiden perceived that through this
circumstance she had become pregnant. She gave birth to a
son, whom she and her father abandoned on a mountain."[2]

Let us return to Kiwai. Another legend relates the history of
Sonare and his six blind brothers. These last, in the absence of
his wife, seized her petticoat and "humbugged" it, the elder
first and then the rest according to age. The wife enters,
changes her petticoat, and puts on the one her brothers-in-law
had humbugged. The same events took place every day for
some time. Signs of pregnancy became manifest, and the
astonished husband interrogates his wife. Then one day he
returned unexpectedly, and saw his brothers "humbugging"
his wife's petticoat. "Oh, I understand now," he said to himself, "that is how my wife has got a child." . . . and he avenged
himself on his brothers.[3] Thus, solely from the circumstance
that she wears a garment that has been "humbugged" by her
brothers-in-law, the wife conceives. The husband who comes
on them by surprise considers them guilty of adultery, and
that his wife is pregnant through them. This is because, to the
mind of these Papuans, the garment worn by a person becomes
an appurtenance. By means of this participation the garment
and the person are henceforth but one and the same individual.

This representation has also given rise to a custom encountered in regions that are widely separated from one another.
To save someone about to be killed, it is enough to cast one's
garment over him. "When a man (a Maori) wished to save
the life of an enemy, during a fight or pursuit, or when a
village was taken, all he had to do was to cast his garment over
nim. If he who did so were a man of standing the act would
be quite sufficient."[4] Similarly in West Africa, during an

[1] R. Decary, "Notes sur les populations du district de Maromandia," *Revue
d'Ethnographie et des traditions populaires* (1924), No. 20, p. 355.
[2] Devallée, "Le Baghirmi," *Recherches Congolaises*, vi (1925), p. 20.
[3] G. Landtman, *op. cit.*, pp. 313-15.   [4] Elsdon Best, *The Maori*, iii, p. 299.

uproar, "Mary Slessor foresaw trouble and disaster, but though her voice was now too feeble to be heard in the babel of sound, she was not yet at the end of her resources. Divesting herself of as many of her garments as was possible, she threw them over the stuff, thus giving it the protection of her own body, according to Egbo law."[1]

From this, too, arises the obligation not to touch the clothing or the personal effects of others, the weapons of a warrior, for instance. It is literally touching him himself, and risking the drawing down his wrath upon the offender. Who knows what bad influence such contact may not arouse? Conversely, putting on the garments of another person is exposing oneself to the chance of acquiring his qualities, whether good or bad. Among the Palaungs of Burma, "when a child begins to walk, one of the first things that it is taught is that it must never in fun put on the clothes of any one else. . . . If a man is addicted to telling lies and some one wears his hat by mistake, that person may catch the lie-telling infection. . . . This also applies to shoes. . . . I once had a Palaung servant who came with me from Namhsan to Burma. A Burmese maidservant, on a muddy day, borrowed my servant's sandals for five minutes, without asking leave. Never had I seen the Palaung woman so indignant. . . . Big tears rolled down the cheeks of my Palaung maid, who said that although the sandals were quite new, she could never wear them again, as she feared that the bad qualities of the Burman" (a liar and a bad sort) "would become hers. The sandals were flung out of doors, where they remained abandoned in the garden."[2]

What is true of clothes is true of everything that has been in close and frequent, if not continuous, contact with the individual. Among the Sema Nagas, "the stool, as the bed, is so closely associated with its owner as to contain some part of his essence, as it were, in virtue of which it is absolutely *genna* (forbidden) at any time to cut or burn a person's stool or bed, while it is very bad form to sit on the bed of a Sema chief unless invited by him to do so."[3] With their neighbours the Lhota Nagas, "if anything intimately connected with the

[1] W. P. Livingstone, *Mary Slessor of Calabar*, pp. 110–11.
[2] Leslie Milne, *The Home of an Eastern Clan*, pp. 37–8.
[3] J. H. Hutton, *The Sema Nagas*, p. 243.

person, such as a cloth or a *dao* (dagger), be sold, the seller
retains a thread from the cloth, or scrapes a tiny shaving off
the handle of the *dao*, for were he to sell the whole of something which was almost part of himself, the buyer might be
able to exercise some magical influence over him."[1]—For the
same reason the Eskimo maintain a similar custom. "When the
natives sold us hunting implements which they had used themselves, or whole skins, they often cut off a small, sometimes quite
a minute fragment, which they preserved themselves. A man
who had sold us a paddle fell ill in spring. Seeing his opportunity, he cut off a splinter from the paddle and extracted some
of the bone nails with which the mounting was fastened."[2]—
In the neighbourhood of the Bering Strait, "when a hunter
sells furs, it is a common custom for him to cut a small fragment from each skin . . . and place it carefully in a pouch."[3]
The interpretation of this circumstance related by Nelson
differs from the others, but it does not exclude the idea we are
considering.

The latter is attested in South Africa also. To the Thonga, the
handle of a man's assegai is an "appurtenance," but not the
blade. "The handle is *he*, the blade is not *he*." (It has not been
impregnated with the perspiration from his body.) . . .
"Should a man have died far away from home, no ceremony
will take place before the news is thoroughly confirmed. Then
all the relatives assemble. A grave is dug, and all his mats and
his clothing are buried in it. These objects which he was using
every day, which have been soiled by the exudations from the
body, are *himself*."[4]—The Zulus "do not eat the flesh of an ox
that has been ridden, because that has united it with the
man."[5] Even vermin are an appurtenance. "It often happens
that one Kafir performs for another the kind office of collecting
these insects, in which case he preserves the entomological
specimens, carefully delivering them to the person to whom
they originally appertained, supposing, according to their
theory, that as they derived their support from the blood of

[1] J. P. Mills, *The Lhota Nagas*, p. 44.
[2] G. Holm, "Ethnological Sketch of the Angmagsalik Eskimo," edited by W.
Thalbitzer, *Meddelelser om Grönland*, xxix, p. 86.
[3] E. W. Nelson, *The Eskimo about Bering Strait*, E.B. Bulletin, xviii, p. 437.
[4] H. A. Junod, *The Life of a South African Tribe*, i, p. 140, note 3, p. 165.
[5] F. Speckmann, *Die Hermannsburger Mission in Afrika* (1876), p. 106.

the man from whom they were taken, should they be killed by another, the blood of his neighbour would be in his possession, thus placing in his hands the power of some superhuman influence."[1]

III

In certain social groups the number of appurtenances is increased by what the individual *owns*, especially when things that he has himself produced or fabricated are in question. These objects are inseparable from his personality: they form part of it, they are the man himself. Property, in such cases, as Thurnwald has remarked, should be called *personal*, rather than *individual*. "As the personal manifestation of the worker, work and the things it produces," says he, "are regarded as of the highest order, as indissolubly bound up with him, like an 'appurtenance' (*Zubehör*). This accounts for the fact that these things perish when he does; they are burnt at his death."[2] This feeling is almost universal. It causes the destruction of a man's belongings when he passes away; and makes any attempt on such objects regarded as the gravest of offences, just as when their owner is alive. "The natives are absurdly sensitive to threats of *burning* anything belonging to themselves. There is no surer way of drawing down their anger than to hint at such a thing as the *burning* of a canoe, a hut, or even a garment. *To chop the property* of another is regarded as symbolical of an intention to *chop his person*."[3]

African negroes hold similar views on this matter. "The appropriation of a thing in some way identifies the object appropriated with the individual. He who fingers a man's possessions really touches their owner. In this respect the Bakongo have a very lively and peculiar feeling of the extension of their personality, though in other domains it is so limited. Seeing how close is the connection between the things possessed and the possessor, it is easy to understand the custom of burying them with him or exposing them on his grave. To keep them for others would be to expose themselves to seeing

[1] A. Steedman, *Wanderings and Adventures in the Interior of South Africa*, i, p. 266.
[2] R. Thurnwald, "Ermittelungen über Eingeborenenrechte der Südsee," *Zeitschrift für vergleichende Rechtswissenschaft*, xxxiii, p. 351.
[3] W. Gill, *Savage Life in Polynesia*, p. 120.

the dead man come and claim them and make reprisals."[1] These expressions are remarkably definite. The "extension of the personality" seems to be an excellent definition of "appurtenance." For their part, Smith and Dale have noted that the Ba-ila people have the same word to denote certain injuries to persons, and also offences against their property: "Since in the minds of the Ba-ila there is a very close connection amounting almost to identity between a person and his possessions, an injury done to his property comes also under this head."[2]

In various districts in South America, this "extension of personality" is to be met with again. "The Jibaro cannot distinguish his own personality from his material belongings, at least not from things he has made himself. When he fabricates a shield, a drum, a blow-pipe or some other delicate object, he has to diet and observe abstinence in other ways; for, according to his own ideas, he actually puts something of his own personality, his own soul, into the object he is making." And again: "The Jibaro always pays great attention to his dress and his ornaments, which form a part of his personality."[3] With the Chimanas of Eastern Bolivia, "it is difficult to acquire objects belonging to little children. The Indians think that if they give away their child's cradle he will die. For certain amulets they most emphatically refused to name a price."[4] It is the same with the Catios Indians of Colombia. "In the funeral procession, they bear in a basket the objects which the dead man used and possessed, that they may be buried with their owner. This is such an inveterate custom with them, that even after they have been converted it costs them a good deal to break with it. I have taken part in the burial of a child a few months old, whose mother and grandmother were both communicants. In spite of their known piety and their renunciation of the other ceremonies, they could not wholly divest themselves of this tradition, and between the folds within which they wrapped the child's little body they placed the feeding-bottle she had used."[5] Guevara notes the same circumstance

[1] Fr. Van Wing, Études Bakongo, p. 129.
[2] Smith and Dale, The Ila-Speaking Peoples of Northern Rhodesia, i, pp. 346-7.
[3] R. Karsten, Blood-Revenge, War and Victory-Feasts among the Jibaro Indians of Eastern Ecuador, E.B. Bulletin, lxxix, pp. 12, 24.
[4] E. Nordenskiöld, Forschungen und Abenteuer in Süd-Amerika, p. 120.
[5] Fr. Severino de Santa Teresa, Creencias, ritos, usos y costumbres de los Indios Catios de la Prefectura apostolica de Uraba, p. 122.

in very distinct terms. "Formerly the Araucans were afraid to part with personal objects made by one who had used them, such as his clothing, weapons, rings, circlets, etc., for these objects were literally identified with their owner, and to place them in the hands of another was equivalent to giving the latter magic power over him." The writer adds a reflection of far-reaching significance: "This magic practice corresponded with the close union existing between a person and his image or likeness."[1]

If indeed primitives in general are so anxious not to let their "appurtenances," whatever these may be, fall into the hands of a stranger, that is, of a possible enemy, it is because he may use them to bewitch the owners. Now, according to Guevara's remark, this bewitching is the same sort of thing as making effigies of them. The appurtenances are treated by the wizard as images, for instance, when they are burnt, or buried with certain substances, etc. We may therefore think that images, in their turn, are conceived of as appurtenances.

Do we need to cite cases of bewitchment of this type? In the New Hebrides "it consists of taking a person's excrement, or the ground where he has urinated, and wrapping it in a leaf of the wild yam. This is then put into a young coco-nut, which is 'charmed' by breathing and uttering prayers over it. Finally, this coco-nut and its contents are buried in a place where a smoke-hole has its vent. The coco-nut becomes warm, and the victim falls ill. Should anyone discover the coco-nut and carry it with tongs and put it into a pool of fresh water, the sick man recovers; if not, he will inevitably die."[2] With the Bakaua of New Guinea, "if someone is to be bewitched, the wizard requires a charm, that is, he must be able to handle some appurtenance of the man who is to be done away with. This may be the remains of a meal, saliva, hair, pieces of skin, grease from his body, or even merely the red dye for his hair, or the stalk of a betel-nut he is chewing. The wizard places the 'soul' of his victim in contact with this object, he *binds* it to the latter, that he may deliver it to the fire with this charm, and thus 'roast' his victim."[3]—Where the bewitching of animals is in

[1] L. Guevara, *Psicologia del pueblo araucano*, p. 174.
[2] J. Bt. Suas, *op. cit.*, p. 767.
[3] R. Neuhauss, *Deutsch Neu-Guinea*, iii, pp. 463-4.

question, the same process is used with their appurtenances. "Till lately the missionaries have not been allowed to use manure for their gardens," writes an early traveller in South Africa, "for it was formerly universally believed that if the manure were removed from the cattle-kraals, the cattle would die of a particular disease."[1]

Sometimes the making of effigies and the bewitching practised upon the appurtenances are combined. Among the Tlinkit Indians, "a wizard acted upon his victim by obtaining a piece of his clothing, some hair, spittle, or a fish-bone from which the person in question had eaten the flesh. Then he made an image of his body, which he treated in the way he wanted the living person to suffer, making it a mere skeleton; deforming the hands, to destroy the ability of a woman at weaving," etc.[2]

IV

The appurtenances may also be used for other purposes besides bewitchment. With the Dschagga, for instance, "when a child is inclined to wander, as growing boys enjoy doing, and disappears from his mother's village for the whole day to roam about the country, they try to attach him to the home by his 'soul.' In the night, when he is soundly asleep, the anxious mother cuts his finger- and toe-nails and a little of his hair. Next day she sends for the medicine-man. He 'binds' these elements, i.e. he spits upon them and, pronouncing certain incantations, he hides them in the framework of the house. In this way the boy finds himself tied to the house and free of his impulse to wander.—When at the end of an expedition a child is brought back to be a slave, the same process is gone through to cure him of nostalgia and the desire to run away."[3] The extension of the personality to the appurtenances—hair-clippings and nail-parings—is quite clearly shown here. They are acted upon, and it is on the individual himself that the effect is produced.

Here is another fact, collected from a Bantu tribe, which is

[1] Rev. J. Philip, *Researches in South Africa*, ii, p. 117.
[2] J. R. Swanton, *The Tlinkit Indians*, E.B. Bulletin, xxvi, p. 470.
[3] Br. Gutmann, *Denken und Dichten der Dschagga-Neger*, p. 65.

no less significant. Among the Ba-kaonde, "if a child cuts its upper incisors before its lower ones (known as *lutala*), it is thrown into the river. . . . After the child has been thrown away, the mother returns without mourning. No one asks any question." (It is known that these children bring ill-luck.)[1]

"There is one way in which the saving of a *lutala* child's life is at times permitted. The mother may be allowed to put all the teeth as they come out, all loose nails, all nail-parings, all hair cut, into one calabash and keep it. After the last milk-tooth has come out, the calabash is taken and carried on the mother's back, like a baby, in the same cloth that she has been wearing to carry the child. She goes to the river and drops the calabash off her back into the water (as she would have done to the baby)—in all such cases of infanticide by drowning, the mother just loosens the cloth and lets the baby fall off without looking round. As the calabash splashes into the water she calls out, 'Here is the *lutala*.' But this 'reprieve' is rare."[2]

Thus, in the minds of these natives, a complete collection of certain appurtenances is the equivalent of the individual himself. It may be substituted for him, even in peculiarly serious circumstances. The interest of the social group demands that the *lutala* which is the bringer of ill-luck should be made incapable of doing harm, that is, that he should disappear. His mere presence in the midst of the group would be a continual menace to the life of its members. As a rule, they do not hesitate to sacrifice him. His mother dares not try to save him— it does happen, however, that the child is sometimes spared, but then a kind of "double," composed of his appurtenances, is sacrificed in his place. In the minds of the Ba-kaonde this double is the child himself. When the mother, letting the calabash fall into the water, says, "Here is the *lutala*," it is not a pious fraud. She is alone, and not trying to deceive anyone. She is expressing the idea, strange enough to our minds, but not so to minds accustomed to think in terms of the law of participation, that the child and its double, although in different places, are one and the same individual. There is no question in the matter for her, or for anyone else in the tribe, since the

[1] Cf. *Primitive Mentality*, pp. 152–4.
[2] F. A. Melland, *In Witch-bound Africa*, pp. 50–4.

double is made up of appurtenances, and the appurtenances of the child are the child itself.

Other appurtenances may hold the same position. Here we have the testimony of a fact taken from the Naguas, a tribe of the Upper Amazon. "At nightfall they dig a trench which, one would surely imagine, is destined to receive the corpse, so carefully do they do it. But it is intended for the burying of all the effects of the deceased—his hammock, arrows, cudgels, knives, feathers, in short, all the utensils he used when alive; these are fastened together and placed in the hammock, and then laid in the trench. . . . Around this grave they clear a little of the ground and plant sugar-cane, bananas, yuccas and papaws in very small quantities, for these products are intended only for the soul of the dead, so that 'he may not come back to look for his utensils, and frighten the living.' The following night, the corpse is put on the fire, roasted, and entirely consumed. Even the bones are made into broth, and mixed with the flour of the yucca that they may be consumed."[1] No portion of the corpse, therefore, is placed in the grave—yet they make preparation near it for the food of the dead man, for fear lest he should return. It must be, then, that he is present there, and, indeed, his appurtenances have been buried. They make part of his personality; they are the man himself. The content of the grave dug with so much care is the dead Indian, just as the content of the calabash, with the Ba-kaonde, is the *lutala* child.

"If an Ewe (in Togoland) dies on a journey, his nails and the hair of his head are cut and taken to his relatives; the man himself is buried on the spot."[2] We should say that the hair and nails "represent" him; to the Togoland native these appurtenances are the man himself, for the participation between them and him amounts to identity.

Lastly, in the Keij Islands, a missionary has observed facts which confirm the foregoing. "The *dandamoer* is a kind of bamboo gridiron, built up about a yard and a half above the floor. They put on it the coco-nut which has been used to sprinkle the departing guests, and then as many coco-nuts

[1] Teniente-Coronel Roberto Lopez, *En la rontera oriental del Perù*, Para (1925), pp. 57–61.
[2] Von François *Mitteilungen aus dem deutschen Schutzgebieten* (1888), i, 4, p. 162.

as there are travellers. They place there too . . . the basket
containing the egg, cigarette ends, and sometimes other small
things that the departing travellers have committed to the care
of the *enkod mangan*. To the natives' minds, these objects . . .
replace the persons themselves. They imagine invisible but
very real relations between these things and the absent ones,
so that all the kindly care bestowed on these will profit them
too. Thus, when their horoscope is about to be cast, they first
of all take the material which will be used for this purpose to
the *dandamoer*, where these objects are left lying, so that they
may put themselves in relation with the absent whom these‑
objects represent."[1] Like the nails and the hair of the dead
Ewe, these objects, the appurtenances of the absent travellers,
are parts of their individuality, in a word, are themselves.
This identity by participation is clearly seen in all the expressions used by Father Guertjens.

To conclude, we can consider that up to the present we have
established the following points:

1. To the primitive's mind, the limits of the individuality
are variable and ill-defined.

2. The "appurtenances" are an "extension of the individuality." They are integral parts of a personality and are
confounded with it.

3. In certain cases, the "appurtenances" are regarded as the
individual's double, and this double is the individual, and can
take his place.

[1] Fr. H. Guertjens, "Le Cérémonial des Voyages aux îles Keij," *Anthropos* (1910),
p. 351.

CHAPTER IV

THE COMPONENT PARTS OF THE INDIVIDUALITY, AND ITS LIMITS (II)

I

AMONG an individual's appurtenances, whether these be separable from himself or not, there are some to which the primitive attributes absolute and exceptional importance. Their soundness and entirety seems to him a *sine quâ non* for his safety and his very life. It is these that an enemy would first of all try to seize, and if he cannot gain possession of them at will, he will try to reach them indirectly. Should he succeed, and the individual be aware of it, the latter regards himself as inevitably doomed.

Such an appurtenance, for instance, according to the oldest authorities, was the *kidney-fat*, in the eyes of the Australian aborigines of Victoria. "The most awful superstition is that they believe that man would never die unless he were killed; that the sick man has been opened, and that his kidneys and fat have been taken out, which has caused death; and that nothing short of the kidneys and fat of another will appease the dead. They also believe that, as the kidneys and fat are the life of man, the eating of the same gives double strength and vigour to those who partake of them: hence they never kill a 'wild black,' as they term him, but they rob the body of that part."[1]—In the same Collection of Letters we find Jamieson writing: "When any black, whether old or young, dies, an enemy is supposed during the night to have made an incision in his side and removed his kidney-fat."[2]

Various passages of Brough Smyth's confirm the testimony of the preceding. When an avenging expedition has found the victims it was seeking, and has surprised and slain them, "they always abstract the kidney-fat and also take off a piece of the skin of the thigh. These are carried home as trophies, as the

---

[1] *Letters of Victorian Pioneers*, p. 68.   [2] *Ibid.*, p. 271.

American Indians take the scalp."[1]—"It has always been the practice among the Aborigines for the warriors of one tribe to make incursions into the territories of another, either to steal lubras, or to surprise and attack males, who, after being struck down, had an incision made in their sides, through which the caul-fat was drawn, which fat was carefully kept, and used by the assassin to lubricate himself—the belief being that all the qualifications, both physical and mental, of the previous owner of the fat were thus communicated to him who used it."[2]

Let us apply to these facts and to those which follow Elsdon Best's concise summing-up: *The native terms denote both material representations of immaterial qualities and immaterial representations of material objects.* Was the kidney-fat, to the Victorian aborigines, what it is to us, namely, a soft, whitish substance, situated in a certain part of the body? Undoubtedly. But at the same time it was something quite different. Although it was a visible and tangible object, it was also an "immaterial quality," in other words, a mystic quality. It was, as the Victorian colonist puts it, "the life of man." As such, exempt from what we call physical laws, it could leave its place in the body and return thither without its departure and return being betrayed in any way. The very incision referred to above is a mystic operation, which does not necessarily leave a trace as the incision of a scalpel would do. Consequently the absence of such a trace on the skin in no way proves that the incision has not taken place and that the kidney-fat has not been removed. Such an argument would avail only for positive minds like our own. It produces no effect upon a mystic mentality. The primitive knows by certain signs which do not err, that an individual's kidney-fat has been removed, and his certainty cannot be shaken, any more than it would need to be confirmed, by the evidence of the senses.

"When an Aboriginal is alone and far distant from his encampments, he is liable to have his kidney-fat taken from him by the spirit of a wild black. The kidney-fat (*Marm-bu-la*) is taken away in some secret manner, and death is certain in the most of such cases, and scarcely to be avoided under the happiest circumstances."

[1] Brough Smyth, *The Aborigines of Victoria*, ii, p. 28 (Upper and Lower Murray).
[2] *Ibid.*, ii, p. 313.

A native returned to his camp saying that his kidney-fat had been taken from him. There was general consternation, and the man regarded himself as already dying. "Malcolm, a wizard—a most learned doctor—who believed he could fly and cut the air as well as any eagle, now commenced his labours. He disappeared in the darkness; boughs cracked and rustled as he took his supposed flight through the trees towards the sky. . . . Malcolm could not at once find the wild black who had taken the kidney-fat and he was at last compelled to take what he made the blacks believe was a lengthened flight. He was absent three-quarters of an hour. . . . He appeared and without speaking a word, seized the dying man in a savage manner, and rubbed him violently; devoting his attentions mostly to the sides of the poor wretch, which he pushed and beat unmercifully. He then announced that the cure was complete. All the men jumped up. . . . The sick man arose, lighted his pipe and smoked composedly in the midst of his friends. . . .

"The blacks firmly believed that Malcolm had flown as the hawk flies, had stooped on the wild black who had stolen the kidney-fat, and had taken it from him, and had replaced it in the body of the patient—and nothing that Mr. Thomas said to them had the slightest effect on their minds.

"They believe that if the wild black who has stolen kidney-fat eats any, even the smallest portion of it, the man whom he has deprived of it will surely die."[1]

This long story, which I have very much abridged, recalls others strikingly similar. At the northern extremity of the other hemisphere, the Eskimo angakok also takes a flight, like the Australian wizard, in order to look for a "soul" which has been snatched from his patient. Like Malcolm, he remains absent for some time, and then comes down again, like him, with the "soul" that he has taken by force from the ravisher. In the same way he, too, at last restores it to the body of the sick man, who at once returns to life and vigour.

This likeness seems to throw strong light on what the angakok calls the "soul," and also on what the kidney-fat of the Australian aborigines really is. In such cases it is a question of *both*

[1] Brough Smyth, *The Aborigines of Victoria*, i, pp. 469–71 (Upper and Lower Murray).

a material object and immaterial qualities, combined in a representation so different from our ordinary ideas that we can scarcely hope to grasp it thoroughly. It is the "life" or, according to others, the "vital principle" or "soul" of the individual. But this vital principle acts only in mystic fashion, and through its presence alone. As long as it is there, the individual remains safe and sound. If he is deprived of it—if the kidney-fat is forcibly carried off, by an enemy, for instance—he dies sooner or later, and nothing can save him from his fate. The only remedy is the one attempted by the native doctors, and that is to recover the "vital principle," the "soul," and, if happily it still remains intact, to restore it to its place in the body.

The same author relates another interesting case. A young woman was wasting away, and she was evidently abandoning herself to death. At last she revealed the secret of her depressed spirits. She told Mr. Thomas that "some moons back, when the Goulburn blacks were encamped near Melbourne, a young man named Gib-ber-ook came behind her and cut off a lock of her hair; that she was sure he had buried it and that it was rotting somewhere. . . . Her *Marm-bu-la* (kidney-fat) was wasting away, and when her hair had completely rotted, she would die. She stated further that her name had been lately cut on a tree by some wild black, and that that was another token of death."[1]

Here we have a very clear instance of bewitchment by means of an appurtenance. The young native woman is wasting away because an enemy, in possession of a lock of her hair, is causing this portion of her individuality to be gradually decomposed. But this very decomposition acts through the progressive wearing-out, the continuous decaying of the kidney-fat, which is the "vital principle." Thus we grasp the process by which the bewitchment leads to death, if indeed the term "process" is not too much at variance with acts that are wholly mystic. The magic exercised upon the hair from a distance reacts upon an appurtenance, and that the most important, the kidney-fat. More simply still, it attacks the second through the first, and indeed both at the same time.

[1] Brough Smyth, *The Aborigines of Victoria*, pp. 468–9 (Upper and Lower Murray).

In New Guinea W. E. Armstrong observed facts analogous
to the foregoing, in which the same ambiguity appears in the
representation of beings and qualities which are at the same
time immaterial and material. "The *Alawai* (witch) kills a
person normally for the sake of food, but exactly what is eaten
seems to be a very vague idea in the native mind. It would seem
to be the "*tantau*" (soul) which is eaten, though they admit
that it cannot be the actual flesh, since this putrefies, and disappears by a natural process; on the other hand, graves are
frequently tampered with by *Alawai*, and the body or part of the
body removed. It . . . would seem that there is confusion
between two ideas—that of the woman in the flesh eating
the actual corpse, and that of the woman as *Alawai* eating the
tantau, or possibly the *earua*." (Both these terms signify the
"soul.") "But the fact of an *Alawai* 'eating' a person does not
prevent the *earua* of the person descending to *Biula* (the Land of
the Dead); the view expressed by an old native was that the
earua is 'eaten,' the eyes alone being left. But such indefinite-
ness of formulation in the native mind," adds Armstrong, "is
quite what one would expect to find. The chief source of error
in this present account is, no doubt, a tendency to give too great
a definiteness to native ideas, which, however, one could hardly
express without being guilty of this form of error."[1] And a little
later he says: "It is not clear to me, probably because it is not
even clear to the native, whether the sick man or his *tantau* is
available for the *Alawai* before he is dead or not. It would seem
that his *tantau* can be used and carried on an *Alawai's iloro*
(pig-pole) before the man is dead, and can even be eaten,
which gives a more literal interpretation to the expression,
'an Alawai is eating me'—a common expression of a sick man,
and falls in line with the belief in the loss of the shadow sometimes in sickness." (The "soul" is also the shadow.)

"The different methods of sorcery employed by witches are
not less instructive. Either the soul (*earua*) 'eats' the person
acting directly by virtue of intrinsic power, without apparently
the use of medicine or spells. (Nevertheless, a woman who is
Alawai is supposed to exert her power mainly by 'talking.') Or
else the *earua* of a person is captured by *Alawai*. The *earua* in
this case appears as a man or woman, and snatches the *earua*

[1] *Annual Report*, Papua (1920–1), pp. 34–5 (Suau Tawala tribe).

of the victim, and binds it, and carries it away like a pig to 'Oiaisa,' a hill near Sagarai, where it remains indefinitely. . . . The dead body . . . remains where the person was attacked, and may be discovered, bearing no signs of violence, afterwards by the relatives. . . . The commonest method . . . is the projecting of 'namo' (small stones, bits of wood, etc.) into a person, from near or from far. There is no wound visible."[1]

These New Guinea Melanesians do not, like the Victorian aborigines, speak of the kidney-fat. With them, that which takes its place is the *earua*, the soul or double of the individual, more or less immaterial, living in the region of the abdomen, or else the *tantau*, a shadow or reflection of the body, and more or less confused with it. This difference is more apparent than real, however. On the one hand, the kidney-fat, in its mystic reality, which alone interests the natives, is the "soul" or "vital principle," and on the other, the *earua* of the Suau Tawala tribe, wholly "soul" as it is, may be affixed to a pole like a pig, and literally eaten. To them, as to the Australian aborigines, a fatal illness consists precisely in this—that this "soul," at once immaterial and material, has been captured and devoured by a sorcerer. With them both, the soul can be carried off without any trace of the operation being left. The removal itself is mystic, and there is therefore no need to make any incision in the body of the victim.[2]

Among Polynesian peoples, who are as a rule much more developed than those of Australia and Melanesia, the idea of the "soul" of the sick man being devoured by a spirit or a god was current. "The theory of sickness and death is that certain gods feed exclusively upon human spirits. Hence the abusive epithet often applied to them: *Atua kai tangata*—man-eating gods, i.e. for trivial offences devouring the souls of their worshippers. If once the soul be eaten by the god, the body—which is regarded as the mere shell or casing of the spirit—must fade away and die. Throughout Polynesia, no one was believed to die a natural death; there was always some special offence

---

[1] *Annual Report*, Papua (1920–1), p. 35 (Suau Tawala tribe).
[2] In the Andaman Isles, "the vital principle is at different times identified with the pulse, the breath, with the blood and with the fat, particularly the kidney-fat."—A. R. Brown, *The Andaman Islanders*, p. 166.

against the gods."[1] Do we not recognize here, in a form which is definitely religious, ideas similar to those just described? Life depends upon a mystic influence, that is, upon the presence of a "vital principle" or a "soul," and when this principle is injured, devoured, life makes way for death. This principle, an essential appurtenance of the individual, both spiritual and material, can, like the kidney-fat of the Australian aborigines and the *earua* of New Guinea Melanesians, serve as food for the spirits whom the Polynesians call gods.

To such representations are attached beliefs which are widespread over the whole surface of the globe: the "soul" can be stolen, eaten, brought back and in certain cases, replaced, put together again, patched up, etc. Frazer's *Golden Bough* has furnished a long and noteworthy list of them, and I refer the reader to those volumes. Sometimes this "soul" appears in the form of a spirit, a breath, sometimes as a bird or other animal, a butterfly, a *homunculus*, and so on. The methods employed to discover where it has been hidden, to recover it and restore it to the body whence it is missing, are also very varied. Nevertheless, beneath this apparently great diversity, one fundamental analogy persists. Like the kidney-fat and the *earua* already studied, this "soul" is always an essential "appurtenance" of the individual. Its presence gives him life, and its absence kills him.

I can say as much of the well-known "external soul" so fully and excellently described in *The Golden Bough*, with the necessary reservations respecting the ambiguity, misunderstanding and contradictions due to the abuse, by many observers, of the term "soul." As a matter of fact, in the most precise testimony relating to the "external soul," the term "soul" is often not even used. The author uses the term "life" exclusively. Here, among others, are two examples of this. Among the Cherokee, "some war-captains knew how to put their lives up in the tree-tops during a fight, so that even if they were struck by the enemy they could not be killed. Once in a battle with the Shawano, the Cherokee leader stood directly in front of the enemy and let the whole party shoot at him, but was not hurt until the Shawano captain, who knew this war-medicine himself, ordered his men to shoot into the branches above the

[1] W. W. Gill, *Life in the Southern Isles*, p. 183.

head of the other. They did this, and the Cherokee leader fell dead."[1]—In South Africa, among the Ba-ila, "one method of self-protection is, by means of a powerful charm, to put one's life into a hiding-place, whether into another person, or into some object. . . . One chief, Mungaila, confided to us once that his life was hidden in the needle on a friend's head: he was careful not to say which friend. Another told us that his was in a friend's finger-nail." The authors then proceed to explain how the doctor starts fixing "the life" of someone in the eye of a servant, in a palm-tree, etc.[2]

This "life" or "external soul" does not appear essentially different from the "vital principle," "soul," and the "kidney-fat," already studied. Like them it is an essential appurtenance of the individual. But it may appear singular that, for his greater security, the individual should himself remove from his person this principle which by its presence alone maintains life. He places it elsewhere, in a coffer, a tree-top, on an animal, in the most unlikely hiding-places. Yet the individual, in spite of the absence of his "life," continues to live. Even more, he regards his existence as more assured, he exposes himself boldly to the gravest dangers. How are we to account for this contradiction?

Paradoxical as the answer may appear, I should say at once: the "life," the "external soul," indeed exerts influence through its presence, but it does so from afar. To the primitive mind there is nothing extraordinary or offensive in this. We have already seen, and we shall see again, many cases of bi-presence, or even of multipresence, in which a being exists and acts in two or more places at the same time. The mystic influence of the "vital principle," placed in surety in a distant hiding-place, makes itself no less felt in the body of the individual, so long as the principle is intact. Like other participations of this kind, this one is realized as easily from afar, as close by.

II

Very often in the collective representations of the primitives, the "vital principle" or "life" of the individual is not to be

---

[1] Mooney, *Myths of the Cherokee*," E.B. Bulletin, **xix**, p. 394. Cf. p. 468.
[2] Smith and Dale, *op. cit.*, i, pp. 256-7.

distinguished from his shadow, similitude, or reflection. Observers constantly report that according to what the natives say their shadow is their "soul," or one of their souls, when they admit that they have several. "Soul," "shadow," these are words fraught with ambiguity, inexhaustible sources of error. Since nearly all these observers know nothing of, or fail to recognize, the special characteristics and orientation of primitive mentality, they attribute to it their own concepts, and in the words the natives use, they believe that they find these. Hence we have inextricable confusion, and to unravel it our only resource is to lay aside the mental attitude habitual to us, and conform as best we can to that of the primitives. Only by doing this can we succeed in reconstituting, up to a certain point, their ideas, which even careful observers have distorted.

In certain of Codrington's passages, for instance, it is clearly apparent that the shadow of an individual is an "appurtenance" essential to his life, like those we have been examining above. Thus, in Florida, "no one would pass a *vunuha*" (a sacred pool) "when the sun was so low as to cast his shadow into it: the ghost would draw it from him."[1] "There are stones of a re-markably long shape called in the Banks' Islands *tamate gangan*, or eating ghosts; these are so powerful from the presence with them of a ghost, not of a spirit, that if a man's shadow fall on one it will draw his soul from him, so that he will die."[2] It seems clear that the "soul" here is nothing but the shadow, and that this shadow is the "life" of the individual, in our sense of the word. Again, still in Banks' Islands, "there is at Valuwa a deep hole into which no one dares to look; if the reflection of a man's face should fall upon the surface of the water, he would die; the spirit would lay hold upon his life by means of it."[3] Here the shadow or reflection evidently holds the same place as the kidney-fat with the Australian aborigines, or the *earua* in New Guinea.

But writings on this subject are not always so easily inter-preted. The unfortunate terms "shadow" and "soul" com-plicate representations which are already themselves obscure. Passages like those which follow show that even Codrington is disposed to let himself be led away by them, sincere as is his

[1] R. H. Codrington, *The Melanesians*, p. 176.
[2] *Ibid.*, p. 184.   [3] *Ibid.*, p. 186.

desire to demonstrate the ideas and beliefs of the natives in the most objective way. "That death is the parting of soul and body, and that the departed soul continues in an intelligent and more or less active existence is what Melanesians every-where believe; but what that is, which in life abides with the body, and in death departs from it, and which, speaking of it in English, we call the soul, they find it very difficult to explain. . . . Thinking, to Melanesian natives at any rate, is like seeing; what is thought of must have some form to be thought of in." And to make this point clearer, Codrington makes use of a sentence of Lorimer Fison, a missionary in the Fiji Islands: "Suppose that there are people who call the soul a shadow, I do not in the least believe that they think the shadow a soul or the soul a shadow, but they use the word shadow figuratively for that belonging to man which is like his shadow, definitely individual and inseparable from him, but unsubstantial."[1]

In other words, when the Melanesians say "shadow," they are thinking of what Codrington himself has in mind when he says "soul." If they make use of the term "shadow," it is because they do not know how to express their thought save by a form known to the senses. They indeed conceive of the soul as imma-terial, but they cannot picture it to themselves except as in material garb.—How does Codrington arrive at such a con-viction? We can easily trace its connection with his own reli-gious ideas. He is not conscious any more than is Lorimer Fison, whom he quotes as an authority, of the influence these exert upon his observations. He alleges that the Melanesians, like the Western peoples, believe that after death the soul continues to exist, and that it retains consciousness of itself. In fact, they believe in an after-life. But this merely means that the individual continues to exist in new conditions. It does not mean to say that, for the Melanesians, there is any "immor-tality of the soul," in the sense in which we understand it. We shall presently see that they have not such an idea of the soul as Codrington attributes to them.

Another excellent observer (and, like Codrington, a mis-sionary), Callaway, who also unconsciously suffers his own convictions to influence him, solves in a directly opposite way this problem of finding out what natives imagine to-day when

[1] R. H. Codrington, *The Melanesians*, p. 247.

they use the term "shadow." "*Isitunzi*, shade"—(says he) "this is, doubtless, a word formerly used for the spirit of a man, just as, among the Greeks, Romans, etc. And scarcely anything can more clearly prove the degradation which has fallen on the natives than their not understanding that *isitunzi* meant the spirit, and not merely the shadow cast by the body; for there now exists among them the strange belief that the dead body casts no shadow; and when they say *Isitunzi si muka*, the shade has departed, they do not mean that the soul has left his tenement, but that the body has ceased to cast a shadow."[1]

Thus, according to Codrington, when Melanesians say that the soul is a shadow they are speaking metaphorically, and they know it. They are not unconscious of the fact that the soul is a wholly spiritual principle. The Zulus, says Callaway on his side, have known this also, for a long time. But they have now become so benighted that they take "shadow" in its literal sense, and no longer for the visible manifestation of a spirit. Both Codrington and Callaway are thus imbued with the idea that there exists a concept of an immaterial soul natural to the human mind, and a common heritage of all peoples. The Melanesians have preserved it, the Zulus have lost it.

Let us set on one side this hypothesis, which probably was bound to seem an evident truth both to Codrington and Callaway, and endeavour to discern what natives really imagine when they speak of the "shadow." This "life-principle," like the other appurtenances of the same kind already studied, is neither properly material nor properly spiritual. With varied shades of meaning in divers social aggregates, it implies at the same time an object which to us is wholly material, such as the shadow projected on the ground, the image reflected in the water, etc., and the mystic virtues inseparable from that object, which give it its importance in the primitives' eyes. In this sense it is correct to say, as Codrington does, that the shadow to them is not merely a portion of surface darker than that which surrounds it, and reproducing the shape of the body in the light, but that it is also a "soul," that is, the "life" or the "life-principle" of the individual. But it is no less true, as Callaway has realized, that this "principle," this "soul," is con-

[1] Callaway, *The Religious System of the Amazulu*, p. 91, note 62.

founded with the shadow taken literally and in a physical sense. To picture the soul to himself the primitive has no need, as the missionary has, to oppose one of these conceptions to the other. He has no idea of choosing between them, nor even the slightest inkling that there should be any need to do so. Nor can we say that he confounds them, since he has never differentiated them. This it is which makes it so difficult for the missionary to understand him, and be understood by him.

Smith and Dale have clearly shown how hard it is for us to get an exact idea of what is in the natives' minds. "Witches can take away a man's shadow—then, he dies. But on the other hand, when the question as to the identity of the self and shadow is pressed home, they will always deny it. We remember talking this matter over with one of our closest friends among the elderly Ba-ila chiefs. He emphatically declared that the shadow was only a thing seen when a person stands in the sunshine, and had nothing to do with the man himself. 'You say,' we went on, 'that when a man is dead he is not done with.'—'Yes, true,' said he. 'He enters the womb and is born again.'—'Well, what is it that enters?—the man's body, or his *chingvule*, or what?' —'I do not know; perhaps it is *muwo*.' *Muwo* is the wind. Sometimes they talk of the *moza* (breath). But we feel sure that all three terms are used metaphorically. They know the difference between a corpse and a living being; they have watched the last breath and know that when it has come out, a change takes place. And that breath is evidently akin to the wind. Breath, wind, shadow—these are not to be regarded as three distinct entities; rather are they words with which the Ba-ila seek to express the mysterious self-evident thing that possesses them. We should be nearer still to their attitude, if we said that they think of a living being as a *muntu*—a person, without asking questions as to what constitutes his personality. There is something strange about him, as mysterious, intangible, as the shadow, or wind, or breath; but what that is they cannot say. Suffice it to call him a person."[1]

These judicious reflections are in accordance with those of another excellent observer, Von den Steinen, who, writing of the Xingu Indians, says: "As for myself, I have simply gathered the impression that, with respect to the 'soul,' Indians think

[1] Smith and Dale, *op. cit.*, ii, p. 162.

sometimes of the shadow, sometimes of the breath, but *they do not take details into account*, always having the idea of the person as a whole, in his 'bodily' individuality."[1]

To these Indians, as to the Melanesians, Zulus, Ba-ila, in fact, to primitives in general, the shadow, like the breath, the blood, or the fat, is an essential appurtenance of the individual. Smith and Dale expressly take note of this. "For the soul, as we speak of the soul, it is doubtful whether the Ba-ila believe in it. Certainly we have never found a word that would be a satisfactory translation. . . . Can we formulate an explanation that will cover all they think and say? Shall we say that a man is full of soul-stuff" (the *Zielstof* of the Dutch scientists, the *Seelenstoff* of the Germans) "just as the world of Nature is pervaded by those mysterious forces manifest in medicines, etc., that this soul-stuff pervades his whole body, but is specially active in some organs—in the blood, heart and genitals? . . . The essence of it may, with the aid of drugs, be separated from the body and be hidden for safety as an 'external soul,' in other things. Into the body comes the spirit from the spirit world, which gives the person his identity, his name, his position, all that we mean by personality."[2]

Later on we shall find this spirit having its lodgment in the body, and see its reincarnation. At the moment we content ourselves with noting that, in the opinion of these careful observers, the Ba-ila have no word which exactly corresponds with the word "soul."

W. H. Nassau had indeed noticed the difficulty which the primitive's idea of the shadow makes for the missionary. "In the Fang, Bakele and other tribes, the same word *nsisim* means not only soul, but also shadow. The shadow of a tree or any other inanimate object and of the human body as cast by the sun is *nsisim*. . . . In my first explorations up the Ogowe River in 1874, as in my village preaching, I necessarily and constantly spoke of our soul, its sins, its capacity for suffering or happiness. . . . I was often at a loss how to make my thoughtless audience understand or appreciate that the *nsisim* of which I was speaking was not the *nsisim* cast by the sun as a darkish line on the ground near their bodies. Even to those

[1] K. von den Steinen, *Unter den Naturvölkern Zentral-Brasiliens*, p. 364.
[2] Smith and Dale, *op. cit.*, ii, pp. 162-3.

who understood me, it was no impossible thought that that dark, narrow belt on the ground was in some way a part of, or a manifestation of, that other thing, the *nsisim*, which they admitted was the source of the body's animation. . . . They said it was possible for a human being to have his *nsisim* stolen or otherwise lost, and still exist in a diseased and dying state; in which case the body would not cast a shadow."[1] The distinction drawn by Nassau escapes them. Neither the spiritual soul as he conceives it, nor the shadow as he defines it in the physical sense, coincides with what they call *nsisim*, which is both a visible object and a mystic principle of life.

III

Up to the present we have seen the shadow or the similitude considered as an "essential appurtenance" of the individual, necessary to his life, and comparable with the other appurtenances which are elements, prolongations, "extensions" of the personality. It is presented, too, in another aspect, and one still more difficult to interpret, when it is called a "double" or a "replica" of the individual. The documents on this point are innumerable; they are as a rule confused, at times vague, and at others too precise, and very often they are contradictory. Rather than entering upon this dark region alone, with the risk of long wandering without much hope of finding a road, we will trust to two experienced guides, Codrington and Elsdon Best. If clarity can anywhere be attained, no way would be more likely than theirs to lead thither.

"The Mota *atai*," writes Codrington, "is no doubt the Maori *ata*, which means a shadow, but *atai* never means shadow in Mota, nor is *niniai*, which means shadow, a reflection, ever used for soul. At the same time, damage was thought to be done to the body by means of the shadow or reflection. . . . But that the shadow was the soul was never thought. So in Saa, they talk of a ghost snatching away the shadow of a child that starts in sleep, and a doctor undertakes to bring it back; but, says Joseph Wate, who tells the tale, 'they say shadow and they mean something else, for the shadow of the child is seen all the while.' " In this passage we find once more Codrington's

---

[1] W. H. Nassau, *Fetichism in West Africa*, pp. 64–5.

usual preoccupation; he expects to find in the Melanesians a concept of the spiritual soul, distinct from the shadow. Nevertheless he does not conceal any of the facts which present difficulty to his hypothesis, and he continues: "The use of the word *atai* in Mota seems properly and originally to have been to signify something peculiarly and intimately connected with a person and sacred to him, something that he has set his fancy upon when he has seen it in what has seemed to him a wonderful manner, or someone has shown him as such. Whatever the thing might be, the man believed it to be the reflection of his own personality; he and his *atai* flourished, suffered, lived and died together. But the word must not be supposed to have been borrowed from this use and applied secondarily to describe the soul; the word carries a sense with it which is applicable alike to that second self, the visible object so mysteriously connected with the man, and to this invisible second self which *we* call the soul.

"There is another Mota word, *tamaniu*, which has almost if not quite the same meaning as *atai* has, when it describes something animate or inanimate, which a man has come to believe to have an existence intimately connected with his own. The word *tamaniu* may be taken to be properly 'likeness,' and the noun form of the adverb *tama*, like. It was not everyone in Mota who had his *tamaniu*; only some men fancied that they had this relation to a lizard, a snake, or it might be a stone. . . . It was watched, but not fed or worshipped; the natives believed that it came at call, and that the life of a man was bound up with the life of his *tamaniu*, if a living thing, or with his safety, should it die, or if not living, get broken or be lost, the man would die. Hence in cases of sickness they would send to see if the *tamaniu* was safe and well. This word has never been used apparently for the soul in Mota; but in Aurora it is the accepted equivalent. It is well worth observing that both the *atai* and the *tamaniu*, and, it may be added, the Motlav *talegi*, is something which has a substantial existence of its own, as when a snake or stone is a man's *atai* or *tamaniu*: a soul then, when called by these names, is conceived of as something in a way substantial."[1]

For the better understanding of this passage, we must place the following beside it. "There is a word used in Mota, never

[1] R. H. Codrington, *op. cit.*, pp. 250-1.

applied to the soul of man, but very illustrative of the native conceptions, and common also to Aurora, where it is used with a remarkable application: this word is *nunuai*. In Mota, it is the abiding or recurrent impression on the senses that is called a *nunuai*; a man who has heard some startling scream in the course of the day has it ringing in his ears; the scream is over and the sound is gone, but the *nunuai* remains. A man fishing for flying-fish paddles all day alone in his canoe with a long light line fastened round his neck; he lies down tired at night and feels the line pulling as if a fish were caught, though the line is no longer on his neck: this is the *nunuai* of the line. To the native it is not a mere fancy, it is real, but it has no form or substance. A pig, therefore, ornaments, or food have a *nunuai*; but a pig has no *atai*, or may hesitatingly and carelessly be said to have one. This word is no doubt the same as *niniai*, shadow or reflection. . . .

"This word, in the form *nunu*, is used in Aurora to describe the fancied relation of an infant to some thing or person from which or whom its origin is somehow derived. A woman, before her child is born, fancies that a coco-nut, bread-fruit or some such thing has some original connexion with her infant. When the child is born, it is the *nunu* of the coco-nut, or whatever it may be, and as it grows up it must by no means eat that thing, or it will be ill; no one thinks that there is any real connexion of parentage, but the child is a kind of echo.

"There is another way in which a child is the *nunu* of a person deceased. Thus Arudulewari is the *nunu* of a boy whom his mother brought up, and who was much beloved by her. This boy died not long before Arudulewari was born, and then the mother believed that her foster-child had wished to come back to her, and that the infant was his *nunu*. But Arudulewari is not that person, nor, as he says, is his soul supposed to be the soul of the dead boy; he himself is the *nunu*, the echo or reflection of him."[1]

Let us set aside this idea of the soul, which evidently is Codrington's own. Since the idea is unfamiliar to the natives —at any rate in the form he gives to it—if introduced into their representations it can only make them still less intelligible. From the passages quoted we have as results simply: (1) the

[1] R. H. Codrington, *op. cit.*, pp. 251–3.

existence of a "second self," a being or an object mysteriously connected with a man; (2) the mystic solidarity of this being or object with the individual who lives and dies at the same time; (3) the definition of this being or object as *atai, tamaniu, niniai, nunuai, nunu,* that is as shadow, reflection, image, echo, double. It is very difficult for us to adjust ourselves to the attitude of primitive mentality here. If these representations clearly admitted the duality of the man and his *atai, tamaniu,* etc., however closely linked their destinies, we could, if not comprehend, at any rate admit, both their distinctness and their solidarity. If, on the contrary, they implied complete identity, we could again extricate ourselves from the difficulty. But they seem to affirm this identity and at the same time to deny it.

Here we have, as we know, one characteristic feature of the thinking which is governed by the law of participation. To primitive mentality two existences can make one and the same being. In the present case, the *atai* or *tamaniu* seems to be an entity distinct from the individual, and at the same time it is confounded with him. At the base of the idea of the appurtenances of the individual, we found a mystic consubstantiality between them and him. This we recognize again at the base of this idea of his shadow, reflection, double, and so forth.

Of the *tamaniu* in Mota, and its relation to the individual, Rivers has given a description which most felicitously completes that of Codrington. "In the island of Mota, there are many individuals who are not permitted by the custom of the island to eat the flesh of certain animals, or to eat certain fruits or touch certain trees. The ground for the prohibition in most cases is that the person is believed to be the animal or fruit in question, his mother having received some influence from the animal or plant at conception or at some other period of pregnancy.

"The course of events is usually as follows: a woman sitting down in her garden or in the bush or on the shore finds an animal or fruit in her loincloth. She takes it up, and carries it to the village, where she asks the meaning of its appearance. The people say that she will give birth to a child who will have the character of this animal or even, it appeared, would be himself or herself the animal. The woman then takes the creature back to the place where she had found it, and places it in its proper home, if it is a land animal, on the land, if a water animal, in the pool or stream from which it had probably come. She builds up a wall round it, and goes to visit and feed it every day. After a time the animal will disappear, and it is believed that that is because the animal has at the time of its disappearance entered into the woman. It seemed quite clear that there was no belief in physical impregnation on the part of the animal, nor of the entry of the material object in the form of the animal into her womb, but so far as I can gather, an animal found in this way was regarded as more or less supernatural, a spirit animal, not a material one, from the beginning. . . .

"It was clear that this belief was not accompanied by any ignorance of the physical rôle of the human father, and that the father played the same part in conception, as in cases of birth unaccompanied by an animal appearance. We" (i.e. Rivers, and his collaborators Fox and Darrad) "found it impossible to get definitely the belief as to the nature of the influence exerted by the animal on the woman. . . .

"When the child is born, it is regarded as being in some sense the animal or fruit which had been found and tended by the mother. The child may not eat the animal during the whole of its life, and if it does so, will suffer serious illness, if not death. . . .

"I inquired into the idea at the bottom of the prohibition of the animal as food, and it appeared to be that the person would be eating himself. It seemed that the act would be regarded as a kind of cannibalism. It was evident that there is a belief in the most intimate relation between the person and all individuals of the species with which he is identified.

"A further aspect of the belief in the animal nature of a child is that it partakes of the physical and mental character of the animal with which it is identified. . . . If the object found has been a fruit, here also the child will partake of its nature. . . .

"In the island of Motlav, not far from Mota, they have the same belief that if a mother has found an animal in her dress, the child will be identified with that animal, and will not be allowed to eat it. Here again the child is believed to have the characters of the animal, and two instances given were that a child identified with a yellow crab will have a good disposition and be of a light colour, while if a hermit crab has been found, the child will be angry and disagreeable."[1]

This is a valuable testimony for more than one point of view. Here Rivers helps us, as it were, to lay a finger on the mystic identity of the child and the animal, which, nevertheless, are at the same time two distinct beings; on the solidarity between all animals of the same species (for the child is identical both with one of them and with all); and lastly, even on the mystic influence of the animal on the mother, which, as he says, could not be definitely ascertained. But it *could* not be. This animal enters into the woman much as the kidney-fat is extracted from the body of the Australian native. The process, which is wholly mystic, escapes the control of the senses, and its effect is all the more infallible. The identity of the child and the animal is of the same order as this process, and must be understood in the same way.

IV

With the Maoris of New Zealand, similar representations have taken shape, but we shall find them still more complex. Maoris, says Elsdon Best, are metaphysicians and theologians. Their subtle thought, however, has not followed the paths along which our metaphysics and theologies conduct us. It has its own methods and its own categories, as it were. How are we to express in our languages the ideas and distinctions at which it has arrived, and of which it makes use? To the highest point of comprehension and clarity to which it is possible to attain, Elsdon Best leads us in his book. Following him, we can enter to some slight extent into the meaning, or, to put it more correctly, the manifold meanings, of a certain number of native terms relating to the shadow, the double, image, etc., of an individual.

1. "The word *wairua* denotes a shadow, any unsubstantial similitude; occasionally it is applied to a reflection, thus it was adopted as a name for the animating spirit of man. . . . We have in Maori another expression similar to *wairua*, and that

[1] W. H. Rivers, "Totemism in Polynesia and Melanesia," *J.A.I.*, xxxix, pp. 173–5.

is *ata*, of which *ata a rangi* is an extended form. Williams's *Maori Dictionary* gives: *ata*, form, shape, semblance, reflected image. *Whakaata*, reflection; Ata ata, shadow." (Here we recognize the word *atai* studied by Codrington in Mota.) . . . "In any case, in Maori, in order to denote the soul or spirit of man, *wairua* is the word in general use."[1]

"The *wairua* is not located in any organ of the body; it is when we consider the terms denoting mental qualities that we note references to bodily organs. The *wairua* seems to bear two aspects; it is supposed to be an immortal quality that survives the body at death, and yet we are also told that certain magic acts were employed in order to destroy the *wairua* of enemies, and so cause the death of their physical bases. The *wairua* can leave the sheltering body during life; it does so when a person dreams of seeing distant places or people; it is the astral body and the immortal soul, certainly a spiritual life-principle."

2. *Mauri* is another term, much more difficult of comprehension, because for us nothing has led the way to it, and the analogies which are evident in the case of *wairua*, seem to be missing here.

"The *wairua*," says Elsdon Best, "has been shown to be a sentient spirit that not only left the body at death, but also during the dreaming hours of its physical basis. The *mauri* is a life-principle that cannot so leave the living body; death alone frees it, or rather it ceases to exist at the death of the body. The *mauri* has been styled the soul by some writers, but this term is assuredly a misleading one. . . .

"The *mauri* may be defined as the physical life-principle. The Greek term θυμός meets the case better than any English expression I wot of, for the Maori viewed the *mauri* as an activity. It is to some extent the source of emotions, for, in case of sudden fright, etc., the *mauri* is 'startled.' . . . Such emotions as love, hate, anger, etc., are not credited to the *mauri*, but to the . . . material organs."

Yet the *mauri* is again and at the same time something else. One of the difficulties of comprehending this concept comes from the fact that it presents three different aspects. "The *mauri* is an activity within us, an active physical life-principle, but under the name of *mauri ora*, it is viewed as a *tapu* or sacred

[1] Elsdon Best, *The Maori*, i, pp. 299–300.

life-principle. If this *mauri ora* becomes polluted in any way, then the consequences are most serious to the person.

"An examination of the third aspect will enable us to see the meaning of this idea somewhat better. That third aspect is the material *mauri*. This may be termed a talisman, a material object that represents the protecting power of the gods; in a sense it may be termed a shrine or medium of the gods. Such material mediums are often alluded to as *taumata atua*, resting-places or abiding-places of the gods. When it was considered advisable to place man, land, food products, a village, or a canoe, etc., under the protection of the gods, it was often effected by means of a *mauri*, a material *mauri*. Some object, in most cases a stone, was procured, and by means of a certain rite, the *mana* of a god or gods was implanted in that stone. As the Maori puts it, the *atua* were located in the stone. The stone was then concealed somewhere about the place or object to be protected. The belief was that the material *mauri* possessed the power of protecting the immaterial *mauri*, or life-principle, of man, land, forests, birds, fish, etc., from all harm. The actual symbol, the stone, is spoken of as the protecting power, but that power was really represented by what our Maori terms the indwelling *atua*."[1]

"Some time ago," Elsdon Best goes on to tell us, "I observed natives erecting a weir for the purpose of taking the lamprey during its upstream migration. Meeting one of these natives in town later on I inquired as to the success of the trapping operations. I was informed that a very poor catch had been made, and that this ill-luck was owing to the abandonment of ancient customs; no *mauri* had been located at the *pa* (weir), as was formerly the case.

"The *mauri ora*, or *tapu* aspect of the life-principle, is an interesting conception, and essentially a Maori one. When the Maori accepted Christianity and discarded the institution of *tapu*, then it was that his *mauri* became vitiated, his old-time gods deserted him, and so welfare, physical or otherwise, abandoned him. All these grievous changes, say my old native friends, were brought about by the contamination of the *mauri ora* of man, which had become common, void of *tapu*, polluted."[2]

[1] Elsdon Best, *The Maori*, i, pp. 304-5. [2] *Ibid.*, p. 366.

Taken separately, each of these aspects of the *mauri* seems comprehensible. We can imagine what a physical life-principle, similar to the Greek θυμός, may be, and a sacred life-principle, *tapu*, sensitive to the slightest contamination. We can conceive, too, that the well-being of a man, a forest, etc., may depend upon a talisman that protects it, and that if this talisman is injured, the man, forest, or whatever it may be, is also in danger. But what proves perplexing to us is that the *mauri* bears all these three aspects at the same time. Let us remember, however, that to Australian natives, Melanesians, Bantus, whom we have been discussing, and no doubt to primitives in general, the physical principle of life is at the same time a mystic principle, and that to their minds these two aspects seem to be inseparable. And as to the relation of the *mauri* in its first two aspects with the material *mauri*, we noted how in Melanesia the destiny of a man and his very life depend upon the well-being of his *tamaniu*. No doubt the differences between these Melanesian representations and the Maori idea are not negligible, yet in both cases participations of the same kind are implied, and they throw some light upon each other.

3. "The word *hau* is another term that puzzles the student of Maori institutions, and one for which there is apparently no English equivalent. As with the *mauri*, we find that there are several aspects of the *hau*, that the term is applied to material objects and also to a quality. The *hau* of a person seems to be his vital personality, or vital principle, or vital *mana*; certainly it represents his vital welfare. It is not located in any one organ of the body, but pervades the whole body. If a man's *hau* be taken, as by means of magic arts, then the magician can slay the person himself. To effect this, the war-lock will obtain something connected with the person he desires to bewitch, as a hair from his head, some of his spittle, or a shred from his garment. This was used as a medium in sympathetic magic, and is called an *ohonga*. Unfortunately this material object is often termed *hau* by natives, which is very confusing to our simple minds. The immaterial *hau* is represented by the material *hau*. It has been seen that the same difficulty exists in the case of the *mauri*. The name of *hau* is also applied to food ceremonially partaken of in certain religious performances, to some object pertaining to a slain person, as a

lock of his hair, taken by the victor in order that a certain rite might be performed over it. . . . The name of *hau* was also applied to branchlets of Coprosma used in certain divinatory rites; all this in addition to the various meanings of the word in vernacular speech, of which there are about eighteen. Can the puzzled condition of European inquirers be wondered at?"[1]

It seems as if *mauri* and *hau* are sometimes almost synonymous. Elsdon Best cites cases where the one term is used for the other. "The material *mauri* of a forest which protects its productiveness, etc., is sometimes called a *hau*, and the welfare, the fruitfulness of forest and land is known by the same name. . . . As an illustration of the *hau* of man, let us suppose that I have an enemy whom I wish to destroy. Should I chance to see him rise from a sitting position, I can take his *hau* by means of a very simple act. I draw my open hand across the seat he has vacated, and so scoop up his aura-like *hau*, some portion of it adhering to the place he has sat upon. A certain rite of black magic performed over that immaterial medium will result in the death of my enemy. . . .

"*Hau ora* is a word denoting vital welfare, physical and intellectual vigour. Any person who has transgressed a rule of *tapu*, i.e. offended the gods, cannot be in a *hau ora* condition. . . .

"A land or a forest can be injured by magic spells, and so lose all productiveness, just as human life can be destroyed by similar means. This is why the *hau* of land is protected by means of a material *mauri*, just as the *hau* and immaterial *mauri* of man are protected."[2]

Since we are ignorant of the other eighteen meanings of the word *hau*, we will avoid making guesses about those which Elsdon Best has introduced to us. Nevertheless it is permissible to note certain points: (1) the bewitchment practised upon a man by means of a part of his *hau* remaining on the seat he has just left, strikingly recalls those which are exercised upon the imprints, tracks, secretions, etc. The analogy is all the closer from the fact that appurtenances such as saliva, hair, garments, etc., called *ohonga* by the Maoris, are also sometimes called *hau*. Elsdon Best says: "The *ohonga* or mediumistic object (a hair, a fragment from a garment, some spittle, anything that had been

---

[1] Elsdon Best, *The Maori*, i, pp. 307–8.   [2] *Ibid.*, pp. 308–9.

in contact with the victim) represents the *hau* or personality; hence we may hear a native say that the *hau* of a person was taken. It is the *ohonga* that was actually taken, but that, representing as it does the *hau* of the victim, gives the sorcerer power over the *hau* and its physical basis." (2) The *hau* or "vital principle" is at once a material object and an immaterial quality. (3) The *hau* of a forest, river, birds, etc., is represented in the type of the *hau* of a man. (4) Finally, to protect the *hau*, whether human or otherwise, natives have recourse to a material *mauri*, which is a talisman both of the *hau* and of the immaterial *mauri*.

Perhaps we shall understand better how these ideas adjust themselves to each other when we have seen how Elsdon Best explains a final one, closely akin to the others, the idea of *ahua*. "*Ahua* means 'form, appearance, character,' etc. It is also used in the sense of 'semblance' " (like the Melanesian *nininai*). "In connection with ritual performances the word frequently occurs. One may take the *ahua* in the form of a stone or branchlet. Such *ahua* may be material or immaterial; the word is applied to a material object representing something material or immaterial, and also to an immaterial semblance of either. The meanings of such a term seem much involved until one has fathomed them, and that may occupy much time. I prefer not to say how many years I sought to grasp the significance of *mauri* and *hau*.

"A man who has had property stolen will take the *ahua* of that property to the priest to be used as a medium in a rite performed in order to discover the thief. Such *ahua* would consist, in most cases, of a sample of the stolen goods. I have known a man to whom a present had been made, simply take the *ahua* of it and return the gift to the donor. The action was simply one of touching the object.—In some cases *ahua* might be rendered by 'personality.' I have myself been frequently greeted as *te ahua*, etc.—the *ahua* of the men of yore—on account of my ceaseless endeavours to acquaint myself with their doings. . . . Again, it was the *ahua* of food offerings that was consumed by the gods, not the food itself."[1]

Lastly, even qualities have an *ahua*. "The Maori mind is nothing if not metaphysical, and so he had evolved a mode

[1] Elsdon Best, *The Maori*, i, p. 311.

of protecting his courage and ability in war from all evil influences that might weaken it. He would take the *ahua* or immaterial semblance of the desirable qualities of the men of a group, and convey it for safe keeping to some *tapu* or secret place."[1]

V

The valuable information given by Elsdon Best about the significance of the terms *wairua, mauri, hau, ohonga, ahua*, in addition to that afforded by Codrington and Rivers on analogous terms, permits of our coming a little nearer to the idea primitives have about individuality.

This idea, as we have already seen, has no very rigid boundaries. Its limits are very indefinite, since they include appurtenances such as secretions, excreta, tracks, imprints, remains of food, garments, weapons, which actually form part of the individual, which are an "extension of his personality." But now it appears that this expression is not altogether exact. The appurtenances would only be an "extension" of the personality, properly speaking, if they were not comprised in it at the outset, if the representation of the self, starting from consciousness, which would be its original home, were later to comprehend them. Such is indeed *our* way of feeling and representing the participation existing between an individual and his appurtenances; it is this that accounts for our veneration for relics, and the emotions we experience when face to face with objects that have belonged to great men. Something of the personality of a Goethe or a Victor Hugo seems to cling to their pens, for instance. A little of Napoleon's, we feel, still exists in his sword or in his well-worn surtout. How much emotion would be aroused in a faithful disciple at the sight of a fragment of the true Cross, or of an actual tooth of Buddha! The veneration and the religious fervour of which the saint or the god is the object is irresistibly extended to his belongings, so that they are no longer thought of as distinct. And thus is brought about that instantaneous psychological transference that Hume has shrewdly observed and analysed.

[1] Elsdon Best, *The Maori*, ii, pp. 227–8. Cf. ii, p. 288.

Can we say that it is the same with primitives? It does not seem to be, at any rate as far as the most intimate of the appurtenances are concerned. To their minds the participation between them and the individual is not the result of a transference, however rapid, effected under the stress of emotion. It is not secondary: it is original, direct; and it is tantamount to what *we* should call identity. The young Australian native who knows that some of her hair is in enemy hands is as dismayed as one of us would be if he found himself confronted with cancerous symptoms in his own body. The Melanesian chief who is aware that the areca nut he has bitten into is now the property of his enemies regards himself as inevitably lost. From the primitive's point of view there is therefore no "extension" of personality to the appurtenances. It would be more correct to say that, in comparison with theirs, our individuality seems to have undergone a "reduction," a kind of shrinking. To the primitive the appurtenances are integral parts of the individual, whilst to us they are only appendages, very close ones, it is true, and in certain cases intimately participating in him, but nevertheless distinct from his personality. His existence is no longer inseparable from theirs; they are still something of him, but they are no longer himself.

What has just been said of the appurtenances applies equally to the shadow, the reproduction or likeness, the reflection, the echo, and so on. These are not "extensions of personality" either. To the primitives the shadow, reproduction, etc., are *originally* comprised in the individual himself. They form a part of him, in the full meaning of the words: the participation is complete.

We have just reached a point of capital importance. The considerations which follow (if they are correct), will help to explain certain disconcerting peculiarities, and to remove more than one misunderstanding. To our minds, resemblance consists in a relation between two objects, one of which is a reproduction of the other. Our likeness or reproduction—just like our shadow, which is our reproduction on the ground—or the reflection of our person in the water, remains something which is outside our person. The likeness is a reduplication of ourselves, it is true, and on this account it touches us very closely. Looking at it, we say: "Yes, that is my very self."

But we know, while we utter the words, that we are thus expressing a resemblance, and not an identity. My likeness—the reproduction of myself—has an existence di$ţ$inct from mine, and what happens to it has no effect upon my destiny.—To the primitive's mind, it is not thus. The picture is not a reproduction of the original, distinct from it; it is itself. The resemblance is not simply a relation that thought has grasped. By virtue of a close participation, the picture, like an appurtenance, is consubstantial with the individual. My picture, my shadow, my reflection, my echo, etc., are literally myself. He who possesses any similitude whatsoever of me has me in his power. Hence is derived the universal practice of "charming" the reproduction, which does not in any way differ from the other very varied methods of bewitching by means of the appurtenances.

But, it will be urged, perhaps, even the most undeveloped of primitives really knows that his likeness or his shadow is one thing, and he himself is another. When his shadow is cast upon the ground, or his figure is reflected in the water, he no doubt recognizes it, and sees it as really distinct from himself. However close he feels the relation between his person and any reproduction of it, he does not confuse them with one another. He perceives them separately just as we do. True.—But this fact does not contradict what has just been said. In the representations of the primitive, that which is generally predominant is not, as in our own, the elements we call objective, which are verified by experience, but the mystic elements. We have already had the proof of this with regard to the appurtenances. Adhering only to the data provided by sense-perception and objective experience, to the primitive as to ourselves, his perspiration, excreta, footprints, the garments he has worn, and the traps he has set, all his appurtenances, in fact, are objects that are external to his person; he cannot be ignorant of the fact. Yet he feels them none the less, he represents them to himself none the less, as integral parts of his individuality. They are his very self, and his actions most incontestably prove that this conviction absolutely governs his mind. It is not combated by objective experience, which, moreover, cannot contradict it. We may even go so far as to say that, in this case, the presence and the power of the mystic

elements in their representations have as a result that the
primitives, despite appearances, do not perceive exactly as
we do.[1]

In the same way, it matters little to the primitive mind that
the reproduction and the original are two distinct things in
space, and that they appear to exist independently of each
other. It perceives this fact, and does not dream of denying it.
It merely neglects it, paying it no attention. It feels the reproduction to be consubstantial with the individual, and it works
entirely with this emotional and mystic representation.

It is not enough, then, to say, as we generally do, that the
shadow or the likeness is a "second self," as if it really had an
existence apart from that of the "first self." It is only another
aspect of the same "self." Or, if we continue to speak of a
"second self," we must imagine it as the primitives do.

The unit, duality, plurality, are not categories, the ordinary
framework of objects for their thinking in the same way as they
are for ours. We are accustomed to an abstract consideration
of numbers and their relations to one another. The logical
contradiction of the one to the many is as familiar to us from
our earliest years as that between the one and the other. The
primitive mind, on the contrary, makes little use of abstraction,
above all, logical abstraction. It does not think in numbers,
properly so called, save with difficulty: when necessary, it has
recourse to concrete numbers, to what I have called "number-
totals."[2] Thus it does not, as we do, oppose the unit to anything
that is not one. In fact, it does not seem to have noticed that
"one" *is* a number. The words signifying "two" and "three"
are generally invariable in all the languages belonging to the
same family, in the Malayo-Polynesian languages from Madagascar to Easter Island, for instance. But it is not the same
thing for "one." On the other hand, many primitive languages
take no trouble to distinguish as a rule the plural from the
singular. They do so merely when it seems indispensable. The
remarks made by Sapir on this subject are extremely
instructive.[3]

It is by no means extraordinary to the primitive mind, as
it would be to ours, that the same thing should be at the same

---

[1] Cf. *How Natives Think*, pp. 35-7.   [2] *Vide How Natives Think*, p. 202.
[3] Sapir, *Language*, pp. 111-15.

time, one, two, or even several. It admits this as being so, without taking note of it, in a great many cases in which the law of participation makes its influence felt, although this does not on other occasions prevent its reckoning in conformity with the principle of contradiction, when it is a question of wages or of barter, for example. To the primitive mind the reproduction is one being, the original another: they are two beings, and yet the same being. It is equally true that they are two and that they are one: two in one, or one in two. The primitive sees nothing extraordinary in that, though we think differently. But the facts prove that we should be wrong in trying to impose our logical exigencies on their collective representations.

Only one part of the problem is thus resolved, however, and a serious difficulty still remains. In the long run we comprehend that the appurtenances may be integral parts of the individuality, that the shadow, the likeness, the reflection, etc., are confused with the man whose form and features they represent. But how are we to explain that the *tamaniu* of an individual, lizard, snake, or stone, and this same individual make but one being? How can the term *mauri* signify at the same time the immaterial vital principle of a man and the stone which is his talisman? It seems as if the white man's mind can never admit this identification of beings so essentially different. He finds himself face to face with the unintelligible.

The absurdity of it will be lessened, however, if he notes that to the primitive mind, every reproduction is a double, but every double is not necessarily a reproduction. In certain cases resemblance expresses participation, but it is not the essence of it. No doubt a portrait, a photograph, is a double. Yet the primitive mind can easily imagine also doubles which do not possess the features of the original at all. It does not attach such preferential importance to resemblance as we do. As a rule, the shadow which is cast by a person on the ground produces his silhouette and his individuality but very faintly, yet primitives do not fail to identify it. When they themselves make an image or likeness of someone in order to bewitch him, the reproduction may be very uncouth and not recall the aspect of the victim in the least. It is clear that a resemblance is not necessary. Even in their drawings and their sculptures, primitives never take especial pains to give the exact form and proportions of their models. Sometimes their productions are strikingly true, and astonish us by the correctness and the animation displayed. But very often, too, if the primitives are not there to explain what their drawings represent, it is difficult and at times impossible to guess at it. They have not aimed at a resemblance, as we understand the term.

Moreover, what interests the primitive most, or even exclusively, when he sees his own image (shadow, reflection, etc.) is not the more or less faithful reproduction of his features, it is the consubstantiality he imagines and feels between it and himself. Now this participation in essence can be also imagined and felt between himself and a being whose outward appearance is different from his own. This being will none the less be his double, his "second self, his replica, his echo," according to the expressions used by Codrington. Hence, between this replica and the individual, at the same time as a real identity, there is a mystic resemblance which does not depend for its existence on a material similitude of form and shape.

Whether his *tamaniu* be an animal, a coco-nut, or a stone, the Melanesian *feels* its mystic identity with him, and sees in this animal or this object not only his protector, as we might say, or his talisman, but also his double, his "second self," and, strange as it may appear, his likeness. For likeness can only interpret and express participation, and where the primitive feels this participation, he does not hesitate to say that there is likeness. It matters little whether his assertion is confirmed or not by the testimony of the senses. Is it not indubitable that the individual and his *tamaniu* resemble each other, in the deepest sense of the word, since this resemblance goes as far as identity?

CHAPTER V

THE DUALITY AND BI-PRESENCE OF THE INDIVIDUAL

I

IN a great many communities, not even excepting European ones, we meet with ancient and tenacious beliefs in which, in a diversity of forms, we recognize ideas closely akin to those studied in the last chapter. I need but mention the werewolf, still a source of dread in more than one of our country districts. In other latitudes the place of wolves is taken by tigers, leopards, panthers, jaguars, etc.

This almost universal belief is often expressed in terms that are more or less distinctly animistic. It is said that the soul of the man who is a werewolf leaves his body and goes for a time to dwell in that of the animal. But even brief analysis of the details of this transformation soon betrays the characteristic features of a different representation, and one familiar to the primitive's mind. Let us refer, for example, to the striking story in which Petronius relates the adventure of a soldier werewolf,[1] which may serve as a type of a number of other similar ones: the man and the animal are in reality one and the same individual. It is not the soldier's soul that leaves him to enter the body of the wolf, for the soldier himself and the wolf make but one.

With the Nagas of North-Eastern India, and the neighbouring tribes, cases of lycanthropy are very frequent at the present day, and we have some very detailed descriptions of them. "The possession is accompanied by very severe pains and swellings in the knees, elbows and small of the back in the human body, both during and consequent on the possession. These pains are said to be such as would result from a continuous marching or from remaining long periods in an unaccustomed position. During sleep at the time of possession the limbs move convulsively, as the legs of a dog move when it

[1] Petronius, *Satiricon*, lxi–lxii.

is dreaming. A were-leopard of the Tizu valley, in a paroxysm at such a time, bit one of his wife's breasts off. When the leopard is being hunted by men, the human body behaves like a lunatic, leaping and throwing itself about in its efforts to escape. Under these circumstances the relatives of the were-leopard feed him up with ginger as fast as possible in order to make him more active, so that the leopard-body, on which his life depends, may have the agility to escape its pursuers."[1] The body of the man and that of "his" leopard thus both experience the same sensations at the same time. In order that the leopard may escape, new strength is procured for the man. They are in reality but one being, present in two places. That is the belief of the neighbourhood, of the pursuers, and of the one chiefly interested himself.

"On one occasion the elders of a large Ao village came to me for permission to tie up a certain man in the village, while they hunted a leopard which had been giving a great deal of trouble. The man in question, who was, by the way, a Christian convert, also appeared to protest against the action of the village elders. He said that he was very sorry that he was a were-leopard; he did not want to be one, and that it was not his fault, but seeing that he was one, he supposed that his leopard body must kill to eat, and if it did not, both the leopard and himself would die. He said that if he were tied up the leopard would certainly be killed, and he would die. To tie him up and hunt the leopard was, he said, sheer murder. In the end, I gave leave to the elders to tie the man up and hunt the leopard, but told them that *if* the man died as a result of their killing the leopard, whoever had speared the leopard would of course be tried, and no doubt hanged, for murder, and the elders committed for abetment of the same. On this, the elders unanimously refused to take advantage of my permission to tie up the man."[2] It would be difficult to imagine a more conclusive fact. Everybody is so convinced that the man and the leopard are the same individual in two bodies that the European administrator is obliged to make his verdict conform to the common belief.

Are other proofs necessary? "Sakhuto, chief of Khuivi" (says

[1] J. H. Hutton, "Leopard-men in the Naga Hills," *J.A.I.*, 1 (1920), p. 44.
[2] *Ibid.*, p. 45.

Hutton further), "showed a wound in his back which was quite new on March 1, 1913, which he said was the result of someone's having shot at him when he was in leopard form. The wound in the human body does not, under such circumstances, appear at once. It affects the place in the human body corresponding to the place of the original wound on the leopard, but takes several days to appear."—"I have known personally a large number of Semas who are, or claim to be, were-leopards or were-tigers. Sakhuto died on July 19, 1916, as a result of the leopard which was occupied by his projected soul (the Sema word is 'aghonga,' which primarily means shadow, but is used normally in Sema eschatology for the soul of a dead person) having been shot by Sakhalu on June 30th of that year. It was reported to the writer on July 4th that Sakhalu had shot a were-leopard, but it was then believed to be identical with one Khozhumo." (Note this word *identical*, from Hutton's pen, which fully confirms what I am trying to establish.) "And it was expected that he would die when the news reached him, as the death of the man concerned does not actually take place till he hears that his leopard body has been killed. It was, however, Sakhuto who claimed the leopard, and who had the honour of dying to prove his claim."—"Zhetoi of Sheyepu has become a were-leopard and eaten a number of animals of his own village and the neighbouring village of Sakhalu, including two of Sakhalu's dogs. In one case in his own village he told the owner of a nuthan calf that he would find the uneaten part of his calf stuck high in the fork of a tree in a certain place, which proved absolutely correct. Sakhalu village one day succeeded in rounding up the leopard that had been raiding the village stock, but an urgent messenger came running from Sheyepu, imploring Sakhalu to let the leopard they had ringed go, as if they killed it Zhetoi would die. After this Sakhalu late one evening shot at a leopard behind his granary in the dusk. Very early next morning a message came from Sheyepu to say that Zhetoi had been shot at the night before by Sakhalu, and would he kindly forbear. I had this account independently from two sources, one of which came from Sheyepu, while the other was Sakhalu himself, who says he will certainly shoot the leopard, if he can, next time."[1]

[1] W. H. Hutton, *The Sema Nagas*, pp. 204-5.

Hutton interprets these facts from the animistic point of view. "Both the Angami and Sema agree," he tells us, "in holding that there is no actual transformation of the body of the lycanthropist into a leopard. What he seems to do is to project his soul into a particular animal with which his human body also thus becomes very intimately associated. A leopard which is thus the recipient (from time to time) of a human soul may be recognized by having five claws on each foot. . . . The 'possession,' if we term it so, is not ordinarily induced by any external aid, but comes on at the bidding of spirits who may not be gainsaid, and under whose influence the man possessed entirely loses his own volition in the matter. The faculty can, however, be acquired by very close and intimate association with some lycanthropist, sleeping in the same bed with him, etc. . . . It is dangerous, too, to eat food or drink that a lycanthropist has left unfinished. . . ." Among the Nagas, lycanthropy appears to be hereditary, or rather, as with many other diseases, a predisposition to it is inherited. "No one wants to be possessed by the habit, and it is, on the contrary, feared as a source of danger and a great weariness to the flesh."[1]

To be able to criticize this explanation, we must first of all endeavour to find out whether the Nagas really imagine that the soul of a man goes to dwell within the leopard. We cannot enter here into a discussion upon these passages, but we seem to gather from them that the Nagas have no more idea of a soul (as Hutton understands it) than the Melanesians, Australian natives, Bantus, etc. It would therefore be wiser to abandon the animist interpretation—even if the language used by the natives sometimes seems to lead thither—and admit the "identity" of man and animal, according to an expression which Hutton himself has not shirked. Although distinct, they make but one individual between them.

"The soul may be conceived of as a shadow," he says again (and we already know how much ambiguity is implied in this word "shadow"), "and is separable from the body, and may occupy the body of a leopard or a tiger during life, in addition to its habitation in the human body, leading, in fact, a sort of dual existence." Is this not stating in animistic terms exactly what we are maintaining? On the very same page Hutton

[1] W. H. Hutton, *The Sema Nagas*, p. 208.

L

lays stress upon the community of essence between man and these animals. "A common origin is claimed for men and tigers (which includes leopards) by all the Nagas of, at any rate, the Western group." He relates the story of a woman who "gave birth to three children: a spirit, a tiger and a man."— "When an Angami village kills a tiger or a leopard, the chief proclaims a non-working day for the death of 'an elder brother.' " . . . "The fear of the tiger among all Nagas is considerable, and they all regard them as beings apart from the ordinary wild animals, and very nearly connected with the human race." Such beliefs are not surprising in minds which find no difficulty in representing the "dual existence" of one and the same individual. For the latter feels himself to be, and he is, at the same time, here a man, and there a tiger.

II

In the Malay Archipelago similar facts have been verified. There is resemblance even as to detail. With the Toradjas of Celebes, for instance, "lycanthropy comes from the gods; it is not learnt. A man is a werewolf by nature, or else becomes one through contagion. A child may become one through eating the remains of his father's rice, if the latter be one. . . . Anything that has been in contact with the werewolf's saliva can transmit the quality. Thus one may be infected through resting his head upon a piece of wood or some other object upon which the werewolf's head has lain. Whilst the animal is asleep, his 'interior' (the noxious principle *lamboja*) leaves his body, and roams about as a stag, pig, monkey, crocodile, buffalo, or some feline species, in search of his prey. . . . When a werewolf that has assumed the form of a pig is pursued by a hunter, it changes itself into a nest of white ants and hangs on a tree."[1]

The following story, which Kruijt relates in the same chapter of his book, clearly brings out the "dual existence" which the Toradjas attribute to werewolves. "One night, whilst his human body was lying asleep in his hut, a werewolf entered a neighbour's home and made an assignation with his wife for the morrow. The woman heard nothing, but the husband was

[1] A. C. Kruijt, *De Bare sprekende Toradja's*, i, pp. 254–6.

awakened, and he recognized the voice. Next day he said nothing about this to anybody. Now that very day all the men of the village were working together putting a roof on a house, whilst the women were in another place, or else preparing the food. After the morning meal, the woman in question, as if drawn thither by an irresistible force, went towards the tobacco plantation which had been appointed the night before as the rendezvous. The husband followed, concealing himself from view. Very shortly afterwards, the werewolf, in human form, appeared, whilst at the same time his material body was still working on the roof. At the critical moment the husband showed himself, and struck a blow at the werewolf, who was immediately transformed into a leaf, which the man seized, placing it in the hollow of a bamboo, and thus imprisoning it. He then aroused his wife, who had fallen fainting to the ground, and returned to the village with her, carrying the bamboo containing the werewolf. When they reached it, the owner of the werewolf (a noteworthy expression, apparently implying that the form in which he manifests himself is an 'appurtenance') was still seated with the other men on the roof at which they were working. Then the man put the bamboo containing the imprisoned werewolf on the fire where the rice had just been cooked. Immediately the owner of the werewolf called out 'Don't do that,' and the husband withdrew the bamboo from the fire. But the moment afterwards, he returned it again, while once more the man on the roof begged him to desist. But the bamboo remained on the fire and, when it was in flames, the owner of the werewolf fell from the roof, dead!"[1]

This man was a wizard, able to assume any form he liked; he changed himself into a leaf as another of his kind changes himself into an ants' nest. The fact that interests us here is that he is present, in his human form, in two different places at the same time. At night, when he entered the woman's house to arrange for a meeting, he was at the same time asleep in his own house. The next day, when he presents himself at the trysting-place, he is at that very moment working upon a roof with other villagers. To the man who tells this story and those who listen to it, this dual existence does not appear incredible. They think it quite natural, too, that the wizard should fall

[1] A. C. Kruijt, *De Bare sprekende Toradja's*, i, pp. 256–7.

down dead when the bamboo containing the leaf begins to burn. And to them it is not a case of a soul abandoning its body to dwell for a brief time in another one. It is simply an individual who is living at the same time in two different forms, either both human, or, again, very different, as among the Nagas, where the lycanthropist exists at the same time in the form of a man and of a leopard.

In the Malay Peninsula, "the power of becoming a man- or were-tiger (as it has sometimes been called) is supposed to be confined to one tribe of Sumatrans, the Korinchi Malays, many of whom are to be met with in the Malay Native States. This belief is very strongly held, and on one occasion, when I asked some Malays at Ingra how it could be proved that the man really became a tiger, they told me the case of a man, some of whose teeth were plated with gold, and who had been accidentally killed in the tiger stage, when the same gold plating was discovered in the tiger's mouth." Many similar stories are current in the country. "The Malays know well how Hadji Abdallah . . . was caught naked in a tiger-trap, and thereupon purchased his liberty at the price of the buffaloes he had slain while he marauded in the likeness of a beast. They know of the countless Korinchi men who have vomited feathers, after feasting upon fowls, when for the nonce they had assumed the forms of tigers, and of those other men of the same race who have left their garments and their trading packs in thickets whence presently a tiger has emerged."[1] We have already seen how widespread is the belief in the "dual existence" of men-animals in the Dutch East Indies.[2]

Many facts, which in some respects can be compared with the preceding, have been collected over a wide area of West Africa, from Sierra Leone to the Congo, and even farther yet, in the south. We know of the men-leopards, the men-panthers, the leopard societies of Liberia, Gaboon, the Cameroons, etc. These secret societies practise ritual anthropophagy. Most frequently, each member in turn must provide a victim, who should be, in the first instance, one of his nearest relatives. The sacrificers clothe themselves in the skins of animals, and so on. Here is the account of a typical case, already fairly old.

[1] W. W. Skeat, *Malay Magic*, pp. 160-1.
[2] Cf. *supra*, Introduction, pp. 38-43.

"A serious occurrence took place in Mellacorée, in 1903. A man of very unusual strength was lying in his hut in the dead of night. Suddenly he felt himself seized, lacerated, stifled. . . . Nevertheless, he struggled fiercely and, succeeding in raising himself, he found that he was fighting at close quarters with a panther of an unusual shape, lighted up by the gleams of the fire which was burning in the hut. Then suddenly, in the heat of the conflict, the panther disappeared; the owner of the hut, streaming with blood, held in his arms a man who no longer offered any resistance, while at his feet a panther-skin was lying. Taken before the Almamy of Morea, this man, who was no less than an Alcali (a chief of the province) of consider-able importance, denounced three accomplices. All four then confessed that at night they assumed a panther-skin which gave them superhuman force. Thus disguised, they entered the huts, and devoured their owners. They did not lose their strength unless someone succeeded in wresting from them the skins they had fastened to their bodies. Before the administrator of the district and another European, they gave the horrible details of their last assassination—that of a woman whom they had devoured, even to the intestines and the hair! In spite of the administrator's entreaties, they persisted in their confession. . . . Among our neighbours in Sierra Leone, the same customs with regard to these societies of men-leopards prevail."[1]

So also, in the Cameroons, the missionary Christol tells us, "this very night men disguised as leopards entered a house and killed a little girl. The head alone of the innocent victim was recovered. . . . Individuals calling themselves leopards go thus disguised into the villages and commit atrocious crimes. They form secret societies and spread terror throughout the district. . . . These barbarous customs have come to life again since the war, and no doubt some examples will have to be made before they disappear once more."[2] The following year another missionary wrote: "There is general belief in men-leopards. With the aid of certain drugs and fetishes, men seem to have the power to transform themselves into men-leopards. In other districts there are said to be men-crocodiles, ape-men, but we never hear of snake-men.

"Whilst real leopards shun man, it is said, the men-leopards

[1] Arcin, *La Guinée française*, pp. 430–1.   [2] *Missions évangéliques* (1917), ii, p. 134.

attack him even inside his hut. . . . At Mbonjo, after a series of seven murders in which the bodies were found lacerated as if by leopards, three men, one of whom was a chief, were shot, and others imprisoned. After this execution of justice, quiet was restored throughout the district. . . . In other cases—we know of some at the gates of Duala and others in the depths of the bush—people have believed it to be cannibalism, or else ritual murders. They are talking, too, of secret societies which kill for sport."[1]—"It is said that they put claws on their feet, and the skins of beasts on their bodies."[2]—"Several villages we have travelled through live in fear of leopards. These leopards are for the most part men organized in a secret anthropo-phagical society. At night, they fall upon solitary persons, kill them, mark the ground with tracks made with a hollow paw of a leopard, leave bleeding scraps of flesh, and then go off and eat their victim."[3]

On his side, Pechuël-Loesche writes: "Besides real leopards, there were false ones committing the same offences. These were men who, concealed in leopards' skins, attacked people, tore their flesh and killed them. The proof of this was demonstrated one day when a courageous hunter, defending himself against one of these monsters, killed him. They then found they were dealing with members of a secret blood-society which, known until that time in the Ogowe district, was advancing south-wards. The terror it caused was universal. . . . Six years later, when I returned to Yumba . . . the 'men-tigers' were worse than ever. There was no possible doubt about it; many of these disguised assassins had been caught red-handed, and executed. To the skin of the leopard with which a man would cover himself were fastened paws in the shape of mittens, furnished with sharp nails and knife-blades—at least, that is what was said."[4]

It is a strange thing that in Peru, in the sixteenth century, the Indians knew of secret societies of the same kind. Their members would enter the huts at night, and suck the blood of their victims, which they called "eating the soul."[5]

[1] *Missions évangéliques* (1918), ii, p. 223 (E. Bergeret).
[2] *Ibid.* (1922), i, pp. 66-7 (Mlle Arnoux).
[3] *Ibid.* (1922), i, p. 136 (P. Galland).
[4] Pechuël-Loesche, *Die Loango-Expedition*, iii, 2, p. 452.
[5] Fr. J. de Arriaga, *La extirpacion de la Idolatria en el Peru* (ed. 1920), 39.

Let us set aside the organization of these secret societies, which is not our present subject. Do we not recognize in these men-leopards and men-panthers the same "duality" as in the werewolves and the men-tigers? No doubt, as a general rule, the latter have no will in the matter, and if they are at the same time men and animals, it is not their fault, whilst the "human leopards" seem to be what they are by their own will, and to retain consciousness of their human nature. They appear to be actual criminals, or, at any rate, diseased persons in the grip of a dangerous form of madness. But let us take care not to exaggerate, from our Western point of view, the importance of this difference. The duality is manifest, in the case of the werewolf, by the simultaneous existence in two different places, of the man and the beast. But to the primitive mind it may not be less real in that which seems to us to make but one individual. We remember those mythical beings, which are men and animals at the same time—not in the fashion of the werewolf or the man-tiger—but because, under their human form, they are also animals, and, in animal shape, they are also men, or indeed men who have the power at will to assume an animal shape, like the bears in the Eskimo story we have already related. If we reflect, moreover, that assuming the skin of an animal is, literally, becoming that animal, the conclusion is forced upon us. The man-leopard of the West Coast of Africa, when he covers himself with a leopard-skin, is not disguised, as we say, as that animal. He veritably *is* a leopard, without ceasing to be a man. From that moment he has its instincts: he has the ferocity and the "superhuman force" that he will lose at once, when that covering is taken from him. He is then both one and dual, like the man-leopard of the Nagas, and the man-tiger of the Malay Peninsula. And, as a natural consequence, the man cannot do away with the responsibility of what the animal has done.

III

We can now briefly pass judgment on the faculty universally attributed to sorcerers—that of assuming and quitting, at will, a form that is not human. This faculty is presented in varying terms, according to whether the primitive societies in question are more or less developed, or else according to the theories which more or less unconsciously occupy the minds of observers. It will often be stated, in animistic language, that the sorcerer sends his soul into the body of the animal, which then carries out what he has resolved upon. In other places the crocodile— or the tiger or lion, or whatever it may be—is the sorcerer himself, in the form he has chosen to assume in order to get rid of his victim. Or lastly, the crocodile in the river and the sorcerer in his hut are but one and the same individual. When we are dealing with "primitives," this last fashion of presenting the matter seems to be the best, or at any rate, the least incorrect. The others seem rather to betray an effort to adapt their representations to our modes of expression, and to the logical exigencies incorporated in them.

Although he does not uphold our thesis, Dr. Malinowski, in his admirable work *Argonauts in the Western Pacific*, makes use of considerations which appear to me to be in favour of it. He very carefully analyses the duplicating of themselves by the witches who, in the Trobriand Islands, "have the power of making themselves invisible, and flying at night through the air. The orthodox belief is that a woman who is a *yoyova* can send forth a double which is invisible at will, but may appear in the form of a flying-fox or of a night-bird or a firefly. There is also a belief that a *yoyova* develops within her a something shaped like an egg, or like a young, unripe coco-nut. This something is called as a matter of fact *kapuwana*, which is the word for a small coco-nut. This idea remains in the native's mind in a vague, indefinite, undifferentiated form, and any attempt to elicit a more detailed definition by asking him such questions as to whether the *kapuwana* is a material object or not, would be to smuggle our own categories into his belief, where they do not exist. The *kapuwana* is anyhow believed to be the something which in the nightly flight leaves the body of the *yoyova* and assumes the various forms in which the *mulu-kwansi*" (witch in action) "appears. Another variant of the belief about the *yoyova* is, that those who know their magic especially well can themselves fly, bodily transporting themselves through the air.

"But it can never be sufficiently emphasized that all these beliefs cannot be treated as consistent pieces of knowledge;

they flow into one another, and even the same native probably holds several views rationally inconsistent with one another. Even their terminology cannot be taken as implying a strict distinction or definition. Thus the word *yoyova* is applied to the woman as we meet her in the village, and the word *mulukwansi* will be used when we see something suspicious flying through the air. But it would be incorrect to systematize this use into a sort of doctrine and say: 'An individual woman is conceived as consisting of an actual living personality called *yoyova*, and of an immaterial, spiritual principle called *mulukwansi* which in its potential form is the *kapuwana*.' In doing this, we would do much what the medieval Scholastics did to the living faith of the early ages. The native feels and fears his belief rather than formulates it clearly to himself."[1] A very similar belief has been verified among the Southern Massim of British New Guinea.[2]

A little further on, Malinowski writes: "A spell expresses the idea that the body of the witch remains in the house, whilst she herself goes out on her nefarious errand. . . . The magician who gave me this spell, said in commentary to the last part: 'The *yoyova* casts off her body (literally, peels off her skin), she lies down and sleeps, we hear her snoring. Her covering (i.e. her outward body, her skin) remains in the house, and she herself flies. . . . Her skirt remains in the house, she flies naked. . . . In the morning, she puts on her body, and lies down in her hut. . . .'

"Here we find another variant of belief as to the nature of the *mulukwansi*, to be added to those mentioned before. Previously we met the belief of the dissociation of the woman into the part that remains, and the part that flies. But here the real personality is located in the flying part, whereas what remains is the 'covering.' To imagine the *mulukwansi*, the flying part, as a 'sending' in the light of this belief, would not be correct. In general, such categories as 'agent,' and 'sending,' or as 'real self,' and 'emanation,' etc., can be applied to native belief as rough approximations only, and the exact definition should be given in terms of native statement."[3]

[1] Dr. B. Malinowski, *Argonauts in the Western Pacific*, pp. 238–9.
[2] C. G. Seligmann, *The Melanesians of New Guinea*, p. 640.
[3] Dr. Malinowski, *Argonauts in the Western Pacific*, pp. 251–2.

This could not be said better. I myself have often insisted, as Dr. Malinowski does here, that our logic and our languages alike do violence to the representations of primitives. I think as he does, that in stating and in interpreting them the greatest caution must be exercised. Nevertheless, I should go somewhat further than he. We are not reduced merely to verifying that the native feels his belief and does not formulate it to himself. If we always bear in mind the fact that his thought is mystic, and that it unhesitatingly obeys the law of participation, undoubtedly everything will not appear *clear*, but yet we shall be able to account for many of the apparent confusions and contradictions.

On the special matter of the *yoyova* witches' nocturnal expeditions, for instance, Malinowski very clearly brings out the vagueness and inconsistency of the native beliefs. Is it the witch herself that flies away, or her emanation? What actually *is* the *mulukwansi* who goes through the air? Who is it that remains behind, asleep in the hut during the expedition? These are questions which never elicit any definite reply, as Malinowski points out. I would add that it would be better not to dwell on them, since the natives do not. There is no reason, as a matter of fact, for asking them if one admits, as they do without any difficulty, the dual existence and the bi-presence of the same individual, many instances of which we have already had. The witch is the *yoyova* asleep in the hut. She is also at the same time the *mulukwansi* flying through the air, and showing herself there as a firefly or a shooting-star. There is no need, therefore, to ask which of the two really is the witch. To primitives, there is no sense in the question.

Junod has mooted the same problem as Malinowski. "Does the native mind think that a true unsheathing of the personality takes place when the *balogi* go to their nocturnal expedition, or that they get out of the hut themselves, as entire things, with their ordinary ego? . . . The Ba-suto say: 'The wizard is going entire, soul and body. . . . The Thonga speak differently. According to them, the *noyi* (wizard) is but a part of the personality. When he flies away, his 'shadow' remains behind him, lying down on the mat. But it is not truly the body which remains. It appears as such only to the stupid uninitiated. In reality what remains is a *wild beast*, the one with which the *noyi* has chosen to identify himself." (These words very clearly bring out the identity of the individual under the varying forms he may assume.)

"This fact has been disclosed to me by the following striking confession of S. Gana, a very intelligent Nkuna. 'Suppose,' he said, 'my father is a *noyi*, and I am not. I want to marry a certain girl because I love her. My father knows that she is a *noyi* because they know each other, and he tells me: "Don't do that! She is *clever*, you will repent!" However, I persist in my idea. He urges me to drop that plan, and threatens me with great misfortune. I marry her. One night my father enters my hut and awakens me. He says to me: "What did I tell you? Look! You wife has gone!" I look at her place and find her sleeping calmly.—"No, here she is."—"It is not she! She is away! Take this assegai and stab her."—"No, father, I dare not."—"Do as I say!' And he puts the assegai in my hand and makes me violently hurt her leg. A cry, the cry of a wild beast, is heard. And a hyena appears instead of my wife, a hyena which deposits its fæces, because it is frightened, and which escapes from the hut howling. My father gives me some powder to swallow, and I shall be able to see the *balogi* and their ways and habits. He leaves me—very much trembling from fear— and goes home. When the sun is going to appear, I hear a noise like that of the wind in the branches, and suddenly something falls down from the top of the hut near me. It is my wife. She lies down sleeping, but her leg shows a wound, the wound that had been made in the hyena!' "[1]

Two themes are blended in this story: that of the woman-hyena, conceived on the type of the man-tiger, the body of the woman and that of the hyena belonging to the same person— and that of the witch who flies away by night, whilst apparently, says the native, she remains sleeping in the hut. If we were to demand of the native that he should be more exact, and tell us whether the real self of the witch is the one that flies away, or the one asleep in the hut, he would be unable to give an answer, even if he understood the question. With his usual way of thinking, he would admit, unreflectingly, regarding the matter as self-evident, that the witch is asleep in the hut and she is far away at the same time. If one persists in interrogating him, one can make him say that she has gone out, or that she is within, or that she has divided herself into two, etc. Nothing would be easier than to obtain from him the reply that he thinks the inquirer expects. But if we hold by the story related by Junod, the dual existence of the witch stands out clearly, and it excludes the questions we are putting to ourselves.

IV

It remains to show that this "dual existence" is not confined to werewolves, men-tigers, men-leopards, etc., and sorcerers of both sexes, and that primitive mentality admits it unhesitatingly in the case of ordinary persons. But does not this directly follow from the belief in the *tamaniu* and the *mauri* we studied earlier, and from similar representations met with to some extent everywhere, of the African conception of a "bush soul," for instance, which Miss Kingsley has described, and which is a mystic identity of the individual with an animal in the bush, so that when the animal dies the man dies, and the man's life ends when the animal perishes? We should not dwell longer upon beliefs that are so general, were it not to show by one or two characteristic facts the duality they imply.

"In Pentecost Island," writes Rivers, "a native, whose animal was a shark, was angry with his son, who had refused to roast a yam for him. When soon after this, the son went out in search of flying-fish, he saw a large shark in the water, which swam round and round the canoe making the sea rough, and then put its nose over the outrigger of the canoe, and upset it. The son cried out with fear and expected to be eaten, but was allowed to swim away while the father, in the form of a shark, took the canoe ashore and hung the paddle, fishing-line, and the fish which his son had caught, over the door of his house. The son was picked up by some friends, and on reaching home was telling the story to his father, when he looked up and saw the things over the door, and was told by his father that he had been the shark, and had given him a lesson not to disobey in the future."[1]

"There is little doubt," says Rivers, reverting later to this

[1] W. H. Rivers, *History of the Melanesian Society*, i, p. 210.

story, when speaking of the identity of the individual with his *tamaniu*, "that when the father was punishing his son, he was both man and shark, although to the eye he had the form of a shark at one time, and of a man at another."[1]—Perhaps, even, I might add, he was at the same time a man in his house and a shark in the sea. This simultaneous duality is evident in the following story, reported by Talbot in Southern Nigeria. "Not long ago, a man of Usun Inyan asserted that his wife, Esiet Idung by name, had told him that her soul sometimes left her and went to dwell in the body of a fish in the Kwa Ibo River. One day she came to her husband, crying: 'I am caught! I am caught and must die, for a fisherman has snared my soul in his trap by the waterside. Go therefore to the place of which I shall tell you and release me before it is too late; for should the man come and kill my affinity, I must die also.' (The husband runs, reaches the trap, and releases the fish snared in it.) Among the others they noticed one of great size which plunged eagerly out into the current. On their return they found that the woman had recovered."[2] The "soul" of which she speaks is undoubtedly a double, i.e. a "second self," which in reality makes but one with the first.

Tauxier has noted similar ideas in French West Africa. Among the Mossi and the Foulsé, "when they kill a crocodile, they kill as a result someone in the village; when they wound a crocodile, a man bound up with it by a subtle and invisible but yet real tie, is wounded at the same time."[3]—Among the Nunumas, "the spirit of every human individual is at the same time in a man and in a crocodile. When the crocodile dies, the man dies the following day. The crocodile is like the person. Should the crocodile lose an eye, the man loses one too, and vice versa. If the crocodile loses a claw, the man becomes lame. The human crocodiles are rather a small species, and at Sapony each man knows the crocodile that corresponds with him. When a crocodile is about to die, it enters the sukhala of the man whose spirit it represents. It is then wrapped in a white loincloth, buried a little apart, and fowls are sacrificed to it. Then the man whose spirit was in the crocodile dies in his turn.

[1] W. H. Rivers, *History of the Melanesian Society*, ii, pp. 364–5.
[2] P. A. Talbot, *Life in Southern Nigeria*, p. 91.
[3] Louis Tauxier, *Le noir du Yatenga*, p. 376.

The Leo people believe that when a crocodile is killed in the marshes, a man in the village is also killed, and this is because the soul of every inhabitant of the village is bound up with that of a crocodile."[1]—" Most Kassufras regard the crocodile as their soul, and think that if one kills a crocodile, the man who is its opposite number dies immediately."[2] Among these same Kassufras, "at Pu it is the iguanas that are venerated and respected. Every iguana has in it, apparently, the soul of a certain person in the village. Therefore if an iguana be slain, a man in the village dies. At the beginning of 1909, a Mossi passing through inadvertently killed an iguana, and the brother of my interlocutor (who was the chief of the village of Pu) died in consequence."[3] Underlying these animistic expressions the real fact shines through. This "soul" which dwells within a crocodile or an iguana is the "bush soul" described by Miss Kingsley; in short, it is the individual's "double," or more precisely, the individual himself in one of his two forms.

According to Nelson's report, this duality of the individual is presented to the eyes in a very striking manner by the Eskimos of the Bering Strait. "It is believed that in early days all animate beings had a dual existence, becoming at will either like man or the animal forms they now wear. . . . If an animal wished to assume its human form, the fore-arm, wing, or other limb was raised, and pushed up the muzzle or beak as if it were a mask, and the creature became man-like in form and features. This idea is still held, and it is believed that many animals now possess this power. The man-like form thus appearing is called the *inua*, and is supposed to represent the thinking part of the creature, and at death it becomes its shade.

"Shamans are believed to have the power of seeing through the animal mask to the manlike features behind. . . . Masks may also represent totemic animals, and the wearers during the festivals are believed actually to become the creature represented, or at least to be endowed with its spiritual essence. Some of the masks of the lower Yukon and the adjacent territory to the Kuskokwim are made with double faces. This is done by having the muzzle of the animal fitted over and con-

---

[1] Louis Tauxier, *Le noir au Soudan*, p. 193.
[2] *Ibid.*, p. 238.   [3] *Ibid.*, p. 239.

cealing the face of the *inua* below, the outer mask being held in place by pegs so arranged that it can be removed quickly at a certain time in the ceremony, thus symbolizing the transformation" (from animal to man).[1]

"Another style of mask from the lower Kuskokwim has the under face concealed by a small hinged door on each side, which opens out at the proper time in a ceremony, indicating the metamorphosis. When the mask represents a totemic animal, the wearer needs no double face, since he represents in person the shade of the totemic animal." This is a noteworthy expression. "Shade" here evidently means double, second self; the animal and the wearer of the mask at this moment are but one, as Nelson himself says in definite terms.—A little later he speaks of a mask which is half human and half bird. "The mask was said to represent the *inua* of the crane. The maker was a shaman, who claimed that once, when he was alone upon the tundra, he saw a sandhill crane standing at a distance looking at him; as he approached, the feathers on the bird's breast parted, revealing the face of the bird's *inua*, as shown in the carving."[2] Such passages reveal a great deal about the participations, the identities even, that primitives feel to be realized between them and the animals represented by their masks.

V

The individual's "dual existence" is not the exclusive property of the human race. Elsdon Best tells us that to the Maoris a forest, river, plantation, animal or vegetable species, even a certain animal, has its *mauri*, just as a man or a group of human beings has. In the facts we have just been reviewing, the consubstantiality between man and animal is such that it is not possible to say whether the man is the double of the animal or the other way about. We now have a very noteworthy observation to consider, one in which an animal has a double in another animal. "Few of the mysterious beings and processes in which the Eskimo believe are very clear and definite

[1] E. W. Nelson, *The Eskimo about Bering Strait*, E.B. Bulletin, xviii, pp. 394-5.
[2] *Ibid.*, p. 402. Cf. E. W. Hawkes, "The Labrador Eskimo," *Geological Survey of Canada*, Memoir xci, p. 127.

in their minds. Thus, though Mamayauk and Guninana talk
freely of *ta-tkok* (souls), they cannot, when pressed, give a
coherent or consistent account of their attributes. Mamayauk
tells (probably from Alaskan sources) that in the case of the
wolf and the arlu (killer-whale?) at least during lifetime
has its double, i.e. every wolf on land has a *ta-tkok* at sea that
is an arlu. If the wolf has trouble in finding food on land he goes
to sea and seeks his double the arlu. Here Mamayauk's knowledge becomes vague. Thus much she has heard, but she does
not know if the wolf remains at sea as a wolf, if it merges with
its double and they become one, or if it becomes an arlu, so
that there are now two arlus, the one that was always at sea, and
the other driven there by hunger.—Guninana says the above
must be information from Western sources. She knows, too,
that arlus are the *ta-tkoks* of wolves; she always supposed that
it was only on the death of a wolf that its *ta-tkok* went to sea
and became an arlu. Still, 'come to think of it,' she had heard
that arlus hunt caribou too, so evidently they are part of the
time in wolf shape. . . . She never heard of a 'wolf voluntarily going to sea to become an arlu because of hunger. . . .
Both Mamayauk and Guninana have heard that bow-head
whales are the *ta-tkokit* of musk-oxen."[1]—According to another
native, "wolves and arlut are *avariksut* (chips of the same block),
equivalent, alike, equal. When wolves starve on land they go
to their relatives in the sea and become arlut. Likewise the
arlut, when unable to find food in the sea, go inland and
become wolves. These wolves, as far as he knows, are in no
way differentiable from ordinary ones."[2]

That these two Eskimo women should not be able to give
more definite information need not surprise us. The natives
who gave Malinowski and Junod theirs could not do so either,
and these two observers rightly say that they should not be
asked for it. But the words of Mamayauk and Guninana,
although vague, become fairly clear when we put them side
by side with other testimony of a similar kind. *Ta-tkok* (soul)
signifies "double," as they themselves say. What they describe,
in terms that no doubt are difficult to translate exactly, is the
duality of existence in the same animal. The wolf on *terra firma*,

---

[1] V. Stefánsson, *The Stefánsson-Anderson Expedition*, American Museum of
Natural History, Anthropological Papers, xiv, p. 357.   [2] *Ibid.*, p. 319.

and the corresponding arlu in the sea are one and the same
being, just like the man and his crocodile or iguana in West
Africa. The point that is peculiar here is that the two aspects
of the individuality (if we may use such an expression) are
both of them animal, and it is the same with the whales which
are "souls," i.e. doubles of musk-oxen. Yet Nelson says expressly that animals have *shades*, and that the Eskimo believe
that nearly all the attributes possessed by the shades of people
are equally possessed by those of animals.[1] If men have doubles
of animal form, there is no reason why animals should not have
them too. All the more so, since primitives very often see but
an external difference between man and animal, and this of
very slight importance.

We must go further yet. Even objects which we regard as inanimate, in certain circumstances or under the effect of a
magical process, may themselves also have a "dual existence,"
or at any rate exist at the same time in two places far away
from each other. Unless we admit this bi-presence, we cannot
understand how the natives represent to their minds certain
magical processes, which are quite ordinary to them. In Torres
Straits, for instance, "the *maidelaig* (wizard) took the large
canine-like tooth of the lower jaw of a crocodile, painted it
red, and filled the hollow base with various kinds of plants, and
finally he rubbed it all over with the fat of a corrupt human
corpse. Next he took a long string of plaited coco-nut fibre, and
tied one end to a young and slender tree, and put the anointed
tooth in the fork of the first branch. Then he said to the tooth:
'You go into that man! . . . do not go all over his body, you
go into his heart. Are you ready? Stand by!' The wizard pulled
the free end of the rope so hard that 'it come thin,' as if it would
break; suddenly he let it go and the rope sprang back, the
recoil of the bent tree causing the tooth to shoot forward—and
the man died.

"Another method, slightly different. The tooth is tied to the
end of the string, and itself fastened to a tree. The string is
pulled, and the tooth flew in the direction of the victim whither
it had been pointed. At the same time a spiritual tooth struck
his victim and entered his body."[2]

[1] E. W. Nelson, *The Eskimo about Bering Strait*, E.B. Bulletin, xviii, p. 423.
[2] *The Cambridge Expedition to Torres Straits*, v, p. 326.

M

This "spiritual tooth," i.e. spirit of the tooth, is, to use the common expression, its "soul," or more precisely, its "double." In other words, it is the tooth itself, inasmuch as, by virtue of the magical operation performed on it, it has become capable of being present in two places at the same time. In the form of its mystic double, the tooth, ten miles away from the place where the wizard has "charmed" it, enters the body of the victim. It penetrates without breaking the skin or leaving the least trace of its passage, and it infallibly kills him.

A native of Fiji very succinctly explained a similar idea to the administrator of his district. "The people of Rewasau, one of the Mboumbutho villages, were losing a lot of their number through some mysterious epidemic, and as usual they came to me about it. They said that a neighbouring clan, the Naiova, whose totem was a malignant little black snake called Mbolo, had the power of the evil eye, and had overlooked them. Consequently their intestines were full of these little black snakes, which were eating them up and causing death. I made a searching inquiry as to the symptoms, etc., of which I made copious notes. Seeing this, the spokesman said to me: 'And now, sir, having asked all these questions, when the next death occurs you will send, I suppose, the District Medical Officer to cut the corpse up and look for the snakes. But he won't find any; they are not real snakes, only spiritual ones.' "[1]

A similar belief is at the base of many practices of black magic. The influence of witchcraft from a distance, which all consider fatal, implies the "dual existence," the bi-presence of the material object which bears death in its train. Without such a conception, the effect produced would remain incomprehensible. Founded upon it, it seems quite simple.

Sometimes the magic may be powerful enough itself to produce the living being who is to carry out the wizard's machinations. Here are two typical cases, in peoples very far apart. In Kiwai Island, a "first" wife, neglected by her husband for a rival, desires to be avenged on him. "She made a model crocodile, and placing it in the Maubo-tiri River, said to it: 'Siváre, come here, you catch him. That's no other man fast here, that's Siváre, you catch him.' She returned home and sat on the gable

[1] A. B. Brewster, *The Hill Tribes of Fiji*, p. 108.

verandah to watch. Siváre donned his war ornaments, and seizing his weapons went on his way to another village. In the act of wading across the river, he was caught by the crocodile, who pulled him under the water and took him into a hole in the bottom."[1]—Nelson relates a similar story. A woman sees her nephew arrive in a piteous state. "When she recognized him, she received his story with words of pity, then words of anger at the cruel villagers. When he had finished telling her of his sufferings, she told him to bring her a piece of wood, which he did; this they worked into a small image of an animal with long teeth, and long, sharp claws, painting it red upon the sides and white on the throat. Then they took the image to the edge of the creek and placed it in the water, the aunt telling it to go and destroy everyone it could find at the village where her boy had been.

"The image did not move, and the old woman took it out of the water, and cried over it, letting her tears fall upon it, and then put it back in the water, saying: 'Now go and kill the bad people who beat my boy.' At this the image floated across the creek, and crawled up the other bank, where it began to grow, soon reaching a large size. . . . It became a terrible bear, and killed all the people in the village."[2]

As a general rule, the wizard who seeks to encompass the death of anyone fashions some image of him. In working at it, he influences him, for the image partakes of the model. By virtue of this participation it is one of his appurtenances, it *is* the model himself. In the stories just told, on the contrary, it is the image which is the original, and the living being is this very image after it has undergone the magical influence. Thus there is to some extent a reversed "doubling." The order given by the incensed wife to the image of the crocodile is carried out by the real animal which this image becomes. So, too, the bear which avenges the wrong done to the boy is the "double" of the image fashioned by him and his aunt. These reversed cases, it seems, allow us to understand a little better the nature of the direct cases. They do not make these more intelligible, but they have the advantage of showing them to us at another angle. They also show how little alive primitive

[1] G. Landtman, *The Folk-tales of the Kiwai Papuans*, p. 142.
[2] E. W. Nelson, *op. cit.*, p. 485.

mentality is to the difference which we perceive between animate beings and inanimate objects.

Would it not be simpler to say: These women, who are witches, are able to give life, or a soul, the one to the model of the crocodile, and the other to the image of the bear?—True; but this would be ascribing our language and, worse still, our ideas, to the Papuans and the Eskimo. In compelling ourselves, on the contrary, to reconstitute theirs to the best of our power —however obscure and contradictory they may appear—perhaps we shall succeed in comprehending a little better what is in their minds when we lend them the ideas of the double, image, replica, shadow, and even "soul" of beings and of objects.

"I dare say," writes Dr. Strong, "many Europeans in Papua have been puzzled by tales such as the following, which have occurred within my experience. Tatakou, a noted sorcerer of the Yule Island district, is known to be at Mou, nevertheless he is accused of committing an offence at Siria, and at the same time, although Siria and Mou are several miles apart. It was, of course, obvious to me that Tatakou could not be in two places at once. It seemed equally obvious to the natives that he could be.

"A native at Cape Nelson has a fit on the station. It is known that he has a brother at Ioma, well over a hundred miles away. The brother is accused of causing the fit by throwing a stone at him . . . alleged stone duly produced, and being very much like thousands of other stones in the district. It was obvious to me that the brother at Ioma could not have thrown the stone all the way from Ioma; it seemed equally obvious to the natives that the brother could have been all the time at Ioma, and yet have thrown the stone (not necessarily thrown it from Ioma) at the brother at Cape Nelson."[1]

The solution of these enigmas has just been indicated. It suffices to note that the Papuans described by Dr. Strong reason as do their neighbours the Melanesians of Torres Straits. They imagine the sorcerer accomplishing his magical operations at Ioma, and there he "points" the stone at his brother, a hundred miles away at Cape Nelson. At the same moment a "spiritual stone"—the corollary of the "spiritual

[1] *Annual Report*, Papua (1921-22), pp. 25-6.

tooth" of Torres Straits—enters the body of his victim, and
produces its deadly result there. To primitive mentality nothing
is simpler than this mystic bi-presence of an object. As for the
stone shown by the natives to the doctor, it was doubtless taken
from the body of the native by a medicine-man.—In the first
story related, things are not quite so clear, because we are not
told what Tatakou had been accused of. If it were an enchantment like the other, the same explanation would hold good.
Tatakou, from a distance, "pointed" a stone, a bone, or a
magic tooth towards his victim. Moreover, the idea that
Tatakou was able personally to be in two places at the same
time, presents no difficulty at all to the natives' minds. They
are quite ready to accept this bi-presence as true when they
picture to themselves the individual and his animal "double,"
his *tamaniu.* It appears no stranger, either, when it is the individual himself who seems to be present both in this place and
in that.

I have quoted elsewhere[1] a fine case of this belief in bi-
presence reported by Grubb. An Indian accused him of having
robbed his garden of some pumpkins, although he knew well
that at the time of this pretended robbery the missionary was
more than two hundred miles away. The native had *dreamt*
of this occurrence, and the fact that Grubb was elsewhere that
day did not prevent his believing the story.

According to Herbert Spencer, E. B. Tylor, and their many
adherents, primitives try to explain how it is that they, whilst
asleep in their huts, can converse with people living very far
away, and they have imagined a double of their own personalities, which can transport itself afar during their sleep. But this
idea of a personal double, both distinct from and identical with
the person, was already theirs, for it is inherent in the way in
which they represent the individual, his appurtenances, his
image, etc., to themselves. It serves them too, in the case of the
dream. They have not invented it expressly to account for this.

Here we have a testimony involving the "double," not only
of the man who is dreaming, but also of the one seen in the
dream. Among the Angami, "nightmares are believed to be
caused by the visit of the wraith of a sleeping friend, which is
stronger than that of the dreamer. A story is told of a man who

[1] *Primitive Mentality,* p. 106.

kept having bad nightmares, and so took to sleeping with his *dao* (dagger) under his pillow. When the nightmare came, he tried to kill it with his *dao*, and getting up to pursue it, saw a butterfly fly into his friend's house. The next morning this friend told some neighbours that he had been horribly frightened in the night by dreaming that a man had tried to kill him with a *dao*."[1]

When the men are at a distance hunting, travelling by land or sea, on a warlike expedition, and so forth, their wives likewise are bound to observe certain inhibitions. They must abstain from special foods, certain occupations, from taking part in diversions, etc. This is a very prevalent custom. Kruijt, who found it among the Toradjas, accounts for it as follows: "The source of these prohibitions is to be found in the notion that the *tanoana* or soul of the warriors who are absent in the body may be able to return suddenly (in a dream, for instance) to its own home, and in such a case it ought to find everything as it should be there. Nothing that might make a disagreeable impression on it or cause it uneasiness must be perceptible. The body of the warrior undergoes the counterpart of all the emotions affecting his soul, and he would run a risk of being incapacitated for the fight."[2] Let us disregard the animistic expressions which Kruijt makes use of, and which the Toradjas themselves have no doubt been led to adopt. The fact remains that, like the other primitives who observe these prohibitions, the Toradjas admit that the warriors are at once far off, on a campaign, and present, at any rate, momentarily, in their homes, whither their doubles, i.e. they themselves, go during sleep.

VI

It would no doubt be convenient to interpret in the same way certain prohibitions which are a concomitant of the "couvade," especially in South America. During the early days following the birth of the child, the father must abstain from all muscular effort and heavy work; he must not handle weapons, tools, etc. Karsten brings forward again the reason usually assigned to such taboos. "The father with his new-born child forms, as it

[1] J. H. Hutton, *The Angami Nagas*, pp. 246–7.
[2] A. C. Kruijt, *De Bare sprekende Toradja's*, i, p. 235.

were, one single personality; the soul of the latter is intimately connected with his own, and everything that happens to the father during the critical days is supposed directly to affect his tender son."[1]

This explanation, no doubt a satisfactory one for certain practices, such as those of the couvade, properly so called, does not suffice for all. According to a report made by Dr. W. E. Roth, for instance, "the father was forbidden to undertake any heavy work or to hunt because his arrow might strike the little infant. If he climbed over a tree-trunk, he always placed two little sticks as a sort of bridge for the child's little spirit that always followed him. If he crossed a river or creek, a calabash or fruit-shell then served to facilitate the passage across of the child. . . . If he by chance met a jaguar, he did not speed away but courageously advanced on the beast. Verily his child's life depended on it. . . . However badly something bit him, he must scratch very carefully, because his nails could harm the infant."[2] These details most distinctly imply, not only that the father and child are so united that what happens to the former reacts upon the latter, as if they formed but one personality, but still more that the child accompanies the father everywhere, and is always close beside him. If the father climbs a tree, the child ascends it behind him, and this is why the father places in the tree little sticks for it to hold on to, for fear of its falling. When the father crosses a watercourse, either by the ford or by swimming, since the child following him runs the risk of drowning, he makes it a little skiff. If he encounters a jaguar unexpectedly, he does not run away as he would at any other time, because the child cannot run so fast as he, and the jaguar would seize it. In short, the father acts in every circumstance just as if the tiny child were beside him. The fact that he does not see it does not prevent him from believing it to be present. Nevertheless, all this time, the baby is lying in its cradle, in its mother's care.

Similar circumstances have been recently noted by a missionary living among the Caribs. "During the first week the father will stay at home; he will do no work at all, for his work

---

[1] R. Karsten, *Contributions to the Sociology of the Indian Tribes of Ecuador*, p. 61.
[2] W. E. Roth, *An Introductory Study of the Arts, Crafts and Customs of the Guiana Indians*, E.B. Bulletin, xxxviii, p. 696. Cf. Bulletin xxx, p. 324.

will make the child's body ache. The second week he will go out to the woods, but not too far, otherwise the child gets too tired. If the path divides itself, he will cover up one path in order that the soul of the child should not take the wrong path and lose its way. Near a creek he will not come at all, lest *okoyumo*, the water-spirit, should take his child, and yet during the first two weeks the baby is with its mother in a little room especially built for the occasion. It is not allowed to take it out. The father himself has not yet seen it."[1]

Therefore, in the view of these Indians the child is both with its father in the woods, and with its mother in the hut, at the same time. To avoid what in such a view is startling to our minds, we should say that whilst the child is lying beside its mother, its "double" is accompanying its father. To the minds of the Indians the child and its double are one and the same individual, whose presence, simultaneously, in two places, is no more surprising than that of the man who is dreaming.

As a rule observers avoid the difficulty by speaking of the "soul" of the child. Nordenskiöld writes: "The Gúarayú Indians in North-West Bolivia told me that when a man went hunting immediately after his wife's confinement, and happened to shoot at a parrot, for instance, he would risk killing his child, for during the first few days of its life, its soul follows its father."[2] And again: "When an Itonana woman has borne a child, she ties its legs with string to prevent it from running after its father. The latter, in the early days of his child's life, must avoid deep water in bathing, otherwise the child might be drowned. He can wash himself only at the water's edge. Here we have once more the idea, so widely prevalent among the Indians, that the child, at the beginning of its life, accompanies its father."[3] Note that it is the "child," as Nordenskiöld very truly says in this passage, and not its "soul." I do not know what word the Indians may make use of, but I very much doubt whether it could be translated "soul," for this "soul" climbs trees, runs the risk of drowning, and may be eaten by a wild beast. It is a double, a replica of the child. It is the child itself, present in two places at the same time.

---

[1] W. Ahlbrinck, *Carib Life and Nature*, Reports of the Twenty-First Congress of Americanists, p. 223.   [2] E. Nordenskiöld, *Indianerleben*, p. 207.
[3] *Idem, Forschungen und Abenteuer in Süd-Amerika*, p. 197.

CHAPTER VI

THE GROUP INHERENT IN THE INDIVIDUAL

I

THE individual, as such, scarcely enters into the representations of primitives. For them he only really exists in so far as he participates in his group or his species. We must now show, therefore, how this participation, described in the second and third chapters, manifests itself in the very constitution of the human individual.

We shall find it profitable to study it in the tribes of Central Australia observed by Spencer and Gillen. While largely making use of their well-known work, we generally prefer to follow the data furnished by Strehlow, who spoke the language of the Aranda and the Loritja, who lived for a long time among them, and seems to have become more fully intimate with them.

In the information he supplies we shall find at once representations and beliefs similar to those which have been analysed already as existing among the native tribes in Victoria. We have the same enchantments practised on the appurtenances of the individual; the same fear of maleficent spirits which seize upon and devour the kidney-fat, the heart and the liver of men, particularly of little children. Strehlow does not identify the "soul" with the kidney-fat, for he says that these spirits seize, roast and eat this fat, the liver, *and* the soul. But this same soul is always comprised in one list with the heart, liver, fat, etc. It is of the same nature. Evil spirits, for instance, "approach a man, put a string round his soul and carry it off."[1]—Others, with the Loritja, "attack men who are alone at night, open their bodies, taking away the soul, liver, heart, and fat."[2] "Soul" here doubtless means, as it does with the Victorian natives, a "vital principle," an appurtenance, which is essential, but similar to the rest.

[1] C. Strehlow, "Die Aranda und Loritja-Stämme in Zentral-Australien," *Veröffentlichungen aus dem städtischen Völker-Museum*, Frankfurt am Main, i, p. 12.
[2] *Ibid.*, ii, p. 5.

Side by side with these representations are to be found others which very notably express the participation of the individual with his group. They are very closely allied with the totemic beliefs of the Aranda and the Loritja, which we must briefly call to mind here. In the legendary period which Spencer and Gillen term the Alcheringa, mythical ancestors were in existence, called *altirangamitjina* (the eternal uncreated, the totemic gods). They had, as a rule, a human form, yet they were endowed with superhuman powers, and possessed the faculty of creating animals whose name they bore. . . . They could also at any time whatsoever assume the form of the animals they created. Many of them wandered about in the forms of emu, kangaroo, eagle, etc. In legends they are also spoken of by their names as animals, and in each of these totemic gods appeared the special characteristics and distinctive features of the particular animal in question. Just like a real kangaroo, the totemic kangaroo god browses on grass, flies from a pursuer, digs a hole in the ground, and so on.[1]

Certain special places where these totemic gods have lived and created their animals, "belong" to them. "Wearied out after their long journeyings they at last throw themselves on the ground, and there their bodies are transformed: partly into stones, partly into pieces of wood called *tjurunga*."[2]

Among the Loritja, the trees into which the bodies of the mythical ancestors are transformed are called *ngana ngamba* (that which has the form of a tree). *Ngana* means tree, *ngamba*, like. This means, says Strehlow, that such a tree indeed has the form of a tree, but it really is the *tjurunga* (i.e. hidden, secret) body of a mythical ancestor.[3] To the primitive's point of view, as we know, the mystic essence of any being matters far more than its outward appearance. To our minds, a tree could not be represented otherwise than as whole, with trunk, roots, branches and leaves, etc., in short, with all that the word evokes in our minds. We can imagine it as being inhabited by a hamadryad or a spirit, but even then it is always the tree that we envisage. To the Loritja, the tree that has shot up where the totemic god disappeared from view is primarily and particularly this

[1] C. Strehlow, "Die Aranda und Loritja-Stämme in Zentral-Australien," *Veröffentlichungen aus dem städtischen Völker-Museum*, Frankfurt am Main, i, p. 15, note 2.   [2] *Ibid.*, i, pp. 2–5.   [3] *Ibid.*, ii, p. 4.

same god. It is certainly true that it presents itself in the form of a tree. But it might equally well have assumed the form of a boulder, or a bush, as some other totemic ancestors have done.

This being so, "in these boulders representing the metamorphosed bodies of ancestors, in these trees and the branches of mistletoe growing on them, in the pools full of fishes, and other like places, live the germs of children, unborn children, called *ratapa*. . . . These *ratapa* are boys and girls, perfectly formed, and of a pinkish colour (like the newborn aborigines); they have a body and a soul. . . . According to the previous connection between the *altirangamitjina* (the mythical ancestor) whose transformed body contains one of these *ratapa*, and such and such an object in Nature, the *ratapa* is also connected with it. In the eucalyptus, the transformation of an ancestor-kangaroo, there is a *ratapa*-kangaroo. So, too, in a tree representing the body of an ancestor-opossum, there is an opossum *ratapa*."[1]

"Conception may occur in three different ways. A *ratapa* . . . may issue from a branch of mistletoe, a fissure in a boulder, etc., and enter the body of a woman passing the spot. Or else the mythic ancestor launches his *namatuna* (a kind of *tjurunga*) at a woman, and this takes the form of an infant within her body. Or lastly (a case that is much rarer), the *iningukua*, the name given to a man's mythical ancestor, may first throw his *namatuna* towards the woman, and then himself enter her. . . ."[2]

In these different forms the participation between the ancestor and the child to be born is already evident, and it becomes more so when we consider what follows. "Every individual necessarily belongs to a definite totem, that he calls his *ratapa*, but as well as this, every individual has yet another totem, called *altjira*, to which he is bound. This is his mother's totem, regarded by every native as an animal (or a plant) which belongs to him. . . . Although the children of one family, of the same mother, may belong to different totems (*ratapa*) they nevertheless all have one in common, the *altjira*, which is that of their

---

[1] C. Strehlow, "Die Aranda und Loritja-Stämme in Zentral-Australien," *Veröffentlichungen aus dem städtischen Völker-Museum*, Frankfurt am Main, ii, p. 52.
[2] *Ibid.*, ii, pp. 55–6.

mother. It may be regarded as their tutelary god, who assures them their food, just as their mother, in their early infancy, feeds and protects her children. This *altjira* appears to a native in his dreams, and gives him any needful warnings. The place where a native has been conceived he calls 'my own place': the one where his mother has been conceived is known to him as 'the place bound up with my totem.'[1]

"By virtue of his union with his *iningukua* (his totemic ancestor), every individual belongs to the same totem as the latter, and this totem, whether animal or plant, is regarded as his elder brother. It is the native's duty to treat it with the greatest respect. . . . He is also obliged, as were his totemic ancestors in their day during the course of their wanderings, to be on the lookout for the prosperity and aggrandizement of his totem, which he does by means of special ceremonies. . . ."[2]

We may now examine into what the sacred objects called *tjurunga* (the *churinga* of Spencer and Gillen) represent to the native. The word means "the secret thing belonging" (to someone). *Tju* is an obsolete word signifying "hidden, secret"; *runga*, "that which belongs, that which is mine." *Tjurunga* may first of all be used adjectivally; for instance, *retna tjurunga*, the secret name. But it is more frequently used as a substantive, and then it denotes the ritual ceremonies of the Aranda, the ceremonies of the emu, known as *ilia tjurunga*, for instance. The name *tjurunga* is especially applied to certain objects of wood or stone, which are oblong in shape and somewhat long and thick, covered with designs and ornaments, and for these religious veneration and immense respect are displayed.[3]

According to Strehlow, "it is believed that a very close bond unites the *tjurunga* with the totemic ancestor and with the man who is his descendant. To put the matter more definitely, the *tjurunga* is regarded as a body common to this man and to his totemic ancestor. It associates the individual with his personal totemic ancestor, guarantees him the protection afforded by his *iningukua*, whilst the loss of the *tjurunga* would call down upon him the vengeance of the latter. Moreover, the *tjurunga* unites the man not only with his totemic ancestor, but also with his

---

[1] C. Strehlow, "Die Aranda und Loritja-Stämme in Zentral-Australien," *Veröffentlichungen aus dem städtischen Völker-Museum*, Frankfurt am Main, ii, p. 57.
[2] *Ibid.*, ii, pp. 58–9.   [3] *Ibid.*, ii, p. 75.

totem (plant, animal, etc., as the case may be), and affords him the opportunity of assuring its prosperity and growth, as his totemic ancestors have done, in times past. . . . This solidary unity (which *I* should term 'participation') between man, his totemic ancestor, and his totem, finds special expression when the ceremonies of the totemic worship are being celebrated. If this participation be not recognized, it is quite impossible to understand the hymns which form part of these ceremonies."[1]

The *tjurunga* is therefore a "double" of the individual, i.e. the individual himself. "It is quite evident that the Aranda (and in this matter we may include the Loritja also), do not conceive of the *tjurunga* as the seat of the soul or of the life. I have frequently questioned the natives with respect to this, and they have always explicitly denied that it is so considered. The *tjurunga* has absolutely nothing to do with the 'soul' (that which is of the same nature as the liver, heart, fat, etc.). The relation between a man and his *tjurunga* is expressed by the saying: '*Nana unta mburka nuna*'—this (i.e. the *tjurunga*) is thy body)."[2]

Thus every man has two bodies, one of flesh and bone, and the other of stone or of wood. This apparent duality does not exclude individuality, for according to the primitive's way of thinking, it is quite compatible with the fact that one and the same being can be in two different places at the same time.

This is not all, however. Besides this *tjurunga* proper to the individual, and regarded as the man's second body, there is still another, the *papa tjurunga*. This one represents his mystic union with his *iningukua*. . . . That it is contradictory to regard these two *tjurunga* as the second body of a man is a fact not perceived by the natives, or else they do not wish to perceive it. Strehlow's editor, Leonhardi, improves upon him in this respect, for he says in a note: "The beliefs of the Arunta and the Loritja relating to the *tjurunga* seem to me to imply very many other contradictions, which exclude any theory capable of comprising them all." This is true from the logical point of

---

[1] C. Strehlow, "Die Aranda und Loritja-Stämme in Zentral-Australien," *Veröffentlichungen aus dem städtischen Völker-Museum*, Frankfurt am Main, ii, p. 76.
[2] *Ibid.*, ii, pp. 76–7.

view, but what is contradictory to us is not so to Australian aborigines. They perceive no inconsistency in their beliefs.[1]

Thanks to Strehlow, we can follow a man's relations with his *tjurunga* throughout the course of his life. "As soon as a woman knows that she is pregnant (i.e. that a *ratapa* has entered her body), the grandfather, on either the father's or the mother's side, of the unborn child, repairs to a *mulga* (an acacia-tree) and cuts from its bark a little *tjurunga*, on which he carves with the tooth of an opossum signs connected with the child's totem ancestor, and with his totem. He smears it over with red ochre, and places it in the grotto in which the other *tjurunga* are preserved. When the child is born it cries incessantly for its *tjurunga*, and to pacify it the grandfather, accompanied by some other men, goes to fetch the *tjurunga* from the grotto. . . . After the circumcision, they put into the youth's hand a large bull-roarer, called *nankara*, and he is henceforth called a *rukula*. This *nankara* represents the mystic body of his maternal totemic ancestor, his *altjira*, who will henceforth accompany and protect him.—After the subincision when he bears the name of *iliara*, they deliver over to him a little bull-roarer, called a *namatuna*, which represents the body of his personal *iliara* ancestor, who from that time will accompany and protect him. . . . Later, when he arrives at manhood, his grandfather conducts him to the *arknanaua* where the *tjurunga* of his totemic ancestor is kept, and shows it to him, saying: 'Here is your body, here is your second self (*iningukua*). If you take these *tjurunga* anywhere else, misery will be your portion!'

"As long as this *tjurunga*, which in some mystic fashion unites the totemic ancestor with the individual, is kept in safety—and of this the *iningukua* in his nocturnal wanderings assures himself —the personal security of the individual is guaranteed. Should it be lost or destroyed, he is in danger of his life."[2] To put it differently, the participation between them is equivalent to a consubstantiality. The very expressions used by the grandfather prove it, although this *tjurunga* is at the same time the *iningukua*, the totemic ancestor, who plays the part of a protecting guardian to the individual, but is ready to play the contrary part should anything serious happen to the *tjurunga*. This same *iningukua* is also the "second self" of the individual.

At the time of the totemic ceremonies, Strehlow tells us, the totem, the totemic ancestor, and the man who is the descendant (he who, by his decoration and his mask, figures as such in the ceremony), appear as one and the same being in the *tjurunga* hymns that are sung. There is, however, no incarnation, properly speaking, of the *altirangamitjina* in the descendant who represents it. If one does not continually bear in mind that the totem, the *altirangamitjina* and the *ratapa* make but one, most of the hymns relating to the *tjurunga* will be unintelligible.[1]

In conclusion, Strehlow himself thus sums up the essential elements of these very complex representations. "A *ratapa* is a little, fully-formed child, which has a body and a soul. When I described it as the 'germ of a child' (*Kinderkeim*) it was for want of a better term, and the word 'germ' must not be taken literally. Here is once again the whole scheme of the subject, as the natives view it: The *altirangamitjina*, in his wanderings of long ago, celebrated ceremonies in various places. In these he lost or left behind him some *tjurunga* (either in stone or wood, *namatuna* or *nankara*, it matters little) which in the course of time can be transformed into *ratapa*, and enter the bodies of the women who pass by. When the totemic ancestor had come to an end of his travels, however, his body was transformed into a boulder, or a tree, or a *tjurunga*. From the body thus transformed, only a single *ratapa* can issue, and this the ancestor himself accompanies and protects throughout its life. *Iningukua* is only another word to denote the personal *altirangamitjina* of a man."[2]

In these beliefs of the Aranda and the Loritja, we have seen once more representations of which we have already spoken—for instance, those mythic ancestors, both human and animal at the same time, assuming either form indifferently, which in both retain their mixed nature. The consubstantial identity of the individual with his appurtenances and with his double is to be found there also. The man *is* his *tjurunga*. The fact is

---

[1] C. Strehlow, "Die Aranda und Loritja-Stämme in Zentral-Australien," *Veröffentlichungen aus dem städtischen Völker-Museum*, Frankfurt am Main, iii, p. 6.
[2] *Ibid.*, iii, p. 7, note 1.

solemnly revealed to him: "This *tjurunga* is your body, it is yourself, it is your second self." There are even two *tjurunga* which form a part of the individuality of the Aranda and the Loritja. Through the one as through the other, he participates in his totemic ancestor. Without there being any reincarnation, properly so called, the ancestor lives again in him. Strehlow lays stress upon the point that the individual, his totemic ancestor, and his totem, make but one.

Not only does the individual participate in his totemic ancestor, with whom in one aspect he is identified: he finds in him a protector also. The *iningukua* accompanies him throughout life, warns him of the dangers threatening him and helps him to escape from them. He is a sort of tutelary deity or guardian angel. But, ought we to say perhaps, since the individual and his *iningukua* are but one, he is himself his own guardian?—Yes, for here participation does not imply that the two beings are altogether blended. No doubt in one aspect, the individual *is* the *iningukua*, but from another point of view, this *iningukua* is distinct from him. It lived before him, and will not die with him. Thus the individual participates in a being who is undoubtedly in him, is himself, makes him what he is, but at the same time surpasses him, who in certain characteristics differs from him, and keeps him in a state of dependency. He feels himself under the protection of his *altirangamitjina* or *iningukua*, of his *tjurunga*, and considers himself safe only when upheld by him. If this protection ceases, he is in danger, and if the guardian be wrathful, the individual believes himself doomed.

This last idea is not necessarily bound up with the totemic organization observed among the Aranda and the Loritja. In varied forms it is to be met with also in communities whose institutions differ from these. Whatever these may be, it is rarely that the individual does not believe in the presence within himself, as an essential part of his personality, of a being upon whom he depends, although he participates in him, and from whom he has a right to expect succour and protection.

II

In West Africa, on the Gold Coast, "the Tshi-speaking negro has arrived at the conclusion that he has a second individuality,

an indwelling spirit residing in his body. He calls this a '*kra*.'
. . . The *kra* existed before the birth of the man, probably
as the *kra* of a long series of men, and after his death it will
equally continue its independent career, either by entering a
newborn human body, or that of an animal, or by wandering
about the world as a *sisa*, or *kra* without a tenement. . . .
The *kra* can quit the body it inhabits at will, and return to it
again. Usually it only quits it during sleep, and the occurrences
dreamt of are believed to be the adventures of the *kra* during
its absence. The 'srahman' or ghost-man only commences his
career when the corporeal man dies; and he simply continues,
in the ghost-world or land of dead men, the existence the corporeal man formerly led in the world. There are, therefore,
in one sense, three individualities to be considered: first, the
man; secondly, the indwelling spirit or *kra*; thirdly, the ghost
or 'srahman'—though in another sense the last is only the con-
firmation of the first in shadowy form."[1]

Major Ellis is then concerned with the possible confusion of
the *kra* with that which we call the "soul." He says: "The
kra is not the soul. . . . Every *kra* has been the indwelling
spirit of many men, and probably will be of many more. The
kra in some respects resembles a guardian spirit, but it is more
than that. Its close connexion with the man is indicated by
the fact of its nocturnal adventures during its absence from the
body being remembered by that man when he awakes. The
latter even feels physically the effect of his *kra's* actions, and
when a negro awakes feeling stiff and unrefreshed, or with limbs
aching from muscular rheumatism, he invariably attributes
these symptoms to the fact of his *kra* having been engaged in
some struggle with another, or in some severe toil. If, moreover,
a man dreams of other men, he believes that his *kra* has met
theirs; consequently the *kra* is held to have the outward appearance of the man whose body he tenants. Hence the *kra* is more
than a mere tenanting, or guardian, spirit. It has, though
doubtless only in a shadowy form, the very shape and
appearance of the man, and both the mind and body of the
latter are affected by, and register the results of, the *kra's*
actions." Although from certain points of view the man
and his *kra* are distinct beings, in other respects they form

[1] A. B. Ellis, *The Ewe-Speaking Peoples*, pp. 15–16.

N

one only, and they are blended in the individuality of the living person.

"When the indwelling spirit leaves the body of the man it inhabits, that man suffers no physical inconvenience; it goes out, when he is asleep, without his knowledge; and if it should leave him when he is awake, he is only made aware of its departure by a sneeze or yawn. . . . When, however, the soul, the vehicle of individual personal existence, leaves the body, that body falls into a condition of suspended animation; it is cold, pulseless, and apparently lifeless. Sometimes, though rarely, the soul returns after such an absence, and then the man has been in a swoon or trance; more generally it does not return, and then the man is dead."[1]

The *kra* receives homage from "his" man. "The Ewe-speaking native offers worship and sacrifice to his indwelling spirit in much the same way as is done on the Gold Coast. In both cases the natal day of the man is the day kept sacred to the indwelling spirit, and is commenced by a sacrifice, either a sheep or a fowl, according to the means of the worshipper; after which the latter washes himself from head to foot, and always arrays himself in a white cloth."[2]

The same ideas are to be found in the neighbouring tribes. "The Tshi-speaking tribes have a word *kra* that is used to designate the spirit of a living man, or, rather, a spirit which ordinarily dwells in a living man, and which expects sacrifice for the protection it grants. Thus, just as there is believed to be an indwelling spirit in certain tangible and inanimate objects, so also is there believed to be an indwelling spirit in the corporeal man, which is similarly distinct from the man himself. This word *kra*, though generally interpreted 'soul,' does not at all correspond to the European idea of a soul; for it is the man himself, in a shadowy or ghostly form, that continues his existence after death in another world, and not the *kra*. The latter is, rather, a guardian spirit, who lives in a man, and whose connection with him terminates at his death."[3]—As with the Ewe-speaking people, those speaking Tshi also believe that the *kra* quits a man's body during sleep, and that when he awakes he can recall the *kra's* adventures during its absence.

[1] A. B. Ellis, *The Ewe-speaking Peoples*, pp. 20–1.   [2] *Ibid.*, p. 105.
[3] A. B. Ellis, *The Tshi-speaking Peoples*, p. 149.

"If the man feels stiff and aching . . . he attributes the pain he feels to the exertion made (by his *kra*) . . . in a conflict, or in some toilsome pursuit."—With them too, "the birthday of a man is the day sacred to his *kra*. If the man be rich, he kills a sheep, if poor, a fowl, and prepares a banquet. He shaves his head, and abstains from all work. In the morning he goes to wash, and, providing himself with an egg, and some new fibre of the kind used as a sponge, he stands before the calabash or other utensil containing the water, and addresses his *kra*, asking for its protection and assistance during the coming year, as he is about to worship it and keep that day sacred to it. . . . Sometimes members of the higher classes, kings or chiefs, keep sacred to their *kra* the day of the week on which they were born."[1]

Other testimony confirms this of Ellis's. Thus, in the Ga-speaking tribes who are geographically situated between the Tshi and the Ewe peoples, "there is something curious about the *okra*. If a direct question on the subject is addressed to a Ga negro, he will answer, after having thought for a moment: 'Is not my *okra* my *susuma*? that is, my soul' (*Seele*). But if this same man narrowly escapes death or some great danger of another kind, he will say: 'If my *okra* had not stood by me, I should never have come through safely.' Or, on the contrary, if some misfortune befalls him, it will be: 'My *okra* turned away from me.' We see, therefore, that according to the Ga negro's view, every individual, beside the soul that is within him (the *susuma*) has another guardian angel who accompanies him day and night, his *okra*. There is this peculiarity, however; all those who are born on the same day of the week call their *okra* by the same name, corresponding with the day. . . . Opposed to the *okra*, the inspirer of all good thoughts and the one who helps to put them to practical use, is the *gbeshi* or *okrabi*, i.e. the black *okra*. The latter leads man into all kinds of evil, and then pursues him day and night, like a guilty conscience. . . . No sacrifices are made to the *okrabi*."[2] This same belief had been noted by Ellis in the Ga-speaking tribes.[3] Possibly it manifests Moslem influence.

[1] A. B. Ellis, *The Tshi-Speaking Peoples*, p. 156.
[2] H. Bohner, *Im Lande des Fetishes*, p. 99 (note).
[3] A. B. Ellis, *The Yoruba-Speaking Peoples*, pp. 125-7.

The same facts have been related in substance by Perregaux. In the terms used by him, it is easy to recognize them, and at the same time we have here an instance of the confusion engendered by the application of the words "soul" and "spirit" to representations that do not correspond with them. "The Tshi believe that the soul of a man exists before his birth, and may have been the soul or spirit of one of his dead relatives." Here the *kra* is evidently in question. "If God grants it permission to return to earth, it receives its marching orders at the same time; its lot is marked out for it beforehand." (Possibly here, too, there is a trace of Moslem influence.) "It is from this idea that the name *okra* is derived, for this name signifies: 'sent on an errand' (with definite orders). . . . During the individual's lifetime the *okra* is considered, either as his soul or his spirit (and it will accordingly be called *sunsum* or *honhom*) or else as a being distinct from himself, who protects and follows him, gives him good or bad advice, makes his enterprises prosperous, or neglects and despises him. In the latter case the *okra* is called *okrabi*, that is, the black soul. . . .

"The Tshi worship their *okra*; they sacrifice to him that he may be favourable to them. . . . If a Tshi escapes death by a miracle, he will say: 'If my soul had not followed me loyally and watched over me, I should not have got off so well.' But if he should be overtaken by misfortune, he will bewail his lot, saying: 'Alackaday! my soul has forsaken me!' "[1] If we did not know, through other channels, the sharp distinction drawn by the natives between the *okra* and the *susuma* or *sunsum*, would it be possible to extract it from this text?

III

While by no means disregarding the vast differences in their institutions, the similarity between these representations of the negroes of the Gold Coast and those of the Australian natives, in some respects, is evident here. For here again, the individual participates in a being which is not entirely blended with him, which existed before him, will separate from him at his death, and which, nevertheless, throughout his life is more than bound

[1] E. Perregaux, *Chez les Achanti*, Bulletin de la Société de Géographie de Neuchâtel, xvii (1906), pp. 266-8.

to him. He is consubstantial with it; it makes part of his personality. Here again, the individual pays his homage to this element of himself which transcends his individuality, and he hopes for help and protection from it. But nothing seems to indicate that this element associates the individual with his ancestors, as does the *iningukua* or the *tjurunga*. Abiding by the observations we have already quoted, it seems as if any sort of *kra* enters any kind of man. The series of men inhabited in turns by the same *kra* might be fortuitous, or at any rate, indefinite, in the natives' minds.

Now it is almost inadmissible that they should represent things to themselves thus. To the mind of the primitive, there is no such thing as chance. If one certain *kra*, and not another, comes to dwell within a human body at his birth, to form part of that individual, *to be*, in some respects, that individual as long as his life shall last, there must be some mystic reason, some participation which accounts for the fact. A man's *kra* cannot be merely any *kra*. Might it not be, on the contrary, although Ellis and the other observers have said nothing about it, the living expression of the solidarity of the individual with his group—his family, clan, or sib?

Captain Rattray's fine book on the Ashanti gives a very decided answer to this question. He has revealed and elucidated the conception of the *ntoro*, which had somewhat escaped his predecessors. No doubt Captain Rattray will tell us more about this in his book on the Ashanti religion to which we are looking forward.[1] Even now, he permits us to recognize in the *ntoro* the essential characteristics of the *kra*, and at the same time to discern its properly ancestral nature.

The *ntoro*, the principle found in every individual, is thus defined by Rattray. "It is the *ntoro* of the man mingling with the *mogya* of the woman that forms the child, and just as the woman transmits her *mogya* or blood, so the man transmits his *ntoro*. Thus each man and woman have in them two distinct elements: *mogya* or blood, and *ntoro*, spirit. . . . The *ntoro* is passed on through the male line as long as there are males, but is immediately lost as soon as it comes into the female line."[2]

---

[1] The book referred to appeared in 1927.—TRANSLATOR.
[2] Capt. R. S. Rattray, *Ashanti*, pp. 36-7.

What exactly *is* this *ntoro*? Rattray says that it "is best translated by 'spirit.' It might almost be called familiar spirit."
(In this we recognize the "guardian angel" of older writers, but
here it is expressly stated that each individual receives his from
his male ancestors.) The author adds: "*Ntoro* appears to be
used at times synonymously with *sunsum*, that spiritual element
in a man or woman upon which depends—not life, i.e. breath,
for that is the *okra* or *kra*—but that force, personal magnetism,
character, personality, power, soul, call it what you will, upon
which depend health, wealth, worldly power, success in any
venture, in fact everything that makes life at all worth living.
. . . Yet again it has been seen that *ntoro* is sometimes used for
semen."[1]

The following facts are accounted for by this latter point of
view. "When a woman marries, she will treat all her husband's
ntoro taboos as her own (still observing those enjoined by her
own *ntoro*), while the converse is not the case. Moreover, the
recognition of the husband's. *ntoro* taboos by the wife lasts only
as long as the woman is of an age to bear children, or as long
as she is living with him as his wife. This is a further proof
of the belief that it is the husband's *ntoro* that is instrumental in
making and building up any offspring that may result from the
union.

"Yet again, in cases of adultery, the offence is greatly
aggravated if committed with a woman who is already enceinte,
as the meeting of the two *ntoro* is supposed to cause the
death of the child in the womb; but should the adulterer
by chance be of the same *ntoro* as the husband, the offence
is much less serious, as the two *ntoro* are really one and the
same spirit, and not so likely to cause fatal results to the
expected child."[2]

"The *ntoro* element in man," says Rattray a little further on,
"seems to be often connected with water or liquid, such as
saliva . . . but I will here only very briefly state that at the
naming of a child, e.g. after its godfather, the infant is taken
to him on the eighth day, and he spits in his godchild's mouth

---

[1] Capt. R. S. Rattray, *Ashanti*, pp. 45–6.
[2] *Ibid.*, p. 50. Here we have one of the reasons why, in so many tribes, the
woman may be the "potential" wife of her husband's brothers. When he permits them to exercise their right, there is no danger attending such a circumstance, if the pregnancy should have already begun.

to strengthen the spirit already there, which is of course his own *ntoro* passed on through his son (not daughter . . . for a godchild by a daughter would not be of the godfather's *ntoro*). The law is irrevocable which insists that only one of like *ntoro* can perform this ceremony."[1]

Thus the *ntoro* is a principle common to a whole group having the same totem, the same sacred day, etc. Whilst being a "spirit," it has at the same time a physical reality, present in each member of the group, which binds them all together. Rattray here shows us the natives under the influence of participations which are perplexing to us. In any object we view we cannot grasp its material reality and its immaterial qualities *without distinguishing between them*. If the *ntoro* be really a man's seminal fluid, or his saliva, whatever its mystic virtues may be otherwise, it is these physical characteristics which first of all are impressed on our minds. It is through them that we define it to ourselves. The mystic virtues inherent in it do not follow until later, and we may admit that they exist without comprehending how it is that such a fluid may contain them. It is impossible for us here, according to Aristotle's expression, to μετάβαλλειν εἰς ἄλλο γένος. To our minds concepts that have nothing in common, far from blending with each other, are mutually antagonistic and exclusive. The Ashanti mind, however, is not dominated by such laws; its methods of thought are different. The physical aspect in which it regards the *ntoro* does not prevent it from being sensible of its mystic virtues *at the same time*, and as the latter are of supreme importance to it, they predominate in the representation. The native sees the *ntoro* transmitting itself, like a spirit, from father to son, and being communicated, through the medium of the seminal fluid, to all who participate in this principle or spirit. In this respect, as in so many others, it is difficult, almost impossible, for us to think as he does. We merely see the path his mind follows, one that we know not how to tread.

"When a person dies, his or her *ntoro* does not accompany the ghost (*saman*) to the *samando*, or spirit-world. It is thought to remain behind and look after those persons of a similar *ntoro* who remain alive, and, I believe, eventually to be reincarnated.

[1] Capt. R. S. Rattray, *Ashanti*, p. 54.

"This disembodied *ntoro* will, in the case of a man, concern itself, for example, with the children of the deceased. This does not hold for a woman, for her children would not be of her *ntoro*, but her husband's; the *ntoro* would not in this case look after her children but (among many possible others) her brothers and sisters by the same father."[1] Thus it plays the rôle of guardian like that attributed to the *kra*. But Rattray shows this rôle of the *ntoro* persisting after the death of the man or woman, and its protection being extended to the members of the familial group, and to them alone.

IV

Similar ideas are prevalent among the Bantus. We shall not lay stress upon them. Edwin W. Smith has summed them up very felicitously in the following passage. "A man named Mungalo will tell you that he is his godfather Mungalo, re-turned to life. At the same time he will tell you that Mungalo is his genius, his guardian spirit. That is to say, a man's tutelary genius is the reincarnated spirit within him, the sovereign part of his soul, within him and yet without him, surrounding him, guiding him from birth to death. This is a very subtle conception, not without its own beauty and value. The Ba-ila address the genius as 'my namesake.' When one of the tribe is minded to go hunting, he rises early and makes an offering of fine meal to his genius and prays thus: 'My namesake, let us go to the hunt together. Bring the animals near to me and ward off from me all danger. Give me meat to-day, oh hunter!' "[2]

Later on we shall examine the Bantus' conception of re-incarnation. What we seize here is that "element" of the individual (retaining Captain Rattray's expression) which forms a part of himself, and which at the same time is exterior and superior to him, which in one respect is not distinct from his own personality, yet to which he addresses his prayers and worship. In other more or less varied forms this element is met with in all parts of the world. It is the *nagual* of Central America, the "soul" of the Indians of New France, described

[1] Capt. R. S. Rattray, *Ashanti*, p. 53.
[2] E. W. Smith, *The Religion of the Lower Races*, pp. 36-7. Cf. Smith and Dale, *The Ila-Speaking Peoples of Northern Rhodesia*, ii, pp. 40-2.

by the Jesuit fathers, the "guardian spirit," "personal god," of many of the North American tribes, the *nyarong* of the Malays, the "personal totem" of Australian aboriginals, and so forth. Such ideas might be arranged upon a long ladder, every rung of which would be occupied. At one extremity, this individual "element" would be so intimately bound up with him as to be almost identical, while at the other end the participation between them is fairly lax, and the "genius" maintains an almost independent life. The intermediate forms are those which we most frequently find described, under various names. Unfortunately the observations at our disposal are often vague, confused, and useless for our purpose. When the ignorance of the European is added to that of the native who is giving the information, and neither of them is really familiar with the language of the other, how is it possible to discern which is the actual object of the representations, and exactly what constitutes the soul, totem (whether personal or otherwise), the protecting genius, the guardian angel, or whatever it may be, that is in question? It is to be desired that in future observers may turn their attention to the necessary precautions to be kept in mind when they are dealing with such subjects. It is essential to address one's questions only to the informed natives who are thoroughly conversant with the traditions and ceremonies of their group, to secure their whole-hearted sincerity by winning their confidence and liking, and lastly, to take down their testimony in their own language, before risking a translation which may not be exact, since the native words and phrases very often have no satisfactory equivalents in our European language.

V

To our way of thinking, however complex an individual may be, his primordial and essential characteristic is that he shall be *one person*. If he were not this, he would not be an individual, but a being compounded of several. But to the primitive, a lively inner sense of his own personality is not necessarily accompanied by a well-defined concept of individuality. Not only are its limits vague and indefinite, since an individual's appurtenances are himself, and his double, reproduction, re-

flection, are also the man himself. There is yet more to consider, for the *tjurunga* of the Australian native, the *kra* of the
Ewe, the Ashanti's *ntoro*, the Ba-ila's "namesake," etc.,
without being completely merged in the individual, is no
longer to be distinguished from him. If this element, which
establishes the individuality by uniting it with the ancestors
whence it has issued, were to be lacking, it could not exist.
The individual is only himself by virtue of being at the same
time something other than himself. Viewed in this fresh aspect,
far from being one unit, as we conceive him to be, he is one
and yet several, at the same time. Thus he is, so to speak, a
veritable "centre of participation."

This very profound difference between the representations
of primitives and our own has nevertheless escaped nearly all
observers. Very often, indeed, it is regarded as a resemblance,
especially by missionaries, Catholic and Protestant alike. It
must be confessed that the attitude of the natives, far from
putting them on their guard against this error, rather en-
courages them in it. In fact, when the missionaries explain that
the corporeal and visible man is not the whole man, and that
in spite of death and the corruption of the body, he continues
to live on, the natives hasten to reply: "That is what we believe
too." When they teach them that man's nature is a dual one,
they at once approve the sentiment: "That is what we have
always held!"

Beneath this apparent agreement, missionaries and natives
are in reality thinking very different things. To the white men's
minds, it is a question of *dualism*, to the natives' minds, of
duality. The missionary believes in a distinction between two
substances, the one corporeal and perishable, the other spiritual
and immortal. United in this life, these two compose the living
individual; death separates them, liberating the spiritual
substance or soul, which is the real individuality. But nothing
is more wholly foreign to the primitive's mind than this con-
trasting of two substances, the attributes of which are antagonistic. He feels, on the contrary, all beings to be homogeneous.
Nothing is purely matter; still less is it purely spirit. All
things are bodies, or have bodies, and all possess in varying
degrees the mystic properties which we ascribe to spirits alone.
Thus where the missionaries see two heterogeneous substances

temporarily united, the natives do not imagine anything of the kind.

Nevertheless, when the missionary states that the nature of man is a dual one, they assent to the proposition, and they can do so in all sincerity, for although the idea of the *dualism* of substances is unknown to them, the *duality* of the individual is a very familiar one. They believe in the identity of a man with his image or picture, his shadow, his double—*tamaniu, atai, mauri, hau,* etc., and in his intimate participation in his *tjurunga, kra, ntoro,* and so on. Thus there is nothing to prevent them from showing their usual complaisance in not contradicting the foreigner, and even in agreeing with him politely. The blunder is later confirmed and intensified by the convenient but misleading use made by the white men of the word "soul" to express native ideas which are widely different from those the word conveys to us.

The "dual" nature of the individual, in primitive representations, seems to assume two forms, and we may ask ourselves whether it might not be better to study them separately. Sometimes the individual comprises what we consider to be two distinct beings, though primitive mentality views them as but one. Such are the werewolf, the man-leopard, the sorcerer-crocodile, etc. Sometimes this duality is in fact a bi-presence. The same individual is found in two different places at the same moment. We have but to recall the Indian who accused Mr. Grubb of having stolen his pumpkins when the latter was more than two hundred miles away, or of Junod's *baloyi,* or Malinowski's *yoyova* witches, who come from afar to kill and devour their victims, whilst still remaining recumbent and asleep in their dwellings. In all circumstances of this second kind, we are dealing less with duality, apparently, than with the simultaneous presence of the same individual in two different places.

Nevertheless, if we examine this matter a little more closely, we find that this difference is more apparent than real, and we do not need to dwell upon it. Or rather, it is formulated in our minds only, and primitive mentality knows nothing of it. For where we think we perceive real duality, that is, two distinct beings united by close participation into a single one, it perceives and feels this unity *first of all*, and it does not attach the same importance as we do to the fact that the two beings —the man and the leopard, for instance—occupy different positions in space. Thus what we call duality is to native minds already a bi-presence, since at the outset they apprehend the same being in both man and leopard. Conversely, what appears to us simply bi-presence is to them duality also. If we say of a dreamer that his "double" has gone away, and returns when the sleeper awakes, they will make no objection. They will admit that the witch flying far away from her hut and the woman asleep there seem to be two persons. To their minds, this duality, even real, does not prevent the fundamental unity of the individual. This making no distinction between one and two, or even between one and many, causes our minds intolerable embarrassment. At the very moment when we try to accept the idea, we instinctively rebut it, or else try to present it in a way that shall make it intelligible. The primitives' mind, on the contrary, accepts it as it is, and delights in it. The idea is implied in their representations of the living, and we shall find it once more at the bottom of their representations of the dead.

PART II

CHAPTER VII

THE LIFE AND THE DEATH OF THE INDIVIDUAL

I

BEFORE studying the way in which primitives picture to themselves the individuality of a dead person, it will be well to review briefly what they regard as the successive stages of a living one. They see, as we do, a newborn infant become in turns a child, youth, adult, and lastly an old man, with powers continually on the wane until life finally leaves him (unless an accident has carried him off earlier). But, as we know, they have no notion either of physiological functioning, or of biological processes. To them, the blossoming out into adult life is not the terminal point of an evolution that has been going on for many years. They are more inclined to believe in abrupt transformations. They will attribute these changes, as well as the functions themselves, to the presence or absence of mystic principles which are themselves complete beings also.

The very young infant does not count. "In obtaining my figures," says an administrator of British New Guinea, "I had a great deal of trouble to get a proper account of each man's family, the father invariably omitting to count the baby, because he did not work in the garden with the other members of the family."[1] The reason thus brought forward is probably not the true one, or at least not the only one. The same circumstance has been noted among a great many peoples, and there the true reason has been given: the very young infant does not, as yet, form a part of the social group. Now since the individual has no actual existence save as a member of the group, the tiny baby is literally not yet wholly born. When a certain time after the mother's confinement has elapsed, above all when certain rites which incorporate the child in its group have been performed, he will have completed the process of birth. All this has been described in detail by Junod in Chapter I of *The Life of a South African Tribe.*

[1] *Annual Report*, Papua (1911), p. 93.

So, too, Father Van Wing says: "A newborn infant is not a *nuana*, a child, he is only a *kimpiatu*. He cannot be a complete *nuana* until he has a name. The word *kimpiatu* signifies grub or chrysalis."[1] And again: "The name, as the Bampangu conceive it, must be added to the three elements which constitute the child when he comes into the world, i.e. the body, soul, and the duplicate soul; these three elements still only make up a *kimpiatu*, a chrysalis; the name added to them makes of it a *nuana muntu*, a child of man. Thus the name is not merely a label. As a constituent element of the personality, it is a characteristic and individuating symbol."[2] We shall shortly see what is signified by the bestowal of this name, which is often of great importance. For instance, of the Kayans of Borneo, Furness remarks, almost in Van Wing's words: "The receiving of a name is really the starting-point of life; and the bestowal of a name by the parents is probably the most serious of parental duties, and to be performed with ceremonies proportioned to their rank. So essential is this ceremony of naming that in the enumeration of a family an unnamed child is not counted, and should a child die before the ceremony of naming, a Kayan or Kenyah mother would mourn for it no more deeply than had it been stillborn. This is true even when an unnamed child lives to be nearly a year old."[3]

In British Equatorial Africa, "if the child should die before being brought out of the house it receives no mourning. The relatives do not shave their heads on account of it, nor do they present offerings to its spirit."[4] With the Ashanti, also, "the infant, for the first eight days after birth, is scarcely considered as a human being, being looked upon as possibly merely 'a ghost child' that has come from the spirit-world, intending immediately to return. If it die before the eighth day, it certainly was such. The little body is then sometimes whipped, it is put in a pot with sharp-cutting elephant grass, and buried near the women's latrine. The parents dress in holiday attire. . . . All this is to shame the little stranger-ghost that had dared to wander down into the world, and to discourage its returning in that form to endanger the life of a human mother."[5]—In

---

[1] Fr. Van Wing, *Études Bakongo*, p. 254.   [2] *Ibid.*, pp. 296–7.
[3] Furness, *The Home-Life of Borneo Head-Hunters*, p. 18.
[4] D. Macdonald, *Africana*, i, p.114.
[5] Capt. R. S. Rattray, *Ashanti*, p. 54 (note).

Madagascar, "the infant had been bathed in accordance with all the rites (on the eighth day). It seems that this operation had, as it were, actually aided it to enter the group as one of its members. Until that time it was a kind of sacred being, somewhat hybrid, semi-human and semi-divine. It had required a certain lapse of time for it to establish itself definitely on earth. A fact that seems clearly to indicate this is the singular prohibition against moving anything, no matter what, in the room, sometimes even in the house, where the birth has taken place, so long as the child has not gone out for the first time. To disturb the place of anything would have been like breaking one of the links about to be formed between the world and the newborn child."[1]

In Gaboon, birth is not completed before a certain time. "The parents are in no hurry to baptize their offspring, if I may express it thus; and on many occasions, I have heard it said of an infant a few days old: 'He has no name yet, he is too little.' "[2]—Among the Bambara, "the falling-off of the umbilical cord marks the end of this seclusion. At Kaarta, the cord, picked up again, is hung round the child's neck in a little pouch. . . . It is only after the cord has become detached that the child is regarded as definitely born."[3]—Finally, in East Africa, among the Akamba, "on the fourth day, the father usually hangs round the child's neck a necklace . . . consisting of one of the fine iron chains made by the Akamba. . . . As soon as it has been hung round the child's neck, the child becomes a real human being; before that it is looked upon as being in more or less intimate connection with the spirit-world, from which it has come, and is called *kiimu* (cf. *iimu*, a deceased relation, a spirit). In order that the newborn child shall be recognized as a real member of the tribe, it is therefore not enough that it is born and receives a name, which is otherwise, among primitive communities, usually the ceremony by which the new individual is taken up as an integral part of the tribe."[4]

The same conceptions are to be found in other continents

[1] G. Mondain, "Raketaka," *Publications de la Faculté des Lettres d'Alger*, lxi (1925), p. 49.
[2] G. le Testu, *Coutumes Bapounou*, p. 30.
[3] Ch. Monteil, *Les Bambara du Ségou et du Kaarta*, p. 211.
[4] G. Lindblom, *The Akamba*, p. 34.

besides Africa. Two examples will no doubt suffice. In North-East India, among the Lhota Nagas, after a confinement "for the next six days in the case of a boy, or five in the case of a girl . . . the child is regarded as in a sense still in the process of being born. The custom until recently was to regard a mother who died during this time as having died in childbirth, and abandon the house and all its contents."[1]—With the Araucans, "the double ceremony (of mourning) was not observed with the bodies of little infants, or children of tender years; their death was an infra-social matter, which did not affect the group."[2]

An infra-social matter: this is almost the expression used by a recent observer in British New Guinea (Mailu). "Most events in village life," he says, "are made the occasion for the village to get a free feed of some kind or other. . . . Strangely enough, childbirth seems to be reckoned an entirely individual and household affair, as though it did not affect the community in any way—no presents, no feast, no distribution of nuts."[3]

According to this widespread belief, therefore, the newborn is still only half born. He as yet belongs, at any rate in part, to the spirit-world. This is one of the reasons why infanticide, especially of children only just born, is so common among these tribes. With them it does no violence to sentiments which we consider quite natural.[4] "I do not know how to reconcile this practice with what we are commonly told, that the love of their young is imprinted on the hearts of men and of animals: these savages give us to understand that such a love is not innate."[5] In their eyes, however, the destroying of a new-born child is not causing its death, because it is not actually alive yet. Only such ideas can account for the singular action of a Fijian chief, reported by Williams the missionary. "Toka-naua," he tells us, "was slain in the last Mbua war, in 1844, leaving a son and infant daughter, who were thrown on the care of their friends, the mother having been strangled and buried with her husband. The orphans were taken to the house of Tokanaua's elder brother, who provided wet-nurses for the

[1] J. P. Mills, *The Lhota Nagas*, p. 146.
[2] T. Guevara, *Psicologia del pueblo araucano*, p. 267.
[3] W. J. V. Saville, *In Unknown New Guinea*, p. 95.
[4] *How Natives Think*, pp. 343–6.
[5] F. de Azara, *Geografia fisica y esferica del Paraguay*, pp. 393–4.

babe. He became, however, dissatisfied with this arrangement, and, as his wife was just then confined, he arranged with
her to murder their own child, that the adopted one might
take its place, and receive her care."[1]

Such an extraordinary solution of the problem appears
wholly reasonable to the Fijian's mind. His brother's child is
also his, for between brothers, children are shared in common.
The baby girl, already some months old, has a sort of right
to be considered as belonging to the family and to the tribe,
whereas the newborn infant does not interest them yet. It is
merely a candidate for life. Is it not better to defer its entry
into life than to risk losing by death a child that is already fully
alive?

II

At the end of a period varying in length, the newborn
child is at last transformed into a definite human being.
Ceremonies, differing according to the tribes, play their part
in this event. As a rule the most important of these consists in
giving the infant a name or, as they often put it, in "discovering" what its name is—that is, which member of the family is
reincarnated in him. Thus we can understand that the name
is not, as Fr. Van Wing expresses it, merely "a label," but a
constituent and "individuating" element of the personality.
To the primitive's mind, being reckoned among the number
of human beings can only signify being a member of the social
group. How may this newborn infant, who is not yet a member,
become one? He has no power of himself to enter their ranks,
for the mystic virtue that is necessary is not his. He acquires
it, however, at the moment when he is given the name of an
ancestor. This latter, who, in a certain sense, lives again in him,
has been and, though dead, still is, a member of the group.
In other words, the bestowal of a name makes the child an
integral part of his group, though in an indirect fashion,
through the intervention of the ancestor.

Neither the life nor the death of a child, even after he has
received his name, has the same importance and entails the

[1] Th. Williams, *Fiji and the Fijians*, i, p. 131.

same consequences as those of an adult, therefore. He certainly belongs to the group already, but he does not fill one whole place in it. He is in a state of "minority," because his integration in the group is as yet only mediate and partial.

At a given moment—usually when the signs of puberty appear—the rôle of the intermediary comes to an end. The youth is about to become, through his own means, a complete and effective member of the social group, and one of its constituent elements. In order that this transformation may be brought about, nothing less than a remoulding of his whole being is necessary. This will be effected by the initiation, in which the presence of the ancestor who until this time has connected him with the group is obliterated, and another takes its place. Here we have the explanation of the capital importance of the initiation ceremonies, to group and individual alike. If they were not celebrated, the community would cease to exist for lack of qualified members. We realize, too, why the novices are always reputed to expire during the course of the ceremonies and to come to life again at their close. The significance of this symbolism is not uncertain. For the young man to be fully integrated in his clan, his tribe, he must first cease to belong to it in a mediate and indirect fashion. Now the primitive mind does not perceive any transition which permits of his passing directly from one of these conditions to the other. To be able to enter the second it is essential to have come out of the first. The novices, separated from their relatives for weeks and even months, subjected to prolonged and often terrible tests, will therefore die, but only to be born again almost immediately, henceforward complete members, we might almost say duly qualified members, of the tribe, by virtue of the ceremonies which have imbued them with mystic essence. Henceforward the group will be perpetuated through them, as they exist through it.

For the same reasons a non-initiate does not count in the tribe. He is scarcely reckoned as alive. Speaking of initiation, Col. Maclean says: "So essential is it deemed, that a person that had not undergone it would be regarded as but a child, however old he might be. He would not be allowed to inherit; he would find no one that would receive him as a son-in-law; and would be treated with universal scorn and ridicule, as well by the women as by the men."[1]—"The difference which in Europe exists between adults and minors, great and insignificant, rich and poor, is nothing compared with that existing in Kikuyu between circumcised and uncircumcised. One might almost say that they are individuals of a different species, with their own laws and customs. Whilst the former enjoy all human rights to an unlimited extent, the latter seem to be only beings without will or rights or social position, liable to any ill-treatment whatsoever, their only safeguards being the remote protection of their fathers. . . . The uncircumcised person, the *kahée*, is not a man, *ti mundu*; he is a nobody, whose small services one accepts, but whom one does not mention, and who counts for nothing in the tribe. . . . He cannot own property, or become a soldier, etc."[2] In fact, this non-initiate has not undergone the transformation necessary to render him an effective member of the social group. Possibly even, the participation which permitted him to form part of it indirectly as a child, has ceased. The ancestor present in him may have withdrawn himself at a given moment, and thus, being no longer an integral part of the group in any way, either mediate or direct, he is nothing; he is a "nobody," for lack of having undergone the tests which, according to the words of an observer of Australian tribes, "change a boy into a man."[3]

For a change which seems so simple and so natural—and which indeed would be so, to the primitives as to ourselves, if the physical life alone were under consideration, but it is not this that is in question here—the young boy has been obliged to return to the state of a newborn infant. A death must therefore be simulated, and then a birth. Mothers have been made to believe that their children really cease to live, that in the camps which they are forbidden to leave, and which no profane person may enter, spirits have carried them off, killed, and devoured them—and that afterwards life has been restored to them. They do not merely regain consciousness, as though they were recovering from a prolonged swoon; in every sense of the word they are newborn. The successive stages of the ceremonies often recall those of a real birth, and the first

---

[1] Col. Maclean, *A Compendium of Kafir Laws aud Cnstoms*, p. 157.
[2] Fr. Bugeau, "La circoncision in Kikuyu," *Anthropos*, vi (1911), pp. 616–19.
[3] R. Brough Smyth, *The Aborigines of Victoria*, ii, p. 271.

few days that ensue, and this period corresponds exactly with that which follows the entry of the infant into life. Very frequently, even, when the initiates return to their fathers' homes, they appear to be like little babies who have to be taught everything; they can neither speak nor walk nor eat, and so on. When the ceremonies are over the novices, henceforward initiated, receive a new name. They are now an integral part of the social group, but this time they have a direct and a personal qualification.

To quote but one example among hundreds, "when the initiation is over . . . in the presence of the whole tribe, the young men are given a public social name, chosen by the *likuda* (operator) and the *bakuda* (father), often after endless delays, and the usual recourse, in case of doubt, to the entire series of divinatory processes. . . . In many Azande tribes, circumcision bears the same name as the midwife—*samba*. There is a resemblance between the rites of circumcision and the natal rites, although the likeness between the two ritual series has never been explicitly owned to me, despite my many questions. We may note, however, firstly, the name *samba* in both cases; secondly, the umbilical cord and the prepuce are regarded as two effective remedies; thirdly, the prohibiting the mention of the name of either father or *likuda*, and other things."[1]

The mystic virtue of the initiation ceremonies has "changed the boy into a man," and also made of the young girl a woman. Henceforward the youths of both sexes participate directly in the nature and principle of the social group. From this time the young men are capable of taking part in hunting or warring expeditions, of being present at the tribal councils and offering an opinion there; in short, they now enjoy all the privileges of the adult. They may also marry, that is, if they have the means to do so or, as is more usually the case, if their family will help them, they can now secure the exclusive and permanent possession of a wife. Only the children of the initiated will in their turn become effective members of the tribe.

That which is here, for want of a better term, called *marriage* (which very frequently corresponds but faintly with what we understand by the term), appears as a rule to be the natural

[1] A. de Calonne-Beaufaict, *Azande*, p. 203.

end of the initiation. It is so, for instance, with the Banaro of New Guinea, studied by Dr. Thurnwald, and with the tribes of North-West Central Queensland, whom Dr. Roth has observed. In the Gulf of Papua, "the actual period of the marriage was determined by the tribe rather than by the families most concerned. The occasion was usually one of many marriages. The betrothals . . . were approved before the boys went into seclusion for their initiation; when they had been duly initiated, and their period of isolation from the everyday life of their tribe terminated, they were free to marry and to resume, as men, the life of their village and tribe."[1]—In Kiwai Island, "initiation covers really a long period and can scarcely be said to be even complete until a youth marries (perhaps not even then), although it is to be noted that marriage invariably takes place very early."[2]

In South Africa, among the Ba-ila tribes, "immediately after the initiation rites come the marriage ceremonies, in most cases."[3] I shall dwell no longer on this well-known fact. Often, even, the marriage is not regarded as definite and irrevocable until after the birth of a child, for only then is a man's personality perfected. Should he have no children, it is in vain that he has been made an integral member of the social group through initiation, his place in it is a very humble one. Some essential quality is lacking in him, and his individuality remains imperfect; therefore it often happens that after his death he does not receive the honours habitually accorded to adults who leave children behind them.

III

Whilst the child, until his initiation, belongs to the social group only in an indirect and secondary way, the old man often plays the principal part in it. As the depositary of the sacred traditions and secrets of the tribe—matters which are communicated only to certain heads of families when they have arrived at a definite age—he is encircled by a kind of mystic halo. He is respected, and often it happens that he is

---

[1] J. H. Holmes, *In Primitive New Guinea*, p. 55.
[2] W. N. Beaver, *Unexplored New Guinea*, p. 186.
[3] Smith and Dale, *The Ila-Speaking Peoples of Northern Rhodesia*, ii, p. 54.

privileged to enjoy the most exalted privileges. A little linguistic detail will throw definite light on the sentiments of
certain primitives in this matter. "An old man, in the language
of the Kowrarega (an Australian tribe in the neighbourhood
of Cape York) is called *ke-turkekai*. *Turkekai* means man; *ke*
(contracted form of *keinga*) is employed as a prefix to denote
the superlative degree (e.g. *kamale*, warm; *ke-kamale*, very
warm)."[1] Consequently, *ke-turkekai*, old man, means "very
much of a man": not exactly "superman," but a man in the
highest degree of the quality of manhood.

The normal life of an individual, therefore, is not pictured
as a curve, ascending during youth, attaining its greatest
height in adult life, and then descending during old age. To
primitives, it is the most advanced age that would correspond
with the highest arch of the curve.

In this way we can account for the respect often paid to old
men, and the authority recognized as theirs. In Australia, for
instance, the testimony of the very earliest observers is almost
unanimous in this matter. In South Queensland, "old, help-
less people were especially well looked after."[2]—In the province
of Victoria, at a meeting with the Yarra-Yarra tribe, the natives
"brought with them an aged head-man named Kul-ler-kul-lup.
He was supposed to be more than eighty years old. He was at
least six feet in height, fat, and with an upright carriage. His
friends—indeed all who saw him—paid respect to him. They
embarrassed and encumbered him with their attentions. . . .
None presumed to speak but in a low whisper in his presence.
. . . Whatever the old man suggested as proper to be done
was done; what he disliked was looked upon with disgust by
all the men of the assembled tribes. . . .

"The aborigines everywhere and on all occasions pay great
respect to old persons. If a number of strangers are going to a
camp, the oldest man walks first, and the younger men follow.
Amongst the Murray blacks, it is considered a very great fault
to say anything disrespectful to an old person. . . .

" 'Respect for old age,' says Sir Thomas Mitchell, 'is universal amongst the aborigines. Old men, and even old women,
exercise great authority among assembled tribes.' . . . In the

[1] J. Macgillivray, *Narrative of the Voyage of H.M.S. " Rattlesnake,"* ii, pp. 294–303.
[2] Tom Petrie, *Reminiscences of Early Queensland*, p. 116.

country occupied by the Dieyerie tribe, says S. Gason, the old men direct the movements of the people.

"On all occasions, when I have seen a number of blacks gathered together, they have shown the utmost affection to the aged persons amongst them. It has always been regarded by the principal men as a privilege to introduce to me the very old men and old women, and I have observed with pleasure the tokens of respect and regard exhibited whenever the old people spoke."[1]

"In the Kurnai tribe," we find Howitt writing, "age was held in reverence, and a man's authority increased with years. If he, even without being aged, had naturally intelligence, cunning and courage, beyond his fellows, he might become a man of note, weighty in council and a leader in war; but such a case was exceptional, and as a rule authority and age went together. The authority of age also attached to certain women who had gained the confidence of their tribes-people. Such women were consulted by the men . . . I knew two of them . . . influencing public opinion very strongly."[2]

Grey had already noted the advantages reserved for old men. "The period of old age must be as happy as any other time in the life of a savage, if not more so. Aged men are always treated with great respect; they rarely take part in any fray, they are privileged to eat certain kinds of food, which the young men may not touch; and they seldom appear to suffer much from the infirmities and diseases to which the aged are generally subject amongst us."[3] Elsewhere he remarks that these privileges often establish abuses which are revolting to European ideas. He tells us that females and young and feeble persons are doomed to a hopeless state of degradation, and to a lasting deprivation of certain advantages, solely because they are defenceless, while the benefits of which they are deprived are given to others, solely because they are old and powerful. This, moreover, is not the result of any personal violence, due to the momentary caprice or the despotic nature of any individual. . . . It is imposed on Australian aborigines by their traditional laws and customs, just as imperative and obligatory in their

[1] R. Brough Smyth, *op. cit.*, i, pp. 136–8.
[2] A. W. Howitt, *The Native Tribes of South-East Australia*, p. 316.
[3] Geo. Grey, *Journals of Two Expeditions of Discovery in North-West and West Australia*, ii, p. 248.

eyes as our laws are to us.[1] For instance, the older men of the tribes take the young women for themselves and set up veritable harems, whilst the young men cannot find wives, or else are obliged to marry old women.

Such customs are not peculiar to these Australian tribes. In many other communities old men have exercised similar domination, founded, as Grey well says, upon force. It may appear surprising that old men should prove stronger than the young or the middle-aged, but it is a question of mystic force here, and against that a man endowed with the most superb physical powers can never hope to struggle. Dread of the misfortunes he would bring upon himself prevents him from rebelling against the authority, even the tyranny, of the old. Their very longevity is already an unimpeachable sign of force. For a man to have so long victoriously resisted all the attempts at sorcery, all the insidious attacks to which he must have been subjected, proves that he must have had a good deal of *mana* or *imunu* or *tondi* within him. "Among the Bihé in South Africa, the respect inspired by these old men in the members of their family is such that the latter do not approach them without using signs of the most profound respect; the women, in particular, prostrate themselves before them. It is believed that these old men are the favourites of the *Kilulu* (spirits), and it is only the counsels given them by these spirits that have enabled them to slip out of and baffle enchantments which must have many a time endangered their lives."[2] No one therefore will risk offending an old man, even if he abuses his power in a way that tradition has moreover at last rendered legitimate. "All investigators familiar with the life of primitive tribes know that the anger of the elders has more influence upon the conduct of the younger members of the family than preaching in the higher classes or blows in the lower classes of civilized nations, for the wrath of the elders may do harm to those against whom it is directed."[3]

Conversely, the favour of the elders is believed very valuable to those who receive proofs of it. Speaking of his old friend

[1] Geo. Grey, *Journals of Two Expeditions of Discovery in North-West and West Australia*, ii, p. 218–19.
[2] L. Magyar, *op. cit.*, pp. 358–9.   [3] W. Jochelson, *The Koryak*, p. 734.

Sorkrark the Eskimo, Rasmussen exclaims: "Strange Sorkrark! When I came to leave your land, to return to civilization, you stroked your hand over my breast at parting and said to me: 'I am an old man. But all within me with forces that grow old is strong yet; and now I stroke thee over the breast to make thee strong for a long life.' "[1] The Eskimo believed that his own longevity was a proof of power, and he wanted the friend who was leaving him to share in it.

Longevity even arrives at being regarded as a quality in itself, which may be detached from the being who possesses it, and which another will seek to retain for himself to give him greater strength. Callaway says so in explicit terms. "When a serious disease invades a kraal, a doctor is summoned, not merely to treat the disease, but to give 'courage medicines.' He selects, among other things, the bone of a very old dog which has died a natural death from mere old age, or of an old cow, bull, or other very old animal, and administers it to the healthy as well as to the sick people, that they may have life prolonged to the same extent as the old animal of whose remains they have partaken."[2]

Extreme old age, however, may become suspect. The man who survives all his generation is possibly a wizard, kept in life at their expense, by making them die. "Up to a certain point, added years are looked upon as conferring honour; but among Ibibio, especially the Efik of Calabar, it is possible to outstay one's welcome in life's caravanserai." Sometimes, in a family where there is a very aged person, several of the young men die one after another. Suspicion is awakened. "Maybe the strength of their young limbs and the breath of their nostrils are drawn out to keep alight the flickering flame of the old life. He is put to death."[3] Usually, however, a man is afraid to injure people like these. Among the Ba-ila, "some old people, tired of their life, ask to be killed, or rail and curse everybody they meet, that they may be put to death. This is not done, for it is too dangerous. What makes it the more dangerous to cut short the life of old men is that in the course of long years they have accumulated perhaps many . . . charms . . . which

[1] Kn. Rasmussen, *The People of the Polar North*, p. 50.
[2] Callaway, *Zulu Nursery Tales*, p. 175, note 16.
[3] P. A. Talbot, *Life in Southern Nigeria*, p. 145.

produce discomfort, emaciation, madness and death in any one who seeks to do them harm."[1]

Finally, the last and not the least important reason for the respect which forbids an attack upon elders, and has helped to maintain their prolonged domination in certain communities, is that the mystic force of which they have given proofs in this life will be no less theirs in the next. Therefore far from getting rid of them by killing them, those who put them to death would be acquiring enemies all the more to be dreaded. Where such a belief exists, it seems difficult to overthrow their prestige. As a matter of fact, however, it is only in exceptional circumstances that this belief secures them effectual power. Usually, deference and respect alone survive.

IV

The grief, which is so poignant in its first moments, caused by the death of a loved child, a father, mother, brother or sister, is felt no less acutely in primitive communities than in our own. It sometimes goes so far as to make life unendurable, and suicides take place. But even if the member of a social group has not been the object of so tender an affection, his death is the source of profound emotion to others. The group is quite overcome by it; this fact has dealt it a serious blow. The survivors are all the more dejected, since death is regarded as contagious.

This word "contagion" has occurred to the minds of several observers. Thus, with the Sakai of the Malay Peninsula, who are fairly low down in the scale of civilization, "two sets of ideas, perhaps both present at the same time, seem to have entered their heads with regard to the death of friends and relatives: (1) that the souls of the dead may do them some evil—probably not wilfully, but through the contagion of death; (2) that the place where anyone dies must, of necessity, have been spirit-haunted before the event occurred."[2]—So, too, with the Sema Nagas, according to Hutton, "it would appear that there is something contagious about dying, and that

[1] Smith and Dale, op. cit., i, pp. 416–17.
[2] I. Evans, Studies in Religion, Folk-lore, and Custom of British North Borneo and the Malay Peninsula, p. 225.

association with death is liable to cause it in itself. . . . Possibly the fact of a man being reported dead gives malicious spirits some hold over him."[1] Such a sentiment, as we know, is universal, and it is unnecessary to multiply proofs of it. Here is just one more. Among the Itonama (Indians of Eastern Bolivia), according to d'Orbigny's report, "when the relatives believe that an illness is mortal, they endeavour to close as firmly as possible the nose, mouth and eyes of the sick man, so that death may not be communicated to another body."[2]

The primitive, however, does not conceive of contagion as we do. He has no notion of pathogenic agents which produce infection, or of the way in which contact may communicate it. He believes—we might just as well say he feels—that death is contagious, for reasons which are both physical and mystic, and which cannot be separated in his mind. Contact with the corpse renders those who touch it, who prepare it for the funeral rites, transport it to the grave and bury it, "unclean." The men and women who have taken a more or less active part in the funeral rites and have consequently been in contact with the corpse undergo a series of purifying ceremonies —or, as we should express it, they have to be disinfected. Yet it is not in this uncleanness (for such contamination is often easily nullified by the appropriate rites) that the most dreadful danger of contagion lies. It is in the dead man himself, for he exercises influence over his relatives. From more or less conscious and egoistic motives; from affection, maintain some, while others pretend it is the contrary; from jealousy of those who are still privileged to see the light of day; from fear of undertaking the long journey alone—from this admixture of emotions, the dead man seeks to carry off others along with him. On this point we have innumerable witnesses, and in spite of the diversity of motives attributed to the dead man, all are agreed in their dread of his efforts to secure the company of one or more of the survivors.

All this is very clearly indicated in an Andaman story reported and explained by A. R. Brown. "Yaramurud, having died through an accident, self-caused," he says, "becomes a

[1] J. H. Hutton, *The Sema Nagas*, pp. 242–3.
[2] E. Nordenskiöld, *Die Itonama Indianer*, quoting D'Orbigny, *L'homme américain*, ii, p. 237.

spirit, but he does so only under the compulsion exercised upon him by his mother, who, now that he is dead, insists that he must go away from the world of the living and become a spirit. The spirit then comes back to see his brother, and by this contact causes the brother's death. The story implies that it was not because Yaramurud was evilly disposed towards his brother that he killed him but, on the contrary, it was his attachment to his relative that caused him to return to visit him, and death followed as a result of the contact of the living man with the spirit. . . . Thus it appears that the Andamanese conceive that the spirits do not cause death and sickness through evil intention, but through their mere proximity, and as the legend very clearly shows, the burial customs are intended to cut off the unwilling spirit from contact with the living."[1]

Of the Bataks, we know from a report made by Warneck, "from the moment of his death, the dead man becomes the enemy of the living, even of his nearest relative." He is angry at having been obliged to "leave the world of light," and he then wishes "to drag other living beings down to death." Warneck gives too a detailed and very animated account of a native burial, taken from a Batak document, and in it we can perceive the anxiety of the survivors at the thought that their *tondi* might be beguiled by the *begu* (the dead man). —A *tondi* who had been drawn towards him was recalled.[2]— It is the same in South Africa, with the Herero. "The object of the homage rendered to the dead is to keep the spirit in a good temper so that he may not carry off the souls of the living to the abode of the dead. One day a native teacher said to a woman who was weeping in the cemetery: 'You can now let your tears fall quietly, for since you are a Christian, you need no longer fear that your relative who is buried here will come and carry you off.' "[3] And in Brincker's *Otji-Herero Dictionary* we read: "*tuerara* means 'to carry something off for oneself.' It is also said of a dying person who is determined to carry away with him someone whom he loves, saying: 'I will not leave you behind me; I am taking you with me.' It often happens, apparently, that the person in question is not long

[1] A. R. Brown, *The Andaman Islanders*, p. 299. Cf. *ibid.*, p. 216.
[2] Joh. Warneck, *Die Religion der Batak*, p. 71.
[3] *Berichte der Rheinischen Missionsgesell chaft* (1914), p. 61 (Kühlmann).

in following the one who wanted to take him to the abode of the dead."[1]

It is especially in the early days after death that the dead suffers most from loneliness, and seeks to procure companions in misfortune to accompany him. Leslie Milne has described this feeling well. "To the relatives who are left the prevailing feeling is of sorrow for the loneliness of the disembodied spirit. Palaungs do not like to be alone. From childhood they are accustomed to be always in the company of others. Children, when they are not playing together out of doors, are with the older people in their homes or in the tea-gardens or jungle. Boys always herd the cattle in company, girls meet each other in the early morning when they go to fetch water from the spring. . . . When they are ill, they are always surrounded by friends, and they seldom sleep in a room alone. It is therefore because of its loneliness that the journey of the ghost seems to a Palaung to be terrible."[2]—The same fears are met with a very long way off, among the Catios Indians of Colombia. "After the death of an Indian, his spirit is always wandering about to find a companion that it may not have to enter the unknown regions of the other world alone. All the living are afraid of being selected by the dead man. This mysterious encounter will infallibly occur if they neglect to place in each corner of the hut or at any rate on the stairs a branch of *tobo*. . . . This precaution must be kept up for about a week. When that period has elapsed the *penarata* (the spirit in the other world) leaves the Indians in peace."[3]

There is another, deeper, though possibly less conscious reason for fearing the contagion of death. The primitive's individuality, as we have already seen, is not a reality in itself, capable of being insulated. It is as it were impacted, or at any rate enveloped in its group, which is the real entity. The subjective feeling that every individual has of his own existence does not prevent his representation of himself from being inseparable from that of other members of his clan or of his sib. Frequently, as we have seen,[4] when one native is ill, the doctor prescribes a treatment or diet for him and his relatives

[1] H. Brincker, *Wörterbuch des Otji-Herero*, p. 229.
[2] Leslie Milne, *The Home of an Eastern Clan*, p. 295.
[3] Fr. Severino de Sta Teresa, *op. cit.*, pp. 56–7.
[4] Cf. *supra*, ii, pp. 87–9.

at the same time. A wife will swallow the medicine that she has come to fetch for her husband. If illness causes consternation to a group it is not because its members dread contagion, in the European sense of the word; it is because the evil influence being exercised upon one member is doubtless already reacting on the rest, by virtue of their mystic union, of the principle that is common to them all.

So, too, if death has struck down a member of the group (usually, like illness, by means of enchantment), the others feel themselves very near being attacked likewise; perhaps, even, they already are. In such a sense, to say that death is contagious is to say that when a death occurs the representation of the intimate solidarity uniting the members of the same group is present in all its force in the minds of each. The feeling of fear is then a reflex, as it were. "In Kiwai Island, natives of Fly River assert that if one of their clan dies some distance from home, at the very moment when his spirit leaves the body, a feeling of unrest comes upon the spirits of the other members of the clan, their bodies become weak, and this weakness is felt for twenty-four hours. The natives call this spirit-sympathy or compassion."[1] Thus they experience, and in their own way they express the fact, that the death of one of them, even at a distance, is "felt" by them all.

Grubb has drawn a vivid picture of the intense horror felt by Lenguas at the idea that a dead body should remain in their vicinity during the night following his decease, their haste to carry away a dying man when he loses consciousness before the day is over, and the desperate efforts he himself had to make to convince them that he was not going to die before sunset. Everything was already prepared to carry him to his grave and bury him there! With Lenguas, as with many other primitives who persist in hasty burial, the chief motive seems to be the fear of the contagion of death. They believe that the presence among them of a recently deceased person will inevitably prove fatal to the living members of his circle. To ward off this danger, the first thing to do is to get rid of the corpse, and at once begin the ceremonies which effectively separate it from them. It is, as it were, the urgent amputation of a gangrenous limb, absolutely essential if life is to be saved, for

[1] E. B. Riley, *Among Papuan Head-Hunters*, p. 297.

in this respect the solidarity of the social group may be compared with the unity of an organic being. The man who has just died runs the risk of communicating—voluntarily or involuntarily matters not—death to one or more of those "belonging" to his group. It is essential therefore to rupture, as soon as possible, the bonds which unite the dead to the survivors, and at once to remove him from among them.

There is at least one other reason for this haste. According to a widely prevalent belief, the person who has just died does not yet wholly understand his present condition. He does not know that he has ceased to form part of the world of living beings. He will not perceive it, nor really be conscious of the fact until after some time, when certain objective signs prove to him that he is no longer living. "The dead of Florida," says Codrington, "go to Guadalcanar. From time to time a canoe came over from Guadalcanar and took the ghosts across to Galaga, opposite to Gaeta. They landed first upon a rock near to the shore, and then for the first time became aware that they were dead."— "At Wanga in San Cristoval, the soul . . . departed from the body becomes a ghost (*ataro*), and the ghost on leaving the body is believed to make its way to three small islands near Ulawa. On his first arrival there the ghost feels himself still a man, and does not realize his condition; he finds friends, and gives them the news of the place he has just left. After some days a kingfisher pecks his head, and he becomes a mere ghost."[1]

In the Indian Archipelago, "the dead man's ghost (*ziel*) will not at once believe that he is dead. The priestess (*walian*) scatters ashes in front of the mortuary, and calls other ghosts from the land of the dead to convince the new-comer of his death. . . . The dead man's ghost converses with them, but refuses to accompany them. . . . Finally, it understands that its body has ceased to live . . . and it weeps."[2] Riedel very frequently refers to a similar belief. In the Watubela Islands, for instance, "if someone dies during the night, they await the dawn before informing his relatives, for the soul (*gamala*) must first of all come to itself. According to popular belief, immediately after death, the soul finds itself in the condition

[1] R. H. Codrington, *op. cit.*, pp. 256–7.
[2] A. C. Kruijt, *Het animisme in den indischen Archipel*, p. 325.

of a man who has fallen from a tree and in the first moments is perplexed and uneasy." In neighbouring islands, "when any-one dies it is customary to make a tremendous noise and bewail the event very loudly, so that the spirit (*nitu*) may become conscious of what has happened to him."[1] Among the Lenguas, too, "the soul on leaving the body is supposed to be astonished, and not to realize quite what has happened."[2]

V

The fear of contagion is but one of the manifestations of the profound uneasiness produced by death in the social group, and the reactions it brings about there. On this subject Dr. Malinowski writes: "Death, among all the coastal natives of Eastern New Guinea, causes a great and permanent disturb-ance in the equilibrium of tribal life. On the one hand, there is the stemming of the normal flow of economic consumption. On the other hand, an innumerable series of rites, ceremonies, and festive distributions, which one and all create all sorts of reciprocal obligations, take up the best part of the energy, attention and time of the natives for a period of a few months or a couple of years, according to the importance of the dead. The immense social and economic upheaval which occurs after each death is one of the most salient features of the civiliza-tion of these natives, and one also which on its surface strikes us as enigmatic, and which entices into all sorts of speculations and reflections. What makes the problem still more obscure and complex is the fact that all these taboos, feasts and rites have nothing whatever to do with the spirit of the deceased. This latter has gone at once and settled definitely in another world, entirely oblivious of what happens in the villages, and especially of what is done in memory of his former existence."[3]

It is no doubt true that the taboos, rites and ceremonies are not concerned with the deceased so much as with repairing the ills and losses that his death causes the group of which he was an integral part. Our difficulty here is to reconstitute the highly emotional representations of which we have no

---

[1] J. S. F. Riedel, *De sluik en kroesharige rassen tusschen Selebes en Papua*, pp. 211, 465.
[2] W. B. Grubb, *op. cit.*, p. 122.   [3] B. Malinowski, *op. cit.*, p. 490.

experience. In European communities the solidarity between members of the same group is no less close than among the Papuans of whom Malinowski is writing, but it is slightly different, and, if we can put it thus, less vital. The death of one of our number entails a blow for all his relatives. But the blow is neither felt nor perceived in the same way as among them. When, for instance, an important member of one of our families is cut off in full vigour, the family frequently has to suffer the consequences of the calamity—a means of subsistence diminished or lost, a lessened social position, an uncertain future for the children left fatherless, health sometimes endangered, and so forth. But serious and painful as these consequences may be, and however prolonged, they are but consequences. Death has directly attacked but *one* individual; all the rest is the result of this first occurrence. In a "primitive" community, the aspect of things is slightly different. When the head of the family or some other important member ceases to exist, the group in a certain sense begins to die also. For the real living being is the group: individuals exist only through it. Thus the group feels itself to be directly affected, for this death means the loss of some of its substance.

This appears to throw some degree of light on the mystery which arrests Malinowski's attention. In a more general fashion this accounts for the paradox we encounter in primitive communities. Though in them the individual is of far less importance in himself than in more civilized ones, the death of an adult among primitives seems to be a far more notable occurrence, and it is the cause of infinitely greater anxiety. This is because death, when it strikes, in reality deals a blow, not at the individual, but, through him, at the group itself. The existence of the group is involved, and this is in danger.

Hence the "immensity" of the reaction noted by Malinowski, the innumerable rites, ceremonies and taboos judged necessary to re-establish the social equilibrium. Hence, too, the widespread custom which demands that the death of a member of a group shall be "avenged" by that of the instigator of his death, or at any rate of one of his relatives.

The natives themselves often say that the dead man claims this vengeance, and that if the survivors neglect it they expose themselves to his wrath, which they have good reason to dread.

They cannot hesitate therefore. *They must* satisfy him in this respect, even if the vendetta entails upon them a war which will cost them dear. Again, if they were to fail in this duty, their ancestors, who watch their acts—and their omissions—very jealously, would not forgive them.

These reasons for the vendetta are clear, but they are not the only ones, nor possibly, despite appearances, the most profound. In the Australian tribes where the necessity of avenging a death seems most insistent, the dead man often has to be satisfied with a mere semblance. The avenging expedition takes place, and at the end of a certain time it returns to camp. Those who have taken part in it do not give an account of what has occurred. No one knows whether they have actually killed a member of the tribe guilty of the death of their relative, or whether they have returned just as they set out, nor will the question be put to them. The affair is over, the act has sufficed. They do not seem to think that the dead can now take offence.

What is absolutely indispensable is not therefore the satisfaction to be afforded to the dead (which will be procured in any case, if there is not too much risk involved); it is a rite which shall re-establish the equilibrium of the social group, the mystic compensation for the wrong it has suffered. In a certain sense, vengeance itself may be regarded as a compensation. Sometimes even, as Thurnwald has pointed out in the case of the Solomon Islands, it does not suffice for itself, and must be accompanied by a definite compensation.

Such was also the idea of those native tribes who could not be persuaded by the French administrator to live in peace with the neighbouring village, since there was a corpse less to their score. They must make the number of the killed equal, and then they will make peace. It is not merely the dead who demands vengeance; it is also the group that cannot do without compensation. It is not a case of demanding a material equivalent alone, for at need that might be forgone, but compensation is of mystic value, and to neglect it might compromise the very existence of the group.[1]

In tribes where the chief or the king is the embodiment and as it were the personification of the social group, as among the Kafirs, for instance, he is entitled to compensation for the death

---

[1] Cf. *supra*, ch. ii, pp. 102–5.

of one of its members, even if this be not due to an outsider. "A singular custom," says Steedman, "prevails among the tribe on the death of a man, his relatives being obliged to present an ox to the chief, by way of consoling him for the loss he has sustained through the death of one of his subjects."[1] The chief is here the equivalent of the group itself, and the "consolation" is a compensation. Col. Maclean writes too: "Kafir law seems to make little or no distinction between wilful murder and any other kind of homicide; unless it be, perhaps, that in purely accidental homicide the full amount of the fine may not be so rigidly insisted upon. All homicide must, however, be atoned for; the principle assumed being that the *persons* of individuals are the property of the chief, and that, having been deprived of the life of a subject, he must be compensated for it. . . . Compensation for all kinds of homicide is so universally insisted upon that should even a person charged with the crime of sorcery die under the torture to which he is always subjected, or be killed without the sanction of the chiefs, the 'Isizi' or atonement must be paid, unless the chief thinks proper to forgo his claim, which he sometimes does in such cases."[2] It would be impossible to illustrate more clearly the idea that homicide is primarily a blow directed at the *group*. The compensation due to the chief who is its embodiment is specially designed to restore the equilibrium that has been disturbed.

A final reason, akin to the foregoing, and bearing the same significance, intervenes here, helping to make this reparation a necessity. To the primitive's mind, one misfortune is the sign that others are about to happen. Now we know that to primitive peoples omens are the same as causes. Here is one example among hundreds. "If a great man dies, or if a large ox dies, it is said to be the beginning of evil accidents, viz., a sign that others of the same kind will follow."[3] This is not merely the popular belief expressed in the saying: "Misfortunes never come singly." In this attitude of primitives in the presence of a misfortune, especially the death of one of their members, are

[1] A. Steedman, *Wanderings and Adventures in the Interior of South Africa*, i, p. 262.
[2] Col. Maclean, *op. cit.*, pp. 60–1.
[3] J. L. Döhne, *A Zulu-Kafir Dictionary*, p. 137.

involved other representations which are more definite and which possibly are the remote and frequently forgotten source of this belief.

As long as the indispensable reparation or compensation has not been effected it is believed that the person or the group that has suffered injury is under malign influence, and consequently is in danger. Among the Dayaks, for instance, "as long as the injured party has not been indemnified—at least, this is their opinion—his welfare and tranquillity in the future are endangered. It is only when the fine has been paid (or the injury atoned for by the vendetta) that his welfare is assured, for only then, say the Landak Dayak, are the evil influences averted."

The author is somewhat surprised at what he observes. "The strange thing about this popular belief with respect to the evil influences arising from a crime or a breach of the law (*adat*), is that it is just those who are the victims that will have to suffer from such influences. It is not a question of the anger of the higher powers directed against the criminal or lawbreaker. This is in very deed a singular phenomenon, and one that contravenes those principles of morality and religion found in nearly all the peoples of the world, even the least civilized. It contravenes the belief, innate in nearly all men, that the higher powers approve of what is good, and hate what is evil. One cannot say that the Dayaks have no idea of morality; their ordinary laws show that their knowledge of good and evil is much the same as ours. . . . And yet they maintain a paradox which regards the injured party as under the domination of the powers of evil, and leaves the guilty unpunished."[1] . . . "Each slight injury, each serious offence, which is suffered brings the victim under evil influences, and not the victim alone, but the whole community. For this reason the malign influences must be made incapable of injury, in the interests of the victim and of all his group, and this is why the Dayaks' penal code demands that not only shall the wrong committed and the damage caused be atoned for through a penalty or compensation, but the evil influences shall also be neutralized."

---

[1] M. C. Schadee, "Bijdragen tot de kennis van den godsdienst der Dayaks van Landak en Tajan," *Bijdragen tot de taal- land-en volkenkunde van Nederlandsch-Indie* (1903), p. 338.

This leads to a singular consequence. "Not only is the person who has been guilty of an offence against another bound to avert the misfortune that threatens the latter; but if fate has already intervened, that is, if, according to popular belief, the person threatened has already been affected, the former is held responsible. If, for instance, the injured person or one of his family happened to die before justice had been satisfied and the evil powers disarmed, the death would simply be imputed to their influence, and the opponent would be held responsible." Schadee found the same belief prevalent in New Guinea, and Dundas noted a similar one in the Dschagga of Kilimandjaro.[1]

We now see why compensation and the vendetta (in so far as the latter is a form of it) are absolutely indispensable to the group that has suffered serious injury through the death of one of its members. It is not merely a case of satisfying an elementary thirst for justice, that demands that one wrong shall be expiated by another, or of relieving the feelings of anger provoked by violence and outrage, or even of re-establishing the equilibrium that has been disturbed. The injury done to the group has placed it, as it were, under the menace of other misfortunes. As long as the first has not been redressed, as long as the group has not been sufficiently compensated, in one form or another, the malign powers will not be "neutralized, disarmed, made incapable of injury," as the Dayaks express it. Once the compensation has been rendered, however, fate ceases to threaten, and security reigns once more.

We may therefore consider the vendetta, on the one hand, as a satisfaction due to the dead man himself and to his ancestors. But in it we must see too, and perhaps primarily, a defensive action on the part of the group against the blow that has affected it, and a means by which it may avert other misfortunes which will inevitably follow upon the first. Understood thus, the absolute necessity for vengeance or for compensation for a death is far more in keeping with the comparatively slight importance which is accorded to the individual, as such, in the primitives' minds.

[1] Ch. Dundas, *Kilimandjaro and its Peoples*, p. 155.

CHAPTER VIII

THE SURVIVAL OF THE DEAD

I

As a rule, the primitive believes in the survival of the individual. According to him, a man, once dead, although he ceases to form a part of the group of living beings, does not cease to exist. He has simply passed from this world to another, where his life goes on for a longer or shorter period, but in new conditions. The European, who very often sympathetically but uncritically ascertains the existence of this belief, hardly ever fails to recognize in it his own faith in the immortality of the soul. To quote but one example only: Taplin the missionary, a really good observer, writes: "Many men strongly question whether the aborigines of the Australian colonies believe in the immortality of the soul. I strongly assert they do; but their belief being traditional, to get a correct idea of what they clearly believe is difficult."[1] Taplin indeed realized that there was some mystery here, but he is no less persuaded that the Australian natives believed, as he did, in the immortality of the soul. They have not, however, the same idea of the soul as he had. Whence therefore did his conviction arise?

We have already indicated the principal reason for it. The difference between the representations of Australian natives and our own in this respect, although profound, is masked by certain superficial yet striking resemblances. These at once attract the notice of observers, who thereupon unhesitatingly conclude that it is a case of identical beliefs. By both mentalities death is, they believe, conceived as a separation, the departure of something, of a being that leaves the body. What they do not see is that the resemblance ends there.

According to the collective representations of communities like ours, that which departs is the "soul," a purely spiritual essence which has nothing in common with matter. The primi-

[1] Rev. G. Taplin, *op. cit.*, p. 26.

tive, on the contrary, has no idea of anything corresponding with our conceptions of pure spirit or of an exclusively material body. To him therefore, when a man dies, it is not the separation of a "soul" from a body.

Let us renounce all hasty and illusive similarities. Do not let us propound to primitives questions which escape their mentality, posed in terms involving a system of metaphysics of which they have not the remotest idea. Let us avoid asking them how they solve problems that they have never even considered. The fate of the individual in the Beyond creates no uneasiness in a primitive's mind, and he has little to say about it. Let us not try to discover in his representations the distinction we make between soul and body. On the contrary, let us endeavour to grasp them without distorting them, if we can, and not force them into the framework which befits our own concepts.

As we know, it is most frequently to present influence that the primitive attributes the circumstances in an entity which arrest his attention. If the compass needle always points to the north, it is because the instrument contains a little "spiritual being" which is always directing it to that quarter. So, too, to the Polynesians, most symptoms of illness are due to the presence within the body of an *atua* which is slowly devouring it. "The absolute ignorance of most natives respecting natural causes and the symptoms of various morbid conditions," says Casalis, "leads them to imagine illnesses, as a rule, in the form of 'a foreign body' in the interior. It is most frequently something that crawls and wriggles and runs from one particular place to another. I have known a sick man who maintained that he had a swarm of humble-bees in his stomach. . . . This false conception is turned to account by certain impostors who pretend that by *suction* they can withdraw the innumerable articles which wizards are able to introduce into the feeble human organism."[1]

In conformity with this habitual attitude the primitive, who is quite conscious of the difference between a living body and a corpse, accounts for the cessation of the vital functions by the departure of a being, a "principle" or "essence," which maintains them. This principle is neither wholly spiritual nor

[1] E. Casalis, *Les Bassoutos*, pp. 295–6.

wholly material, if we may make use of such terms here; it is both at once. Its presence acts like a mystic virtue. We recall, for instance, the "kidney-fat" of the Australian aborigines. As long as it is present or at any rate intact, it guarantees the life of the individual. It may be removed by a wizard without any wound being apparent. It may also waste away as a consequence of one of the appurtenances of the individual—his foot-track, sweaty garments, nail-parings, some of his saliva, or of his hair, etc.—having undergone the machinations of a wizard. There are manifold ways of injuring this kidney-fat and causing its present influence to cease, and then death, of a necessity, supervenes. In other parts, the rôle of the kidney-fat is attributed to the heart, the liver, blood, etc.

Nevertheless, this condition is not the only one upon which life depends. If a man's image or likeness, his double, his *atai* or *tamaniu*, his *wairua* or *mauri*, etc., be injured or destroyed, he dies, just as the man-leopard dies when "his" leopard is killed. By virtue of their consubstantiality the disappearance of the double as a rule involves that of the individual himself, since he is not really distinct from it.

In very many tribes, too, the individual comprises within himself, though without complete identification with it, a being which has its own life, and yet is himself. Such is the *iningukua* of Central Australia, the *kra* and the *ntoro* of West Africa, the *nagual* of Central America, the Malays' *nyarong*, and many other forms. Of this being, too, it must be said that as long as it is present the individual exists, but when it definitely withdraws, death at once takes place.

Moreover—and this has been the cause of endless confusion —these present influences are not independent of one another. The bewitchment of a man by means of magic practices exercised on one of his appurtenances, or on his image or likeness, while arresting the vital functions, determines the departure of his protecting genius. Conversely, the definite departure of this *kra*, *ntoro*, or whatever the genius may be, involving the individual's death, puts an end to the presence of the principle which maintained the vital functions, and which is distinct from the genius. In both cases the individual *dies*, and yet he *subsists*; it is only his condition that has changed. Cut off from the society of the living, henceforth he forms part of another group, that of the dead of his family or his clan, and by them he is received in some fashion or other. Most languages have a word to denote the individual who has passed into the state of death—*tamate* in Melanesia, *begu* to the Battak, and so forth. We have no term that corresponds exactly with these, because we do not so picture the state it expresses. "Spirit, shade, phantom, spectre, ghost, *Geist*," etc.—all these words, as well as "soul," far from interpreting the thought of primitives, misinterpret and disguise it. To render it faithfully, we shall henceforward abstain from using these fallacious terms, and we shall say "the dead man," or simply "the dead."[1]

II

Nearly everywhere primitives believe that the dead have gone somewhere else to lead a life which is fairly similar to life here below. Its details differ with different communities, but there is the same fundamental conception at the base of them all. I shall give a few examples only. In the Kai tribe of New Guinea, "as men continue their existence in the form of ghosts (*Geister*), and as they take with them to the life beyond all their qualities and powers, it is the most warlike, violent and brutal . . . that are most dreaded after their death."[2]—Among the Kayans of Borneo, "the word *urip*, in common speech, means 'alive,' but it is applied also as a prefix to the names of those recently deceased, and seems to mark the speaker's sense of the continuance of the personality as that which has life, in spite of the death of the body."[3]—In Africa, certain Bantus have the same conception. "They do not mean that at death a person is utterly extinct. It is the resurrection of the body that is denied. The person himself lives on."[4] In Uganda, in former days, the dead king was still alive. "These women in the temple were not called widows, nor considered as such, but were wives of the departed king, who was spoken of as still living. . . . In a royal temple daily inter-

---

[1] Cf. C. G. Seligmann, *The Melanesians of British New Guinea*, p. 610, and Schreuer, "Das Recht der Toten," *Zeitschrift für vergleichende Rechtswissenschaft*, xxxiii, p. 341, note 3.　　　[2] R. Neuhauss, *Deutsch Neu Guinea*, iii, p. 142.
[3] Hose and Macdougall, *The Pagan Races of Borneo*, ii, p. 34.
[4] Smith and Dale, *op. cit.*, ii, p. 103.

views were given as though he were alive, and the assembled crowds sat in front of the royal dais where the king was said to be invisibly present."[1]—With the Kikuyu, "the act of stepping over a corpse is probably considered a serious insult to the *ngoma* (spirit)."[2] (It is a serious misdemeanour on the part of the living.)—"Women," says Fr. Van Wing, "wash the body of the corpse all over," and the writer adds: "This expression *mvumbi* is a noteworthy one. It does not denote what we mean by a dead body. To the Bakongo the soul (*moyo*) is still present. By the form of the word *mvumbi* indicates a personal, living being. . . . It must be remembered that one cannot use the word *mvumbi* for the dead man as long as his body remains in the mortuary. The dead is always spoken of as if he were alive. *Mvumbi* also means 'the late' So-and-So; *Mvumbi* Nzeza, the late Nzeza."[3] This last feature is the finishing stroke that shows that in the Bakongo estimation, the dead are still alive. They are even supremely alive. "They are endowed with a life that persists, and with superhuman powers that allow of their quitting their villages underground to influence, for good or evil, the whole of nature, men, animals, plants and minerals. The most mighty chiefs on earth are also the most mighty underground."

"At the moment of burial, scarcely has the funeral procession started than the bearers totter; the dead man becomes restless, and a relative is obliged to intervene to quiet him and beg him to allow himself to be carried to the cemetery. . . . He is very carefully lowered into the grave by means of ropes and lianas. He must be laid very level, and once placed, disturbed no more, for fear of drawing down his vengeance. . . . A near relative, either man or woman, says to him: 'Give our ancestors news of us. . . .' A woman gives him some message, saying, 'You hear me, although you are no longer breathing.' "[4]

[1] J. Roscoe, *Twenty-Five Years in East Africa*, pp. 150–1.
[2] C. W. Hobley, *Bantu Beliefs and Magic*, p. 107.
[3] Fr. Van Wing, *Études Bakongo*, pp. 276–7. Cf. the ideas of the Ceylon Veddas. "A definite period elapses before the spirit becomes a *yaka*; for it appears that, properly speaking, the word *yaka* should not be applied to the spirit of the dead, for the first few days after it has left the body. During this short period, the term *prana karaya* (living one) should be used for the spirit of the deceased, for it has not yet attained the condition implied by the word *yaka*."—C. G. Seligmann, *The Veddas*, pp. 132–3.   [4] *Ibid.*, pp. 283–4.

To the Herero, "the dead man is not dead; he hears, feels, sees, thinks of the living, and punishes them. If one Herero says to another: 'God (i.e. the ancestor) is a witness of this, I shall complain to him,' the other is certain that the complaint will be heard. For this same reason they take vengeance even upon enemies who are already dead and resting in their tombs; they disinter their bodies for this express purpose."[1]—Among the Ba-ila, "I promised to send an ox," Capt. Dale writes, "and Kakobela, before he died, said he would wait for it *below*, and ordered that no one was to kill it until it came or he would be displeased. . . . The corpse was put on three dry skins, and wrapped in a blanket. . . . Fat was put all over him and his pipe put into his mouth. Then finally the people addressed him: 'Speak out your complaints now (if you have them); do not take them with you below to destroy your community.' As there was no answer, he was taken to be satisfied, and the funeral proceeded."[2]—So, too, with the Kiziba: "Priests are not buried; their bodies are taken into the woods, wrapped in cloth made of lace-bark. . . . There the body is uncovered and placed upon a seat. A pipe is put in the dead man's mouth, and near him are deposited a calabash and a reed for drinking, just as if he were still alive. They give him a covering of lace-bark, and a leopard-skin. . . . They say that wild beasts do not attack the corpse, because they take it for a living person."[3] For a final example, among the Mossi tribe, "when the body (of the *Moro-nabi*, or king) is in the grave, half a bar of salt is placed on his head, a living dog on his right, and a living cat on his left. A cock and a canister of millet are added. The cock is put there to crow in the morning, to warn the dead *naba* to get up early. The cat chases away the rats and mice; the millet and the salt are to serve the dead man for food. All this done, the pit is covered in with earth, burying living and dead alike."[4]

We might prolong our list of proofs indefinitely. We will conclude this part of our subject by quoting Grubb's words. "The Lengua cannot conceive the possibility of man's per-

[1] J. Irle, *Die Herero*, pp. 130, 198.
[2] Smith and Dale, *op. cit.*, ii, p. 110 (note).
[3] H. Rehse, *Kiziba, Land und Leute*, p. 121.
[4] L. Tauxier, *Le noir du Yatenga*, p. 351.

sonality ceasing to exist. The after-life is to him simply a continuation of the present, only in a disembodied condition."[1]

The dead, like the living, may be present at the same time
in different places. This duality and bi-presence of an individual
is no more difficult of conception to the primitive in the case
of a dead man than it is with a living man; he even accommo-
dates himself to it better. He appears to regard it as quite
natural that the corpse on the one hand and the dead man
still surviving are one and the same individual. To our minds
death ruptures the union of body and soul. The soul leaves
the body, with which it had nothing in common, and henceforth it alone lives; the body decays. But the primitive has no
conception of these as two heterogeneous substances. He knows
nothing of the independent existence of spirit as opposed to
matter, which is at the base of our metaphysics and our
religions. He does indeed perceive that the softer parts of the
body are destroyed, and he will not hear of the resurrection
of the body. Nevertheless, since the transition from life on
earth to the after-life is merely a change of condition and of
surroundings, the dead man, to him, is just what he was when
alive.

Through not having recognized this fact, the best observers
are often mistaken and run the risk of leading us into error.
"In true death," says Codrington, "for instance, the separation
of soul and body is complete." (We must remember that,
according to him, the Melanesian idea of the soul is the same
as ours.) "The *atai* or *talegi* becomes a *tamate* or *natmat*, a dead
man, and the corpse also is spoken of by the same word."
(This means that the dead man and the corpse are one and
the same being, whose duality and presence in two different
places does not prevent individuality, a significant circumstance which Codrington unconsciously notes.) "The ghost,
however, does not at first go far, and possibly may be recalled.
The neighbours therefore bite the finger of the dead or dying
person to rouse him, and shout his name into his ear, in hopes
that the soul may hear it and return."[2] What Codrington calls
the "soul" here is evidently the dead man, to whom he elsewhere gives the name of "ghost." He himself has once remarked

[1] W. B. Grubb, *op. cit.*, p. 116.   [2] R. H. Codrington, *op. cit.*, p. 226.

this fact, although its bearing escaped him. "It is a strange thing," he says, "that in the islands of the New Hebrides nearest to Aurora, in Pentecost and Lepers' Island, the word *tamtegi* is used for soul, for this is no doubt the Mota *tamate*, dead man; the natives, however, have persisted in their assertions that they have no other word."[1] This is exactly what I say, too. The natives do not know what the soul or spirit is; they know only the man, whether alive or dead, with his appurtenances, his *atai, tamaniu,* semblance, etc.; they have a name to designate him when he has ceased to live here below, and has entered upon his post-mortal state. This name means "dead man," and there is no good reason for translating it "soul."

The dead man, after having quitted his relatives, remains in their neighbourhood for the first few days. Most frequently he is invisible, though he may sometimes appear in the form of an animal. He does not definitely remove himself until certain ceremonies have been carried out.[2] His vicinity is disturbing to the survivors, and their grief is mingled with dread. They are afraid of contagion, and they fear that the dead man will carry off with him companions in misfortune. They endeavour therefore to pacify and cajole him, to allay his irritation—for at this time, the dead is often very hostile to the living, because he is jealous of them—and they are careful to do nothing that may afford him a pretext for punishing them. How does this anxiety of theirs show itself? By the care bestowed upon his corpse, either when it still remains where it was when the body turned to clay, or where it has been exposed or buried. The corpse, then, lying in the hut or buried in the earth, and the dead man wandering about the bush, are to the primitive one and the same individual—he who yesterday was a living being in their midst, and who to-day is living another life elsewhere.

Thus the seeming duality of the corpse and the ghost by no means excludes their consubstantiality. Just as the wound inflicted on the leopard appeared on the body of the man-leopard, so too, whatever affects the corpse is felt by the dead

<hr />

[1] R. H. Codrington, *op. cit.,* p. 253.
[2] Details on this subject will be found in R. Hertz's "La representation collective de la mort," *Année sociologique,* x, p. 120, *et seq.*

man himself, even if far away. There are numerous rites and customs the real significance of which is due to this point of view. The unconscious, non-sentient body, already in the first stages of decomposition, is treated as if still living; it is warmed, fed, etc.; what is more natural, if it is but one with the absent dead who continues to live? What other means can there be of satisfying the needs of the latter? To offer the corpse what is supposed to be desired by the dead man is literally offering it to himself, since the two are but one. This is no mere hypothesis. The facts which follow, by way of example, prove that in addressing the corpse, it is really with the dead man, living elsewhere, that the native believes him-self to be treating.

In Queensland, "a space in the ground underneath the body, about four feet square, would be cleared bare of grass, and at one side of it a small fire would be built. This was that the spirit of the dead might come down in the night and warm himself at the fire, or cook his food. If the body was that of a man, a spear or waddy would be placed ready, so that the spirit might go hunting in the night; if a woman, then a yamstick took the place of the other weapon, and her spirit could also hunt, or dig for roots."[1] Roth says, too: "For a week or two" (after the death) "the nearer relatives . . . go in parties to the burial-place, being afraid to go singly on account of seeing the deceased's *Moma* (shade, ghost) possibly. Tobacco, matches, food, a pipe, etc., may be left each night at the grave-side, and the individual departed openly informed to that effect."[2]—In the New Hebrides, "the existence of the soul (*Seele*)—that is, the dead man—is conceived in a wholly material fashion. The deceased is interred in his hut that he may not be without shelter. Food is brought him to support life, and in places where the corpses are wrapped in matting, it is because the matting has become a kind of money, and the dead man must be accompanied to his grave by his wealth."[3]

The dead appear to be extremely sensitive to cold and damp when their bodies are exposed to them. In the Dieyerie tribe,

---

[1] Tom Petrie's *Reminiscences of Early Queensland*, p. 31.
[2] W. E. Roth, *Ethnological Studies among the North-West Central Queensland Abori-gines*, No. 289, pp. 164–5.
[3] F. Speiser, *Ethnologische Materialen aus den Neuen-Hebriden und den Banks-Inseln*, pp. 312–13.

"should the weather be cold when a native dies, fires are lighted near the grave, so that the deceased may warm himself, and often they place food for him to eat."[1] In Victoria, in August 1849, a native who had died of consumption had been buried by his companions in ground belonging to a colonist. "In the month of November following a great storm of wind and rain swept through the country, and almost as soon as it had cleared off, Georgey's friends again presented themselves and begged for the loan of spade and shovel. In reply to my inquiry . . . I was told that 'poor fellow Georgey was too much cold and wet and miserable' where he was buried, and they wished to remove him. Having exhumed the body, they wrapped an additional blanket and comforter round it, placed it on a bier . . . and carried it across the creek to another spot in the paddock, and placed it in a hollow tree, all the openings in which they carefully stopped with dead sticks so that no animals could get in."[2]—"In the Trobriand Islands, I was discussing, on one occasion, with a chief the cause of the crop failure. 'It is the fault of the Government,' said he. 'In the old days we buried our garden medicine-men at death in the village; now we are compelled to carry them well outside, away out in the cold of the bush. Naturally, treated like this, their spirits refuse to look after the gardens, and famine comes.' "[3]

Among the Indians in New France, we find the same conceptions prevailing. "One thing, however, did not please them. When they were about to put the body in the grave, they saw that there was a little water in the bottom, because the snows were then melting and some water had dripped into it. That struck their imagination, and as they are superstitious, it saddened them somewhat."[4] The same Father elsewhere relates: "He tried to find out why the woman made so much difficulty about giving up the body of her son. She gave three reasons, the first being that the cemetery in Quebec was very damp."[5]

The dead man, through the intervention of the corpse, not only feels the cold; he is also hungry and thirsty. He must

[1] R. Brough Smyth, *The Aborigines of Victoria*, i, p. 126.
[2] *Ibid.*, i, p. 108.   [3] *Annual Report*, Papua (1912), p. 124 (Dr. Bellamy).
[4] *Relations de la Nouvelle-France* (1634), p. 20 (Fr. Le Jeune).
[5] *Ibid.* (1637), p. 56 (Fr. Le Jeune).

therefore be nourished, and it is to the corpse that the food necessary to the dead will be served. This is a universal custom, with which classic antiquity has familiarized us. But among the Greeks and Romans the gesture tended to become symbolical. To most "primitives," the dead literally are in need of food and drink—not with the same regularity or in as large a quantity as the living, or one could never have enough for them. But yet it is necessary to bring them food and drink at certain intervals. Otherwise they will suffer and they will wreak their wrath on the relatives who neglect them.

Thus in Kiwai Island, "a hunter once killed three pigs in the bush, after which he lost his life somehow, without ever being found. The people carried away two pigs but left one for the dead hunter, speaking among themselves, 'Ghost belong him, you me no savy, him he *kaikai* (eat), poor fellow he hard work, no good people take him pig altogether. Ghost belong him he look round, by and by get nothing, by and by hard up.' "[1] In Kiwai, too, "on the evening of the burial food is placed on the grave by members of the clan to which the person belonged. When this is completed, a fire is lighted upon the grave. The person supplying the food addresses the spirit of the departed as follows: 'This food is for you. We leave it here. We have also made a fire for you.' . . . Food is placed on the grave for five consecutive days. . . . On the sixth day the director of the sacred rites . . . addressing the unseen spirit says: 'These plants are for you. This is the last day we shall make food for you. Go.' "[2]

In many primitive communities, as long as the body is still there, its share is served out at every meal. From time to time, after the funeral, food is brought to the spot where it now rests. "It is believed that the deceased is still present after his death. This is proved by the fact that as long as the body is still in the house, the dead man has his usual share put before him at every meal."[3]—"During the time that the dead person remains in the house," says Mrs. Leslie Milne, "lacquer bowls filled with food are set at both sides of the body, near the head, at the usual hours for meals. The food at one side is for the spirit

[1] G. Landtman, in Beaver's *Unexplored New Guinea*, p. 304.
[2] E. B. Riley, *op. cit.*, p. 167.
[3] A. Hueting, "De Tobeloreezen in hun denken en doen," *Bijdragen* . . . *Nederlandsch-Indië* (1922), p. 147.

ɔf the dead person, that at the other for his guardian spirits (of whom there are two)."[1] Lastly, not to dwell longer on facts that are well known, among Akamba tribes, "the sacrifices consist entirely of food, and stress must be laid on the fact that the spirits are thought really to need material nourishment. They feel hunger, thirst, and cold, just as human beings do." The missionary, Brutzer, reports this advice given by a doctor to the elders of the tribe: "Go to N.N.'s place of sacrifice. . . . Build up again N.N.'s hut, which has fallen to pieces. He is sleeping in the open air, and because he is obliged to sleep outside, no rain will fall, lest it should cause him inconvenience. Take him something to eat, too, for he is very hungry. Give him some seed to sow also."[2]

In short, whatever is given, or refused, to the corpse will be used by, or lacking to, the dead man. The honours rendered to his body are accepted by the dead man, and so forth. . . . Upon this latter point our feelings are somewhat akin to those of primitives. If we believe that our dead are being outraged through their tombs being violated, for example, or their bodies ill-treated, we react with as much indignation as do the Melanesians, the Indians or the Bantus. Nevertheless, it seems strange to us that food and drink should be given to a dead man, that he should be covered to keep him warm, and that hunting implements should be placed within his reach, etc.

III

Seeing that the dead man's individuality is of the same type as that of the living, its limits similarly will be indefinite and indeterminate. There can be no question of the traces of his footsteps, the remains of his food, his secretions and excretions, etc. The liquid matter which oozes from the corpse, however, like the living man's saliva and perspiration, seems to be regarded as his appurtenance, and in this sense, it *is* the dead man. In this way we can account, at any rate partially, for horrible customs that have been noted in more than one place —in the Indian Archipelago, for instance, according to Riedel's

---

[1] Leslie Milne, *The Home of an Eastern Clan*, p. 294.
[2] G. Lindblom, *The Akamba*, pp. 183-4.

report. "In the Aaru Archipelago, when an adult dies, he is washed all over, dressed in accordance with his state, and coral, gold, and silver ornaments are put on him. For two days and nights he remains, in a sitting position, wedged between two pieces of wood, with his feet upon elephant tusks, and most frequently he is placed under the house and looked after by the members of the family. On the third day he is placed on a small craft (*bor*), lying on his back. That day his blood-relations come and tear off with their nails pieces of flesh from his cheeks, ears and chest, that they may swallow them down with some sirih-pinang. As long as the body remains in the house, a drum is beaten. When the *bor* has been placed on a platform outside the house, a hole is made in it, to receive the *humores cadaveris* in a gong or basin, to be able to consume them with sago, as a token of attachment to the dead, or to remain in permanent communion with him. This repulsive custom does not seem to be followed by any disastrous consequences."[1] In other places, the widows are sometimes forced to drink these humours from the corpses of their husbands.

The hair is a particularly important appurtenance of the deceased. We know that the North American Indian used to expose himself to serious danger in the hope of carrying off an enemy's scalp. It was not only to satisfy his pride in showing others the proof of his bravery, and to exhibit a trophy. The scalp possessed the same mystic value that so many primitives, in the Indian Archipelago and South America, for instance, attribute to heads and skulls. To gain possession of this appurtenance belonging to another was the same thing as becoming his master, and from the mere fact of possessing it an enemy was transformed, if not into a protector, at any rate into an ally or a servant.

But the most essential appurtenance of the dead man, as it were, the one which is in the front rank in primitives' imagination, is undoubtedly his bony framework, especially his skull. The softer parts of the body rapidly decompose and putrefy, particularly in warm, damp climates, unless there is some means of preventing this by embalming the body, as was done in Egypt and in Peru. These two countries, moreover, are very dry. As a rule, in the communities we are dealing with here,

[1] J. S. F. Riedel, *op. cit.*, p. 267.

there is no way of preserving the flesh of a corpse indefinitely; therefore the bones are all the more prized. Their very hardness, and the fact that in most regions they are immune from the influences of time, increases the religious respect in which they are held. Evidently they contain within them much of the *mana* or the *imunu* of the man himself.

To minds thus biased, the way in which dead bodies are treated, the place where they are provisionally or definitely deposited, often bear a different meaning from that which they would have in our minds. Interment, for instance, is not always for the purpose of securing their safe repose. Dr. W. E. Roth has remarked upon this very circumstance. "For the very general custom of exhumation and the uses to which the bones were generally subsequently put, it is very probable that burial of the body was not regarded in the same light as it is by more civilized people, a convenient method for its final disposal, but rather as a means toward an end, namely, the cleaning and preservation of the bones. . . . All the main Indian nations, previous to contact with European influences, practised exhumation. . . . The Warrau attained the same object by leaving the body for some time in water to be exposed to the ravages of flesh-eating fish. It is therefore a matter of but little surprise that earth burial varied from an excavation or pit to a shallow grave uncovered, or to a surface burial, etc."[1]—Fr. Colbacchini says, too: "The dead man is buried meanwhile in shallow earth and sprinkled with water. Every day at sunset his relatives come and pour water over him so that the decay of the flesh and the cleaning of the bones may be hastened."[2]

As Hertz has shown us, other motives are sometimes added to these, especially in the Indian Archipelago and Melanesia, to account for the haste shown in causing the softer parts to disappear that the bones may be liberated. "While the body is rotting," says Codrington, "the ghost is weak; when the smell has ceased, the ghost is strong."[3] And again: "In these methods of disposing of the distinguished dead, whose ghosts

[1] W. E. Roth, *An Introductory Study of the Arts, Crafts and Customs of the Guiana Indians*, E.B. Bulletin, xxxviii, p. 640.
[2] Fr. A. Colbacchini, *I Bororos orientali*, p. 156.
[3] R. H. Codrington, *op. cit.*, pp. 260, 263.

are expected to be *lio'a* possessed of power, there may be seen very probably the effect of the belief, of which mention has been made, that the ghost continues weak while the corpse continues to smell; the *lio'a* of the dead man sunk in the sea, burnt, enclosed in a case, or rapidly denuded of flesh, is active and available at once. . . . At one time they did at Saa what now they do in Bauro; they poured water on the corpse until the flesh was consumed, and then took the skull. . . ."

If so much trouble is taken to separate the bones from the decaying matter as quickly as possible, it is because, as an appurtenance, the bones *are* the dead man himself. Codrington himself explicitly says so. "Inland (at Santa Cruz) they dig up the bones again to make arrow-heads, and take the skull to keep in a chest in the house, saying that this is the man himself, and setting food before it. . . . Not long ago there was a man in Aurora, who out of affection for his dead brother dug him up and made arrows of his bones. With these he went about speaking of himself as: 'I and my brother'; all were afraid of him, for they believed that his dead brother was at hand to help him."[1] The presence of the bones was the presence of the dead: to Melanesians it is the same thing.

These representations are connected with practices, the significance of which will now be clear. In the islands bordering on Neu Mecklenburg, for example, "when the corpse buried in the ground is in a state of decomposition, the relatives dig up the skull and carefully cover it with leaves; the same is done with the bones of the humerus. On this occasion a great feast is prepared, and the skull is displayed along with the food to be eaten at the festival. Then the women are heard howling with grief as at the burial. When the feast is concluded the skull is buried once more, and it will not be disinterred again. The humerus bones will be used to fashion special spears, and these will be for the service of the relatives only. A superstitious belief attaches to this custom, for it is thought that during a fight the ghost remains beside the man who bears such a spear."[2] As in Aurora, then, the presence of the bones ensures that of the dead man himself. At any rate, the possession of this appurtenance gives the user the mastery over the dead,

[1] R. H. Codrington, *op. cit.*, p. 309 (note 1).   [2] R. Parkinson, *op. cit.*, p. 308.

and guarantees his support. In the Admiralty Islands, "when a Moa'nus dies, the corpse on his bier remains in the house until total decomposition has been accomplished. . . . When the skeleton alone remains, the women wash it carefully in sea-water. The bones of the humerus, femur and tibia are placed in a basket, and this basket and its contents are buried in a certain place. The skull, ribs, ulna and radius bones are put in another basket, and steeped in the sea for some time that they may be thoroughly cleaned and bleached. Then they are put, along with fragrant herbs, on a wooden platter which is placed in the house which the dead man inhabited when alive. Formerly the teeth were detached from the skull, and the dead man's sister made herself a necklace with them. After some time the ribs are divided up among them, the son being chosen to do this. The chief wife receives two, and the nearest relatives one each. In memory of the dead, everyone wears his rib-bone underneath his arm-ring—a custom which recalls that in Berlinhafen in New Guinea."[1]

The custom of wearing a dead relative's bones on one's own person is easily explained. The presence of this appurtenance guarantees that of the dead, and there are various motives for desiring this, even if for affection only. "It was one of the oldest native customs to cut out the tibia and fibula to make into lime sticks, also the lower jaw (worn later, when cleaned, as an ornament round the neck). This was done, curious as it seems, from feelings of alleged affection. Certain it is that they prized these bones of their dead relatives very much. Three days ago I was approached by the chief of Kavataria, who lost a ten-year-old child some little time ago. He said: 'You have put a taboo on the bones. You know my child is dead. My wife cannot sleep day nor night. She sends me to you to ask leave to open the grave and take, not a bone, but just one tooth—one little tooth.' "[2] When she is in possession of this tooth, the bereaved mother will feel that her child is beside her once more.—At San Cristoval, "in each house relics of the dead are preserved, the skull, or jawbone, a tooth, or hair. These are placed in a coco-nut-leaf basket, and hung up at the top of the main post of the house. Sacrifices are burnt below, and the smoke and savour of the burnt sacrifices ascends and

[1] R. Parkinson, *op. cit.*, pp 404–5.   [2] *Annual Report*, Papua (1913), p. 117.

is pleasing to the ghost. These ghosts are probably lately deceased members of the household, a beloved wife or child."[1]

Since the bones, especially the skull, *are* the dead man, they will be consulted, just as he himself would have been. Any question put to them is addressed directly to him. In a story related by Landtman, "the man . . . dug up the skulls of his dead parents, washed them in the water, and left them to dry in the sun. In the night he lay down to sleep on his back with one skull in each armpit, for he wanted the spirits of his parents to come and speak to him in a dream. By his side he had a heavy stick. In the middle of the night he woke up, seized the stick, and called out: 'What's the matter you two no come quick, tell me? I been sleep long time. Suppose you no come, I break him head belong you.' Then he lay down again, and after a while the parents came and spoke. . . . In the morning, the man woke up and thought, 'Oh, mother, father he been come, he been talk along me good.' And he put the skulls back into the grave."[2] A similar story has been reported from Torres Straits. "That evening Sesere went into the bush and picked a quantity of scented leaves, with some of which he thoroughly rubbed the skulls of his father and mother, and placed the skulls on the remainder. Then he lay down with the skulls close to his head, but before he went to sleep he told them what had happened to him on that and the previous day, and inquired what fish it was that ate the grass, and how he could catch it.

"When he slept the skulls made a small noise, and spoke to Sesere, telling him it was the dugong which ate the grass, and how he could take it."[3]

In another story from Kiwai Island, we hear of a man who had disappeared, whose wife had been grieving for him. With the lapse of time the body decayed, leaving the bones only. One night the corpse appeared to his wife, telling her where she would find his bones. She awoke her parents and told them of her dream. The following day the people all went to find the dead man. (We should note the significance of this

[1] C. E. Fox and F. H. Drew, "Beliefs and Tales in San Cristoval," *J.A.I.*, xlv., p. 166.   [2] G. Landtman, *op. cit.*, p. 285. Cf. *Ibid.*, p. 509.
[3] *Reports of the Cambridge Expedition to Torres Straits*, v, p. 41.

expression; the dead man and the bones are the same thing.) The wife knows the way, and the bones are found.[1]

Elsdon Best gives a portion of an address to the remains (i.e. the bones) of a man who had been buried in the territory of another tribe or clan, delivered by a man of his own tribe. "He had exhumed the remains and escorted them back to the home of the defunct one. 'Farewell, O sir! I have returned you to your people, to your very home. Farewell. Go to your ancestors, to your elders, who will welcome you.' "[2] It is the bones that he is contemplating, but the dead to whom he is speaking. The consubstantiality between the dead man and his bones is so real to the Maori that he does not distinguish between them. When his thinking becomes more logical he will say that the bones "represent," or take the place, or are a symbol, of the dead, and so on. But this symbolic way of thinking began by being realistic and emotional, and possibly as long as it is in any sense powerful, it always remains more or less so.

Conformably with these ideas, the food offered to the dead is sometimes put in front of his bones. Among the Toradjas, "the whole sacrifice to the dead should be considered as a last meal taken in their company. To realize this conception more fully, they have baskets filled with boiled rice placed in contact with the bones, after which all who are participating in the sacrifice take a part of the offering and eat it."[3]—In the Nicobar Islands, the great feast of the dead, which lasts for a month, is celebrated every three or four years. "At Nancowry, in the Central Islands, the skull is washed by the widow, or some near relation of the deceased, in the liquid of the unripe coco-nut, just in the stage when it is best for drinking. The skull is also rubbed with saffron, and afterward put on a plate on a kind of altar specially prepared for it. A hat is also placed on the skull—the kind of hat varies according to the sex of the deceased. On the hat are fastened cigarettes, about which strips of red and white cloth have been wound. Food is also served to the skull. . . ."[4]

The possession of bones, especially of skulls, may be very

---

[1] G. Landtman, *op. cit.*, p. 381. [2] Elsdon Best, *The Maori*, ii, p. 73.
[3] A. C. Kruijt, *De Bare sprekende Toradja's*, ii, p. 125.
[4] G. Whitehead, *In the Nicobar Islands*, pp. 205-6,

advantageous, since it entails the use of the mystic force attaching to the dead. This, as we know, is one of the reasons which make head-hunting such a widespread and persistent custom. "The tribe occupying the portion of New Guinea opposite Tauan and Sabai is continually at war with its neighbours. The chiefs of Sabai and Tauan ornament their dwellings with strings of skulls of New Guinea bushmen. The owners of these ghastly trophies were very averse to our touching these *malakai*, i.e. ghosts, as they called them."[1] *Malakai* or *markai* actually means "dead." In this instance the skull is therefore explicitly identified with the dead man.—In Kiwai Island, the ownership of an enemy's eyes gives the same power. "At one end of the central hall (of the darimo)[2] will be seen two circles, in which are two dots. Two small holes are made in the flooring-boards with fire. In each hole is placed a dried eye of an enemy put to death in battle. The dot-marks represent the two eyes. . . . Spirits of slain enemies are supposed to inhabit the two eyes, and when the builders of the house go forth to war, the spirits have the power of capturing those of the enemy, thus making them weak and impotent, and giving the attacking party an easy victory."[3]—In Borneo, among the Kenyahs, "Bo Adjang Ledja, before his death, had often communicated his uneasiness to me. He was afraid that the Sultan of Kutei would have his skull taken secretly out of his grave, for this sultan was already preserving the skulls of several other chiefs in a chest in his palace, as he wanted the ownership of them to give him power over the Bahan tribes."[4]—Again, in Espiritu Santo, in the New Hebrides, "people utilize the hollow human bones, particularly those of their relatives and of men of high rank in the *suque* or secret society, to make into spearheads. It is thought that the *mana* of the deceased will pass into the possession of the owner of the spear with his bones. Spears made from the bones of chiefs are specially prized."[5] And a little farther on we are told: "Strangers naturally tried also to procure for themselves spearheads made from the bones of mighty warriors or men of high rank in the *suque*, so that they, too,

[1] *Reports of the Cambridge Expedition to Torres Straits*, v, p. 298 (quoting W. W. Gill, *Life in the Southern Isles*, p. 267).   [2] The Sacred House of the men.
[3] E. B. Riley, *op. cit.*, p. 88.
[4] A. W. Nieuwenhuis, *Quer durch Borneo*, ii, p. 324.
[5] F. Speiser, *op. cit.*, pp. 205–14.

might participate in the *mana* of these dead men."—"At Ra-
kaanga and Manihiki, islands lying six hundred miles due
north of Rarotonga, if a king, priest or distinguished fisherman
died, the body, after lying three days in the grave, was exhumed,
and the head cut off. . . . The head was deposited in a finely
woven coco-nut-leaf basket, and placed in the fore-part of the
canoe as a sea-god. When overtaken by unfavourable winds on
a voyage, or drenched with heavy tropical rains, the head
would be taken out of the basket and held aloft by the hair,
whilst prayers were offered to it for favourable weather. The
hands and feet of defunct chiefs, priests, and fishermen were
used for the same purpose by people of inferior rank."[1]

The same beliefs with respect to the potency of skulls,
whether of friend or foe, is encountered in regions very far
away from the Pacific. In Gaboon, for instance, "in the case of
an 'oga' or great chief, the body was buried near the village,
sometimes even in the room in which he had died. This was so
that he might be more easily disinterred, and his head taken
away to be transferred to the fetish-case containing the remains
of his ancestors. Thereby the dead man became the protector of
his village and of his family."[2] In Siberia, in one Chukchee tale,
"a young man goes to the dead body of his father for protection.
But the corpse says: 'I cannot keep you near me. I am dis-
integrated and my house is very cold.' After that the 'spirit'
instructs the young man how to win the young daughter of a
rich reindeer-breeder. In still another very characteristic and
widely known tale, a young girl finds in the country a bare
skull, and takes it home. She conceals it in her clothes-bag.
. . ." (The mother finally finds it.) "The whole family are
panic-stricken. They flee, leaving the girl alone and without
any means of subsistence. The girl begins to lament before the
skull, and in a paroxysm of despair, she even kicks it with her
toes. The skull departs in search of its body, and soon comes
back in the shape of a fine young man, bringing along a large
herd and a long train of sledges."[3] In this story, the body, skull
and individual himself are all one.

In South America, the Jibaros of Ecuador are anxious above

---

[1] W. Gill, *Savage Life in Polynesia*, p. 104.
[2] Abbé André Walker, "Funérailles chez les anciens Mpongoués," *Recherches
congolaises*, vii (1925), p. 99.   [3] W. Bogoras, *The Chukchee*, p. 519.

all things to gain possession of the heads of their enemies. Karsten has described in detail the ceremonies of which these trophies (*tsantsa*) are the occasion and object. He says: "They (the Jibaros) do not find anything contradictory in the thought that the spirit of the slain enemy on the one hand entertains feelings of hatred and revenge against the slayer, and always looks for an opportunity to harm him, and on the other hand, at the same time, as it were, plays a rôle as his friend and adviser. The latter, it must be understood, he has become under the influence of the magical conjuration, through the ceremonies performed. . . ."[1] To possess the *tsantsa*, and to have had it treated thus, is to have the enemy himself at one's service. Elsewhere Karsten says: "That Indians actually believe that the dead can be made to live again by means of their bones was the experience of Nordenskiöld with the Guichua of Queara. When he was on the look-out for skulls and skeletons, the natives thought that he wanted to take them away to his country to bring them to life again and thus discover secrets about the gold-mines of the Incas."[2] Possibly even the natives thought it was not necessary to revive these dead men, but that the possession of their skulls would suffice, for we have just had instances where the skulls made known to those who interrogated them what they desired to learn.

Finally, since primitives recognize very little difference between men and animals, it is to be imagined that the bones, especially the skulls, of animals—above all of those possessing great mystic value—will be preserved, honoured, consulted, entreated, like the human bones and skulls. Such a custom is, as a matter of fact, practised in many different places. I shall cite but one instance only. In the islands of Tanembar and Timorlao "turtle-catching is the chief occupation of the male population. The turtle shells are preserved in the festal house, and the skulls hung up in a tree near their owner's dwelling. When they come back from turtle-catching, they offer these skulls a sacrifice of rice, sirih-pinang, tobacco and palm-wine. At the same time they invoke them thus: 'Oh, comrades, ascend the tree higher yet and call your friends! Here you have

---

[1] R. Karsten, *Blood-Revenge, War and Victory-Feasts among the Jibaro Indians of South Ecuador*, E.B. Bulletin, lxxix, p. 46.

[2] *Idem*, "Der Ursprung der indianischen Verzierung in Süd-Amerika," *Zeitschrift für Ethnologie*, xlviii (1916), p. 204, note 2.

all sorts of things to eat, rice, sirih-pinang, tobacco, whilst in the sea your friends only eat two kinds of herbs with stones, uk, uk, uk!' "[1] To us, these skulls "represent" turtles; to the natives, skull and turtle are but one.

IV

It may perhaps be convenient to differentiate what, in each community, is strictly an "appurtenance" of the dead, forming part of his personality, from that which, in a wider sense, "belongs" to him, being more akin to his "property," as we should understand the word, although at the same time implying a more or less intimate participation between possessor and possessed. Such a line of demarcation will often be very difficult to trace. In this case, as in that of the living, the limits of the individuality are very indefinite.

With the Greenland Eskimos "private property" (that which I have called "appurtenance") "is most fully recognized in the *kaiak*, the *kaiak* dress and the hunting weapons, which belong to the hunter alone, and which no one must touch. They are very rarely lent. . . . Snowshoes may almost be regarded as belonging to implements of the chase; but, as they were introduced by the Europeans, they are not considered matters of private property. . . . Next to clothes and hunting implements come the tools which are used in the houses, such as knives, axes, saws, etc. . . . Many of these, and especially the women's sewing materials, are regarded as altogether private property. Other household implements are the common property of the family or even of all the occupants of the house. . . . The Eskimo knows nothing of private property in land."[2]—Thalbitzer writes too: "The man makes his working and hunting implements himself, this being the first condition for the right of possession. . . . The weapons and implements made by the man himself are buried in his grave and are not inherited. The son inherits, however, his father's tent and *umiak*. . . . But the small personal implements closely connected with the owner's work follow him to the grave, as, for instance, the sealer's *kaiak*. Thus the personal right of possession

<hr>

[1] J. G. F. Riedel, *op. cit.*, p. 288.   [2] Fr. Nansen, *Eskimo Life*, pp. 108-9.

of these things is so strongly developed, that it has a religious character."[1] In other words, these things are appurtenances.— With respect to the Cameroons, Von Hagen expresses the same idea very forcibly. "Upon the grave are heaped up the shattered hut of the dead man, together with all its furnishings, for in even the tiniest object that he had ever used in his life, his soul (*lauona*) continues its existence."[2] And a little later he says: "In every implement used by a man there exists some portion of his soul."

In the eastern islands of the Torres Straits, the dead man's "appurtenances" are very strictly defined. "Mr. Bruce defines the term *keber* as the spiritual essence of the deceased. It was represented either by the body of the man or by any object which was regarded as his during his life or after his death. Thus, in the 'theft of the *keber*' it mattered not how insignificant were the object stolen, so long as it was regarded as part of the deceased himself. The theft of any portion of the body, or even of a post, or part of a post, used in the funeral ceremonies, was considered equivalent to disturbance of the ghost of the deceased himself. In this connection Mr. Bruce adds that by such theft the ghost of the deceased was made restless and was inclined to give trouble to his living relations . . . until they regained possession of the stolen *keber*.[3] And again, "attempts were made, usually but not invariably, by enemies of the deceased, to get possession of some part of the corpse. The proper *keber* to steal was the desiccated body or—if the body had not been mummified—the skull, and considerable strategy was often necessary to capture it. But anything might serve as a *keber*, a pebble or a piece of wood from the grave; it might even be sufficient to cut a chip from a piece of wood marking the place of burial, or break off a neighbouring twig or leaf." Therefore all these objects represent the "spiritual essence" of the deceased, by virtue of the same claim, even if not so completely, as his corpse or his skull. A man possessing them has the *keber* also within his power. The dead will not rest in peace, nor will he allow his relatives any, until these things have been restored to him.

[1] W. Thalbitzer, "Ethnographical Collections from East Greenland," *Meddelelser om Groenland*, xxix, p. 524.
[2] G. von Hagen, "Die Bana (Kamerun)," *Bässler Archiv*, ii (1911), p. 108.
[3] *Reports of the Cambridge Expedition to Torres Straits*, vi, pp. 127–8.

In another passage the author establishes a very close connection between this *keber*—these appurtenances—and the double or shadow or some sort of likeness of the individual. "The word *mar*, or more frequently *lamar*, was used to express a shadow, reflection, ghost or spirit, but it does not follow that any one of these ideas was confounded in the native mind with one of the others."[1] The accuracy of this observation has been proved more than once during our study of these matters. Primitives know nothing of distinctions which appear wholly natural to us, but on the other hand, they have some which escape our understanding. "There is another word, *keber*, which is employed very frequently in connection with death and with funeral ceremonies, but it is very difficult to gain a conception of its exact significance. Anything that is actually connected with a man in life or after death, no matter how insignificant, is looked upon as a part of the deceased, one might even consider that the natives regarded it as a part of the *lamar*: such an object is called *keber*. The pantomimic funeral ceremonies were termed *keber*, and the performers who personated ghosts were called *keber le*."[2]

From these passages it appears that the objects denoted by the term *keber* form part of the man, or rather, of the *lamar*, i.e. the man in his post-terrestrial existence. We have here, then, a very characteristic type of the dead man's appurtenances. *Keber*, moreover, comprises much more than does "appurtenance." It extends not only to everything that constitutes the personality of the deceased—his corpse, image or likeness, shadow, etc., but also to the stones and wood of his grave and even of the trees near it. These objects, as we are expressly told, form a part of him. We find it difficult to consider them true appurtenances, like the elements of the individual himself, and in this we no doubt are wrong. Perhaps here again we are imposing on that "participation" which so preoccupies the primitive mind laws which pervert it, and when we try to adapt it forcibly to a conception of individuality unknown to the primitive, we are only distorting it.

In these same islands, "if a man died who had no family, his

---

[1] *Reports of the Cambridge Expedition to Torres Straits*, vi, p. 251.
[2] As with so many general terms of this kind, which have not undergone the same logical development as our own concepts, *keber* seems to be employed as noun or adjective indifferently.

widow handed over all his effects to his male relations, who broke them up and burnt them; even stone-headed clubs were chipped into small pieces and thrown into the fire. . . . If an only son died, all his goods, and his father's also, were broken up and destroyed in the same manner; sometimes the parents collected them all inside the house and burned it down with the contents. Then they would ask their friends to go and destroy the food in their gardens, yams were dug out of the ground and chopped up, all growing food was destroyed. . . ."[1]

Such practices are very widespread and, although showing a great variety of detail, they are singularly uniform. Almost everywhere, either at the moment of death or at the first or second funeral ceremony, the relatives destroy everything that "participates" of the dead. We cannot say that all the objects thus sacrificed are "appurtenances" of the dead man, in the strict sense of the word, and that they actually form part of his individuality, but this difficulty possibly arises more from our ways of thinking, our language and our concepts than from the real underlying idea. Here, for instance, we have Seligmann's words with reference to the house of a dead man, in one of the New Guinea tribes. "It may be suggested that the house of a married individual has been so intimately associated with the deceased man or woman, a member of a strange clan, that it may be regarded as having in some measure become identical with the dead stranger, so that after the death it becomes unfit to continue in existence among the folk of the hamlet."[2] If we say that the house becomes "identical" with its inhabitant, are we not saying, as precisely as we can, that it is an "appurtenance" of his? This accounts for the frequency with which we find natives believing themselves obliged to abandon or destroy it. "The house of the deceased," says Macdonald, "is always taken down, whether he died in it or not. No one will live in that house on any consideration."[3]

It is the same thing with the house as with the other personal effects of the individual. If any one took them or used them he would not only be depriving the dead of something to which he had a right. His offence would be a much graver

[1] *Reports of the Cambridge Expedition to Torres Straits,* iv, p. 159.
[2] C. G. Seligmann, *The Melanesians of British New Guinea,* p. 13, note 2.
[3] D. Macdonald, *Africana,* i, pp. 108–9.

one, for he would be injuring the dead man's very individuality, he would be wounding and mutilating it, attacking it in its essential part, just as he might attack a living man through one of his appurtenances, and who would venture to draw down upon himself thus the wrath of the dead?

Thurnwald has expressed this idea very felicitously. "In Buin a large share of a man's possessions disappears during the funeral ceremonies. Provisions are consumed, taro plantations and coco-nut palms, which were for the dead man's personal use, are destroyed, as if they formed part of his person, and ought, with him, to pass into the Beyond where the dead live."[1]

In a way which we find very difficult to define, but which is yet beyond doubt, the dead man's individuality is implied in these objects which participate in him. Therefore the primitive does not even ask himself whether he shall keep them or not. To appropriate them for himself would be the same as mangling the dead; from motives of prudence if not from affection, such an act cannot be contemplated.

Very frequently the origin of these customs is obscured or even lost, and yet they persist. Thus, with the natives of the Purari Delta, "it has long been a custom to destroy certain coco-nuts or sage palms belonging to the deceased soon after his death. . . . No informant was ever able to supply a rationale for this practice. It does not appear to be regarded as in any way beneficial to the deceased, nor is it thought that the palms are in any way infected or rendered harmful by his death. It seems much more like a sacrifice made in grief or despair. As an informant said: 'These coco-nut palms belonged to So-and-So, who used them during his life. Now that he is gone, we do not wish to keep them.' "[2]

Often, too, Europeans obtain even from the natives' statements explanations that are incorrect. Grubb, for instance, writes: "The personal belongings and animals of the deceased are destroyed at his death, evidently with the idea that they may prove useful to him in the after-life. The reason given by the Indian for doing this is that the ghost would otherwise

[1] R. Thurnwald, "Ermittelungen über Eingeborenenrechte der Südsee," *Zeitschrift für vergleichende Rechtswissenschaft*, xxxiii, p. 346.
[2] F. E. Williams, *The Natives of the Purari Delta*, p. 219 (Territory of Papua. Anthropology. Rept. No. 5).

haunt the relatives. Now, if the ghost had no interest in these things, why should it do so?"[1] Certainly, it has an interest in them, and even greater than the Indian proclaims it. For it is not merely a case of the possible utility of these things to the dead man; it is a question of his own personality, for the objects partake of his nature, just as the appurtenances of the living are the man himself. Dobrizhoffer's Abipones acted like Grubb's Lenguas, and from similar reasons. "All the utensils belonging to the lately deceased are burnt on a pile. Besides the horses killed at the tomb, they slay his small cattle, if he have any. The house which he inhabited they will pull entirely to pieces."[2]

Nordenskiöld has noted similar very characteristic circumstances in the north-west of Bolivia. "When an Itonama dies, his soul (*mbola*) remains near the place where he lived, and it is called *chokihua*. His fields are abandoned, no harvest is reaped, for everything in them belongs to the dead. This, however, applies to adults only; no one is afraid of the dead children.

"These *chokihua* live in the forests. Every place, every once-cultivated field, and every tree has its owner, its *chokihua*. In every undertaking one runs the risk of robbing one or other of them. After their death men continue in possession of all they have owned when alive. . . . The safest way is to clear a piece that has never been cultivated.—An Itonoma never meddles with a relic that has been unearthed, or a clay utensil or any other object from old houses or former tombs, for they all belong to the *chokihua*. If excavations are made there, death will be the result." And a little later, he says: "Many Itonoma widows refuse to sell the baskets and tools made by their husbands. . . . An Itonoma may keep objects which have belonged to his dead father or mother in his possession, however. But if he wants to use them, he must ask their permission. Should he require an axe, for instance, he will say: 'I will bring it back directly.' "[3]

The following story comes from the same district. A widow without means of livelihood had become engaged again.

[1] W. B. Grubb, *op. cit.*, pp. 122-3.
[2] M. Dobrizhoffer, *A History of the Abipones*, ii, pp. 273-4.
[3] E. Nordenskiöld, "Die religiösen Vorstellungen der Itonoma Indianer in Bolivia," *Zeitschrift für Ethnologie*, xlvii (1915), pp. 106-7.

"When she came to the cross-road which led to another plantation . . . her husband stood there, and he said to her in a
threatening tone: 'So you are going to marry again, are you?
And I have not been dead a year, not even a month!' Paralysed with fear, she could find no answer to this. Then she
perceived a man coming from his field in the other direction,
and cried: 'Come and help me; my dead husband is here!'
The man hastened to her side with his bow and arrows, but the
dead man had already vanished. 'Look out!' said the man, 'he
will come and find you to-night!' The body of the dead man
was disinterred and burnt (the burning shows that he was
regarded as a sorcerer). The widow married, and two days
later, when her new husband had gone hunting, she stayed
behind in the camp. When she was alone, her dead husband
arrived, took her in his arms, and she immediately fell down
dead."[1]—Here it is not merely a case of sexual jealousy, as we
might think it. The husband takes his revenge because he has
been injured through that which "belongs" to him. His wife
is one of those "appurtenances" which may not be interfered
with, and above all which cannot be appropriated without
wronging his own personality. With nearly all primitives,
adultery is an attack on property, understood, certainly, in a
more or less mystic sense. If it is punished, it is because it is a
theft, and also for the mystic injury it involves, an injury
which may even jeopardize the life of the husband.

It is in this way that we can explain, too, the prohibitions
and often horrible obligations imposed upon widows. If they
are to be treated exactly like the other appurtenances, they
should be put to death. As a matter of fact, in the Fiji Islands
and in other places, one or more of them would be strangled,
even before the husband had breathed his last.[2] As a rule they
are allowed to live, but in a very miserable state, under the
constant supervision of the dead husband, ready to take offence
at the very slightest breach of the taboos and regulations for
mourning. Frequently the widow is obliged for many weeks
to keep company day and night with the decaying body of
her husband. Sometimes she lives the life of a recluse for
months or years. The dead man's brothers take it in hand to

[1] E. Nordenskiöld, *Forschungen und Abenteuer in Süd-Amerika*, p. 308.
[2] F. Speiser, *op. cit.*, p. 320.

see that the obligatory rites are scrupulously carried out, down to the smallest detail. They feel themselves responsible, for on them, rather than on the widow, the vengeance of the incensed man would fall. Sometimes even, before the widow can marry again, she must accomplish a rite of "disappropriation," which definitely detaches her from her dead husband.[1]

[1] Cf. *How Natives Think*, pp. 331–5, and Smith and Dale, *The Ila-Speaking Peoples of Northern Rhodesia*, ii, p. 62.

CHAPTER IX

THE DUALITY AND BI-PRESENCE OF THE DEAD (I)

I

AMONG a great many primitive peoples, if a person desires to strike at a dead man who is remote and invisible, he acts upon the body which remains. This dead man, therefore, is at once present and absent, or rather, he is present in two places (if not more) at the same time. The corpse that can be seen and the dead man who has disappeared are felt to be one and the same individual. There is abundant testimony with respect to this, and we are merely embarrassed by the difficulty of selection.

In the Brisbane district, "in the case of adults, immediately after death, some old medicine-man, not necessarily a relative, would cut off the whole genitalia of a male, the clitoris only of a female, wrap them in grass, and place them high up in the fork of a tree: this was significatory of the sexual instinct being finished with, and to prevent the spirit (*nguru*) of the dead entering into sexual relations with the living."[1] Thus the mutilation of the corpse reacts upon the dead, just as the wound inflicted on the leopard appears upon the body of the man-leopard. In both cases individuality is consistent with duality and bi-presence.

The Dieyerie tribe did not like to leave the dead to wander. "Some of the younger men were sent off to dig a grave, and the elder ones proceeded to tie the great toes of the body together very securely with strong, stout string, and then tied both the thumbs together behind the back, the body being turned face downwards whilst the latter operation was going on. . . . One would think that even a strong healthy living man could not break or rise from such bonds. In reply to me, they said the tying was to prevent him from 'walking.' . . .

---

[1] W. E. Roth, *North Queensland Ethnography*, Bulletin ix, No. 13 (*Records of the Australian Museum*, vi, 5 (1907), p. 399).

Every night for one moon (four weeks) two old men went to the grave about dusk, and carefully swept all round it; each morning for the same period they visited it to see if there were any tracks of the dead man on the swept place. They told me that if they were to find tracks, they would have to remove the body and bury it elsewhere, as the footmarks would denote that the dead man was 'walking' and discontented with his present grave."[1]—"I have already stated the very general belief that the spirit of a deceased assumes a fresh corporeal form; but I think some tribes must have thought that the re-embodiment took place sometime after death, for they displayed great care in the interment of a dead man, by firmly tying the thumb of the right hand to the great toe of the left foot, the body being doubled up, with the knees touching the chin. . . . A fire was kept burning before it for several days, and a hut was sometimes built over it. The natives seemed to think that, notwithstanding their efforts to keep their friend down, he got up and warmed himself."[2] The contradictions which the author finds perplexing arise from the fact that he does not see that the dead man's individuality comprises both the body in the grave and what he calls the "spirit," which is at a distance. The native accepts as self-evident that the body is the same individual as the "spirit" which is far away, and also that the latter has a body proper to itself. (He does not conceive of spirit as purely spiritual, nor body as purely material.) He finds no difficulty in the idea that the dead man should come to warm himself in the hut whilst his corpse is resting in its grave, where, moreover, it feels the benefit of this warmth. For the dead man and his corpse, although separated in space, in reality make but one.

The Lengua witch-doctors were very anxious to get rid of Mr. Grubb, but as he was a very powerful white magician they were doubtful what to do with him after they had killed him. They were trying to find some way of making him leave the country, once dead, even although his body would have to remain there. "They concocted the following plan, which, fortunately for me, they did not carry out, probably because they felt doubtful of their ability to do so successfully. They

[1] R. Brough Smyth, *The Aborigines of Victoria*, i, p. 119. Cf. Eylmann, *Die Eingeborenen Süd-Australien*, p. 232.   [2] *Ibid.*, ii, p. 273.

intended to surround my hut with dry brushwood after they were sure that I was asleep. At a given moment they were to fire this fuel and then, knowing that I should be blinded by the smoke and confused by the sudden danger, they intended to kill me as I rushed from the flames. But before carrying out this part of the scheme, their plan was to build little huts at suitable distances along the route I usually took to the River Paraguay in the east. They knew that when travelling I always made them prepare a rough shelter to protect me from the sun and weather, whenever time permitted. They concluded that my spirit, wandering about the neighbourhood, would be attracted by these huts, and thus be induced to take the road to the east, their great desire being that my spirit should leave their country. . . ."[1] By Mr. Grubb's "spirit," they evidently understand the dead missionary, who will be inconvenienced by the sun and the rain, although his body has been burnt.—In this there appears a belief that we shall encounter again when we treat of witch-doctors. Even though the participation, the consubstantiality, between the dead man and his corpse be ever so intimate, even though their duality be only bi-presence, the people can never be absolutely certain that when a corpse has been destroyed the dead man is altogether disposed of.

At any rate, however, they may try. Primitives will endeavour to make the dead incapable of doing injury, and therefore they will mutilate the remains, dismember the body, etc. "I was told of one tribe in the upper course of the Ogowe who, in their intense fear of ghosts, and their dread of the possible influence of the spirits of their own dead, sometimes adopt a horrible plan for preventing their return. With a very material idea of a spirit, they seek to disable it by beating the corpse until every bone is broken. The mangled mass is hung in a bag at the foot of a tree in the forest. Thus mutilated, the spirit is supposed to be unable to return to the village, to entice into its fellowship of death any of the survivors."[2] Thus, according to Nassau's explicit testimony, it is the corpse that is reduced to pulp, and the "spirit" (which we call the dead) that has gone far away, that is paralysed and unable to return. It cannot be more

[1] W. B. Grubb, *op. cit.*, p. 124.
[2] W. H. Nassau, *Fetichism in West Africa*, p. 234.

clearly shown that the two are but one.—Among the Ba-ila, "the old woman had said just before she died: 'You people neglect me, you do not bring me water and food as you ought; when I am dead I will come back and trouble you.' So a noted doctor was sent for from a neighbouring village, and after various incantations had been gone through and the people protected by his various medicines from the power of the old woman's ghost, the corpse was taken into a lonely place in the veld. And there a huge pile of firewood was collected and set alight. The doctor then cut up the corpse and threw it on the fire bit by bit. . . . When the process of cremation was completed, the ashes were scattered to the winds so that the old woman's purpose might be completely frustrated."[1] Due precautions have been taken. The body has been first dismembered, then burnt, and lastly, the ashes have been scattered to the winds. The dead woman, one with the corpse, must feel the counterpart of all this. It is hoped that she has now been rendered incapable of "coming back," but it is not possible to be quite sure about it.

So too, the Eskimo, when they have reason to dread a dead person, try to protect themselves from him by destroying his body. Three murderers have killed a man. They cut his body up in pieces and abandon it in a clump of willows. The cutting-up, etc., was done for fear of the dead man's *nappata* (soul).[2] Rasmussen tells the story of a sorcerer who had killed his second wife. "Then he cut her up, dismembered every joint, severed her head from her body, and threw it into the sea. But before he left the body, he cut out her warm heart, and ate it. Then he dragged her along the ground, a little way from the beach, and left her there." He commits another murder. "Outside the house, Christian opened the body and cut it into pieces just as he had done with Sakua's. He ate Katiaja's heart too: he did this to prevent the soul of the dead avenging itself upon him. Then he covered up the corpse with a few stones."— Lastly, having, with the aid of accomplices, killed yet another person, "as usual, they cut the body to pieces, put the head in a

[1] Smith and Dale, *op. cit.*, ii, p. 116.
[2] V. Stefánsson, *The Stefánsson-Anderson Expedition*, American Museum of Natural History, Anthropological Papers, xiv, p. 334.

kayak bladder, and threw it into the sea. The rest of the dismembered body was covered up with stones. But the eyes
were cut out of the head, and . . . Christian's mother had
them in her stone lamp all the winter. This was to blind the
soul, if it wanted to avenge itself."[1] Thus to the Eskimo mind,
as to that of the Bantu, the mutilation of the body places the
"soul" (or, as we prefer to call it, the dead) in a state of in-
capacity for revenge: we have not two distinct beings here, but
a single one. Nelson has noted the same fact. "In ancient
times, the sinews in the arms and legs of a dead person who had
been of evil repute during life were cut in order to prevent the
shade from returning to the body and causing it to walk at night
as a ghost." The same thing was done with animals. A hunter
had just brought a red fox into the *kashim*. They cut its tendons,
opened its navel, etc. "The people told me that by this ceremony the shade of the fox was dismissed either to the land
of the dead or back to the tundra, where it would be harmless.
If this should not be done, it might remain with the body and
go about in that shape, doing evil to the hunters or others in
the village. The legs must have the tendons cut. . . ."[2] The
most general custom is to pacify the animal that has been
killed. Here, for some reason that does not appear, they
endeavour to paralyse it, and the methods pursued indicate
that the dead animal and its body are but one.

II

The case of witch-doctors is very significant. We know what
terror they inspire. Often the natives desire to be rid of them
at all costs. They are made to submit to trial by ordeal, they
are tortured, put to death, but will that suffice? Will not the
dead magician be yet more powerful? When prepared to kill
Mr. Grubb, the Lengua witch-doctors asked themselves this
question, hesitated, and finally abstained from action. Would
not there be some means, if not of annihilating, at least of
paralysing the magician when dead? They frequently think so,
and it is by destroying his body, for the dead man and his
body make but one individual. Thus, with the Kai of New

[1] Kn. Rasmussen, *The People of the Polar North*, pp. 397, 300, 303. Cf. p. 336.
[2] E. W. Nelson, *The Eskimo about Bering Strait*, E.B. Bulletin, xviii, p. 423.

Guinea, "it is frequently not enough to kill the sorcerers; they are cut to pieces and their remains strewed around."[1]—In the Nicobar Islands, "the bodies of such unfortunates, being regarded as unfit for burial, were usually taken out to sea and sunk with stones, in the belief that there was thereby less risk of their spirits haunting the island; the apparent needless cruelty of maiming their victim before strangling him is seemingly explained on the like grounds."[2]

In most Bantu tribes the rule is to burn the witch-doctor, whether alive or dead. With the Ba-Kaonde, for instance, the suspected individual is obliged to undergo the ordeal of poison. "After the divination and conviction the *mulozhi* is tied up and a kind of inquisition follows to find out why he killed So-and-So, and also what manner of witchcraft was used. . . . After the inquisition the *mulozhi* is speared to death and his body is burned." A little later Melland reports that a lion, suspected of being a wizard, was completely burned.[3] In Uganda, "underlying the custom of burning people there appears to be the idea of annihilation, for the ghost is supposed to be destroyed with the body, and all fear of further trouble from it ceases."[4]

Is this quite certain? As far as the Ba-fioti are concerned, Pechuël-Loesche expresses doubt. "In destroying the body" (by fire) "or leaving to wild beasts the task of dismembering it, whilst its tissues are naturally decomposed by exposure to the air, natives believe that they have entirely avoided all danger. But what becomes of the *tschinyemba* (soul)? The destruction of the corporeal sorcerer only produces a spiritual sorcerer who, being in the after-life, is less easily reached, and therefore all the more formidable." This idea caused much consternation among the people, for they had never thought about that; it was enough for them to wreak their vengeance on the monster himself, and refuse him a grave. The *nganga* (witch-doctors) were of opinion that the evil principle was to be found in the body itself, and that it was destroyed with it, or even before it, by the poison administered, and that that was precisely

---

[1] R. Neuhauss, *Deutsch Neu Guinea*, iii, p. 102.
[2] Extract from E. H. Man's *Report on the Penal Settlement in Nancowry Harbour* (Census of India, 1901), iii, p. 193.
[3] F. H. Melland, *In Witch-bound Africa*, pp. 206-7, 221.
[4] J. Roscoe, *Twenty-Five Years in East Africa*, p. 87.

what killed the sorcerer. Others were certain that if the body were not put in the ground, but dismembered and destroyed, it would be the same with the soul, i.e. the double.[1] These replies made by the witch-doctors are significant. The first assurance recalls the well-known belief that a wizard or witch contains within his or her body an evil principle, often discovered in the stomach or intestine when the post-mortem takes place. This principle is revealed and killed by the mystic virtue of the ordeal, and it is destroyed by the fire which consumes the sorcerer's body. The reply of the others amounts to saying, though not quite openly: "The sorcerer who survives death and the corpse are one and the same being. Therefore, when we destroy the latter, we are also free from the former."

During their lifetime sorcerers have sometimes not been detected. When dead, they continue their nefarious deeds, and finally they are suspected. They are disinterred and burnt, and it is, strangely enough, discovered that their bodies are still intact. The corpses of sorcerers do not decay. This belief is found in regions that are very widely separated. Pechuël-Loesche mentions it. "The bodies of sorcerers whose malevolent activities have not been discovered, and who have received honourable burial, do not decay in the ground."—"It sometimes happens," writes Talbot, "that through superior cunning or good fortune a witch or wizard manages to elude suspicion, and dies in odour of sanctity, lamented by all. After death, such ghosts seem no longer able to conceal their evil nature, but come back to their old haunts to play all sorts of mischievous tricks upon those left behind. For example, after the death of a certain chief, many small misfortunes happened to his relatives for some years. Someone chanced to notice a small hole at the corner of one of the rooms, just above the grave. At once suspicion was aroused; since it is by such apertures that ghosts are usually thought to return. His body was disinterred (after six years) and it was stated to have been found quite fresh. . . . Upon this uncanny discovery a consultation was held as to what was best to be done. The body was burnt."[2]

According to the same author, these maleficent dead are

---

[1] Dr. Pechuël-Loesche, *Die Loango Expedition*, iii, p. 338.
[2] P. A. Talbot, *Life in Southern Nigeria*, pp. 60-1.

not necessarily sorcerers, but sometimes merely discontented, embittered people who desire to avenge themselves on the survivors. "When young men are cut off by some violent death, it has been noticed that misfortune usually befalls those left behind. . . . Sometimes sacrifices are demanded to appease the manes of the departed; but more often it is pointed out that the dead man is too angry, because of his untimely death, for his spirit to be softened by offerings. Then the only way for the family to secure themselves from further molestation is to dig up and burn the corpse, that there may no longer be the wherewithal for the spirit to work its evil will. For as the body is consumed and turns to dust, so the astral also disintegrates and can no longer come back to earth, or meddle with human affairs." Talbot's language here is tinged with "spiritism," but the natives' thought is not matter of doubt, for they believe that in burning the corpse they are at the same time liberating themselves from the dead man whom they cannot reach.

Mrs. Leslie Milne has observed a similar belief in the Palaungs of Burma. Here it is modified by Buddhist influences, but still recognizable. "If a *kar-bu* (spirit) does not go to eat of the fruit of forgetfulness, it may make its home in the dead body, sometimes leaving the graveyard to try to torment the people in the place where it lived. The body that it inhabits does not decay, but remains as it was on the day of death. A story is told of an old woman who died of fever. After her death one person after another died in rapid succession. The tenth dying person was asked, 'Who art thou?' and the answer was, 'I am X,' naming the old woman who had died. The *kar-bu* of the old woman had made its home in her body in the grave, and coming out at night it drove the *kar-bu* out of one person after another" (to take its place), "really killing them. A wise man went to the graveyard, and with the aid of some men, lifted the coffin out of the ground. They opened it, and a tiny hole through which she was supposed to have emerged was found in the coffin, exactly above her heart. Her body looked as if she were sleeping" (i.e. it was not in any way decayed). "They carried it to the jungle and cut it into small pieces, burying the pieces here and there. Then the plague ceased." And the author adds: "As the *kar-bu* of the old woman was presumably free to take up its abode elsewhere, it is difficult to understand why the epidemic ceased, unless the *kar-bu* could not find its way back to the village."[1] But the *kar-bu* was not thus free; it is bound to its body by the most intimate of participations, and the destruction of the body annihilates it. It is therefore natural that the epidemic in the village should cease when the body had been cut up into small pieces.

Let us return to West Africa. We know that in the Lower Niger district, as with many Bantu tribes, children born with teeth already through are not allowed to live: they are "Jonahs" (*porte-malheur*).[2] "I have found this custom at Brass" (says de Cardi), "but with an exception, i.e. I knew a pilot in Twon Town who had had the misfortune to be born with his upper front teeth through; whether it was because it was only the upper teeth that were through, or whether it was that the law is not so strictly carried out in the case of a male, I was never able to make sure of. However, he had been allowed to live, but it appears in his case some part of the law had to be carried out at his death, viz. he was not allowed to be buried, but was thrown into the bush, to fall a prey to the wild beasts, and any property he might die possessed of could not be inherited by any one, but must be dissipated or thrown into the bush to rot."[3] Thus this child, this bird of ill-omen, was a danger to his group, like all his kind who are, along with the sorcerers, bearers of a malevolent principle. Nevertheless, for some unknown reason he is allowed to live, probably on condition that he lives at a distance from his relatives. But this is merely a respite. Since, once dead, he may be yet more maleficent than when alive, he must be definitely rendered incapable of working ill. How is it to be done? His body is exposed to the wild beasts of the bush, and when it has been destroyed, the ill-omened dead man, one with it, will have disappeared also.

III

To the primitive the dead man's existence does not cease. It is only his life on earth that has come to an end: his life continues elsewhere, and the barrier dividing the two con-

---

[1] Leslie Milne, *The Home of an Eastern Clan*, p. 341.
[2] Cf. *Primitive Mentality*, p. 249.
[3] Mary Kingsley, *West African Studies*, p. 487.

ditions is not an insurmountable one. The living may be imagined as already dead, and the dead as alive again. Nordenskiöld very truly says: "To die one instant and to be alive again the next is a condition that constantly arises in the Indians' legends. This affords us a view of their conception of death as a mere change of form. When a man sleeps, he meets the dead, and when he dies, he is sleeping for a long time. The survivors can never be sure that the dead will not return. To the Indian, death is not a portal through which he can never return, once he has crossed its threshold."[1]

Such an attitude is not peculiar to the Indians of Bolivia. In various districts there are many tales of dead people who have returned to life, and even of others who, having every appearance of life, are in reality dead. A wizard has killed them. He considers it advantageous for himself to restore to them the appearance of life for a longer or shorter time. At first nothing in them has changed, although he has deprived them of an essential appurtenance without which they cannot continue to live long, that is, according to a current expression, he has "eaten their soul." As a matter of fact they are already dead, but their friends and relatives, and often they themselves, do not realize it. They are, as it were, "respited" dead, and their position may be likened to that of the shell to which a time-fuse has been applied.

In the south of Queensland, for instance, according to the testimony of a very early observer, "death is always caused by a *turrwan* (great man) of another tribe. When a man dies, they think that at some previous time he has been killed before without its being known to any one, even himself. Verily a strange belief! They think he was killed with the *kundri* and cut up into pieces, then put together again; afterwards dying by catching a cold, or perhaps being killed in a fight. The man who killed him is never blamed for the deed—'he had to die, you see!' (This means that he had been already 'doomed,' or even killed, without its being seen, by some wizard's agency.) But they blame a man from another tribe for the real cause of death, and do their best to be revenged. . . ."[2]

Similar ideas are found among the Papuans of the Koiari

---

[1] E. Nordenskiöld, *Forschungen und Abenteuer in Süd-Amerika*, p. 297.
[2] Tom Petrie's *Reminiscences of Early Queensland*, p. 30.

tribe in British New Guinea. "The 'Vata tandia' whom I have met have all belonged to the Koiari tribe, at the back of Port Moresby. They have the power of making themselves invisible by means of a certain dance. . . . While . . . invisible some of them enter a house, catch one of the inmates, and throw him to their friends outside, who beat him to death, not with ordinary clubs, but with a special kind of club with a very long handle. Having killed their man they proceed to bring him to life by rubbing him with their hands and muttering incantations, but he only lives for a day or two at most, and during that time he has forgotten all about the attack that was made upon him, and consequently cannot warn his friends. But after death you can distinguish a man who has been killed by 'vata,' because if you feel his limbs you will find that his bones have all been broken." Murray adds: "The practice of bringing the dead to life is not restricted to the Koiari or the Vata, but is found elsewhere in the territory."[1]

Among the Toradjas, "when a werewolf, in its animal form, approaches a man, the latter seems irresistibly overcome by sleep. When it has come right up to its victim the werewolf takes its human form once more (although its body has remained in the house). The victim has fallen down in a swoon, and the werewolf tears his body to pieces, opens the abdomen, takes out the liver and eats it. Then he puts the body together again, closes it up, and licks it with his long tongue. The man returns to his former state, and knows nothing of what has happened."[2]

To comprehend such strange conceptions, in which the primitive mind sees nothing extraordinary, we must set aside the significance we attach to the word "death," and try to arrive at the primitive's meaning of it. To him death is not an irreparable breach separating the individual from the world of the living for ever, since his body returns to dust, whilst the soul, spiritual and immortal, alone survives. It merely signifies an abrupt and profound change in the individual, which does not prevent him from continuing to exist in spite of the decay of his body. It is such a "death" as this that the young men die in the course of their initiation tests, to be born again imme-

---

[1] J. H. P. Murray, *Papua*, pp. 216–17.
[2] A. C. Kruijt, *De Bare sprekende Toradja's*, i, pp. 255–6.

diately afterwards: it is a mystic change of individuality. So, too, at a certain stage in the initiation of the Aranda medicine-men, the candidates are put to death, and their bodies denuded of their organs. Then they are recalled to life and provided with new organs: another mystic change, which has made them a kind of supermen.—It is in this same sense that we are to understand that sorcerers make their victims "die," and then revive them.

Often in these cases of unperceived death (*mort larvée*), the life that does appear is very precarious, and the sorcerer has taken care that the man should not be long in actually dying. Often, too, to secure a personal advantage for himself, he has merely sought to transmute the individuality of his victim. Junod has described such a circumstance in detail. "Their object may be, not to kill their victims, but *to use them as servants*, for ploughing their fields, cutting their wood, and so on. One day footprints of a leopard were seen in a mealie garden near the Shiluvane station. People were convinced that this was nothing but a bewitched person, sent during the night under the form of an animal to serve the owner of the field; it is said that the *baloyi* (sorcerers), when assembled in the *hubo*, choose those whom they like amongst the victims they have overcome by . . . their magical inspiration, and change them into leopards, hyenas and snakes, compelling them either to till the fields or to uproot mealies in the gardens of others, and to 'lead' the stems and plant them in the gardens of *baloyi*. A Nkuna of Thabina once pretended having witnessed such a case of nocturnal theft—and he was expelled from the country because, as people said, he could not know of such deeds if he were not himself a *noi* (sorcerer)."[1] This last feature pertinently calls to mind that all these events occur on the mystic plane and escape the perceptions of the ordinary man. How could this Nkuna have been able to see what is invisible to all, except sorcerers? The death of the victims, their transformation into animal-servants, their work in the fields, are of the same order as the wound caused by the tooth or bone that has been "pointed" from afar by the sorcerer, and which has entered the victim's body without his skin bearing the slightest trace of it.

[1] H. A. Junod, *op. cit.*, ii, pp. 470-1.

Instead of killing persons thus, and restoring their lives by transforming them, the sorcerer may find it easier and more advantageous to duplicate them. With the Ba-Kaonde, for instance, "the doctor puts some special medicine inside a reed-buck horn, and then places the reedbuck horn inside a roan antelope's horn. This renders himself and the horns and the clothes he wears invisible. . . . When he wants a person— say, as his slave—he goes, unseen, to where that person is. Arrived there, he places his hand on the person, and jabs the point of the roan horn into the ground by him, so that it sticks there—upright. The horns then assume the shape and attributes of the person, who simultaneously becomes invisible like his captor. The doctor can thus remove him easily.

"Both invisible, they proceed to a big pit which the doctor has previously dug. . . . In this 'dungeon' the invisible captive is placed.

"Meanwhile the substitute man, though it looks like the real man, behaves like him and talks like him, is very weak: he soon gets ill and dies. The doctor—still invisible—has been watching for this, and is present at the mourning and at the burial. When the burial party leaves the grave, he puts medicine on it: the grave opens and he thus recovers his horns and medicine. He takes them back. . . . His prisoner is now visible again and is sold as a slave. (He will never be missed, as the people all think he is dead and buried.) A Kaonde chief says he had a brother-in-law stolen in this way."[1] Another witch-doctor, instead of antelope horns, uses a stick surmounted by a human head in miniature, made from human flesh. This stick becomes the "double" of the victim.

With the Ba-ila it is pretty much the same as with the Thonga described by Junod, but without the victims being transformed into animals, however. "The man may be alive at the time, but the witch abstracts his 'soul,' and what is left is only the empty shell, and of course that soon withers, and the man dies; or the warlock waits until the actual death, and then impresses the disembodied spirit into his service. . . . He may send it to fetch the grain out of another person's field. The owner does not notice the theft, for to all appearance the grain is still there. But it is only phantasmal; the essence has

[1] F. H. Melland, op. cit., pp. 214–15.

S

been abstracted."[1] In other words, all these proceedings have taken place on the mystic plane.

It is the same in the Congo. "The Baluba sorcerers assert that they can steal away a man's personality, and leave his body a mere mindless automaton, 'an empty ear of corn.' They pretend to accomplish it thus:

"A negro is walking calmly and thoughtlessly along: suddenly he hears his name, looks round and sees nothing; slightly disturbed, he pursues his walk, but hears himself called again; again he looks round and sees nothing. He is now filled with the paralysing dread that his soul has been called out of him, stolen by an invisible Muloshi; he is no longer more than a shadow of himself, an image which before long will dissolve, unless he betakes himself in all haste to a magician. Meantime the sorcerer who has cast the spell or played the trick pretends to have deposited the wraith of his victim in a carefully closed jar or in a hollow figure."[2] Here the sorcerer exercises no other outrage on his victim than to call him by name without letting himself be seen. This is enough to be able to rob him of his "soul," as other sorcerers rob a man of his liver or his heart. This "soul," like the heart and the liver, is an essential appurtenance: if the individual be deprived of it, or if it be affected, he can no longer remain alive. But the sorcerer can arrange for the man's death to be respited.

Sometimes, even, he makes himself master of the dead whom he himself has not killed. He brings them out of their graves to appropriate them to himself. "Among the Anang people, north of Ndija, a strange superstition obtains. The inhabitants are credited with going to the graves of those newly dead, and there making a sacrifice to ensure the aid of evil spirits. After this they beat upon the mound with a plantain stem—the African tree of life—calling, at each stroke, on the name of the corpse till, at length, the dead man is said to arise from his grave. Then the sorcerers bind him at once, and sell him into captivity far away."[3]

[1] Smith and Dale, *op. cit.*, ii, p. 96.
[2] Sir H. H. Johnston, *George Grenfell and the Congo*, ii, pp. 660-1.
[3] P. A. Talbot, *op. cit.*, p. 63.

IV

Side by side with these cases in which, by the act of a sorcerer, individuals, apparently alive, are in a state of unperceived death, there are others, more rare, in which a dead man, exceptionally mighty as a magician, himself comes back to life, spreading terror around him. Grubb gives us an excellent example of this, which we interpret after a somewhat different fashion from his. Seriously wounded by a native, he had managed, despite extreme weakness and loss of blood, to regain the mission station. "On getting near the mission," he writes, "the Indians appeared shy and frightened, although not so much as they afterwards became. The fact of the matter was the people had had time to think, and reports had been circulated and had reached them that I had actually died, but that in some mysterious way I had been resuscitated. This was a possibility of which they had no precedent, and could only be accounted for in their minds from the fact that I belonged to a class to which they attributed abnormal powers. . . . But, more than this, the doubt had arisen as to whether the being inhabiting my body was really mine or that of another. Many for a time doubted my real identity, and attributed the marvellous way in which, in my critical condition, I had managed to cover the sixty miles between the scene of the attack and their village, to the probability that the soul animating my body was other than human."[1]

The missionary then brings forward several facts to support this interpretation of the Indians' belief. "I was sitting one day, resting in a deck-chair in the shade, and as the position of the sun changed it was necessary for me to move farther into the shade. I was far too weak to carry the chair myself, although strong enough to raise myself up and crawl a few paces, so I beckoned to a girl . . . to come and move the chair for me. She had known me for many years, and was moreover somewhat of a pet of mine, yet she approached with evident caution, and keeping at a respectful distance from me, she caught hold of the chair, placed it hurriedly in the shade and then, with an unmistakable look of fear, ran off to the village.

"On another occasion a man to whom I was very well known

[1] W. B. Grubb, *op. cit.*, p. 264.

inquired, at a safe distance, after my health. He then said: 'What is your name?'—'Yiphenabanyetik, of course,' I replied. (This was Grubb's Indian name.)—But he, with an incredulous look, said: 'I know it *was* Yiphenabanyetik; but who are you now?' The people seemed assured of the identity of my body, but the puzzle to them was, who was inside?

"One day, when sitting in the same spot in the shade, I saw a party of Kisapang approaching. They had arrived in the village on a visit of courtesy to me, and were now being formally conducted into my presence by Esoabyabam, one of the Lenguas, who led them to within about twelve paces of me. Waving his hand in my direction, he turned to the Kisapang, and introduced me by saying in a very solemn voice: 'There sits the soul of Yiphenabanyetik.' My visitors respectfully stood at a safe distance, and after conversing in whispers for a few minutes, retired, evidently glad to leave my uncanny presence.

"These incidents afford evidence that the Indians believed I had actually died, but doubted whether or not I was the living embodiment of my former self. Some years after, Mechi, the chief, actually assured one of us that although he knew I was still the same Yiphenabanyetik, nevertheless he was convinced that I had died."[1]

It appears as if this chief had very well expressed what was in the minds of his people. The missionary, who knew the Lenguas wonderfully well, would not have been mistaken if, in this respect, his mind were not previously biased. He takes it for granted that, to them as to himself, the soul is a spiritual guest that abandons the body when a man dies, and that this spiritual being is the person's real ego. According to his view the Indians, persuaded that he had actually died, consequently believed that his "soul" or "ego" had left his body at the moment of death, and since he was once more alive, were wondering whether it was the former "soul" or "ego" which now inhabited his body, or whether it were another. But the Lenguas, like all other primitives, have no idea of such a psychology or metaphysics. To their minds the person who dies survives as he is, but in another place, and in other conditions, than those that were his in the land of the living. In the case we are considering, what frightens them is that, contrary

[1] W. B. Grubb, *op. cit.*, pp. 266–7.

to the usual state of affairs, the dead man seems to be continuing to live as he did before. Mr. Grubb at a given moment ceased to live, yet his body is not decayed: this dead man goes on breathing, walking, talking. Such a thing is unprecedented. The missionary must be a magician of unheard-of power; what may he not be able to accomplish?

This fear explains the attitude of the Lenguas in the instances quoted. The little girl who hesitates to approach is afraid of Mr. Grubb because, living as he appears to be, he is really dead, and a powerful magician. The man to whom he is known, and who asks his name, wants to know whether the Yiphenabanyetik who has passed through the gate of death is indeed the Yiphenabanyetik whom they had formerly known. Lastly, to interpret as well as we can the mind of the Indian who introduces the Kisapang to the missionary, saying solemnly: "Here sits the soul of Yiphenabanyetik," we will disregard the word "soul," which is the writer's own. No doubt the Indian merely wanted to say: "Yiphenabanyetik, who has died, and is alive again, sits here." The feelings of dread and uneasiness experienced by the Indians at sight of him are not a matter of doubt, and Grubb is quite right to lay stress upon them. But they do not arise from uncertainty as to his actual identity, as he imagines, attributing to them his own belief in the soul as the spiritual tenant of the body. What they fear is a dead man with all the appearance of a living one, or (which amounts to the same thing) a living being who has actually experienced death.

Mrs. Leslie Milne recounts a similar circumstance. "I was told that arrangements were made one afternoon to bury a Palaung who was believed to have died that morning. A tremendous rainstorm began before the coffin was closed, such a tempest of rain that it was decided to put off the funeral till next day. After a few hours, to the surprise of everyone, the dead man sat up in his coffin. From that time he was given the name of A-jung. (The Palaung word *jung* means rain.) His family, who had believed him to be really dead, must have often wondered if another spirit had entered his body, although he appeared to be the same.[1] "This is the question which Grubb believes the Lenguas to be asking about *him*. Mrs. Leslie Milne's

[1] Leslie Milne, *op. cit.*, p. 292.

note is too much abridged for us to be able to get anything really precise out of it, but in any case it is not rash to believe that the Palaungs, like the Lenguas, are disturbed by the presence of a dead man returned to life.

V

The mind of the primitive recognizes no fundamental difference between entities, even between those which we call animate and inanimate beings. In varying degrees, all participate in the same *mana, imunu, tondi*, and so on. For all of them life and death are pictured as of the same general type. As a matter of fact, animals, plants, inanimate objects, all have "doubles" like men, and these "doubles" form part of their individuality, really are themselves. What has been said above regarding the relations of the human individual with his double, likeness, reflection, etc., is no less true, *mutatis mutandis*, when we are considering animals, plants, and inanimate objects.

This serves as an explanation of apparent peculiarities in the usual behaviour of primitives—for instance, in the way in which they dispose of the offerings and sacrifices made to ancestors, spirits, and gods. When they themselves consume the ox or the fowl they have offered to an ancestor, we are tempted to think that they have merely accomplished a symbolic ritual action before proceeding to their own repast. But such symbolism is hardly natural to the primitive. He usually gives all his actions their natural and full significance. The dead suffer from hunger, thirst, cold, etc. They must have clothing, they must be provided with warmth, and given food and drink. Nevertheless, it is only in very rare cases that they have found that the dead have lightly nibbled the food put within their reach. How, then, do they feed on it?

In British New Guinea, "the food of the feast *kairi pei* (sky-food) was dedicated to the spirit of the deceased in whose honour the feast had been made. During the night preceding the first day of the feast, the spirit was supposed to extract from the food its *aipo*, likeness, form, essence, and what was left of the food was regarded as minus the essentials of ordinary food, but good enough for such an occasion."[1] Likeness, form, essence—

[1] J. H. Holmes, *In Primitive New Guinea*, p. 162.

these are the very same expressions as those used by Codrington and Elsdon Best to denote these "doubles," that are integral elements of men's individuality. The ancestor who receives the offering of food and consumes its "likeness," really appropriates its essential reality, and thus he is in communion with the one who offers it and who eats the flesh itself.

Some observers see only cunning and trickery in this. "The Torres Straits Islanders hold feasts in honour of the dead, who are supposed spiritually to partake of the *essence* of these offerings. The cunning offerers, after entreating the good offices of the dead in consideration of these gifts, eat the food themselves, pretending that the essence is gone."[1] But, at least as long as the conceptions retain their original significance, as long as faith in the presence and the power of the ancestors maintains its empire over the primitives' minds, there is no trickery in this. Those who sacrifice do not pretend to offer the food to the dead; the latter partake of it as actually as the living who eat it afterwards. To these natives who find no difficulty in accepting the double existence of one and the same object, and its presence in two different places at the same time, the "essence" or "likeness" of the ox or fowl is the animal itself. The dead man—who can no longer eat meat as the living do—is entirely satisfied with his share. If he considered himself the victim of a hoax, his vengeance might be a terrible one, and the "primitive" would never run the risk of provoking it.

Speiser has rightly laid stress upon this point. "When the native seems to combat the idea that pigs and inanimate objects have a soul" (the writer is referring to a passage of Codrington's) "he does so, possibly, because he feels that there is a difference between the soul of man and that of a pig. But on the other hand, he does believe in a 'shadow-soul' of pigs and inanimate objects; otherwise, the funeral offerings that he brings to the dead for his life beyond the grave would have no significance."[2] And again he says: "In Maevo, the funeral feast of a dead man of exalted rank will be held on the fiftieth day. . . . The villagers kill pigs, the dead man's brother takes the tips of the liver from all the pigs sacrificed, carries them

[1] W. W. Gill, *Life in the Southern Isles*, pp. 202–3.
[2] F. Speiser, *op. cit.*, p. 318.

into the forest, calls the dead man by name and says: 'Here is something for you to eat.' . . . When several pigs are thus sacrificed, it is auspicious for the dead; but if there are not any his life in Hades will be a miserable one. . . . This is clearly admitting that the pigs sacrificed are for the nourishment of the dead in the next world, and that their souls follow him thither also." Here "soul" is evidently synonymous with "double, likeness, essence," that is, from the primitive's point of view, the equivalent of the animal itself.

Some examples, taken from different localities, will no doubt suffice to show that these same representations, though more or less distinct, and to some extent modified, are current everywhere. "Of the manner in which offerings are supposed to be received by the deity to whom they are offered," writes Skeat, "it is difficult to obtain very much evidence. I have, however, frequently questioned Malays upon this subject, and on the whole think it can very safely be said that the deity is not supposed to touch the solid or material part of the offering, but only the essential part, whether it be 'life,' savour, essence, quality, or even the 'soul.' "[1] This is precisely what the Papuans and the Melanesians have just given us to understand.

Among the Eskimo whom Stefánsson studied, in the course of the treatment of a sick man, "each time the *keyugak*" (a spirit in the shaman's service) "is to return to a fresh attempt after failure, he must be made some small present of something he specially asks for to pay him for each effort. If he asks for a pair of mittens, mittens will be made, often of miniature size, and put under the sick person's bedding, hung over his head, or given to the shaman. The spirit (*keyugak*) will then have new mittens, which are the *ta-tkoit* (souls) of the mittens made for him."[2] It is the same with the Eskimo of Bering Strait. "The persons who are making the feast . . . take a small portion from every dish and cast it down on the floor as an offering; then each takes a ladle of water and pours a little on the floor so that it runs through the cracks. In this way they believe that the spiritual essence of the entire quantity of food and water from which the small portions are offered goes to the shade. This essence of the offerings is believed to be transported

[1] W. Skeat, *Malay Magic*, p. 73.   [2] V. Stefánsson, *op. cit.*, p. 375.

mysteriously to the abodes of the shades and thus supply their wants until the time of the next festival. After these offerings have been made the festival maker distributes the food that is left among the people present, and all eat heartily."[1]

The Indians of New France had the same ideas. "They bury, or enclose with the bodies of their dead, biscuits, oil, skins, hatchets, vessels and other implements, in order that the souls of their relatives may not be in poverty and need in the after-life, for lack of these things, for they imagine and believe that the souls of these cooking vessels, hatchets, knives, etc., and all that they dedicate to them, especially at the great feasts in honour of the dead, go to the other world to help the souls of the deceased, whilst the bodies of these skins, hatchets, cooking vessels, etc., remain in the graves and tombs with the bodies of the departed. This was their usual reply when we told them that the rats and mice ate the oil and the biscuits, and that rust and decay did away with the skins, the hatchets, and the other tools they buried with the bodies of their friends and relatives in the grave."[2] The Indians derived no personal advantage from the food and the objects they thus placed at the disposal of the dead. They were not ignorant of the fact that these offerings were the prey of animals or eaten up by rust and corruption, but they were none the less persuaded that the dead would make use of them. These foodstuffs and these objects therefore had an invisible existence in addition to the visible one. It was this invisible existence, wrongly termed "soul"—it would be better to call it image, likeness, essence, double, or some such term—which, being consubstantial with the thing itself, would be of use, as the missionary Sagard tells us, to the dead in the other world.

In South Africa, this "likeness" of the foodstuffs to the food itself is so strong that a sorcerer can use it to cause his victim's death. "Food is worked upon. The verb here used is *kuindanka* (meaning, to turn over and over, reshape, transform). The reference is not to the poisoning of food in the ordinary sense of the word, though we do not deny that some witches may be mere poisoners. The meaning is this: the warlock takes food in his hands, says some incantation over it, and sends

[1] E. W. Nelson, *op. cit.*, pp. 364–5.
[2] Fr. Sagard, *récollet*, *Le Grand voyage au pays des Hurons* (1632), pp. 233–4.

forth a phantom of the food, which appears in the man's dish as if it were his own food, but which in reality is full of a deadly essence that, entering his body, will kill him. So when the account speaks of a chief being killed through his milk, it does not necessarily mean that it was poisoned; but in some way the milk was 'worked upon' by the witch, either by actual contact or by *actio in distans*."[1] Does not this "double" of the milk very closely recall the "spiritual tooth" that the sorcerer of Torres Straits sends from a distance to enter his victim's body?

Like plants, animals, and men, inanimate objects are therefore capable of bi-presence, and their individuality is compatible with a dual existence. This it is which permits the primitives to believe that the dead and the ancestral gods have consumed their offerings, even though they appear intact and they themselves feed upon them later.

[1] Smith and Dale, *op. cit.*, ii, p. 96.

CHAPTER X

THE DUALITY AND BI-PRESENCE OF THE DEAD (II)

I

THE dead, as a rule invisible, appear to the living in varied circumstances, and there are very few primitives who have not seen some of them, or at least do not believe that they have been seen close at hand. Since such apparitions usually cause intense emotion to those who witness them, or even wholly overcome them, we must expect to find very little respect paid to logical exigence in the representations of this class. Contradictions which would be altogether impossible in our eyes are unperceived by primitives and, in particular, the simultaneous appearance of the dead in two widely separated places at the same time seems quite natural to them.

At the very moment of death, this bi-presence may already occur. Here is a particularly definite instance. In Raketta, Fischeliinsel, Kaiser Wilhelmsland, New Guinea, "a man said to his cousin: 'We will go fishing together to-night.'—'Agreed,' replied the cousin. Night fell, and whilst they were sleeping, the first man was laid low by fever. His 'soul' (*Seele*) arose, went out, and waked the other, saying, 'Get up, cousin, day is breaking, we must go fishing.' The cousin arose, and both embarked and set off during the night.

"At this instant, the man in the village died. They adorned his mortal remains in the usual way, and decorated him with ochre; whilst his soul in the boat (i.e. his 'double') put on the same adornment. The two fishermen rowed on, approaching Tagalip. Then the man said to the 'soul': 'Cousin, row on this side; there are fish here.' The soul did so; the man did not look round him at all, his gaze was wholly fixed on the fish, but as they passed along a cliff the man said: 'Come and sit here, and look after the fish, and I will sit at the back.' Then it was the 'soul,' the ghost (*Gespenst*) that was watching the fish while the man rowed.

"They reached Tagalip, when the man who was rowing slowly at last perceived that it was a ghost with whom he was associated, and he thought to himself: 'This ghost is going to devour me!' So, whilst they were passing along under a cliff, the man laid down his oar gently and noiselessly, got on to the outrigger of the boat, and climbed up the rock. The ghost continued to drift on alone in the boat, while the man was already going in the direction of the village.

"A little later, the ghost saw a fish and said, 'Cousin, stop paddling; there are plenty of fish here.' The fish swam away, and nobody stopped the boat. Then the ghost looked round to see what was happening, and now he found that the man had disappeared and he was all alone. He started up, fastened his teeth in the prow, broke it off and let the boat sink. He jumped out on to the cliff, climbed it and began running after the man. . . . But the man had already reached his house and shut the door, and he kept inside. The ghost first of all sought him in the village, but without success. Then he retraced his steps, and came to his own place in the village of the dead (*Geister*). A little later, his body was brought out of his house and placed in the grave.

"Then the man said: 'You wanted to subdue me with cunning, but your soul (*nitu*) was not able to devour me. You have done for yourself, however; go to your village empty-handed.'"[1]

From this story we gather that the duality and the bi-presence of the dead merely continue as they were in his life-time. The man who suggested a fishing expedition to his cousin is kept away by fever. He remains at home, and it is his "soul" (a very unsuitable expression, but we have no exact equivalent for the native word; it would be better to say his "double") that goes to wake the other, and sets out with him. Thus the man is in his hut and in the boat at the same time. He dies, and is prepared for burial, and at the same time his double is also found to be decorated with the funeral trappings and painted with the ceremonial ochre. Could the participation which makes one and the same person of the man lying dead in his hut and his double in the boat be more clearly shown?

---

[1] O. Dempwolff, "Eine Gespenstergeschichte aus Graged, Deutsch Neu Guinea," *Zeitschrift für Kolonialsprachen*, ix, pp. 120–1.

And now the man is dead and his double has become a ghost. (The word *Gespenst* used by Dempwolff, possibly does not render the native word exactly.) Suddenly, probably because day has dawned and the funeral trappings become visible, the living cousin realizes that it is a dead man, that is, the "double" of a dead man, who is accompanying him and, seized with dread, he escapes without attracting attention. The dead man's "double" does not perceive his flight until later, and after an unsuccessful pursuit, he reaches the village of the dead; therefore when the obsequies are taking place, he is far away. At this moment the corpse is being carried out of the house and laid in the grave. The man who has escaped from the "ghost" says to the dead man who is being buried: "You wanted to devour me, but you have not been able to." He is of opinion, therefore, like the rest of the spectators, that the corpse just laid in the grave, the dead man himself, and the dead man's double, who has pursued him and who is now in the village of the dead, are one and the same individual only. The dead man and his double are confounded at one time and recognized as distinct at another, just like the living man and his double.

II

Very often the dead, especially in the first few days after the decease, appear in the shape of animals. Codrington has reported several instances of such a belief. "In Florida a man planted in the bush near Olevuga some coco-nut and almond-trees, and not long after died. Then there appeared among the trees a white kandora cuscus, a great rarity. This was assumed to be the appearance of the dead man, now a *tindalo*, and was called by his name."[1] Thus the ghost was at once a *tindalo*, i.e. a man continuing his existence in the other world, and an animal manifesting itself in the midst of trees that he had planted when on earth.—"Upon the grave (at Motlav) was set a bamboo vessel of water . . . and a little dish with a roasted yam in it; as the food was eaten by rats they removed it, for the rat might be the deceased himself, at any rate during the five days that the ghost remained about the place." In the

[1] R. H. Codrington, *op. cit.*, p. 177.

Solomon Islands, "sharks are in all these islands very often thought to be the abode of ghosts, as men will before their death announce that they will appear as sharks, and afterwards any shark remarkable for size or colour which is observed to haunt a certain shore or rock is taken to be someone's ghost and the name of the deceased is given to it. . . . Sharks are very commonly believed to be the abode of ghosts in Florida and Ysabel and in Savo, where they are particularly numerous; hence, though all sharks are not venerated, there is no living creature so commonly held sacred as a shark, and the *tindalo* of the shark . . . seem even to form a class of powerful supernatural beings."[1]

Yet other animals may be dead men who are manifesting themselves. "There was a story current of an alligator which would come out of the sea and make itself at home in the Florida village in which the man whose ghost it was had lived; it was called by his name. . . . A lizard seen to frequent a house after a death was taken to be the ghost returning to his old home. . . . The sacred character of the frigate-bird is certain. . . . Just as many ghosts take up their abode in sharks, many also, and powerful to aid at sea, are those who abide in these birds."—"In the New Hebrides," says Codrington again, "some men have the power, as the natives believe, of changing themselves into sharks."[2] We have already seen what these men-sharks are. This duality, this animal and human coexistence which primitives recognize in certain individuals, is believed by them to extend also to the dead. The presence of the latter, in the shape of sharks or of frigate-birds, does not prevent them from dwelling at the same time in the "land of the dead." This bi-presence does not arrest the primitive's attention, and if anyone remarks upon it to him, it does not worry him. Codrington has said that the "ghost" spirit of the dead man has its abode in the shark, alligator, or whatever it may be. But the ghost (*tindalo*) is not the "spirit" of the individual; it is the individual himself, passed from the living to the dead state.

In San Cristoval "a great many ghosts become incarnate into animals. It may be wondered in what way natives determine the particular animal into which the *ataro* of a dead relative has entered. It depends partly on where the man is

---

[1] R. H. Codrington, *op. cit.*, pp. 179–80.   [2] *Ibid.*, p. 187.

buried. It is a common practice to bury in the sea both chiefs and common people, and their *ataro*" (i.e. they themselves, now dead) " naturally become incarnate in fish, especially in sharks. . . . It may be also an octopus, a skate, a turtle or a crocodile. . . ." [1]

The same authors describe how certain men participate in certain animals, without presenting this participation as an identity of substance. They show this intimate connection being established during the individual's life-time, and persisting after his death. "When a man or woman grows old, natives watch to see whether any animal persistently associates itself with them. This is often a bird. The bird comes to the house and perches on the old man's shoulder. It must be a young bird. It is fed and treated respectfully as the future home of the man's soul. His children will not eat any bird of that sort. This taboo seems to last only for a generation. There is a man now living at Raumae whose father's *ataro* went into a hawk. This man cannot kill any hawks or eat them, though other people do so quite freely. . . . Or again the *ataro* may go into a stone or a tree. This is known by dreams after a man's death. . . . A man will say, 'I cannot eat such and such a fish or bird, because it is my father or my mother.' Such beliefs of connection with animals should be compared with the Banks' Islands beliefs in a *tamaniu*."[2] The resemblance is, indeed, evident. If, as I think I have shown, the individual and his *tamaniu* are consubstantial, if both, as primitives conceive of them, are one and the same individual, is it not natural to say as much of the living or dead individuals in question and the animals with which they are "associated," or within whom they "have their abode"?

"At Ulawa there were two familiar sharks who were widely known and respected. . . . One of them has been slain, but his rival is still said to exist. These ghost-sharks did not harm their worshippers, but were often sent by them to kill men at a distance. . . . The following account of the proceedings in such a case comes from Ulawa, but it applies equally well to San Cristoval. At the village where Huaahu (one of these sharks) was venerated, if it were decided to send a shark on such an

---

[1] C. E. Fox and F. H. Drew, "Beliefs and Tales of San Cristoval," *J.A.I.*, xlv. (1915), p. 161.   [2] *Ibid.*, pp. 161–2. Cf. *supra*, ch. iv, pp. 142–6.

errand, Huaahu was called by the priest, and told to go for his servants. Presently he returned with the other ghost-sharks, who would then fall in, their noses in a straight line. The next thing was to select one of them for the job, and this ghost-shark was given some of the earth on which the victim's spittle had fallen, or some of the earth from his footprints in the sand. The ghost-shark named then went off accompanied by a ghost-skate, his helper," and finally the man is killed.[1] These sharks *are* dead men, existing moreover at the same time in the abode of the dead. They are not merely the home of the *ataro* or of the "soul" of the dead : they are the dead man himself, and are not distinct from him. "One of these sharks, known throughout these islands, was partly human. The head was that of a shark, but part of the body, and the legs, were those of a man." Is not this the exact counterpart, among the dead, of the men-animals and the animal-men we have met with among the living?

In Samoa the presence of the dead in an animal, or rather, his apparition in animal form, is implicit in the custom here related. "Another singular custom was that they would go to the spot where any of their friends had been killed, and would spread a piece of native cloth on the road. Then they would wait until some animal such as an ant, lizard, spider, or anything living, crawled on it, when they would at once fold it up in the cloth, and take it away for burial. What the exact meaning they attributed to this is, I do not know, but it was always done when possible."[2] Turner reports the same fact, but in greater detail. "The unburied caused great concern. . . . On the beach, near where a person had been drowned, or on the battlefield, where another fell, might be seen, sitting in silence, a group of five or six, and one a few yards before them with a sheet of native cloth spread out on the ground before him. Addressing some god of the family, he said : 'Oh! be kind to us! Let us obtain without difficulty the spirit of the young man!' The first thing that happened to light upon the sheet was supposed to be the spirit. If nothing came, it was supposed that the spirit had some ill-will to the person praying. That person after a time retired, and another stepped forward, addressed some

[1] C. E. Fox and F. H. Drew, "Beliefs and Tales of San Cristoval," *J.A.I.*, xlv. (1915), p. 163.   [2] G. Brown, *Melanesians and Polynesians*, pp. 170-1.

other god, and waited the result. By and by something came, grasshopper, butterfly, ant or whatever else it might be; it was carefully wrapped up, taken to the family, the friends assembled, and the bundle buried with all due ceremony, as if it contained the real spirit of the departed."[1]—This account is very instructive, and its concluding words, rightly interpreted, give its significance. In Samoa, as elsewhere, it is not the "spirit" of a dead man that is buried, it is the dead man himself. He it is, therefore, who appears in the form of grasshopper, ant, or whatever it may be, and to him the funeral honours are accorded. Yet to the Samoan mind, this does not imply that he is being incarnate in such an insect exclusively. The likeness between this and other facts of the same kind leads us to think that we have here bi-presence. The dead is the insect that appears on the native cloth, and at the same time an inhabitant of the other world. In the Indian Archipelago, the belief in animals that are at the same time human beings has been frequently attested. In many parts of Java and Sumatra "it is commonly believed that the souls of men from time to time pass into the bodies of crocodiles. These crocodiles possessed of human souls are not only harmless in themselves, but they even protect the inhabitants of the place. They are their relatives. . . . In Bangka, the crocodile is the object of great veneration. . . . To kill it is considered a great crime. . . . The natives hope to become crocodiles after death."[2]—This last feature shows that these ideas hold good for the dead also, and if freed from the animistic form in which they are couched, we can recognize in the representation of these crocodiles bearing a human soul within them the "doubles" of men, i.e. these men themselves.—Among the Battaks of Si-Baloengoen, "to very aged men who have always led exemplary lives is attributed the power to disappear suddenly and to be metamorphosed into tigers, elephants, or snakes; these wander about the world without ever doing any harm to men, and they leave to their congeners the task of punishing the bad and incorrigible."[3] Between these very aged men and the dead the transition is a very easy one.—Riedel says too: "The *nitu* or *natmate* are the

---

[1] G. Turner, *Nineteen Years in Polynesia*, pp. 223-4.
[2] Dr. T. Epp, *Schilderungen aus holländisch Ostindien*, quoted by A. C. Kruijt, *Het animisme in den indischen Archipel*, pp. 189-90.   [3] A. C. Kruijt, *Ibid.*, p. 198.

spirits of the ancestors (in Tanembar and Timorlao), honoured as guardian and domestic gods. When invoked, they come from the island of Nusnitu (north-east of Seelu), and passing through an opening made in the roof, they enter, for a time, their skulls, or the wooden or ivory effigies made to represent them and placed on the top of the house, in order to consume the sacrifices and to lend their aid to the people of the house. The *natmate* can also assume the forms of kangaroos, birds, pigs, turtles, dugongs, crocodiles and sharks. Many people meet their death through not having sacrificed to the *natmate* they have encountered in their dreams."[1]

The dead very frequently reappear as birds. "At Silindoeng in Sumatra I was told that the little birds that steal the rice in the fields are the souls of the dead who gather together to feast upon the rice cultivated by their descendants."[2]—The Toradjas have the same belief. "Mice, black snakes, lizards, frogs are all incarnations of the souls of the natives' ancestors, who appear in this shape to claim their share of rice, and on this account the natives hesitate to drive them away."[3]—In North Borneo, among the Dusuns of the up-country villages, "I noticed in 1915 that in one of the fields on the hillside near Tambatuan, a single tree was left in the middle of the clearing. Guessing that this was not preserved without some good reason (according to native ideas), I made inquiries and was told that it was customary to leave a single tree standing 'lest the birds, having no perching place, should curse the crop.' A similar custom obtains among some of the Dyak tribes of Sarawak, where it is said that the tree is left as a refuge for the spirits of the jungle which has been felled."[4] Thus these natives are torn between the desire and the need to protect their harvest from predatory birds on the one hand, and the fear of offending the dead who come in this very form to feed upon it, on the other. The latter sentiment is the more powerful, for we have seen that the natives dare not neglect to provide the dead, who have become birds, with their share.

This is far from being an isolated instance. In all latitudes the behaviour of the natives with respect to such and such

[1] J. G. F. Riedel, *op. cit.*, p. 281.
[2] A. C. Kruijt, *Het animisme in den indischen Archipel*, p. 176.
[3] *Id. Die Bare sprekende Toradja's*, ii, p. 256.   [4] I. Evans, *op. cit.* pp. 38–9

animals in many cases appears at times strange and even inexplicable. We must, however, remember the representations of which we have given some examples. In forms of being in which the white man perceives only *animals*, the primitive discerns at the same time *men*, and if in addition these animal-men are dead, the fear and respect they inspire are doubled. It is by this consideration that the primitive regulates his action.

Hutton reports the following circumstance: "I was going up from Zubza to Kohima with Srisalhu of Khonoma, when we met a large snake in the road. I started to beat it, but Srisalhu would not join in. When I had killed it, he said that it was *kenna* (taboo) for him to kill snakes. The reason was that his home in Khonoma, or rather his father's home, had been inhabited by a snake. When Srisalhu removed to a new site, the snake appeared in the new house. It still lives in Srisalhu's house, and is frequently seen, having survived two rebuildings. This fact impressed Srisalhu, who talked it over with the other men of his kindred, who considered that a man who had a snake like that in his home ought not to kill snakes at all. . . . If Srisalhu's descendants are prolific, this *kenna* will doubtless in time affect a whole kindred. In conclusion, I cannot do better than quote Mr. Hodson. 'What these facts seem to prove is the existence in this area, not so much of totemism, as of a mental attitude, a *Weltanschauung*, which in other parts of the world has permitted totemism to flourish and prosper.'"[1] What they prove, at any rate, is that in the minds of the Nagas there are always present ideas which relate to men-animals and to the bi-presence of the dead.

Among the Lhota Nagas, "no member of a household in which a death has occurred may take the life of any creature, whether animal, bird, or insect, till the days of *genna* (taboo) are accomplished and the soul has finally left for the Land of the Dead, in case the creature killed should be the dead man in another form." This is very clearly put, and to this passage Hutton adds a note: "All the Naga tribes that I know hold these two conflicting beliefs as to the life after death, regarding the soul as inhabiting a butterfly or other insect, and also as continuing an anthropomorphic existence. The discrepancy

[1] J. H. Hutton, *The Angami Nagas*, p. 397.

does not seem to occur to them till pointed out, and not to worry them much then. 'Who knows?' is all they say.' "[1]—Why should it worry them? What is a discrepancy to Hutton is to them merely bi-presence. It is not in the least surprising to them that the same individual should be both a man and a butterfly at the same time, and whether it is a case of the living or of the dead, conceptions of this kind are equally familiar to primitives.

III

According to the belief of a great many Bantus, especially in South Africa, the dead appear chiefly in the form of snakes. In Döhne's *Zulu-Kafir Dictionary*, for instance, "*i-hlozi* means apparition; the ghost of a deceased person. (This word expresses the transmigration of souls. A person is supposed to become an *i-hlozi* at his death, and enters into a kind of snake, in which form he appears after death whenever it is necessary to commune with those he left."[2] Let us set on one side this transmigration of souls, for the Kafirs, before knowing any missionaries, had no idea of the "soul." But even from Döhne's comment it is clear that the snake is indeed the ancestor himself, and to the Kafir the two make but one, for he adds: "Everything good or evil is ascribed to the *i-hlozi*—for the good he is praised, and for the evil he is offered sacrifices."

For his part Callaway writes: "It is said that men turn into many kinds of animals" (after their death). "It is said that one becomes a wasp, another an *isalukazana* (kind of lizard), another an *imamba* (poisonous snake), another an *inyandezulu* (green *imamba*), but the greater number turn into the *umthlwazi* (harmless snake), which may be green or brown." And in another place he says: "These snakes are known to be human beings when they enter a hut; they do not usually enter by the doorway . . . they do not eat mice, etc. If the snake has a scar on the side, someone who knew a certain dead man of that place who also had such a scar comes forward and says: 'It is So-and-So. Do you not see the scar on his side?' "[3] This last

---

[1] J. P. Mills, *The Lhota Nagas*, pp. 118–19.
[2] J. L. Döhne, *A Zulu-Kafir Dictionary*, p. 140.
[3] Callaway, *The Religious System of the Amazulu*, pp. 196–7, 200–1.

feature recalls the leopard-man on the corresponding part of whose body was to be seen the wound that "his" leopard had received.[1]

The presence of these men-snakes reassures the living about the feelings of the dead with respect to them. If they do not show themselves, anxiety is felt. "After the dead man has been interred, and the snake has been seen on his tomb, it is expected in the house that he has occupied in life. If it does not appear, a buck or a bullock will be sacrificed to invite it to visit the house. Should the snake still remain invisible the witch-doctor is sent for, and he cuts the buck's throat. If the animal cries out it is a good sign. . . . We say: 'Come back to your house, so that we may now see you.' We ask, too, 'Why are you angry with us? All our cattle are yours, and they always will be. Do you want more meat? You have only to say so, and we will kill a bullock at once for you; we shall not refuse you that.' Then the charm is fixed up in the rafters, and the witch-doctor assures the family that the *itongo* will soon appear in a dream. All this having been accomplished, as soon as ever a snake enters the house, they all regard it with close attention, to note whether it will escape when it perceives people near it. If it does so, it is not the *itongo*. If it remains quiet, it is then known as the house snake, the tame snake, the *itongo* of the house."[2] It is the snake hoped for; the dead to whom sacrifices are offered, and who is entreated to come. The natives do not differentiate between the two. A little further on the author adds: "When a tribe or part of a tribe goes to another place, and the *itongo* is not seen in the new village, they believe that it has remained behind in the old one. Then they cut down a bough of wild mulberry and carry it to the old home. They offer a sacrifice, singing the *itongo's* favourite song, so that it may say to itself: 'My children do indeed feel they are forsaken, seeing that I am not in their midst!' Then the bough is dragged towards the new village, and possibly the *itongo* will follow in its tracks, or reveal in a dream why it withdraws its presence." Throughout this passage Dr. Wangemann has not once used the word "soul." It is merely a question of the dead (*itongo*) in his snake form.

[1] *Vide supra*, ch. v, p. 160.
Dr. Wangemann, *Die Berliner Mission im Zululande*, p. 17.

Among the Xosa Kafirs, "after the death of a great chief, his house and all his personal effects are destroyed. The grave is surrounded by a hedge, and every year, when the grass is burnt, people watch to see that the fire does not come within a mile of it, so that the black-spotted green snake, which is said to be harmless, in which the spirit (*Geist*) of the dead dwells, may not go away. This snake is distinguished from the others in that it is not afraid to visit the kraal, and when the latter is moved, it accompanies the village people to their new home. It is recognized 'as a friend is recognized.' "[1]

"The *Amahlozi*," Wangemann tells us, "do not all become *Amatongo*, but mainly the dead chiefs alone, for the *itongo* has a higher rank in the Land of the Dead (*Geisterwelt*) than the ordinary *ihlozi*." But both *Amatongo* and *Amahlozi* present themselves in the guise of snakes.

Are these reptiles really the ancestors or are we to understand that the latter, being distinct from the snakes, only assume their form to appear to the living? If we are to believe Callaway, the Zulus have put this question to themselves, and they realize the difficulties it involves. "Old men, when we ask why it is said that the *Amahlozi* are snakes, say: 'Because they are *Amadhlozi*.' And we ask, saying: 'Just tell us if dead men have tails?' They are puzzled there, and cannot tell us. And so we say: 'O, how is it that you do not tell us whether the *Amadhlozi* are snakes?' So they repeat the same words; they are puzzled and do not tell us, that we may understand. We understand if they say: 'The *Amadhlozi* are in snakes,' we do not understand if they say: 'The snake is an *Idhlozi*.' "[2]

The problem is succinctly set forth by these young Kafirs, pressing the old men, whose language seems unintelligible to them, for a direct explanation. If Callaway has interpreted their thought aright, and if we are not dealing here with young men in whom contact with white people has aroused a spirit of criticism, we have here, in the making, a transition from "prelogical" mentality to that which appears natural to us, because it is our own. The old men cannot account for their conception of dead men-snakes, but they adhere to it, and the logical difficulties invoked by others do not affect them, for

---

[1] A. Kropf, *Das Volk der Xosa-Kaffern*, pp. 158-9.
[2] Callaway, *op. cit.*, pp. 134-5.

this conception is solidary with the tribal traditions. How could they get away from it?

To conclude this part of our subject, here is another missionary testimony, which doubtless will appear conclusive. "The dead are changed into snakes, and people call them *amadhlozi*. . . . Nevertheless . . . some are transformed into mammals such as weasels, for instance; the very old women into a certain kind of lizard; others again, into insects: this is not very clear, however. These *amadhlozi* live underground, and it is *there* that the Zulu, in thought, conceives all his ancestors to be. . . . The life of the dead is a continuation of their life on earth. The dead have their kraals and cows, their sheep and goats, they eat and drink, and so on. . . .

"Yet with all this, they are snakes! The Zulus' idea is not that the *spirits* (*Geister*) of the dead *enter into* snakes, etc. . . . If that were how they represented the matter to themselves, it would not be so irrational and perplexing as it now is. . . . Natives who are working for white men may admit that it is the spirits that enter into the snakes, but in this they are merely repeating a word they have heard the missionaries use. *Before they have had any Christian teaching the Zulus absolutely do not know that they have a spirit.* Accordingly there is no word for *Geist* in the Zulu language. For 'spirit,' missionaries are obliged to use words which mean 'breath' or 'wind' and to introduce the idea of 'spirit' into it, and they have almost inconceivable difficulty in making natives understand that they have not only the breath of their nostrils, but also an immortal spirit that, at death, leaves the body and goes back to its own place. Zulus do not say: 'The spirits of men enter snakes.' They simply say: 'Men are changed into snakes.' Nor, when they see an *Ihlozi*-snake, do they say: 'there is a man in it,' but, 'there is a man.' One day, when the missionary Schroeder had killed a snake-*idhlozi* at Ekuhlengi, a native presented himself, and accused him of having killed his grandfather. Another time, Reinstorf, in company with a young black servant, encountered a snake on the road to Esiklengeni. The boy ran forward to kill it, but when he came close up, he started back in terror, saying, 'It is a man, Baas!'

"If they are asked the question, 'How can the dead man become a snake? Do you not bury him, and does not his body decay?'—some of them will reply: 'It is the shades (*isitunzi*) of the dead that become snakes.' Others say: 'It is the spinal cord (*umfunkulu*) that becomes the snake,' and yet others own that they do not know how it happens."[1]

With this, the hearing of the case comes to an end. This "irrational" representation which it is impossible to make clear, of dead men leading in the other world a life similar to their life on earth, who are at the same time tame snakes frequenting the house wherein they have lived, should not surprise us. It is absolutely similar to those which we studied in Chapter V. It merely implies, as they do, the bi-presence of individuals who are men and animals at the same time. To these natives the individuality of the dead is simply of the same type as that of the living.

Junod tells us that, to the neighbouring tribe, the Thonga, the dead do show themselves in human shape in the sacred forests, but very rarely. Far more frequently they appear in animal guise, as the praying mantis, for instance, or the small blue-grey snakes. These graceful and harmless little reptiles are often seen in the huts, climbing up the thatched roof, or up the reed walls. He gives the story of a sacrifice to the dead, told by a native. " 'When a man wants to offer a sacrifice, he gives a piece of native cloth, or some mealies, or some food of any kind. Even Kafir beer may be prepared, and it is all carried to the sacred wood to be given to the gods' (i.e. ancestors). 'Formerly guns and elephants' tusks and hippopotami's teeth used to be placed on the graves. You can still see them, but they have all become rusty and decayed. Yesterday and the day before this is what happened. I went to the wood, too, and then *that came out*. It was a snake, the father of Makoundjou, the master of the forest, Elephant-Face. The women fled away, scared to death. And yet it merely came to thank us; it had no intention of striking at us. It thanked us, saying: "Thank you, thank you, you are still here, children? You came to bring me presents, to provide me with food; very good indeed!" It was a huge python, as big as my leg there' (here he pointed to his ankle). 'It came right up to me and remained quite still, without attacking me. As for me, I looked at it too. It said, "Thank you, grandson, you are here again." ' '

[1] F. Speckmann, *op. cit.*, pp. 165–6.

" 'But,' I said to Nkolélé, 'is what you are telling me a fancy or a fact?'

" 'It is most assuredly a fact! These are great truths I'm telling you!' "[1]

Junod, however, does not think, as Speckmann did, that these snakes are the ancestors themselves. "It sometimes seems," he says a little later, "that the snakes are confused with the gods themselves. As a matter of fact, in the Ba-ronga religion reptiles hold a high place. The huge python that appeared to Nkolélé was, in his eyes, in close and intimate relation with his revered ancestor, since he said: 'This animal was Mombo-Wandhlopfou!' "—Is anything more needed to draw the same conclusions as Speckmann did, and recognize that the large python and the ancestor, by virtue of a close participation (or, as Junod says, relation) make but one and the same individual? —Junod continues: "On the other hand, there are pretty little blue and green snakes, quite harmless ones, too, which frequently glide into the natives' huts and which they take great care not to injure. They are all convinced that these come 'from the gods,' and sometimes they are allowed to wander about the thatch of the hut for weeks at a time without being touched. Sometimes it happens (as Spoon has told me), that one person, less prejudiced than the rest, begins to tire of this embarrassing vicinity, that he brings down the snake with his stick, kills it and throws it outside, saying, 'Now you're done for; we have had enough of you!' which is certainly treating the divinity very cavalierly.

"This last is a very significant fact, for it proves to us that it is contrary to reason to *identify* the snakes sent by the gods with the gods themselves, or to assert that the black races believe in a regular metempsychosis. That the reptiles of the sacred wood and the tiny blue snakes are regarded as *temporary incarnations* of the *chikouembo* is probable. . . . They have never had any idea of worshipping a snake."[2]

We shall have no difficulty in admitting that the Ba-ronga do not believe in metempsychosis, and that they are not snake-worshippers, but we may ask ourselves whether the person who is "less prejudiced than the rest," and who kills one of these snakes, has not been under the influence of the white men, and

<hr/>

[1] H. A. Junod, *Les Ba-ronga*, pp. 392–3.   [2] *Ibid.*, pp. 397–8.

whether this isolated circumstance sufficiently counterbalances the common belief (according to Junod himself) that the snakes are in "intimate relation" with the ancestors, that is, are the ancestors themselves. Junod concedes that they are "temporary incarnations," and this conception of the matter is one that we can more easily understand. Yet the facts in their ensemble incline us to think with Speckmann, that we are dealing here with a dual existence and bi-presence. The natives feel it to be real, even without conceiving it clearly, and they do not see the difficulties it raises. "The Zulu Kafirs," writes Casalis, "imagine that their ancestors visit them most frequently in the guise of snakes. . . . This does not prevent their addressing the spirits of their ancestors directly, or recognizing that they may exist elsewhere in a different form from that of a snake."[1]

In East Africa, among the Akamba, "a python which comes to a village is not killed, but milk is set out for it, since it is considered to bring good luck and increase to the cattle; this belief is shared by many Bantu tribes. . . . According to some Akamba the *aimu*, or spirits of departed kinsmen, sometimes take up their abode in a python or green mamba, and for this reason these snakes are not killed when they are found in the neighbourhood of the villages. . . . On the other hand, a python which is encountered in the woods is killed out of hand. All pythons are not inhabited by spirits, but only those that, by going into a village, show that they indubitably take a special interest in it."[2] Lindblom would readily admit, as Junod does, that these are "temporary incarnations" of the dead. "It does not seem that the natives think that the spirits dwell permanently in these animals, but they only occasionally avail themselves of this method of visiting their living relatives. A wild cat used sometimes to come in the evenings near the mission station of Mulango, and a little food used to be thrown to it. The people said it was a deceased relation, and even mentioned the name. . . . When a wild animal so far departs from its usual habits that it approaches human beings fearlessly, it is thought that a special reason must exist. It cannot be an ordinary animal. These animals must not be confused with the totem animals . . . which are not considered to be

---

[1] E. Casalis, *Les Bassoutos*, p. 259. [2] G. Lindblom, *The Akamba*, p. 119.

reincarnated *aimu*."[1]—To the primitive's way of thinking, as we have seen,[2] *any* animal which behaves in an unusual way is not merely an animal, like the others; it is at the same time a human being. To this we must now add: this human being is sometimes a living being, and sometimes a dead one. Bi-presence is as natural to the one as to the other. Here we have one more proof, if proof were needed, of the fact that the life of the dead is a continuation of that of the living.

Among the Tongas, "in returning to the land of the living, spirits were supposed most commonly to take other than human forms. They might visit their former haunts either in the form of snakes, lions, leopards, crocodiles or other animals, and by such transmigrations either express their wishes regarding the living or work on them their revenge. If some few days after the burial of a man or woman a snake was seen to haunt the *makunthu*, the relatives made no doubt about its being their deceased relative returned in this guise. On no account would it be interfered with; they rather left it to come and go as it chose, even if it entered their houses. . . . If any of these creatures, tenanted for the time being by a spirit" (which means, regarded as the dead man himself) "was killed accidentally or on purpose, there followed both wailing and strife. The offence was serious. . . . One day, meeting one of these snakes . . . I seized a stick and promptly killed it, when, looking very reproachfully at me, the woman said: '*Wabaya chiwanda*,' i.e. 'You have killed a spirit.' " (The writer had already said that the word *chiwanda* was also used to designate a corpse.) "She meant, I believe, not that I had killed the spirit itself, but cut off its chance of visiting former haunts by killing the form it made use of."[3]—By the light of what has gone before, this woman's reproaches are comprehensible. The *chiwanda* is the dead man himself, appearing in the form of a snake, and one with it. By killing the snake, the writer had killed the dead man, just as in wounding a tiger, the hunter wounds the man who is its double. To kill a dead man is no absurdity to these natives, believing as they do that life in the next world continues the life on earth, and that there a

---

[1] G. Lindblom, *The Akamba*, p. 180.   [2] Cf. *supra*, Introduction, pp. 43–49.
[3] A. G. MacAlpine, "Tonga Religious Beliefs and Customs," *Journal of the African Society*, v (1906), pp. 264–7.

man eats, drinks, suffers heat or cold, and also dies. Do not let us confuse survival, which is universally admitted by primitives, with immortality, of which they have no idea.

To conclude the subject of these Bantu representations regarding the individuality of the dead, I cannot do better than quote E. W. Smith's reflections on the matter. "We speak of our beloved dead as if they were in heaven, while at the same time many of us think of them as ever near us. Some among us also naturally cling to the idea that they sleep their last long sleep in God's acre. So the African will say, in almost the same breath, that the dead have gone to a great village under the earth, where everything is pure and where they till the fields and reap abundant harvests; that they have gone to some far country in the east or north; that they are in the forest surrounding their earthly home; that they are in the house inhabited by the living; that they are wandering about in the guise of wild animals; that they are in the grave, which is the house of the dead. When we recall the fact that most, if not all, Bantu believe that the dead for the most part return to be reborn, we shall get an idea of what some people call the confusion of thought which characterizes the Bantu; others with perhaps equal reason regard it as metaphysical subtlety."[1] This very striking summary, coming from a man who has made a profound study of Bantu thought, shows us how far we still are from having penetrated all its recesses. Perhaps the task may become a little easier if we adopt as the guiding principle of our research the idea that the law of participation governs this ensemble of representations, and that in their minds individuality is readily compatible with multipresence.

[1] E. W. Smith, *The Religion of the Lower Races*, p. 32. Cf. H. A. Junod, *The Life of a South African Tribe*, ii, p. 250.

CHAPTER XI

THE CONDITION OF THE DEAD—THEIR END

I

THE dead are living. Of this fact primitives everywhere are convinced, and their actions testify to the strength of this conviction. But if they are asked what constitutes their present life, their conceptions of it will prove vague, confused, and often contradictory. Practically every investigator of the subject will admit that it is impossible to get to the bottom of it.

In the islands of the Torres Straits, for instance, "it was extremely difficult, indeed practically impossible, to get any very definite information respecting the belief as regards spirits.

"There is no doubt that the soul or ghost, *mari*, of a person (man, woman or child) left the body at death, but for several days it did not wander far from the corpse. . . . The *mari* were believed to go to Kibu, an unknown island that lies to the west, but they could come back and walk about at night-time. The word *mari* means the ghost, or soul of a person after death, as well as shadow, reflection. *Markai* is considered by Mr. Ray as derived from *mari-kai*, ghost person, and as practically synonymous with *mari*, but applied to a 'ghost' of a dead person rather than to a 'disembodied spirit.' He draws attention to the circumstance that till the *mari* becomes a *markai* he is a very intangible sort of thing."[1] We shall soon find, when we come to analyse popular legends, that *mari* and *markai* practically denote the dead.

In Neu Pommern, according to Parkinson's report, "after his death, a man's soul arrives at a place called Mlol. About the life that he leads in that place (conceived as being in the earth's interior), the Sulka have only very vague and obscure representations."[2]—From Elsdon Best we gather that there are one, two, and even three spirit-worlds: in the sky, under the

---

[1] *Reports of the Cambridge Expedition to Torres Straits*, v, pp. 355–6.
[2] R. Parkinson, *op. cit.*, p. 187.

earth, and far away to the west. . . . The myths regarding them are very difficult to reconcile with each other. . . . "In one case," he says, "the same person gave me an account of how the spirits of the dead descend to the under-world, and also told me that spirits abide in the tenth heaven."[1]—"Concerning the condition of the souls of the dead, we find that the Dayaks have only quite vague and obscure conceptions and legends and, what is worse, these often differ widely and contradict each other. Most of them agree in the main upon the following points, however. As soon as a man dies, his *liau* begins its life." (This *liau* is the individual himself in his dead state.) "At first this is more or less a shadowy existence. It goes at once to the *Lewuliau*, the spirit-world (*Geisterland*), but it does not yet occupy its own place there. It often returns to the earth, wanders about in the woods, etc., and watches over the grave and the tomb in which its body is lying, etc."[2]—Of the Sema Nagas Hutton says : "The views of what happens to the soul" (i.e. the dead) "when it does take its final departure from its present habitations are not very consistent. The dead go to the west, or to the east, they turn into butterflies or other insects, a common Naga belief; but the commonest and best known theory (the holding of which, however, does not apparently preclude belief in one or both of the others) is that the souls go to the Hills of the Dead, and from there pass into another world, sometimes conceived of as celestial, more often as subterranean, where they continue to exist much as they did in their mortal lives."[3]—At a distance widely separated from this, among the Copper Eskimos, a careful observer also writes: "Although there is a universal belief among these natives in an existence after death, their conception of that existence is very vague and indefinite. . . . Direct questions as to the fate of the individual after death invariably received the answer: 'I don't know.' Occasionally, when pressed more closely, a native would say : 'Perhaps he is still alive in some other place, we have no knowledge.' One woman told me that the dead sometimes go to the moon."[4]

[1] Elsdon Best, *The Maori*, i, pp. 314–16.
[2] A. Hardeland, *Dayaksch-Deutsches Wörterbuch*, v, *liau*, p. 308.
[3] J. H. Hutton, *The Sema Nagas*, p. 211.
[4] J. Denness, *The Life of the Copper Eskimo*, the Canadian Arctic Expedition, 1913–18, xii, pp. 177–8.

Need we be astonished at all this vagueness and contradiction? As long as it is a case of the influence the dead exercise upon the living and vice versa, primitive conceptions, even while thoroughly emotional, do not lack clarity. The dead are alive, and upon their good pleasure depends the happiness or unhappiness of their relatives still upon earth. They are the real owners of the soil; they retain their rights over what has belonged to them; they desire to be honoured, sustained, and so forth. Upon all these points, which are of vital importance to him, the native is in no manner of doubt. He does not imagine that anyone *can* think in any other fashion than that imposed by tradition. Among primitive peoples sceptics are rare, and incredulous persons still more so. But setting aside all their relations with the living, how do they conceive of the condition of the dead *per se*? It is extremely difficult to find out, for the primitive has no reason to trouble about it, and he is satisfied with the vaguest of beliefs. Where is the spirit-world to be found, for instance? "They" (the Bantus) "have no inclination to go into this question. But they are a polite people, and if you insist, they are more likely to be polite than truthful. . . . When you ask questions like this, why, you are 'only talking.' In a general way, as far as I can make out, they think of it as 'down' rather than 'up.' "[1] Others regard it as up or down indifferently, and the inconsistency does not worry them. "According to the Berg Damaras, the dead inhabit little huts in the sky. An old native who was superior to the rest in intelligence told me that these little dwellings of the dead are graves to which a rounded shape is given, and that they are filled in with earth and stones. As I remarked that the dwellings of the dead were in the sky, and asked how these two assertions could be reconciled, he answered: 'You are separating the two ideas in your mind too much. With us, it all coincides (*zusammenfällt*).'"[2] This is the very crux of the matter, and it would be impossible to indicate it more unerringly than this old Berg Damara has done.

One feature nevertheless is almost unvarying. The world of the dead is the exact reverse of that of the living. Everything

[1] W. C. Willoughby, *Race Problems in the New Africa*, pp. 65–6.
[2] Vedder, "Religion und Weltanschauung der alten Bergdamara," *Berichte der rheinischen Missionsgesellschaft* (1920), p. 121.

there is just the opposite. "In the lower-world conditions are in every way the reverse of those in this world. There, for instance, the sun and the moon travel from west to east, they being the same orbs, however, which illumine our world."[1] Everything is done the wrong way round. "When the dead go downstairs, they go head first. . . . They go to market, but the market takes place at night. Their meetings and, in a general way, all their activities, are nocturnal. In the daytime they sleep; at night they wander around, preferably in the earlier phases of the moon."[2]—In Aua Island in the Pacific, "canoes in the spirit-world float below the water, bottom uppermost, above the spirit-hamlets, so canoeists sit head downwards in their canoes."[3]—"They speak the same language as the living, but every word has exactly the opposite meaning: black means white, white black, and so on."[4]—"In the spirit-world the spirits (*zielen*) speak the same language as on earth, but every word means exactly the contrary to what it meant before; for instance, sweet means bitter, and bitter sweet. There, to stand up means to lie down, etc."[5] This belief of the primitives is by no means confined to natives of the Indian Archipelago, and it helps to account for the fact that undeveloped peoples, almost everywhere, have a dread of finding themselves out in the open when it is really dark. They will hardly consent to go out unless in parties, and bearing a light of some kind. It is not so much that they are afraid of the wild beasts that might attack them as of the dead whom they risk encountering, for our night is the daytime of the dead. As soon as dawn appears, the danger is over, for the dead in their turn seek repose.

II

Yet despite all this, the condition of the dead cannot but be of interest to the primitive. However concerned about his present relations with them he may be, is he not obliged to ask

[1] S. A. Barrett, *The Cayapa Indians of Ecuador*, ii, p. 352.
[2] Joh. Warneck, *Die Religion der Batak*, p. 74.
[3] G. L. Pitt-Rivers, "Aua Islands, Ethnographical and Sociological Features of a South Sea Island Pagan Society," *J.A.I.*, xlv (1925), p. 434.
[4] A. C. Kruijt, *op. cit.*, p. 380.
[5] W. G. Schadee, "Het familieben en familierecht der Dayaks van Landak en Tajan," *Bijdragen* . . . N.I. (1910), p. 413.

himself, at any rate at certain times, what is to become of him personally in the other life, where he will be, in whose company, what he will be doing, what there is to fear or to hope for in that Beyond to which a sorcerer can send him immediately if he wishes to do so?—He does, in fact, question himself about this subject, but his questions are not those which would be the most important in our eyes. To us the problem of our individual destiny is the predominant one. "What is to become of me? Am I to be saved or damned to all eternity?" The man who belongs to the primitive races knows nothing of this anxiety, for to him there is scarcely any individual destiny or eternity. In the world of the dead as in that of the living, the veritable existence is that of the group, clan, or *Sippe*: what we term individuals are "members" of it, in the strict sense of the word. Death makes no change in a social solidarity which is almost organic in its character.

Thus the individual does not ask himself what is to become of him in the next world, for he knows the answer already. The clan is in existence there as it is here. To say that a man dies is to say that he is going to take his place, according to his rank, among the dead members of his group. The idea of punishment or recompense for his personal conduct during life does not occur to his mind. "After death ghosts of both men and women" (or the dead of both sexes, as we term them) "returned to their own clans, those of women who had married returning to their original homes and not to the clans of their husbands."[1]—"In the early days of Christian missions an attempt was made to have the Christian dead buried in the churchyards, to distinguish them from the heathen by having a religious burial according to Christian custom, and to disregard the clan custom and burial grounds. A few Christians agreed to this rule, and had their dead buried in the common church burial grounds, but after a time the clan members of those who had died begged leave to remove all the male dead, and took their bodies to their own burial grounds. . . ."[2] They could not bear the idea of a separation which would destroy the unity of the clan.

If the thought of a future life *does* disturb the primitive it is

---

[1] J. Roscoe, *The Bagesu*, pp. 148-9.
[2] *Idem.*, *Twenty-Five Years in East Africa*, p. 148.

U

when he asks himself how he will be received yonder. The clan, according to Smith and Dale's felicitous expression, is a natural Mutual Aid Society, comprising both living and dead members. Every living person therefore has a duty with respect to both. What will happen to him when he dies, if he has not fulfilled his obligations? What reception will be accorded him? Supposing the clan in the next world should refuse to receive him? The very thought is terrible. To be thus excluded from his group after death is to the primitive the nearest approach to what we call damnation.

In this we find one of the reasons, and by no means the least important, why, in so many communities, it is considered the greatest of misfortunes to have no children. The individual no doubt has need of them in the next world for his own purposes, but since the dead members of the clan cannot dispense with worship, offerings and sacrifices, which their descendants alone are able to secure for them, children are still more indispensable. None but a descendant is qualified in this respect, and no other would trouble about it. The first duty of a member of the clan, as soon as initiation has fully incorporated him with it, is to have one or more male children who, after him, can see that the requirements of the dead members are satisfied. This is the reason that marriage is so frequently the natural end and, as it were, the crowning ceremony of initiation. If a man has no male heirs, bad luck to him in this life and, still more, in the life to come! In the Fiji Islands, "men who were unfortunate enough to be childless were most unhappy. They feared to die and face the forbears of their race, who would be enraged with the wretch who had failed to supply posterity for the continuance of the family worship. Barrenness of wives was a frequent source of application to the courts for divorce, and British law was considered harsh and inapplicable in that it took no cognizance of such a grievance."[1] It did effectually prevent the fulfilment of the duty regarded as of paramount importance.

If one cannot have children by one wife, it is absolutely necessary to take another. This is as a rule understood by the barren wife herself, and it is often she who will bring the second wife to her husband, seeing in her, not so much a rival of her own, as the mother of the children who are indispensable.

[1] A. B. Brewster, *The Hill Tribes of Fiji*, p. 69.

Among the Ababua, "it is interesting to note that barrenness is not a ground for the repudiation of a wife. If after the lapse of a few years an Ababua woman finds that she does not present her husband with a child, she will go to her brothers and beg them to give him her younger sister, to live in the household and endeavour to replace her as the mother of a family. Should this substitute . . . give birth to a child, the elder will go to the husband, saying, 'You see this child; he is ours, just as if I had given him to you.' "[1]

To the Ashanti, the extinction of the clan is the worst calamity that can befall. "Not only are human beings divided into exogamous clans and *ntoro*, but in the spirit-world (*samando*) the ghosts continue to be concerned with and able not only to confer good upon but to receive benefits from those members of the human community alone who were their clansmen on earth. I believe also it may yet be shown that the only hope the inhabitants of the 'cold, shadowless spirit-world' have of reincarnation upon the 'warm, sun-bathed earth' lies in being born again into that *abusua* (and just possibly also *ntoro*) of which they were members on earth. The extinction of the clan would therefore mean the extinction of all hope of return to this world."[2]

The reception accorded to a dead man in the next world by the men of his group does not depend solely upon the descendants he may leave behind him. There are many other elements which intervene; in particular, the rank he occupied in life, the way in which his life ended (by a good or bad death),[3] and the funeral honours accorded him. If his body has not been the object of ceremonial ritual, if he has not been interred, or immersed, or burnt, etc., as he should have been, they will turn their backs on him. He will be despised and disgraced, possibly turned out of his group and banished. Here we have another motive, and one that is not less urgent than the first, for ensuring that male children shall be left behind him. According to the Batak view, "the *begu* (dead) live by families and tribes in a community. To reach the *begu* who are akin to him, the dead man must have been buried with his deceased relatives. . . . The more descendants a man has

---

[1] A. de Calonne-Beaufaict, *Les Ababua*, p. 76.
[2] Capt. R. S. Rattray, *Ashanti*, p. 80.   [3] *V. Primitive Mentality*, pp. 274-9.

left behind him on earth, the greater is the consideration shown him in the land of the dead. . . . Childless men, like slaves, occupy the lowest rung of the social ladder. This is why the Batak regard it as so terrible a thing to have no sons."[1] The Bantu think the same. "The most important reason" (for the Banyankole) "was that it was the duty of a son to perform the funeral rites after his father's death, and to see that all the necessary observances were paid, so that the ghost might take its proper position in the other world. If no one attended to this matter, the poor ghost was despised by its ghostly clan-fellows and other ghosts completely ignored it."[2] In West Africa, on the Lower Niger, "as a rule, the burial customs depend for their character upon whether the deceased has children or not; in a certain number of instances childless people are buried with the same ceremonies as those who have left descendants, and this whether they are men or women; but as a rule the heir-less man or woman receives treatment little or no better than the child, who is simply thrown into the bush."[3] The very worst experience for the dead is to be kept apart from the rest. "To be forced to inhabit the Land of the Dead alone is the supreme dread. 'Die, and may you find none of the other dead at home!' is a sinister imprecation, and another form of curse is 'May you find no dwelling among the dead!' "[4]

The anxiety not to be parted from one's relatives and the strong feeling of the solidarity existing between individuals in the Beyond are very clearly expressed in the *Relations de la Nouvelle-France*, where we find, too, the naïve conviction that the next life is merely a continuation of this. "An old Indian chief always vented his wrath against Christianity. . . . His wife died a Christian. Her husband, who loved her tenderly, thought he could not show his affection for her better than by becoming a Christian too. . . . He resolved to join her as soon as he could, went frequently to visit her grave, two miles from here, and, concealing his designs from us, he urgently begged us to baptize him. We put him to a test of two years before granting him this privilege. . . . He once asked me whether Christians who were weary of life were not allowed

[1] Joh. Warneck, *Die Religion der Batak*, p. 15.
[2] J. Roscoe, *The Banyankole*, p. 108.
[3] N. W. Thomas, "Notes on Edo Burial Customs," *J.A.I.* (1920), p. 379.
[4] Br. Gutmann, *Denken und Dichten der Dschagga-Neger*, p. 128.

to hang themselves, that they might go all the sooner to rejoin the blessed dead. . . . At length he was baptized. The very next night he hanged himself in the place where he usually slept."[1] By becoming a Christian his wife had been separated from her group in the next world. He could not bear the idea that she should be alone there. Here is another story of the same kind. "Last year I baptized a young woman belonging to one of the most influential families of Tsonnontouën, and the day after her baptism she died. The mother could not control her grief at this loss, for our savages love their children very tenderly, and when I tried to console her by depicting the endless bliss that her daughter would enjoy in heaven, she said to me artlessly: 'You did not know her. Here she was mistress, commanding more than twenty slaves who are still in my service. She never knew what it was to go to the forest to fetch wood, or to the river to draw water; she had not to trouble about any household affairs. Now, since she is the only one of our family in Paradise, I am afraid she will find it hard to get used to being alone, for she will have to cook for herself, fetch her own wood and water, prepare everything that she has to eat or drink. Is it not indeed pitiful that she should have nobody to wait upon her where she is now? Here is one of my slaves who is ill; I beg you to teach her well and put her on the road to heaven, so that she may not lose her way and she can go and live with my daughter and help her with the housekeeping.' "[2]—"One day," the same Jesuit missionary tells us, "a girl whom we had just baptized happened to die. Her mother, seeing that one of her slaves was at the point of death, said to me: 'My daughter is all alone among French people in the Land of the Dead; she has neither relatives nor friends with her, and here is the spring-time coming on; she must plant some maize and some pumpkins: baptize my slave, so that he can go to the French country too, and then he can do it for her.' "[3] These Jesuit fathers often tell us that what the Indians dislike most about baptism is that it separates them for ever from their relatives after death. They are lost to each other, and the clan is accordingly maimed. Besides, when they go to the Indian Land of

[1] *Relations de la Nouvelle-France*, lxii (1682), pp. 62–4.
[2] *Ibid.*, liv (1669–70), pp. 92–4.
[3] Fr. L. Hennepin, *Description de la Louisiane* (1687), p. 94.

the Dead, they know what awaits them there, and that they will lead the same lives as they do upon earth. But in the Frenchmen's heaven, in their Paradise, what will be the lot of the lonely Indian? "These benighted folk have all the trouble in the world to get hold of ideas about heaven. Some of them are prepared to renounce its joys when you tell them that there are no cornfields there, that people do not go hunting or fishing, and that they do not marry there. One of them told us he thought it a bad thing that people did not work in heaven, for it could not be right to be idle, and for that reason he did not want to go there."[1] They are never lacking in excuses for avoiding the baptism that would send them there. They do not desire this "passport to the skies." "Some say that as their legs are feeble they would never be able to undertake so long a journey; others are afraid of falling from so great a height, for they cannot imagine how they could hold on so long without tumbling down. You will find that some are anxious as to whether there is any tobacco there, for they say that they could never do without it."[2]

The following story will again prove how strong is the desire to rejoin their relatives in the next life felt by the Indians. "Whilst I was living amongst them," says a traveller, "a husband and wife, whose hut was next my own, lost a four-year-old child. They were so overcome with grief at the death of this child, and practised their mourning customs so rigorously, weeping and cutting themselves with knives, that the father at length died as the result of it. But what astonished me was that the wife, until then inconsolable, had no sooner seen her husband expire than she dried her tears and seemed in some way comforted, despite her double loss.

"As I did not know how to account for such a change of front, I took a favourable opportunity to ask her about the matter, telling her that I had supposed that the loss of her husband, far from moderating her anguish, would have increased it.

"She told me that as the child they had lost was too young to be able to get food for himself in the spirit-world, she and her husband had feared his lot there would be a very miserable

---

[1] *Relations de la Nouvelle-France* (1637), p. 121.
[2] *Ibid.* (1638-9), pp. 110-11.

one, but since her husband, who loved him as devotedly as she did, and who was a good hunter, had also gone to the same country, she could now feel comfortable about him. There was no longer any cause for tears, for her son must be happy while protected by a father who loved him dearly, and now she had no desire but to join them both as soon as possible."[1]

III

In the next world the dead man lives with the defunct members of his group, but his interest in those who are still on earth does not cease. They are aware of this, and they act accordingly. In all the important circumstances of life, the living are concerned to know what the dead will think about them. Accordingly, among certain Bantu tribes of East Africa, "when a man has a younger brother, the latter does not marry until his elder has taken to himself a wife. But if the elder should die, it is *his* name that is given to the woman his younger brother is marrying: only on such a condition can she become his wife. It is believed that if the elder saw his brother marrying whilst he himself had died a bachelor, he would be as annoyed as if the thing had happened during his lifetime."[2]— The same custom prevails among the Dschagga. "When an adult has died unmarried, they seek a wife to give him in the Land of the Dead. His father goes to find a man whose daughter has died unmarried, saying: 'Give me your dead daughter for my dead son, who is all alone!' . . . The usual sacrifices are offered. A poor man does not pay the dowry save by symbols; he will bring the young girl's father a piece of wood instead of the customary beer and goats. After this marriage of the dead man and the dead girl, the girl's father says: 'I must help my daughter to prepare her meals.' He brings all sorts of food in small portions so that those who are henceforth her parents-in-law may feed on them.

"With rich people it may happen that a father does actually marry a wife for his dead bachelor son. The marriage is cele-

[1] J. Carver, *Voyage dans l'Amérique septentrionale*, pp. 306-7.
[2] J. Raum, "Die Religion der Landschaft Moschi am Kilimandjaro," *Archiv. für Religionswissenschaft*, xiv (1911), p. 179.

brated as usual, without anything to show that it is a dead man who is in question, but the new wife is called by his name. If the father is called Muro, and the dead son Nsau, she is known as Nsau's wife, and her children are Nsau's children.

"The first male child receives the name of the living father, as if the latter were his grandfather, and the first girl bears the name of her mother as if it were her grandmother. In this way they conform to the custom which gives the firstborn the name of their grandparents, never that of their father."[1] This last circumstance is highly significant. If the child is given the name of his living father, it is because the latter is not really his father, but his grandfather, for the real father is the dead man to whom the wife has been married. The physical parentage, which in our eyes is the only true one, here gives place to the mystic paternity, which primitives rate very much more highly. For the well-being and the consideration of the adult who has had the misfortune to die unmarried, and consequently without children who can perform the necessary sacrifices to the dead, the posthumous marriage is his salvation. By marrying a wife for him, his father procures him the children that he cannot do without. When they are born they will therefore be the grandchildren of their mother's actual husband, and in this way the dead man will have sons of his own.

Let us recall here that in many communities, notably in several Bantu tribes, a man's first wife is not chosen by him. It is his father, acting with the familial group, who selects her for him. Later, if he is wealthy enough, he can marry one or more to his own taste. "The father of the young man, fearing scandals and lawsuits (for adultery, as an attack upon property, is punished like theft, with substantial damages), does all he can to marry him very early, at from eighteen to twenty years of age. He selects a wife for him, and in the Sesuto tongue, she is *the wife of his father*; later on, if he can afford it, he will choose a second wife for himself."[2] The first marriage is a transaction, not between the married pair themselves, but between the two families. "The young girl," says the same missionary, "henceforth belongs to the family of her husband, who has given so many head of cattle for her, for according to the Sesuto expression

---

[1] Br. Gutmann, *Denken und Dichten der Dschagga-Neger*, pp. 81–2.
[2] *Missions évangéliques*, lxvii, p. 26 (Christeller).

(and this is a very important point) it is the young man's father who is marrying."[1]

The circumstance reported by Gutmann, therefore, seems less surprising. What the father does for his dead son corresponds exactly with what he would have done for a living one. Here again we realize how closely the life of the dead is intertwined with that of the living, and how the individual, whether alive or dead, is always thought of in relation to the group of which he forms a member.

IV

What becomes of the dead at long last? When no more sacrifices or offerings are brought to them, when the years in their passing have gradually obliterated the recollection of them, is their individuality still preserved and, if so, for how long?

If it were purely spiritual souls in question they would be also immortal, but in primitive peoples that know nothing of such souls we do not find any belief in immortality. Everywhere primitives believe in survival, but nowhere do they regard it as unending. Perham has noted this fact among the Dyaks of Sarawak. "The future life does not, in their minds, extend to an immortality. Death is still the inevitable destiny. Some Dyaks say they have to die three times; others, seven times; but all agree in the notion that, after they have become degenerated by these successive dyings, they become practically annihilated by absorption into air and fog, or by a final dissolution into various jungle plants not recognized by any name. Maybe, they lack the mental capacity to imagine an endless state of liveable life."[2]

To nearly all primitives, indeed, the dead are neither "spirits" nor "souls," but beings very similar to the living, having suffered decline and deterioration in one respect, yet still powerful and redoubtable in another. As a rule they can be neither seen nor touched, and when they do appear, it is rather as phantoms or shadows than as real beings. Nevertheless they have a body like ours, although it has neither substance nor solidity. They

[1] *Missions évangéliques*, lxxvi, p. 205 (Christeller).
[2] Ling Roth, *The Natives of Sarawak*, i, p. 213.

go hunting or fishing, or else they cultivate their fields; they eat and drink, they marry, and so on. In short, it is literally true that the next life is the continuation of this one, on another plane. There a man finds a social position that corresponds with the rank that has been his on earth, and physically he is still like himself.

Such is the belief that the Lenguas, for instance, explained to the missionary Grubb as follows. "The *aphangak* or departed souls of men in the shade world . . . merely continue their present life, only of course in a disembodied state." (That is, they have not their terrestrial body, but they have one all the same, as we shall see.) "The souls of the departed are supposed, in the ethereal state, to correspond exactly in form and characteristics with the bodies they have left. A tall man and a short man remain tall and short as spirits; a deformed man remains deformed. . . . The spirit of a child remains a child, and does not develop, and for this reason is not feared."[1] Grubb uses the terms "souls" and "spirits"; we prefer to say "the dead": it is a matter of terminology. But from his own showing the exterior of these souls and spirits is as similar as possible to that of living beings. A little later he adds: "An Indian professes to be able to recognize an *aphangak*, because it retains the same appearance as it had when in the body."

Consequently the primitive, as a rule, will not hear of amputation. He will consent, sometimes even eagerly, to receive the ministrations of the white doctor, but he will energetically refuse the surgeon's attentions, for any mutilation that the living body has suffered will reappear on the dead. Now it is of supreme importance that a man should be able to present himself in the Beyond without any physical blemish, and above all, with all his limbs. "Once a native" (a Maori) "had his arm badly crushed. He was taken to the nearest hospital, but would not hear of having the limb amputated without his father's consent, and the old fellow flew into a fearful rage when he was consulted, saying his son would want his arm in the next world, and it was better for him to die with it and keep it, as it could not be sent after him."[2] Innu-

---

[1] W. B. Grubb, *op. cit.*, p. 120.
[2] Goldie, "Maori Medical Lore," *Transactions of the New Zealand Institute*, xxvii (1904), p. 88.

merable facts of this kind have been noted. Here is another one. In Uganda, "the idea of passing into the unseen world of ghosts without a limb, or in anywise mutilated, was terrible to the native mind, and this made men anxious to retain a limb whenever possible. In battle men preferred to die with a shattered limb rather than have it amputated and live."[1] And again: "It is only a few years since amputations have become possible, for the native idea was that the loss of a limb involved a similar loss to the ghost, and that such mutilation debarred the ghost from joining its clan members." As we have just seen, nothing could be more dreaded by a ghost than this exclusion. "This belief made more terrible the frequently in- flicted punishment of mutilation for various offences, such as theft and adultery. The person whose hand was hacked off was known as a thief, the person whose eye was gouged out as an adulterer, while the loss of an ear was the mark of stubborn disobedience. These marks gave the unfortunate person pain and inconvenience in this life, cutting him off from all chance of promotion, and degrading him to a low social position, while in the next world his ghost was expelled from the society of his relatives. These beliefs hindered surgical work, because men preferred to die with a limb intact rather than to live without it."[2]

The same idea often prevails with respect to marks on the body, whatever these may be. In Assam, "among the northern Tangkhuls, the poorest of them and the only Naga tribe in Manipur that tattoos, I was told that the women were tattooed in order that they might be identified hereafter by their husbands. The same belief is found among the Daflas. . . . In the Mao Heaven there is a special compartment for those whose ears have been split during life, and the Tangkhuls inflict a wound upon the head of the corpse in order that on his arrival he may be received as a warrior. Obviously the ghost carries all these marks and we may find in eschatological belief the explanation of other cases of mutilation *inter vivos*."[3]

---

[1] J. Roscoe, *Twenty-Five Years in East Africa*, p. 147.   [2] *Ibid.*, p. 174.
[3] T. C. Hodson, " Mortuary Ritual and Eschatological Beliefs among the Hill Tribes of Assam," *Archiv. für Religionswissenschaft*, xii (4), pp. 454–5.

V

The dead who may thus be disabled, mutilated, tattooed, does not escape, any more than the living, from the inevitable decay that time will bring about sooner or later. His life is too closely akin to that of mortals for it not to end in the same way. He too, as a rule, must end by dying. The primitive, however, has no very clear idea of the analogy perceptible in his conceptions, and moreover, even in this world, death is not always regarded by him as necessary. In certain communities, there is no "natural" death.[1]

Nevertheless it is nearly everywhere admitted that, save in the case of reincarnation, which may occur periodically, the dead do at last disappear. In Australia, in North-West Central Queensland, the native has "a hazy notion" of survival, at any rate in the Boolia tribes, but it is very obscure, and he does not assign any lengthened term for it. The Boolia vaguely imagines the corpse "getting older and moving about elsewhere," when he stops bringing food and tobacco to the burial place.[2] So, too, in the neighbouring district of Cloncurry, after a burial, "when night falls, a fire is lighted at a few yards' distance from the grave, and some meat, etc., hung up on a neighbouring tree. This may be repeated for three or four nights following, and occasionally now and again during the next few months, until it is believed in fact that the deceased 'has got too old, has gone away somewhere else.' "[3] It seems as if his image becomes dim fairly soon, and that they thus cease conceiving of him as alive.

With the Aranda and the Loritja tribes, whilst the family is lamenting, "the ghost approaches and speaks to them. 'Why are you weeping? I am alive. I shall go away for a short time only; then I shall return to you. Wait patiently meanwhile.' After the funeral ceremonies he goes away towards the north and reaches the seashore. . . . When several months have elapsed, he returns in a great black cloud, goes into his son's body, where he remains for some time. If he has no young son, it is over his grandson's growth that he watches. When he leaves the body he has tenanted, he says to his relatives: 'Stay

---

[1] V. Primitive Mentality, pp. 37–43.
[2] W. E. Roth, Ethnological Studies among the North-West Central Queensland Aborigines, No. 279, p. 161.   [3] Ibid., No. 291, p. 165.

here; I shall not come back.' " (He returns to the Island of the Dead, and weeps much, because he will never see his kindred any more.) . . . "Finally, he is destroyed by lightning, and this time his existence has really come to an end."[1]

Codrington relates the story of a Melanesian who had gone down to Panoi, the land of the dead, and who wanted to bring his wife back with him. "That, she said, was impossible, and she gave him a shell armlet by which to remember her. He took her by the hand and began to drag her; her head came off and her body came to pieces. . . . For . . . ghosts in Panoi have something more of body and substance than they have when they come back into the world; else the man could not have taken hold of his dead wife's hand. When a ghost comes into the world, it is but a *tagangiu* that is seen, and something circumscribed by an outline like a shadow. But the ghost in Panoi" (i.e. the dead man) "of which the other is probably again the ghost, has a *tarapei*, a body, which has not only form and colour, but a certain consistency."[2] This passage broaches interesting views upon the way in which certain Melanesians conceive of the dead. It expressly confirms the idea that they have bodies, and are not purely spirits or mere shadows. It shows, moreover, that bi-presence appears as natural in the case of the dead as of the living. When a dead man "comes back" and shows himself to the living, it is usually in the form of an animal. Of this we have had numerous examples, especially in Melanesia. But he may also reappear in his human guise, and whilst this resemblance, this double, astonishes the living, the dead man is none the less still in Panoi. The apparition (the double) and this dead man are but one.

According to these same Melanesians, "this ghostly life (like that of the living, but paler) is not eternal. The *mere akalo* soon turn into white ants' nests, which again become the food of the still vigorous ghosts; hence a living man says to his idle son: 'When I die, I shall have ants' nests to eat, but then what will you have?' The *lio'a*, ghosts of power, last longer—but at last they turn into ants' nests like the others."[3]

In the New Hebrides, according to Sommerville's report, "the soul dies only three times in Hades, each time getting

[1] C. Strehlow, *op. cit.*, ii, p. 7. [2] R. H. Codrington, *op. cit.*, p. 278.
[3] *Id., The Melanesians*, pp. 260-1.

more and more ethereal, finally fading away altogether. In the first stage, immediately after life, it inhabits a region below the earth and where it has still a semi-corporeal existence, and to which region the sacred men have often been and know all about it. Here the dead order the affairs of earth. . . . The soul enjoys that existence for thirty years, and then comes the second death, and so on as mentioned. . . . At Fate, the soul died six times. Finally it dissolved entirely."[1]—Among the Dyaks of South Borneo, we find both a belief in the death of the dead and in their reincarnation. "According to the unanimous testimony of the natives, everything in *Lewuliau* (the abode of the dead) occurs as it does in our world. People marry, plant rice, and *die* there. But in that world they do not die once, but *seven times*, after which they return by re-incarnation to the world of the living, die again, and so on."[2]

The Ainu of Japan have a very curious belief, according to which the dead "look upon persons who have not yet crossed the river of death as ghosts, and consider themselves to be the natural and substantial people. They think of us, in fact, just as we do of them."[3] In *How Natives Think* (p. 304) I have quoted a passage by de Groot, which mentions a similar idea in China.

It is the same in Africa, in certain Bantu tribes. With the Wakonde, "a dead person dies in the under-world too, according to the missionary Jauer's notes, and there, when one dies, it is definitely the end of him."[4]—Among curses quoted by Gutmann we find this: "May you die yet once more among the dead."[5] Casalis noted a similar imprecation used by the Basutos. "A horrible curse only too often heard upon their lips is: ' May you die among the dead, or in the Land of the dead!' "[6]—Lastly, among the Akamba, "the *aimu* (dead) are considered to be subject to the laws of mortality. Those who have existed for a time are believed to disappear and to be replaced by new ones, who vanish in their turn."[7] Without continuing this list any further we may, I think, admit that a

[1] F. Speiser, *op. cit.*, p. 323.
[2] *Berichte der rheinischen Missionsgesellschaft* (1882), p. 102.
[3] Batchelor, *The Ainu of Japan*, p. 226.
[4] Fr. Fülleborn, "Das deutsche Njassa und Ruwumagebiet," *Deutsch Ost Afrika*, ix, p. 323.   [5] Br. Gutmann, *Denken und Dichten der Dschagga-Neger*, p. 128.
[6] E. Casalis, *Les Bassoutos*, p. 258.   [7] G. Lindblom, *The Akamba*, p. 182.

belief in the death of the dead is practically universal. Seeing what the primitives' usual idea of dead people's way of living is, they could but die as do their congeners.

The dead, then, can also be killed. In a popular story from the islands of the Torres Straits, for instance, a young girl, Uga, persecuted by her brother, heard that a young man, a stranger named Tabepa, had come to Pulu, and she learnt where he was staying. "Now Tabepa was a spirit come from Kibu, the island home of spirits. She went to find him; they went back to Pulu, and he married her. . . . When the young people had been in Kibu for some time, it was evident that Uga was expecting. The brother Dagi, who had found their whereabouts, was plotting to kill Tabepa when he and his wife returned to Mabuiag." (Here we have, then, a dead man married to a living girl, who is about to have a child by him.)

"The company of *markai* (the dead) arrived, and among them Uga and her fine-looking husband, who were heartily welcomed. When all were comfortably seated and were talking unsuspectingly Dagi reached for the *lut* and hit Tabepa across the nose. Thereupon the Mabuiag men rose and killed all the *markai*, who swam back to Kibu (their home) as porpoises and garfish.

"The following month, the whole of the *markai* returned to avenge themselves, all armed with waterspouts. Seeing them approach, the Mabuiag men began to feel very uncomfortable, as they recognized that there was now a state of war between them and the spirits.

"When the *markai* came, they devastated the island with their waterspouts, and the storm carried away to Kibu the men, and houses, and canoes, and dogs, and Uga, too, as if they were so many pieces of paper. Uga was now a *markai*, and lived with Tabepa in Kibu."[1]

Stories of this kind are numerous. During a battle, "one Mabuiag man . . . shot at a boy in the scrub and killed him, and shooting through a leaf he hit a *mari*" (dead man) "in the eye and killed it; he cut off both their heads . . . and carried the long narrow head of the *mari* in his hand."[2] This story, says

[1] *Reports of the Cambridge Expedition to Torres Straits*, v, pp. 83–5.
[2] *Ibid.*, v, p. 319.

Dr. Haddon, was given me as a true narrative, but the *mari* episode was not explained. It seems, indeed, as if it were self-evident to the natives, for there is nothing to prevent a *mari* (dead man) from being killed by an arrow that enters his eye. The dead who fight with the living run the same risks as they, and they can receive the same fatal wounds.

Lastly, among the Kai of New Guinea there is a story told of Gololo, the frog, who is a "spirit" (dead man). Gololo summons other spirits and they go with him to attack a tree upon which two women have taken refuge. One of them was to sit down on the ground, a second would mount on his shoulders, and so on, until they could reach the crown of the palm-tree. "At this moment the women seized their sticks, the spirits swerved to avoid the blows, and the whole column tottered and fell. In this fall, one of the dead men was crushed to death. . . . The day dawned and surprised the dead. Then the women came down, called the other inhabitants of the village, who soon arrived with torches and wood and set fire to the palm-tree. All the dead (*Geister*) hiding in the grooves of the tree were then roasted to death, and furnished food for living men."[1]

Killed, roasted, and eaten—these dead are treated exactly as living men, of flesh and blood, in like circumstances, would have been.

[1] R. Neuhauss, *op. cit.*, iii, 161–3.

CHAPTER XII

REINCARNATION

I

LIFE in the next world does not necessarily end as ours does in this. There are dead who do not die, and their desire to return to earth is satisfied by periodic reincarnations. In the opinion of many primitive peoples, the children who are born have already lived on earth, and even more than once previously. They are born but to die, and they die, to be born again after a longer or shorter interval. What happens to their individuality in the course of these successive transits through the portals of death? Once more we find ourselves faced by conceptions that seem obscure, vague, and even contradictory to us. The primitive's thought proceeds along a path in which we find it very difficult to follow it.

We shall study the facts that relate to reincarnation preferably among the Eskimo of the Mackenzie Delta, and those living around the Bering Strait. Thanks to Stefánsson and to Nelson, we have detailed descriptions at command, and these are as precise as the nature of such conceptions allows of their being.

Stefánsson had more than once observed, and not without surprise, that the parents of a little girl bore patiently with all her whims, even the most outrageous. They never rebuked her, and consequently they never punished her. "I had noticed ever since I knew them that Mamayauk (the mother) in speaking to Noashak" (the tiresome little girl) "always addressed her as 'mother.' When one stops to think of it, it was, of course, a bit curious that a woman of twenty-five should address a girl of eight as 'mother.' . . . One day another Eskimo family came to visit us, and, strangely enough, the woman of the family also spoke to Noashak and called her 'mother.' Then my curiosity was finally aroused, and I asked, 'Why do you two grown women call this child your mother?' Their answer was: 'Simply because she is our mother,' an answer which was for the moment more incomprehensible to me than the original problem. I saw, however, that I was on the track of something interesting, and both women were in a communicative mood, so it was not long before my questions brought out the facts that furnish the following rational explanation, which shows not only why these women called Noashak 'mother,' but also why it was that she must never, under any circumstances, be forbidden anything or punished.

"When a Mackenzie Eskimo dies . . . the soul (nappan) remains in the house . . . for four days if it is a man, and for five days if a woman. At the end of that time a ceremony is performed by means of which the spirit is induced to leave the house and to go up to the grave, where it remains with the body, waiting for the next child in the community to be born.

"When a child is born, it comes into the world with a soul of its own (nappan), but this soul is as inexperienced, foolish and feeble as a child is and looks. It is evident, therefore, that the child needs a more experienced and wiser soul than its own to do the thinking for it and take care of it. Accordingly the mother, as soon as she can after the birth of the child, pronounces a magic formula to summon from the grave the waiting soul of the dead to become the guardian soul of the newborn child, or its atka as they express it. Let us suppose that the name of this dead person is John. . . .

"The spirit of John not only teaches the child to talk, but after the child learns to talk, it is really the soul of John that talks to you, and not the inborn soul of the child. The child, therefore, speaks with all the acquired wisdom which John accumulated in the long lifetime, plus the higher wisdom which only comes after death. Evidently, therefore, the child is the wisest person in the family or in the community, and its opinions should be listened to accordingly. What it says and does may seem foolish to you, but that is mere seeming, and in reality the child is wise beyond your comprehension.

"It must, then, never be thwarted, for if incensed, the guardian spirit might leave it. Then it would die, become deformed, or something of that kind. Public opinion would deal very severely with parents who should refuse their child anything or punish it. . . .

"As the child grows up, the soul with which he was born (the *nappan*) gradually develops in strength, experience, and wisdom, so that after the age of ten or twelve years it is fairly competent to look after the child, and begins to do so; at that age, therefore, it becomes of less vital moment to please the guardian spirit (*atka*), and accordingly it is customary to begin forbidding children (things) and punishing them. . . ."[1]—"If you see a man who is bow-legged, or humpbacked, or whose ears are big, and if you ask . . . why . . . the answer will usually be: 'It is because his parents forbade him things when he was young and offended his guardian spirit.' "[2]

"The natural consequence of the fact that it is the spirit of John that does the thinking and talking for the child, is that the child is addressed as a relative by all the relatives of John (for it is indeed to John that they are talking). If John was my father and your uncle, then I speak to the child as 'father' and you speak to it as 'uncle,' irrespective of the child's age or sex. There was, for instance, a couple I knew who had for a child a boy of seven years, whose father called him stepmother, and whose mother called him aunt, for those were their respective relationships to the woman whose soul was the boy's guardian or *atka*. . . . A boy may find himself in the position of being at once his father's son and his father's mother, which relationship he will, of course, find perfectly natural."[3]—Charlevoix, in speaking of the name, says too: "Among many peoples, the child is given the place of the last bearer of the name, and it sometimes happens that a child finds himself treated as a grandfather by one who might be his own."[4]

As we have seen above,[5] the *atka* and the name are one and the same. We remember Rasmussen's definition—"Man is composed of body, soul (*nappan*), and name (*atka*)." We understand it better now that we know more definitely what the *atka* is. It is the guardian soul, the tutelary genius of the child, i.e. the ancestor of whom he is the reincarnation. If it should happen that the name is incorrectly given, in other words,

[1] V. Stefánsson, *My Life with the Eskimo*, pp. 394–400.
[2] *Ibid.*, p. 399. Cf. Stefánsson, *The Stefánsson-Anderson Arctic Expedition*, American Museum of Natural History, Anthropological Papers, xiv, p. 282.
[3] *Ibid.*, p. 401.
[4] Charlevoix, *Journal d'un voyage dans l'Amérique septentrionale*, iii, p. 280.
[5] Cf. *supra*, ch. vii, pp. 208–11.

that the relatives have been mistaken about the reincarnation, it will soon be perceived, by the state of the child. "A small boy in this house, now about four years old," says Stefánsson, "was born a short time before his uncle died. After the uncle's death the baby became very restless, and became quiet only after he got the uncle's name. This was given him as a second name, and he at once became quiet. He had been crying for the name. Formerly, when a child was very restless and cried, a medicine-man was called in to determine whose name he was crying for; when the right name was found, the crying stopped. On being questioned, all the people of the house (three) agreed that not only did the child want the name, but in all probability the name was equally anxious to get into the child, i.e. they seem to think of the name as an entity."[1] There is no doubt about it. Here, the name of the uncle is the dead uncle himself, or at least that which the observer calls his "soul." Once again, "a child is named Keyuk from one of several Keyuks; the one from whom the child is named is *oma atka* (that one's name); the others are not the child's 'name,' though they bear the same name."[2]

These comparatively simple conceptions may lead to complications which appear hopelessly confusing to our minds. "It happens sometimes that between the occurrence of one death and the occurrence of the next, several children are born. Each of them can and does receive the soul of the dead man as his guardian. This is another case of the Eskimo's unclearness of thinking, for they seem to look upon each child as being the abode of the soul of the dead. How a single soul of a single man can, after his death, become three souls or thirteen, inhabiting simultaneously three children or thirteen children, is a metaphysical question in Eskimo theology. They cannot explain the fact, but they know it is so."[3]

We are not so astonished as Stefánsson, for we know that the participation implied in duality or plurality of existence or in bi-presence leaves the primitive's mind absolutely undisturbed. He considers it a thing that is quite simple and natural. To us, from Plato downwards, participation is a metaphysical

---

[1] V. Stefánsson, *op. cit.*, p. 202. Hardeland says too: "The word *ara*, name, is treated like a person. A man is asked 'Who is your name?' " *Versuch einer Grammatik der Dayakschen Sprache*, p. 110.   [2] *Ibid.*, pp. 286–7.
[3] Stefánsson, *My Life with the Eskimo*, p. 402.

problem, but to the Eskimo, we may say that it is a self-evident fact.

The converse of the last case considered may also occur; there may be many deaths in the interval between two births. What becomes, then, of the "souls" of all these people recently dead?—They will all enter the body of the one newborn child. Thus it is that the intolerably tiresome child, who is the mother of her mother Mamayauk, is also the mother of another woman, whom she calls her daughter (which she does not do for her own mother). She is the reincarnation of these two persons, who died just before her birth.

Here is Mamayauk's explanation of the matter. "Mamayauk says the name is the same thing as the *nappan* of some dead person, another name for the same thing." Then *atka* would be for the dead what *nappan* is for the living. "When a child is born, it has a *nappan* of its own; when it gets one or more names, the *nappatait* of those dead people come and 'live with' the child. The child gets as many 'souls' to live with (or by) it as it gets names, but none of these are its soul properly speaking. The child's own soul is the one it was born with. When the present Norosak (Noashak?) shall die, and her name shall pass to a Norasak III, the *nappan* that goes to that child will not be the *nappan* of Norasak I, but will be the *nappan* with which Norasak II was born.

"Mamayauk and Guninana" (another woman of the same tribe) "agree on this story. They have no idea what will become of the soul of Norasak I when Norasak II dies, nor the other two souls (Norasak II has three names) which now 'live with' Norasak II. This means that of the four souls of Norasak II she now has only the one which 'from always' was hers. At her death this will be provided for by having a child named for it."[1]

From this it follows that we are not dealing here with a reincarnation, in the full sense of the word, for the child that comes into the world is not really a dead person born again. It has its own *nappan*, and it is only after several days have elapsed that they procure for it the *atka* that will henceforward take care of it and secure its growth and progress. This *atka* does not mingle with its person; up to a certain point it remains a separate thing. "The *atka* is sometimes in a child, sometimes

[1] Stefánsson, *My Life with the Eskimo*, pp. 357–8.

near it, sometimes it goes quite away. When a child's *atka* gets farther from it than a fathom or so, the child will begin to cry, and will not cease till the *atka* returns."[1] In this *atka* we recognize an element of the individuality studied earlier under the names of tutelary genius, *iningukua, kra, ntoro, nyarong*, and so forth, although differing in some respects from these.

Unfortunately it is very difficult for us to reconstitute ideas implying that a certain being is, and at the same time is not, another being. Stefánsson remarks: "Mamayauk's story that the child is born with a soul which is its own, as opposed to others which merely live near the child, is partly discredited by the following fact. The words '*uwaña kait kain*' (used on sneezing) mean 'I myself, come here.' If a mother uses this formula for her infant child, she says, '*Nogasak kait kain*,' where the Nogasak addressed is not the child Nogasak, but the dead person of that name, or the soul of that dead person. Later, when Nogasak has learned to speak, and can use the formula for herself, she says '*uwaña kait kain*,' I myself, come here, yet *uwaña* is not what it would be with us, but—the dead Nogasak, or her soul. The *atka* (name, soul) of the dead person is therefore *I myself*, somewhat as our ancestors used to speak of *my mind* and *my body*, as if the mind and body were not *I*, but merely something belonging to me."[2] This very noteworthy passage does not prove that Mamayauk is contradicting herself. It shows that between the *atka* and the individual there is something other and something more than an association, a cohabitation, intimate as we can conceive it to be. It is a case of participation, consubstantiality, which, though not entire, is none the less real.

Other testimony, though certainly less detailed, confirms Stefánsson's. "Mr. Brower says that he has noticed, though he never tried to explain it to himself, that almost every person calls some younger one 'father' or 'mother,' irrespective of the sex of the child."[3] There he is dealing with the Eskimo of Barrow Point. On his side, Rasmussen writes: "Originally the Eskimos regarded the name as a kind of soul, with which was associated a certain amount of vitality and dexterity. The man

---

[1] Stefánsson, *My Life with the Eskimo*, p. 363.
[2] *Ibid.*, pp. 339, 364. [3] *Ibid.*, p. 389.

who was named after one deceased, inherited the qualities of his name, and it was said that the dead man had no peace, and that his soul could not pass to the land of the departed, before his name had been given again. . . . After the death of the body, the name takes up his abode in a woman who is about to bear a child. . . . It is born with the child. . . . The child cries at birth . . . because it wants its name."[1]

Widely removed from this district, among the Eskimo of Hudson's Bay, similar conceptions have been found. "A week after the birth comes the giving of the name. There is a magic séance for the purpose of consulting the spirit that is supposed to live again in this child. If this spirit says that it consents to live again in this child, that is, to guide and protect it, etc., the child will bear its name. *The dead man lives again through his name*, as the Eskimo express it. To complete the fancy of this survival the child will bear the name of the dead man, sing the same *ayaya*, still more, it will be given the same family name as the dead man possessed ; for instance, if a little boy is named after his grandmother, the whole family will call him granny, and he will wear woman's dress. A little girl named after a man will hear herself called father, brother, uncle, as the case may be, and this will last all her life. . . .

"This survival in the name prevents the parents from reproving their children; they think they would be wanting in respect for the spirits, so that *practically* the difference between survival through the name alone and the true reincarnation of souls is almost nil, although in theory the Eskimo admits the one and denies the other. . . .

"Care is taken to give names to quite young puppies lest they should die. . . ."[2]

Among the Labrador Eskimo, "the babe . . . early attains a knowledge of his power, and acquires a habit of speaking with authority which cannot be misunderstood. He is treated with great respect by his parents, and his smallest wishes gratified.

"The custom of treating a child with all the deference due to an adult, and asking his will or opinion with mature respect,

[1] Kn. Rasmussen, *The People of the Polar North*, p. 116.
[2] Mgr. A. Turquétil, O.M.I., "Notes sur les Esquimaux de Baie Hudson," *Anthropos* (1926), xxi, 3–4, p. 421.

is perhaps due to their idea of the namesake (*at'itsi'ak*), by which the child receives the name of the last person who has died in the village. It does not matter if the child is of different sex. . . ."[1]

In Kamtchatka, in the eighteenth century, "they do not give a child a name until after one or two months. If he is very restless at night, they consult the shaman, and always allege the reason to be that the child has not received the name he ought to have had, and that such and such an ancestor is tormenting him. Accordingly they at once change the child's name. He is given that of one of his dead relatives, disclosed by the female shaman."[2]—Among the Chukchee they discover the name by divination. . . . "The mother, while holding the suspended object in her hands, enumerates one by one the names of all deceased relatives, saying with each name : 'This and this has come?' When the object loses its balance and begins to swing, the name is selected. Then the people say aloud : 'Such and such a one has returned to us.' This is more than a mere verbal formula. For instance, I met on the Wolverine River a Reindeer Chukchee family who, two years before, had lost their chief, who was much beloved by his sons and nephews. Immediately afterward the wife of the oldest son of the deceased man gave birth to a son, to whom was given the name of his grandfather. He was considered, in a way, as a reincarnation of the deceased one, and therefore was always spoken of as the house-master. At one time, when the youngest and favourite daughter of the deceased one—but who, nevertheless, had a violent temper—began to abuse her oldest sister, the mother said, 'Tell the house-master' (meaning the small boy). 'Let him try and make her silent. She is his favourite child.'

"Often the name fixed upon does not agree with the child, who then grows slowly, and is sickly, or, as the Chukchee say : 'he has heavy bones.' Then a shaman, or a 'knowing person,' is invited, and proceeds to change the name. This process is sometimes repeated five or six times during the first few years of the child's life."[3]

[1] E. W. Hawkes, *The Labrador Eskimo*, p. 112 (Geological Survey of Canada, Memoir 91).   [2] Steller, *Beschreibung von dem Lande Kamtchatka*, p. 353.
[3] W. Bogoras, *op. cit.*, p. 512.

II

Facts observed by Nelson among the Eskimo of the Bering Strait throw a little light upon the reincarnation studied by Stefánsson in the Eskimo of the Mackenzie Delta. "The first child born in a village after a person dies is given the dead one's name, and must represent that person in subsequent festivals which are given in his honour. This is the case if a child is born in the village between the time of the death and the next festival to the dead. If there be no child born, then one of the persons who helped prepare the grave-box for the deceased is given his name and abandons his own for that purpose.

"Shades of people who die from natural causes go to the underground land of the dead. There also go the shades of all dead animals, where each kind lives in a village of its own. In this underground world the shades of people depend entirely on the offerings of food, water, and clothing made to them by their relatives in the festivals given to the dead. Even the shades in the land of plenty (shamans and those who, having suffered death by violence, go to the skies) can be made happier by being remembered with presents in these festivals."[1]

Here there does not seem to be any question of reincarnation, properly speaking. The "shades" of the dead, i.e. the dead themselves, live in their underground retreat. The living who bear their names represent them. Nevertheless, between these dead and their "representatives" there is real participation, from the fact that the latter bear the "name "of the dead.

At long intervals, the great festival of the dead is celebrated, and between two of these ceremonies, the minor funeral festivals will take place. When enough food has been collected for the great festival, the dead are invited to it. "At the holding of the next minor feast to the dead, each relative plants his invitation stake before the grave of the one he wishes to honour. The invitation stake consists of a slender wooden rod, four to six feet high . . . and topped by a small, painted wooden image of the totemic animal of the deceased; this stake is supposed to notify the shade of the dead of the approaching festival. Still further to notify the shades, a song of invitation is sung at the minor festival to the dead given the year before the great feast,

[1] E. W. Nelson, *The Eskimo about Bering Strait*, E.B. Bulletin, xviii, pp. 423, 377.

and as the shades are believed to be present at these festivals, this song is supposed to be heard by them. . . .

"When one of these festivals begins with its opening song of invitation, the shades are in their graves, and come thence to the *kashim* (house of the men), where they assemble in the fire-pit, under the floor. At the proper time they ascend from their place beneath the floor, entering and possessing the bodies of their namesakes in the *kashim*, and thus obtaining for themselves the offerings of food, drink and clothing which are made to their namesakes for the benefit of the deceased. It is by means of such offering that the shade is believed to obtain the supplies necessary for its wants in the land of the dead."[1]

Thus during these festivals there is established between the dead man and the living one who bears his name a participation, such that anything offered to the namesake is in reality received by the dead. The garments that the namesake puts on are actually clothing the dead. The food his namesake takes gives the dead strength, and what the living man drinks quenches his thirst. At one of these festivals, "two men among the namesakes were given suits of clothing, also loaded guns, flasks of powder, caps, filled bullet pouches, and similar articles. After receiving their gifts these men danced wildly about, flourishing their guns and shouting in great excitement. One man cried: 'You don't believe me. You think I lie, but I will guard and protect the village from danger,' at the same time firing his gun towards the roof. The other man who received a gun went through a similar performance."[2]

The offerings made and the songs finished, the "shades" are sent back to their usual dwelling-place. They return thither, wearing the "essence" of the new clothing, "for it is believed that when the old clothing is removed from the namesake and the new put on, the spiritual essence of the new garments goes to the shade." Such a belief is in accordance with what we have already learnt [3] about the "doubles" of objects in general, especially those offered to the dead.

A story related by Nelson shows how far the existence of the dead may be compared with that of the living, and the namesake's life confounded with that of the dead. There is so close

---

[1] E. W. Nelson, *The Eskimo about Bering Strait*, E.B. Bulletin, xviii, pp. 363–5.
[2] *Ibid.*, p. 377.   [3] Cf. *supra*, ch. ix, pp. 278–82.

a participation between them that what happens to the one
reacts upon the other, and in this sense, although very different
in appearance, the two have nevertheless but one individuality
between them. This is the exact counterpart of the conception
we have noted so often in the case of the living, with the werewolves, men-leopards, *tamaniu*, bush-souls, for instance. "A
young woman living at a village on the Lower Yukon became
ill and died. When death came to her, she lost consciousness
for a time, then she was awakened by someone shaking her,
saying: 'Get up, do not sleep, you are dead.' When she opened
her eyes, she saw that she was lying in her grave-box, and
her dead grandfather's shade was standing beside her. He put
out his hand to help her rise from the box and told her to look
about. . . ." (She travels past the village of the dogs, and
arrives at her grandparents', and they give her food and
drink.)

(Being invited with her grandparents to the festival of the
dead, she goes thither in their company, and the ceremony
takes place.) "Then the shades went outside the *kashim* to wait
for their names to be called for the ceremony of the putting
of clothing upon namesakes of the dead.

"As the shades of the girl and her grandparents went out of
the *kashim*, the old man gave the girl a push, which caused her
to fall and lose her senses in the passage-way. When she recovered, she looked about and found herself alone. She arose
and stood in the corner of the entrance-way under a lamp
burning there, and waited for the other shades to come out,
that she might rejoin her companions. There she waited until
all the living people came out dressed in fine new clothing, but
she saw none of her companion shades.

"Soon after this, an old man with a stick came hobbling into
the entrance, and as he looked up he saw the shade standing
in the corner with her feet raised more than a span above the
floor. He asked her if she was a living person or a shade, but
she did not reply, and he went hurriedly into the *kashim*. He
told the others, who hurried thither; some of them took down
the lamp, and by its light she was recognized, and hurried into
the house of her parents.

"When the men first saw her, she appeared in form and
colour exactly as when alive, but the moment she sat down

in her father's house, her colour faded, and she shrank until she became nothing but skin and bone, and was too weak to speak.

"Early the next morning her namesake, a woman in the same village, died, and her shade went away to the land of the dead in the girl's place, and the latter became strong again, and lived for many years."[1]

Thus, during the great festival of the dead, in which those who are explicitly invited thereto take part, the identification between them and their namesakes is such that at a given moment it is no longer possible to distinguish which of the two is actually present. The namesakes themselves feel sufficiently conscious of this actually to mistake themselves for the dead. Nevertheless this participation, no less real though not so complete, at ordinary times, does not prevent the dead from dwelling habitually in their underground retreat, to which they must return when the festival comes to an end. It appears therefore that the Eskimo think of the dead as both in their underground dwelling, and at the same time mysteriously bound to their namesakes. This is a case of bi-presence such as we have already seen, but with this difference, that the individuals are present on the earth and beneath it at the same moment.

Is it not the same with the dead women mentioned in such a way as to excite Stefánsson's curiosity? The little girl, whom her own mother calls "mother," and who is also the mother of another woman, of a different family, is not the reincarnation of these two dead women in the complete sense of the term. Nevertheless, they are united with her, present in or about her, to guide and protect her. The importance of the part they play in her life will gradually diminish until the day comes when the grown-up girl will need them no longer; then they will leave her. May we not believe, though Stefánsson says nothing about it, that the dead who are the *atka* of living beings are none the less in their underground abode? When he asked his two informants what became of the *atka*, when their rôle as guardians came to an end, he obtained no reply, yet their silence does not prove that they may not have some dim conception of this idea. The bi-presence of the dead under the earth and at the same time in their namesakes, seems to be implied among the

[1] E. W. Nelson, *The Eskimo about Bering Strait*, E.B. Bulletin, xviii, pp. 489–90.

Mackenzie Delta Eskimo no less than among those around the Bering Strait, through their collective representations with respect to the "name."

As Stefánsson has remarked, these beliefs help us to understand why children are never to be thwarted or punished, and nothing is to be forbidden them. Now this custom is not peculiar to the Eskimo, for it is found, as far as we know, among nearly all "primitives." There is scarcely one missionary who has not been shocked at the unvarying indulgence shown by natives with regard to their children. Everything is forgiven them. "These savages cannot bear anybody to chastise their children, even to speak sharply to them, for they can refuse nothing to a crying child."[1]—In South America, according to Dobrizhoffer, the Abipones "love their children very tenderly. . . . They must, however, be blamed in this, that when their children are disobedient or do wrong, they do not venture to rebuke them and still less to punish them."[2]— With the Dayaks of South Borneo, a man, by punishing one of his children, got himself into trouble. The outraged mother left him and returned to her own family, who took her part. She did not return until he had begged pardon and paid a compensation.[3]—In South Africa, again, among the Ba-ila, "you must not be severe with them, however naughty. Children are precious in their eyes, and they are constantly haunted by the idea that the child may make up its mind to return to the spirit-world whence it came, if it is not treated properly."[4]

Without laying further stress upon a well-established fact, I note that Smith and Dale account for this as Stefánsson does. The dread of seeing the child decide to return to the spirit-world (probably, the land of the dead) is not very different from the fear of offending the *atka*, the name, i.e. the spirit of the dead person who is the "guardian soul" of the child. It is not, therefore, very rash to conclude that where we find that children are neither to be rebuked nor punished, the parents are obeying conceptions very similar to these.

If this be so, we understand a little better, too, what is going

---

[1] *Relations de la Nouvelle-France* (1634), p. 42 (Le Jeune).
[2] M. Dobrizhoffer, *Historia de Abiponibus*, ii, p. 226.
[3] Wallmann, *Leiden und Freuden rheinischer Missionäre*, p. 187.
[4] Smith and Dale, *op. cit.*, ii, p. 17.

on in the minds of the natives when they try to prevent the "soul" of the little child from straying, or to recover it when it has gone. Here, as we know, we have one of the reasons alleged to account for certain practices connected with the couvade.[1] Among the Tami of New Guinea, for instance, "the mother must be very careful not to lose the 'soul' of her infant. She may not go out, for the child's soul follows her, and if something should frighten it very much, it might lose its mother. Even inside the house the mother may throw nothing away, for fear of throwing the child's soul away with it. When the baby cries unceasingly, it is a sign that its soul is lost, and in such a case, it must be recovered."[2]—In a Dimuga village in British New Guinea, where no white men had previously been seen, Saville passed a very uncomfortable night. "What made things worse was the continual screaming throughout the night of a young child in one of the women's houses close by. I learned afterwards that this woman would not allow the child to sleep while I was there, lest some calamity might befall his *iau*, or spirit, after it left the body in sleep."[3]

In facts of this kind, which are extremely common, this term "spirit," so ambiguous and deceptive, no doubt sometimes means what the Eskimo call *nappan*, the true "soul" of the child, and sometimes *atka*, i.e. the ancestor or the person recently deceased who, whilst living in the land of the dead, lives again also in the child. Probably, it is more often the latter that is in question. I have endeavoured to show above[4] that the child does not at once form part of the social group. He belongs to it only indirectly, by the intermediary of an ancestor present in him until the rite of initiation establishes him therein, making of him a "member" of the clan or of the "*Sippe*" in the full sense of the word. These conceptions seem very closely allied with those which I have just analysed among the Eskimo.

III

With the Bantus, the "name" plays a part very similar to that we encountered among the Eskimo. The Ba-ila recognize

[1] *V. How Natives Think*, pp. 259–62. [2] R. Neuhauss, *op. cit.*, iii, pp. 517–18.
[3] W. J. V. Savile, *In Unknown New Guinea*, p. 300.
[4] Cf. *supra*, ch. vii, pp. 207–11.

that "there are various kinds of names. The birth-name is the one given to a child soon after birth, when by the aid of the diviner it has been ascertained of which of its forbears it is the reincarnation. . . . This name is *tonda*, not to be lightly used, and though it remains with him all his life, it is strictly *tonda* for him to pronounce it. . . . The child is therefore given another name for everyday use."—The authors say that the reason for this taboo "is, that by pronouncing a name you may bring misfortune down upon the person or upon yourself. It is the same sort of feeling that prevents some people speaking of a ghost when passing through a churchyard at midnight. Talk of the devil . . ."[1] According to the Ba-ila, the dead can just as easily be reincarnated in animals as in human beings, sometimes in a single one, and again in several at a time. "Curiously enough, it is only more or less dangerous beasts that men choose to become: the lion, leopard, hyena, wild dog, elephant, a snake, and the fabulous Itoshi monster. Sometimes a person may choose to become all the first four or five of these. A doctor provides the necessary medicine. . . .

"Two points must be noticed. The person does not enter into an already existing animal, but becomes an animal. The animal is not born; it simply develops out of the worm. The ghost of the man has already taken its course, gone to the east, and taken up its abode near the grave. While the hyena or lion" (that the man has become) "is wandering about, the people will still come to the grave to make their offerings. And the fact of having become a lion is no bar against being reincarnated.

"It was like this with the old chief Sezongo at Manzela. Some time after his death we visited his grave, and found some men sweeping the hut in which he was buried. There was a tortoise in the hut, and we were informed that it was Sezongo. They scraped some earth from the grave, disclosing a potsherd, which they moved, showing the orifice of a reed. It was along this the tortoise had come, so they said, but they meant that worms had come along the reed and changed into the tortoise. We heard subsequently that two lion-cubs had appeared in the hut, and it was an accepted fact that Sezongo had become two lions. A year or so later a number of lions, ten or a dozen, came

[1] Smith and Dale, *op. cit.*, i, pp. 365–8.

one night and made the earth shake with their roaring. The people were much impressed. They said the lions had come from afar to salute the two who were Sezongo.

"Some time afterwards, Sezongo's son had a son born to him, and it was proved to be the old chief who had returned to earth.

"The question occurs to a European—it did not occur to a native—where is Sezongo? At the grave where to-day he is 'worshipped,' in the tortoise, in the lions, or in the boy roaming about the village? There seems to be a curious confusion of thought, or a conception of the 'soul' as bipartite or tripartite. . . . What is the relation between the lion who is Sezongo and the boy in the kraal who is also Sezongo?

"Some people would answer that the lion was the boy's external or 'bush' soul, and the relation between the two was so close and intimate that the well-being of the one depended upon that of the other. But the Ba-ila have no such belief. As we shall see presently, the boy has a guardian which seems at first almost like a fourth Sezongo, but which certainly is not the lions.

"To the community that lion is more or less sacrosanct. They will not kill it if they can avoid doing so, and, further, they will seek to prevent a European from killing it. Should it, however, take to man-eating they will give their scruples to the wind; be he ten times their chief, they are not going to let him devour them!"[1]

Why does the question that intrigues the European not occur to the native's mind? How is it that he does not ask himself: Who really is Sezongo? Is he the tortoise, the lion-cubs, the little fellow, or the dead man near his grave?—The preceding chapters of this book, I venture to think, furnish the clue to the enigma. The case noted by Smith and Dale is very clearly one of multipresence. To the Ba-ila the same individual may find himself at a given moment in various places and in different forms. This is a matter of experience. Sezongo is at the same time near his grave, in the lion (or lions), in the tortoise and in his little grandson. He even is these lions and this child. The thing is self-evident and does not need any explanation. It is a mystery to minds like ours only.

[1] Smith and Dale, *op. cit.*, ii, pp. 125–8.

At what period, and how, does the dead man reincarnate himself in a human being? "Some hold that it is at the mentioning of the name in the ceremony of divination that the child becomes So-and-So, or rather, that So-and-So becomes the child. . . . But we have again and again heard men say: 'I am my grandfather; I entered my mother's womb to be born.' In that case, either at conception or sometime later, the spirit enters the embryo. If there were unanimity upon this point, it would help us to determine their ideas of the soul. If the spirit only comes at the naming ceremony, then, before it, has the child no soul, or has it a secondary, a nutritive, sensitive soul, and the spirit comes as the rational soul? What is the relationship between the ancestral spirit and the body? Does it simply live in it as a guest, or does it animate the body, making it perform its functions? These are questions to which they can supply no answer."[1]—How could they give any, if the terms in which the questions are propounded have never entered their minds? They would not know what to say. Let us give up pursuing researches that can yield no result, and rather endeavour to bring out clearly the participations involved in their beliefs regarding reincarnation.

The same individual may reappear in two others at the same time. "A discarnate spirit" (or, as I should say, a dead man) "may return to earth in two bodies. Suppose there are two brothers who separate to live in different districts, and each has a child born to him in about the same time. They go to the diviners in their respective districts, and each is told that it is the grandfather who has returned in the flesh; the child confirming it in the way we have described. They are satisfied, then, that this is so. Up to this time no communication has taken place between the brothers as to the children, but now that the names are given each sends to the other to say: 'Our father has returned to our home.' No conviction arises in their minds that a mistake has been made; they simply accept the situation. If a spirit so wishes, why should it not occupy two bodies? It does not occur to them to question the possibility of one person being in two places at once."[2]

By certain indications, however, we realize that the term "reincarnation" does not exactly render the primitives' con-

[1] Smith and Dale, *op. cit.*, ii, p. 153.   [2] *Ibid.*, ii, p. 154.

ception. Rather is it with them, as with the Eskimo, an intimate participation between the living and the dead who has entered his body. "No man can remember what he was when he lived on earth before, or what he was and did in the spirit world. The memory—shall we put it so?—and all intellectual activities are outside the scope of the spirit, which determines who the man is, not what he is. . . . To the Ba-ila, it would seem the soul—the man himself—is more like a tenant, a lodger in a house where all the daily avocations are carried on apart; he has no share in them, but is like a star and dwells apart."[1] Thus the reincarnated man must not be confused with the reincarnating. It is not quite exact to say that he is his spirit, his soul, that it is the man himself, as these authors do here, but it would not be correct either to say that there are two distinct beings. Here we have a participation that we cannot render clear, nor are we bound to do so. We have already studied it above, when examining the relations between the individual and his tutelary genius.

A little farther on, Smith and Dale describe this participation in very striking terms. "The namesake upon whom the native calls for help, and to whom he makes his offerings, is the one whose name was given him after birth—his grandfather probably. Thus a boy will be named Mungalo after consultation with the diviners; and by his solemn act of accepting the breast at the mention of the name, he shows his acquiescence. Mungalo was his grandfather, and when he speaks in his prayers of his namesake, he means Mungalo, his grandfather.

"But he was named Mungalo because he actually was and is Mungalo, that is, his grandfather reborn! Quite so! He is Mungalo, and Mungalo is his grandfather, and Mungalo is also his guardian spirit. That is to say, a man's guardian spirit, his tutelary genius, is the reincarnate spirit within him: shall we say? is himself. The genius is not only within him, but, in a sense, external to himself, protecting and guiding him."[2]

"Whatever good fortune a man may have—wealth, fame, escaping from danger, etc., it is ascribed to the good offices of his namesake. . . . Accidents, of course, happen; a man may have his life endangered in a thousand ways. When such happens, he wonders what his *musedi* (guardian spirit) was

[1] Smith and Dale, *op. cit.*, ii, p. 155.   [2] *Ibid.*, ii, p. 157.

doing to allow him to get into danger like that. He makes an offering and reproaches his *musedi*, saying: 'Why did you leave me? I nearly died. Where were you? See, I make you an offering; do not leave me again.' . . . As for the way the guardian spirit conveys his admonitions, he comes in dreams or speaks in a low voice heard only by the man himself within his breast.—Every individual, as soon as his name has been given him, has his own guardian spirit."[1] Does not this spirit, which among the Ba-ila is the reincarnation of a dead relative, strikingly resemble the West African *kra* and the other spirits of the kind, that we have found existing in nearly all primitive communities? And do they not all, though in varying forms, represent the participation of a dead man in the individuality of a living one?

With the Ba-kaonde, neighbours of the Ba-ila, Melland noted most of the beliefs just described. There too we find the name given to the child after the diviner has discovered which dead relative reappears in him; we have the chief manifesting himself in several lions, issuing from the worms of his decaying corpse; the dead man reincarnated in several children or in several animals, and so on. Melland, wishful of making the bi-presence and the multipresence of the dead intelligible, observes that we have no word which exactly expresses what is in the natives' minds. To them, he believes, it is not a question of true reincarnation, but merely of an "emanation" of the soul or of the "spirit" of the dead. Hence there would be nothing absurd in imagining that one "soul" can have many "emanations," and each of these may enter a different being. This interpretation does indeed rationalize the Ba-kaonde beliefs, but if we want to render such representations unimpeachable from the strictly logical point of view, do we not run the risk of distorting them, and overstepping the mark? From the native point of view, if not from our own, neither bi-presence nor multipresence appears contradictory. Should we not distrust any interpretation that effectually disposes of them?

Finally, in the Bantu tribes studied by Roscoe, beliefs which are much akin to the preceding ones are current. "The child was named as soon as possible after its birth, by the father if it was a boy, and by the mother if it was a girl. In either case it

[1] Smith and Dale, *op. cit.*, ii, pp. 158-9.

was called after some deceased ancestor of the father's clan, whose ghost was then expected to look after it. If the child did not thrive, the parents consulted a medicine-man, who took an augury, and would sometimes advise them to change the child's name."[1]—With the Basabei, "the ghost took charge of the child. Though it used its influence generally for good, it might also punish the child for any failure in clan duties or observances."[2] Among the Busoga, "Walumbe was the name of the god of the dead. To him all the departed souls went after death to report themselves. Singularly, Walumbe was also the god who gave women children. Each newly-married woman went to ask his blessing in order that she might bear children."[3] Do we not find here, in a clearly mythological form, the idea that the dead are born again in their children? "The ghost of one of its ancestors became the guardian of a child, though it was never supposed to enter it as its animating spirit,"[4] which means that with this tribe, as with the Ba-ila, biological and psychic functions are accomplished without its aid. The names given at birth were retained until puberty, and at the close of the initiation ceremonies young people, of both sexes, received new ones.[5] In other words, the guardian spirits who had watched over their childhood now quitted them. By initiation they passed through death and a new birth. Their new names affiliated them with their ancestors, and henceforth they were directly incorporated in their social group.

From the facts studied in this chapter, it is clear that the relations between the living and the dead are still closer and more complex than is usually stated. It is not enough to state that the dead are constantly present to the minds of the living, who do nothing without consulting them; that the well-being, prosperity, and very existence of the social group depend upon the good will of its dead members, and that these in their turn cannot dispense with the worship and the offerings of their descendants. The solidarity existing between them is yet more profound and more intimate, and it is realized in the very essence of individuals. The dead "live with" the members of their group who are born into the world.

---

[1] J. Roscoe, *The Bagesu*, p. 24. [2] *Ibid.*, p. 59.
[3] *Ibid.*, pp. 104–5. [4] *Ibid.*, p. 106. [5] *Ibid.*, pp. 77–9.

Whilst still dwelling in their subterranean or their celestial abode, they are nevertheless at the same time present in the children, from whom it is difficult to distinguish them, since they are their "names," and, in a certain sense, their "souls." When this indwelling presence comes to an end, as it usually does when initiation is accomplished, it gives place to a more complete participation of the individual, now an adult, with his ancestors. The rites of initiation often seem to have as their essential aim to weld the new member of the clan definitely and finally into the mass of his ancestors. Henceforward it is his right and his duty to assure the permanence of the group by providing it with descendants.

Through this symbiosis of the living and the dead, a symbiosis which is both mystic and concrete, the individual is not wholly himself except by virtue of the ancestors who live once more in his personality.

INDEX